# SPRING BOOT
# MICROSERVICES

# SPRING BOOT MICROSERVICES

## Design, Implementation, and Deployment

Andres Sacco

MERCURY LEARNING AND INFORMATION

Boston, Massachusetts

MERCURY LEARNING AND INFORMATION
121 High Street, 3rd Floor
Boston, MA 02110
info@merclearning.com

A. Sacco. *Spring Boot Microservices: Design, Implementation, and Deployment.*
ISBN: 978-1-5015-2338-0

Library of Congress Control Number: 2025943217
242526321   This book is printed on acid-free paper in the United States of America.

Our titles are available for adoption, license, or bulk purchase by institutions, corporations, etc.

All of our titles are available in digital format at various digital vendors.

*To my grandparents, who taught me the importance of always learning new things.*

*To my wife and children, for supporting me while I was writing this book.*

# CONTENTS

*Acknowledgments*                                                                 *xiii*

*Introduction*                                                                    *xv*

**Chapter 1: Getting Started with Spring Boot**                                   **1**

What Is Spring?                                                                   1

What Is Spring Boot?                                                              3

The Methodology of This Book                                                      4

    Defining the Scenario                                     4

    The Approach to Making Decisions                          6

Creating an Application                                                           7

    How to Use Alternatives                                   8

    What Is the Structure of the Application?                 11

    How to Add Logic to the Application                      13

    How to Run the Code                                      19

Best Practices                                                                    23

    Reducing Possible Conflicts                              23

    Formatting the Source Code                               25

Summary                                                                           26

**Chapter 2: Creating the Domain of the Application**                             **27**

Introduction to Microservices                                                     27

    Problems Associated with Monoliths                        28

    Problems and Solutions Relating to Microservices          30

    Impact on the Developer's Day to Day                      32

Defining the Architecture                                                         34

    Which Types of Architectures Exist?                       34

    Which Is the Best Alternative for Each Scenario?          38

    How Does a Spring Boot Application Work?                  39

    Implementing the Architecture                             41

Creating the Application Logic    41
Manage the Exceptions    53
Add Validators    59
Summary    66

**Chapter 3: Configuring Basic Aspects**    **67**
How Is the Application Configured?    67
Why Is This Relevant?    67
What Aspects Are Configurable in an Application?    67
How Can Multiple Configurations Be Used?    72
What Is an Actuator?    73
How Does Spring Boot Implement an Actuator?    74
Using the Actuator Endpoints    78
What Are the Steps to Customize the Actuator?    88
Summary    95

**Chapter 4: Interacting with the Database**    **97**
What Ways Exist to Preserve Information?    97
Relational Databases    98
Non-Relational Databases    101
Both Types of Databases    101
Which Is the Best Alternative for Each Scenario?    104
Persisting the Information    105
Object Mapping    105
Repositories    106
How Can Information Be Persisted Within a Relational Database?    110
How Can Information Be Persisted in a Non-Relational Database?    120
Versioning the Changes    130
Which Tools Exist to Do It?    132
Which Is the Best Alternative for Each Scenario?    133
How Can It Be Implemented on a Spring Boot Application?    135
Summary    138

**Chapter 5: Communication with External Services**    **139**
What Does Communication Between Applications Mean?    139
Which Components Are Connected with Communication?    139
Which Protocols Exist?    141
Which Types of Communication Exist?    144
Which Is the Best Option for Each Scenario?    145
How to Implement Communication in Spring Boot    147
How Can Communication Be Carried Out?    149
How to Reduce the Impact of Errors    159
What Is Resilience?    159
How Can Resilience Be Implemented?    160
Patterns    161

How Can the Impact of the Request Be Reduced?                       168
   Methods to Minimize the Impact                    168
Summary                                                             182

## Chapter 6: Testing Different Aspects   183

What Does Testing Applications Involve?                             183
Which Kinds of Tests Exist?                                         183
   Unit Tests                                        184
   Integration Tests                                 190
   Performance Tests                                 206
   Other Types                                       211
   Which Is the Best Option for Each Scenario?        222
Summary                                                             223

## Chapter 7: Documenting the Endpoints   225

What Does Documenting Microservices Mean?                           225
   Which Options Exist to Do It?                      225
   What Is the Best Way to Do It?                     227
How Are the Endpoints on the Application Documented?                228
   Documenting the Different Endpoints                231
   Adding Examples to the Documentation               236
Checking the Documentation                                          239
   Which Mechanism Exists to Check the Documentation? 239
   Which Is the Best Option?                          239
   How to Implement the Validations in the Application 240
Summary                                                             246

## Chapter 8: Externalizing the Configuration   247

Internal Configuration                                              247
   Problems with This Approach                        248
External Configuration                                              249
   What Are the Main Benefits?                        249
   What Ways Exist to Do It?                          250
   What Is the Best Option for Each Scenario?         250
What Implications Do the Modifications Have on the Application?      252
   Creating a New Config Server                       252
   Adding Queues to Detect the Changes                264
Summary                                                             268

## Chapter 9: Build and Package the Application   269

What Is the Idea Behind the Build and Package Processes?            269
Build                                                               269
   Code Format                                        270
   Prevent Dependency Conflicts                       270
   Detect Unused Dependencies                         270

Code Analysis and Auto-Fix                                          272
Update Dependencies                                                 275
Upgrade Application                                                 276
Packaging                                                          278
What Problems Could Appear During This Process?                    278
How to Build an Image                                              279
Summary                                                           293

**Chapter 10: Observability and Monitoring**                       **295**

What Is Observability and Monitoring?                              295
Logging                                                           296
What Ways Exist to Expose Logs?                                    297
What Is the Best Option for Each Scenario?                         298
What Implications Do the Modifications Have on the Application?     299
Traces                                                            306
What Ways Exist to Collect Traces?                                306
What Is the Best Option for Each Scenario?                         307
What Implications Do the Modifications Have on the Application?     308
Metrics and Alerts                                                311
What Ways Exist to Collect Metrics and Create Alerts?             312
What Is the Best Option for Each Scenario?                         313
What Implications Do the Modifications Have on the Application?     314
Summary                                                           318

**Chapter 11: Securing the Information**                            **319**

What Does Securing the Information Mean?                           319
Which Mechanism Is Used to Secure the Information?                320
What Things Are Possible to Restrict?                             320
Securing the Applications                                          321
How Can This Library Be Integrated into the System?              322
Summary                                                           350

**Chapter 12: Discovering, Exposing, and Balancing**               **351**

Exposing                                                          351
What Does Exposing All the Endpoints Mean?                        351
What Ways Exist to Do This?                                       352
What Is the Best Option for a Scenario?                           355
How Can This Pattern Be Integrated into the System?              355
Discovering                                                       366
What Does Discovering the Different Instances Involve?            366
What Ways Exist to Do This?                                       367
What Is the Best Option for a Scenario?                           369
How Can This Pattern Be Integrated into the System?              371
Load Balancing                                                    377

What Does Balancing Requests Mean?   377
What Ways Exist to Do This?   377
What Is the Best Option for a Scenario?   380
How Can This Pattern Be Integrated into the System?   380
   Summary   382

**Appendix A: Setup Enviroment Tools**   **385**

**Appendix B: Recommended and Alternatives Tools**   **391**

**Appendix C: Opening a Project**   **393**

**Appendix D: Install and Configure Relational Database**   **395**

**Appendix E: Install and Configure Non-relational Database**   **401**

**Appendix F: Further Readings**   **409**

**Index**   **413**

# ACKNOWLEDGMENTS

I would like to thank my family members and friends for their encouragement and support during the process of writing this book:

- My wife, Gisela, has been my rock, always patient and understanding when I spent long hours at my computer desk working on this book.
- My little daughter, Francesca, helped me relax between writing each chapter.
- My baby, Allegra, is the newest family member and inspired me to write this book.
- My dear friends, German Canale and Julian Delley: Your unwavering trust in me and support during my lowest moments have been invaluable.

My sincere thanks to the wonderful team at De Gruyter Brill for their support during the publication of this book. Thanks to Steven Elliot for providing excellent support.

# *INTRODUCTION*

The Java ecosystem has evolved over the last twenty-five years. Previously, creating a simple application meant downloading and including the libraries inside the project, but fortunately, in 2002, Maven[1] automated this process.

Another significant issue was connecting to a database or creating a Web application that exposed a specific number of endpoints, as this required using different libraries to tackle each problem independently. This introduced another issue, namely, the interaction between different libraries; the developers needed to understand how each library worked behind the scenes, and in some cases, there were conflicting versions. The appearance of Spring[2] created the foundations on which Spring Boot[3] later solved all of these problems, generating an ecosystem where integrating a database, connecting to an external service, ensuring availability, and documenting an application can be done simply.

Nowadays, creating a new application is straightforward thanks to Spring Boot. This simplicity, however, can lead to overlooking essential concerns, such as ensuring the application is resilient and performs well. This book addresses these challenges by guiding the reader through crucial tasks, such as persisting data in a database. It also offers practical tips, recommended practices, and useful libraries to support the development of robust and efficient applications.

## WHY WRITE THIS BOOK?

Numerous articles, books, and other resources are available on using Spring Boot to create a simple application from various perspectives. Some offer outstanding detail, while others focus on aspects related to choosing one approach over another for persisting information.

With all these arguments, why did it seem necessary to write this book? The idea behind this book is not merely to present concepts found in other resources; it aims to teach best practices for each new concept through real-world scenarios, rather than simply presenting applications that expose a few endpoints without further depth.

---

[1]https://maven.apache.org/
[2]https://spring.io/
[3]https://spring.io/projects/spring-boot

Some questions that arise with the everyday use of applications are:

- How can an application be created to expose endpoints following a specific architectural strategy?
- What are simple ways to preserve information, reduce complexity, and maintain database agnosticism?
- How can an application handle errors related to itself or problems arising from communication with other applications?
- What strategies can minimize the impact of multiple requests made to obtain information from another application?
- How is the application packaged and distributed?

This book answers these questions throughout its various chapters.

The book's limited scope allows it to focus on the various concepts rather than exploring possible alternatives for implementing the business logic.

Explaining all concepts related to a topic in depth, such as optimizing a query to retrieve information from the database, is beyond the scope of this book. Appendix F lists various books and resources to refer to for more information on each topic covered in the book.

## WHO IS THIS BOOK FOR?

This book is for developers with a Java programming background who want to learn about the fundamental aspects of creating microservices or applications using Spring Boot. To achieve this, the book presents an example scenario of a fictitious company.

No prior experience with Spring or Spring Boot is required. The book guides the reader through creating a project from scratch, with each layer assigned a specific responsibility.

## PREREQUISITES

Java JDK[4] 21 or higher, Maven[5] 3.8.x or higher, and an IDE must be installed on the machine. Suitable IDE options include Eclipse[6], IntelliJ IDEA[7], and Visual Studio Code[8]—select the one that best fits your requirements.

NOTE *Appendix A contains all the information about the different options available for installing these tools.*

Some chapters mention using a database such as MySQL[9]. To simplify the installation of the database on a local machine, it is recommended to install Docker and use it to run the database.

---

[4]https://jdk.java.net/
[5]https://maven.apache.org/
[6]https://www.eclipse.org/downloads/
[7]https://www.jetbrains.com/es-es/idea/
[8]https://code.visualstudio.com/
[9]https://www.mysql.com/

The use and installation of Docker are beyond the scope of this book, but tutorials[10] and cheatsheets[11] with the most common commands are available.

## How to Check the Prerequisites

After installing all the tools listed in the previous section, verify that they are correctly installed before proceeding with the chapters.

To check Java, run the following command:

```
➜  ~ java -version
openjdk 21 2023-09-19
OpenJDK Runtime Environment (build 21+35-2513)
OpenJDK 64-Bit Server VM (build 21+35-2513, mixed mode, sharing)
```

Next, verify whether the Maven version is correct by running this command:

```
➜  ~ mvn --version
Apache Maven 3.9.1
Maven home: /usr/share/maven
```

Finally, to ensure Docker runs correctly on the machine, use the following command:

```
➜  ~ docker --version
Docker version 26.1.2, build 211e74b
```

Docker is necessary to run other applications used for various purposes, such as validating the existence of certain information. It can also be used to reduce the complexity of installing a database on a local machine.

## How Were the Prerequisites Chosen?

In many cases, there are different reasons for choosing one technology over another. For example, the author of a book or article may prefer one version of Java or a specific configuration manager based on their personal experience. In this book, the election of the different prerequisites is connected to different surveys or metrics accessible to anyone; for example, some excellent surveys are Synk[12], JetBrains[13], New Relic[14], Stack Overflow[15], and Spring[16].

Most of these surveys recommend that developers use only long-term support (LTS) versions of Java in production environments, such as versions 8, 11, 17, or 21. The use of the oldest LTS versions is decreasing annually. For example, according to a 2022 JetBrains survey, only 30% of applications used version 17, but by the end of 2023, that percentage had increased to 45%. The increase in the rate could be due to many reasons. One relevant point, however, is that Spring Boot version 2.x.x has been deprecated, so to maintain application security and benefit from performance improvements, upgrading to a newer version of Java is necessary.

---

[10]https://docker-curriculum.com/
[11]https://docs.docker.com/get-started/docker_cheatsheet.pdf
[12]https://snyk.io/jvm-ecosystem-report-2021/
[13]https://www.jetbrains.com/lp/devecosystem-2023/java/
[14]https://newrelic.com/resources/report/2024-state-of-the-java-ecosystem
[15]https://survey.stackoverflow.co/2023/
[16]https://spring.io/blog/2024/06/03/state-of-spring-survey-2024-results

NOTE   *Spring Boot, since version 3.0.0, requires the use of Java 17 or higher.*

According to the same surveys, 73% of developers use Maven as a dependency manager for some applications, rather than other options, such as Gradle. Note that the examples in the chapters can be translated to Gradle with minimum changes.

## SOURCE CODE

The source code for this book is available to readers under the Source Code/Downloads tab on the book's home page, which is located at *https://github.com/andres-sacco/deguyer-spring-boot-microservices*.

## HOW THIS BOOK IS STRUCTURED

The book has twelve chapters and six appendices, set out as follows:

- The first block of chapters (1–3) provides a basic understanding of how to create an application. It covers various strategies for organizing logic; configuring different aspects, such as ports and URLs; and exposing metrics that specific tools can collect.
- The second block of chapters (4–6) explains how an application can integrate and interact with external resources such as databases or other applications. Additionally, this block outlines how to test applications by considering all aspects, not just the creation of unit tests.
- The third block of chapters (7–9) provides a brief overview of documenting the endpoints exposed by an application and validating whether the documentation adheres to a standard. It also explains how to externalize the application's configuration to avoid redeploying the application each time a change is required.
- The final block of chapters (10–12) explores advanced topics, including application monitoring, introducing a gateway to access multiple applications, and implementing security at the endpoint level.
- The appendices cover various topics intended to provide support throughout the book—from configuring the development environment to offering recommended resources for further reading.

# CHAPTER 1

# GETTING STARTED WITH SPRING BOOT

I n early 2002, creating simple applications meant considering which libraries or frameworks to use, as some were incompatible with each other. These decisions and the associated problems meant that developers spent many hours analyzing and finding solutions to particular situations, which could be frustrating given that, at that time, resources now widely available—such as Stack Overflow[1] and ChatGPT[2]—which assist in these tasks, did not exist.

When Spring and Hibernate[3] were released, some problems started to disappear because they offered the possibility of simplifying many tasks. For example, Hibernate reduces the complexity of accessing a database, preventing developers from having duplicate code in their applications.

This chapter provides a brief overview of Spring Boot, its various modules, and their purposes, to enable the creation of a simple application by the end of the chapter.

## WHAT IS SPRING?

Spring is a framework that provides a container for creating and managing various components. These components can be defined using annotations or XML. Although XML is less commonly used today, it was a novel option when the first version appeared because Java didn't have annotations.

**NOTE** *The first version of Spring was released in 2004, and since then, the framework has grown significantly in terms of developer adoption and the range of supported features and technologies. Today, a large community of developers works on fixing the issues encountered in each version of Spring. An annual conference is also held to showcase the latest features to the developer community.*

Spring defines a context responsible for managing the lifecycles of all the different internal components. The framework implements two distinct patterns: dependency injection (DI),

[1]https://stackoverflow.com/
[2]https://chatgpt.com/
[3]https://hibernate.org/

which involves delegating to someone else the task of assigning a concrete class instance, rather than performing it manually. Spring manages the state of these dependent objects without requiring any developer intervention.

Figure 1.1 illustrates the different types of DI implementations.

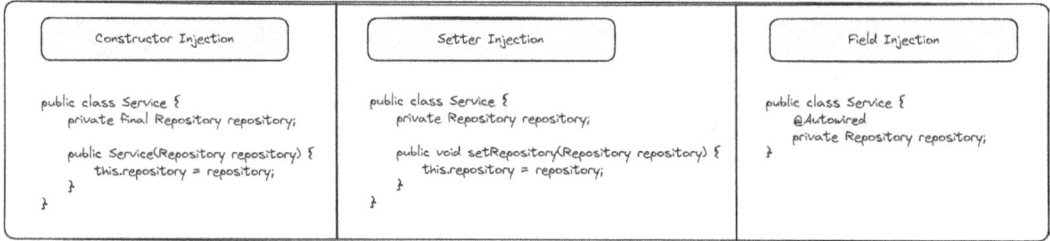

**FIGURE 1.1** Different ways to implement DI.

The second relevant pattern that utilizes Spring is inversion of control (IoC), which delegates to the framework the responsibility of creating and managing the various objects that a class requires, similar to the DI pattern. Figure 1.2 shows the approach to defining objects with and without using IoC.

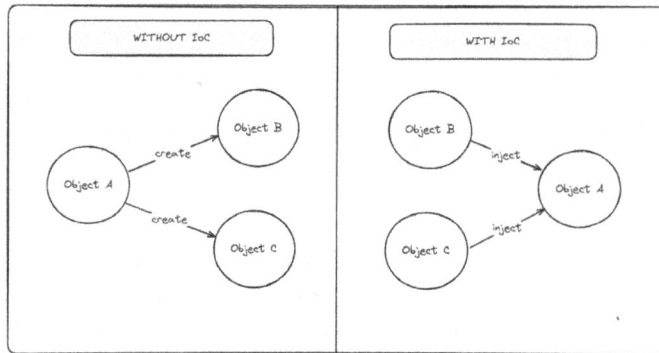

**FIGURE 1.2** The main difference in the use of IoC.

One of the main attributes of Spring is that the framework is split into different modules, each of which has a specific purpose; the most relevant modules are shown in Figure 1.3.

The different modules have specific purposes:

- Data Access: This set of essential tools enables the persistence of information in various storage systems, including relational and non-relational databases.
- Web: This group supports the development of Web applications that process HTTP requests.
- Container: This group contains all the core functionalities Spring uses across its various modules, such as DI and component lifecycle management.
- Test: This group supports creating tests to ensure that all code developed using Spring functions correctly.

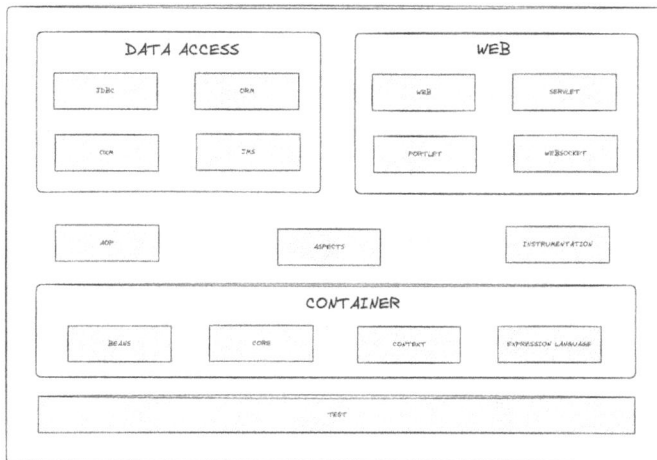

**FIGURE 1.3** Main modules of the Spring Framework.

**NOTE** *Please note that this book does not cover every topic related to Spring, as many other books listed in Appendix F explore these subjects in greater detail. The following section provides a brief definition of some key concepts to offer a general understanding.*

## WHAT IS SPRING BOOT?

Released in 2014, this project aims to simplify the creation and development of Java Web applications by leveraging the Spring Framework. Some key features of Spring Boot include auto-configuration of components, rapid startup without requiring deployment artifacts on a Web server, and various tools for monitoring and ensuring everything functions correctly.

Spring is organized into different modules; Spring Boot follows the same approach, reducing, at a minimum, the complexity of adding support to access a database. This framework comprises numerous modules, with additional ones being added each year to support other tools and streamline the configuration process. Table 1.1 provides a brief overview of the various Spring modules, highlighting some that are explored in more detail throughout the book.

**TABLE 1.1** Explanation of the different modules of Spring Boot.

| Module | Description |
|---|---|
| Starter | This module contains a set of dependencies that reduce the application's configuration when interacting with other modules. |
| Actuator | This module provides features to expose information and metrics about the application that some tools, such as Prometheus[4], could consume. |
| DevTools | This provides features that help the developer improve the experience of developing a Spring Boot application. One notable feature is the application's hot reload capability. |

*(Continued)*

---

[4]https://prometheus.io/

*TABLE 1.1* Continued

| Module | Description |
| --- | --- |
| CLI | This is a tool designed for rapid application development using Groovy scripts. |
| Testing | A set of classes and interfaces is provided to create tests and check different aspects of the application. It's possible to combine this module with JUnit[5] and Mockito[6]. |
| Configuration Processor | This module generates metadata from the project files, enabling the IDE to provide suggestions and guidance on where to develop specific components. |
| Web | This module provides the logic to expose endpoints and create reactive applications. |
| Data | This provides a consistent and straightforward way to access relational and non-relational databases with minimum changes. |
| Security | This provides a way to reduce the code to authenticate and authorize the different users in an application. |
| Messaging | This provides a standard interface in the same way that the data module interacts with different providers of asynchronous communication, such as Kafka and RabbitMQ. |
| Scheduling | This provides features to process a high volume of information using cron jobs or batch processing. |
| Cloud | This provides tools to implement the most common patterns (service discovery, gateways, and contract testing) in distributed systems. |

The current version of Spring Boot at the time of writing, 3.x.x, incorporates numerous improvements over the previous version, leveraging all the features that Java version 17 offers developers. One of the most significant features is that it enables the application to be built natively using GraalVM[7], which was previously experimental in Spring.

Check the support calendar on the official Spring Boot Web site regularly. It also provides extensive information about when a version will be deprecated.

## THE METHODOLOGY OF THIS BOOK

While it all may sound ideal in theory, applying a solution in a real-world scenario often reveals unexpected challenges. To bridge the gap between theory and practice, this book presents each topic through a realistic scenario that illustrates the development of an application designed to interact with other systems.

### Defining the Scenario

Welcome to Travel World Agency (TWA), the world's largest travel agency! It sells flights and has offices in countries including the US, UK, and Germany. The company utilizes technologies such as Java/Spring Boot for the backend and Node/Angular for the frontend. All the platform's logic is contained within a single extensive application, which has numerous responsibilities and utilizes a database to persist client reservation information. Additionally, the application integrates with an external system to retrieve information on flight availability from various airlines.

---

[5]https://junit.org/junit5/
[6]https://site.mockito.org/
[7]https://www.graalvm.org/

*Travel World Agency does not exist in the real world. The name represents a fictional travel agency featured as the case study of this book.*

The flight team, one of the most influential in the company and responsible for 80% of the sales, is a high priority. Therefore, the manager suggests reviewing the current structure of the microservices before proceeding. The platform's structure is depicted in Figure 1.4.

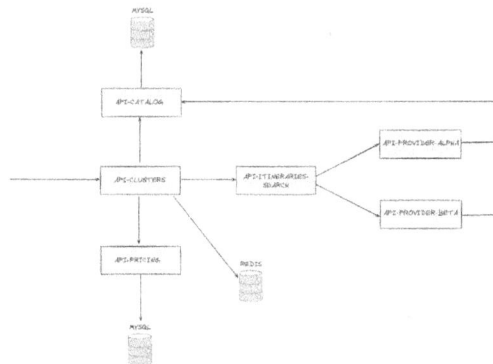

**FIGURE 1.4** Diagram of the different microservices that comprise the flight team.

As shown in Figure 1.4, the platform consists of several components, each serving a distinct purpose. Table 1.2 provides additional context about each application:

**TABLE 1.2** Explanation of the responsibility of each component.

| Application | Description |
| --- | --- |
| api-catalog | api-catalog is a microservice that contains all the information about valid cities for finding flights. This API returns a specified number of flights as requested, allowing users to navigate to the next page of results without initiating a new search. All results are saved in a database with a time to live (TTL). |
| api-clusters | api-clusters refers to the microservice that handles all validations for search parameters. It also calls api-pricing to retrieve the final price for each itinerary. |
| api-pricing | api-pricing is a microservice that contains all the rules for adding a markup to each itinerary and calculating the final prices. |
| api-itineraries-search | api-itineraries-search is a microservice that contains all the logic for determining which providers to call to retrieve all itineraries. Additionally, this microservice removes duplicate entries. |
| api-provider-alpha / api-provider-beta | These APIs simulate retrieving information from an external provider. |

After reviewing the figure and the table, it becomes clear that the platform currently only provides the ability to browse and purchase flight tickets. The goal throughout this book, however, is to develop an application that encapsulates all the logic required to manage reservations.

The new application will have the following responsibilities:

- Validate the existence of the flight information that some users want to buy.
- Provide all the methods to save, modify, or retrieve the information of a specific reservation. This means saving all the information about a particular flight.

In Figure 1.5, the primary entities represent the reservation information. The image does not include all the attributes that will appear in the section related to application creation.

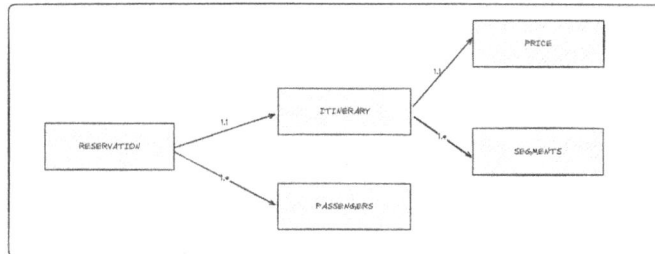

**FIGURE 1.5** The structure of a reservation.

The requirements of this new application are straightforward, as the goal is to simplify the business logic and allow focus on other aspects.

## The Approach to Making Decisions

When working at a company that develops applications, deciding on the architecture is one of the most common situations. This process involves changes that significantly impact the source code and the developers, such as selecting a language or framework, switching to a different database, and determining the best way to solve complex code.

Most architectural decisions are made without proper documentation or consideration of alternative options and their trade-offs. This approach negatively impacts developers, as they must understand why a particular library or tool was chosen over another. If the developers who made these decisions leave the company, it becomes challenging for others to answer these questions.

A way to solve all these problems appeared some years ago with the appearance of ADR, or Architectural Decision Records, in 2014, with Michael Nygard[8] as one of the first promoters of this solution. The relevance of this technique increased each year, to the point that it was included on the Thoughtworks[9] Technology Radar.

This technique aims to create a concise document written in Markdown, with sections that explain the problem and possible solutions. The idea is that someone could read the document and know which alternatives to consider to make the final decision and who is participating in the process. One aspect to consider is that an ADR can invalidate a previous one due to changes in the technological context; therefore, it is necessary to explicitly specify the name of the ADR that is being invalidated by the new record.

---

[8]https://adr.github.io/
[9]https://www.thoughtworks.com/radar

The ADR contains specific sections, as illustrated in Figure 1.6. The format can be modified or expanded by adding additional sections, but it is essential to maintain a concise document.

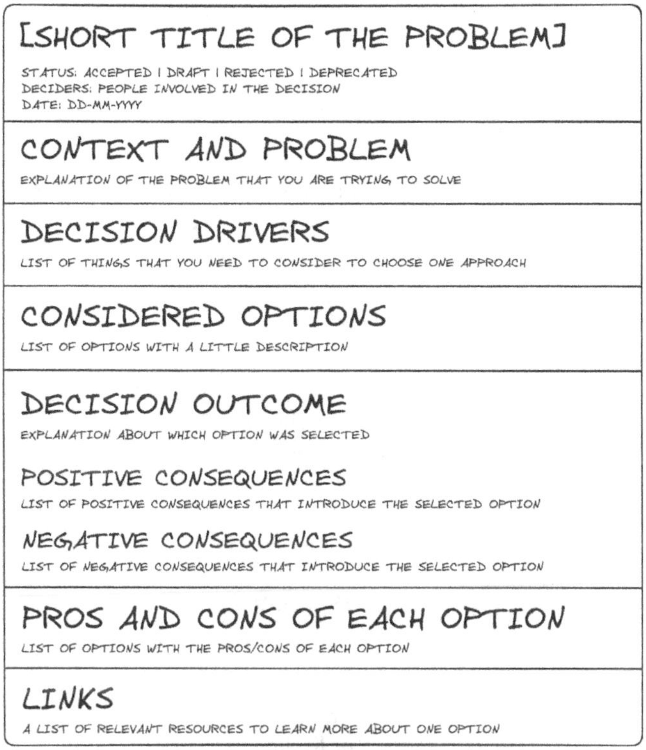

**FIGURE 1.6** The ADR approach that will appear in all of the chapters.

This book presents various libraries and approaches to solving specific problems. To illustrate the trade-offs involved in choosing one approach over another, different ADRs are included, highlighting multiple alternatives beyond the one implemented in the book.

## CREATING AN APPLICATION

In certain situations, creating an application can be time-consuming due to the manual addition of dependencies and the need to verify version compatibility. With Spring Boot, this issue is resolved by providing various options to create a project that automatically includes all of the necessary dependencies.

Nowadays, the alternatives that exist to create a Spring Boot application with some level of assistance are:

- Using Spring Initializr[10] from the Web site
- Using the plugin available on different IDEs, such as Eclipse, IntelliJ, and Visual Studio Code
- Using a command line to create the application

---

[10]https://start.spring.io/

This chapter explores multiple ways to create the project, focusing primarily on using plugins. The IntelliJ plugin is highlighted, as it is the most popular IDE choice according to the Snyk and JetBrains surveys.

**NOTE** *This decision depends on the reader's experience in building a project from scratch; therefore, this section does not include an ADR.*

### How to Use Alternatives

All alternatives lead to the same result; this section can be skipped if creating a Spring Boot project is already known.

### Using Spring Initializr

This alternative enables creating a project directly on a Web page and previewing the results instantly, without the need to download any files.

When visiting the Web page *https://start.spring.io/*, the configuration management, language, Spring Boot version, and all project metadata—such as group, artifact, name, and Java version—must be specified. Table 1.3 provides detailed information on the purpose of each field and the required values.

**TABLE 1.3** The data necessary to create a new project.

| Attribute | Value | Description |
|-----------|-------|-------------|
| Project | Maven Project | The kind of project to generate: either Maven Project or Gradle Project |
| Language | Java | The programming language to use: Java, Groovy, or Kotlin |
| Spring Boot | 3.3.0 | The version of Spring Boot to build against |
| Group | `com.twa` | The project's group ID, for the sake of organization in a Maven repository |
| Artifact | `api-reservation` | The project's artifact ID, as it would appear in a Maven repository |
| Name | `api-reservation` | The project name; this is also used to determine the name of the application's main class |
| Description | `API that manages everything to do with reservations` | The project description |
| Package name | `com.twa.flights.api.reservation` | The project's base package name |
| Packaging | `jar` | How the project should be packaged: either `jar` or `war` |
| Java | 17 | The version of Java to build with |

The next step involves including all the necessary dependencies for the project. To accomplish this, click the ADD DEPENDENCIES button, located in the left corner, and add the following dependencies:

- Spring Configuration Processor[11]: This generates the metadata for developers to use in configuration files such as YAML or `properties`.
- Spring Web: This dependency enables the application to support creating a RESTful API with an embeddable server, such as Tomcat.
- Spring Boot DevTools[12]: This library offers valuable features for developers, such as fast application restarts and remote debugging.

After including the dependencies, pressing the Generate button packages the application into a ZIP file. This file can be decompressed in any preferred directory. Then, open the project in the IDE following the instructions in *Appendix C*, and continue with the steps described in the *How to add logic to the application* section of this chapter.

### Using a Plugin

Another way to create a Spring Boot application and add dependencies is by using the plugin that most IDEs have preinstalled. For example, in IntelliJ—the default IDE used in this book—no additional setup is necessary.

Opening IntelliJ and selecting File -> New -> Project from the top menu displays the window shown in Figure 1.7, allowing the selection of the JDK version and the Spring Boot initializer location to create the application.

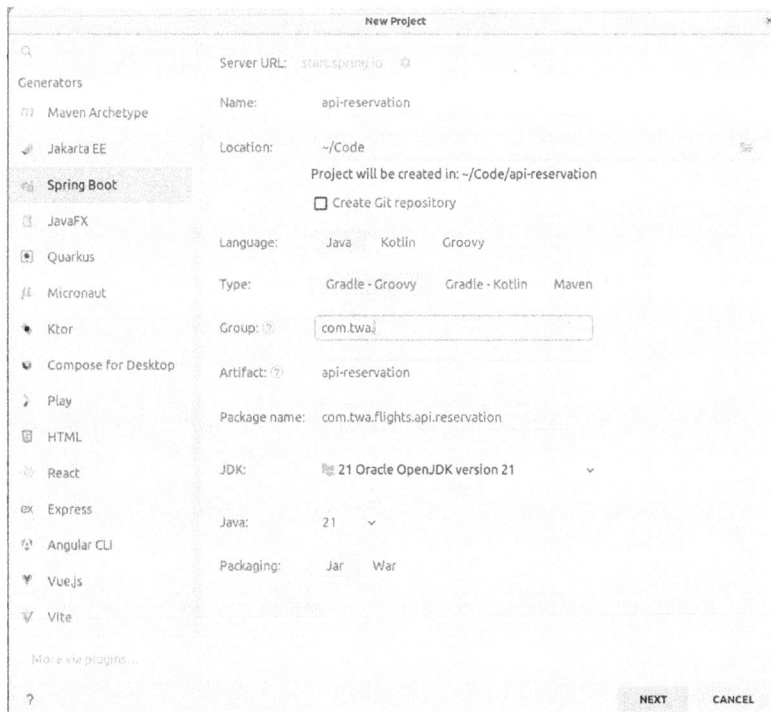

**FIGURE 1.7** Modal to create a new project using the IDE.

---

[11]https://docs.spring.io/spring-boot/docs/current/reference/html/configuration-metadata.html
[12]https://docs.spring.io/spring-boot/docs/current/reference/html/using-boot-devtools.html

As shown in the previous figure, most of the required information matches what is displayed in Spring Initializr.

The next step involves adding all of the necessary dependencies to ensure the project functions correctly. As mentioned earlier, Spring DevTools, Spring Configuration Processor, and Spring Web should be selected. Unlike Spring Initializr, here, dependencies are organized into groups, making them easier to locate, as illustrated in Figure 1.8.

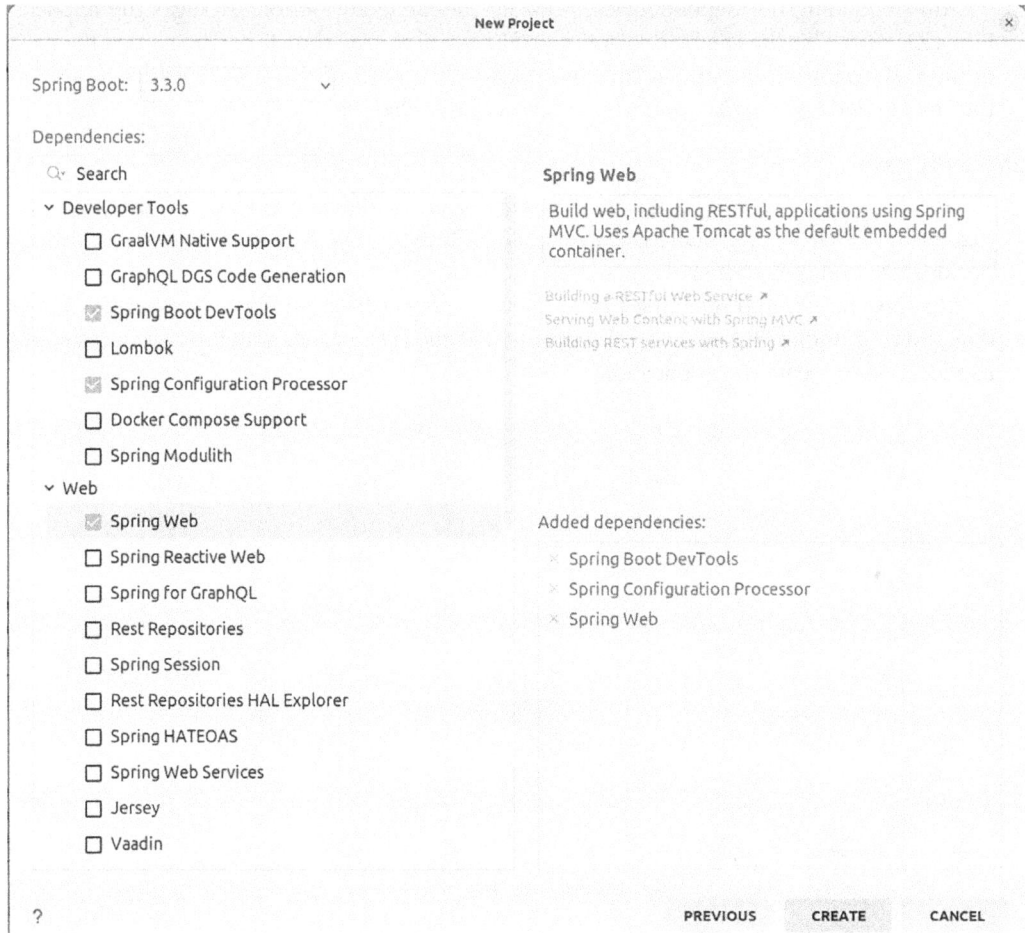

**FIGURE 1.8** Modal to add the dependencies to the project.

After completing this process, the result is the same as when using Spring Initializr.

## Using the Command Line

The last option uses the command line to create a project that uses the same engine as Spring Initialzr behind the scenes. This option is simple because it involves entering the same information as the other options but as parameters, similar to those listed in Listing 1.1.

```
→  ~ curl https://start.spring.io/starter.zip \
   -d type=maven-project \
   -d language=java \
   -d bootVersion=3.3.0 \
   -d baseDir=api-reservation \
   -d groupId=com.twa \
   -d artifactId=api-reservation \
   -d name=api-reservation \
   -d description="API which manages everything about the reservations" \
   -d packageName=com.twa.flights.api.reservation \
   -d dependencies=web,devtools,configuration-processor \
   -o api-reservation.zip
```

**LISTING 1.1** Command to create a project.

After executing the previous command, a ZIP file will be generated containing the same structure and files as a Spring Initializr project. The next step is to decompress the file and import it into the IDE, following the instructions detailed in *Appendix C*.

### What Is the Structure of the Application?

The project's structure comprises files and folders that represent configuration, tests, and application logic. This structure remains consistent regardless of the method used to generate the project, as the outcome is always the same.

To view the application's structure clearly, run the `tree` command from the root directory. This will produce an output similar to Listing 1.2.

```
→  ~ tree

├── HELP.md
├── mvnw
├── mvnw.cmd
├── pom.xml
└── src
        ├── main
        │       ├── java
        │       │       └── com
        │       │               └── twa
        │       │                       └── flights
        │       │                               └── api
        │                                               └──
reservation
        │                                                       └── ApiReservationApplication.java
        │               └── resources
        │                               ├── application.properties
        │                               ├── static
        │                               └── templates
        └── test
                └── java
                        └── com
                                └── twa
                                        └── flights
                                                └── api
                                                        └──
reservation
                                                                └── ApiReservationApplicationTests.java
```

**LISTING 1.2** Structure of the Spring Boot application.

The project's structure is similar to how it would look in Maven and Gradle. Only some files in the `root` folder are changed, but the main structure is not modified. Table 1.4 provides a brief explanation of the various elements that comprise the project.

**TABLE 1.4** Explanation of each part of the application.

| Element | Description |
|---|---|
| mvnw<br>mvnw.cmd | This script serves as a wrapper in case Maven is not installed on the machine. |
| pom.xml | This contains all the specifications Maven needs to build the project, such as dependencies, plugins, and repositories. |
| ApiReservationApplication.java | This is the main class of the application. |
| ApiReservationApplicationTests.java | This is a simple test class that verifies the application's correct operation. |
| application.properties | This file starts empty but serves as a place to define all the application's configuration settings. Alternatively, a file with the same name and a YAML extension can be used to configure the application. |
| templates<br>static | These folders will contain all the files related to exposing a Web page. |

One of the main components of any application is the file containing all the dependencies—in this case, the POM file, which contains all the dependencies necessary for executing the application. Listing 1.3 displays the file's contents.

```xml
<?xml version="1.0" encoding="UTF-8"?>
<project xmlns="http://maven.apache.org/POM/4.0.0" xmlns:xsi="http://
www.w3.org/2001/XMLSchema-instance"
    xsi:schemaLocation="http://maven.apache.org/POM/4.0.0 https://maven.
apache.org/xsd/maven-4.0.0.xsd">
    <modelVersion>4.0.0</modelVersion>
    <parent>
        <groupId>org.springframework.boot</groupId>
        <artifactId>spring-boot-starter-parent</artifactId>
        <version>3.3.0</version>
        <relativePath/> <!-- lookup parent from repository -->
    </parent>
    <groupId>com.twa</groupId>
    <artifactId>api-reservation</artifactId>
    <version>0.0.1-SNAPSHOT</version>
    <name>api-reservation</name>
    <description>API which manage everything about the reservations</
description>
    <properties>
        <java.version>17</java.version>
    </properties>
    <dependencies>
        <dependency>
            <groupId>org.springframework.boot</groupId>
            <artifactId>spring-boot-starter-web</artifactId>
        </dependency>
```

```
        <dependency>
                <groupId>org.springframework.boot</groupId>
                <artifactId>spring-boot-devtools</artifactId>
                <scope>runtime</scope>
                <optional>true</optional>
        </dependency>
        <dependency>
                <groupId>org.springframework.boot</groupId>
                <artifactId>spring-boot-configuration-processor
                </artifactId>
                <optional>true</optional>
        </dependency>
        <dependency>
                <groupId>org.springframework.boot</groupId>
                <artifactId>spring-boot-starter-test</artifactId>
                <scope>test</scope>
        </dependency>
    </dependencies>
    <build>
        <plugins>
                <plugin>
                        <groupId>org.springframework.boot</groupId>
                        <artifactId>spring-boot-maven-plugin</artifactId>
                </plugin>
        </plugins>
    </build>

</project>
```

**LISTING 1.3** Structure of the POM file.

Listing 1.3 shows an additional dependency, `spring-boot-test`, which wasn't explicitly selected because, by default, any Spring Boot application archetype includes this dependency along with a simple test to ensure the application works correctly.

One last thing to mention about the POM file is the `parent-pom` at the beginning of the file's definition, which contains all the information related to building the application and the definitions of the versions of the different libraries that Spring Boot and the other modules can use. This approach reduces the possibility of conflicting versions of the dependencies because it delegates the responsibility of indicating which version of a specific library is best to Spring Boot.

## How to Add Logic to the Application

Creating the application's skeleton does not mean the project is complete; it is just the starting point, as the project only includes a class responsible for running the application, similar to what is shown in Listing 1.4.

```
import org.springframework.boot.SpringApplication;
import org.springframework.boot.autoconfigure.SpringBootApplication;


@SpringBootApplication
public class ApiReservationApplication {
    public static void main(String[] args) {
        SpringApplication.run(ApiReservationApplication.class, args);
    }
}
```

**LISTING 1.4** Structure of the main class.

As shown in Listing 1.4, the case study presented in this book initially lacks endpoints or specific logic. The following section introduces the logic required to ensure the application exhibits its intended behavior.

## Creating the Domain

The first step in the application process is to define the classes that represent the application's domain and contain all the information the endpoints need to perform their tasks. Two methods are available for this: the traditional approach of creating a class with attributes, setters, and getters, or using a newer feature introduced in Java 14 called records.

**NOTE** *Records reduce the amount of code required to create a class by providing automatic access to the data contained in each attribute, eliminating the need for explicit setters and getters.*

To begin, create a record that represents the information required for each passenger taking a flight, as shown in Listing 1.5.

```
package com.twa.flights.api.reservation.dto;

import java.time.LocalDate;

public record PassengerDTO(
        Long id,
        String firstName,
        String lastName,
        String documentNumber,
        String documentType,
        String nationality,
        LocalDate birthday) {
}
```

*LISTING 1.5* Passenger class definition.

An alternative way to define the same block as Listing 1.5 is shown in Listing 1.6.

```
package com.twa.flights.api.reservation.dto;

import java.time.LocalDate;

public class PassengerDTO {

    private Long id;
    private String firstName;
    private String lastName;
    private String documentNumber;
    private String documentType;
    private String nationality;
    private LocalDate birthday;

    // Default constructor
    public PassengerDTO() {
    }
```

```
    // Constructor with all fields
    public PassengerDTO(Long id, String firstName, String lastName,
String documentNumber, String documentType, String nationality,
LocalDate birthday) {
        this.id = id;
        this.firstName = firstName;
        this.lastName = lastName;
        this.documentNumber = documentNumber;
        this.documentType = documentType;
        this.nationality = nationality;
        this.birthday = birthday;
    }

    // Getters and Setters
}
```

**LISTING 1.6** Passenger class definition without records.

The record's name ends with DTO, following a standard convention designed to keep the class simple, serving as the data structure that the application receives from or returns to a client making a request.

**NOTE** *DTO, or data transfer object, is not a new pattern; it's a pattern that has been around for more than twenty years and appears in the book Patterns of Enterprise Application Architecture by Martin Fowler[13].*

*On Martin Fowler's official Web site[14], there is a short description of the pattern.*

After creating the passengers who will take the flight, the next step involves creating a class that contains all the contact information for the reservation owner in case any issues arise, as illustrated in Listing 1.7.

```
package com.twa.flights.api.reservation.dto;

public record ContactDTO(
        Long id,
        String telephoneNumber,
        String email) {

}
```

**LISTING 1.7** Contact class definition.

The last step is to create a class that represents a flight reservation, including the passenger information and contact details, as shown in Listing 1.8.

```
package com.twa.flights.api.reservation.dto;

import java.util.List;

public record ReservationDTO(
```

---

[13]https://martinfowler.com/books/eaa.html
[14]https://martinfowler.com/eaaCatalog/dataTransferObject.html

```
            Long id,
            String itineraryId,
            String searchId,
            List<PassengerDTO> passengers,
            ContactDTO contact
) { }
```

**LISTING 1.8** Reservation class definition.

The goal is to maintain a simple domain model. As a result, no attributes related to the flight are included—only two IDs associated with the flight search are present.

## Creating the Endpoints

An application that contains only domain classes without any access points, such as endpoints, lacks meaningful functionality. Therefore, it is necessary to create a class that exposes at least one endpoint, as shown in Listing 1.9.

```
package com.twa.flights.api.reservation.controller;

import com.twa.flights.api.reservation.dto.ReservationDTO;
import org.slf4j.Logger;
import org.slf4j.LoggerFactory;
import org.springframework.http.HttpStatus;
import org.springframework.http.ResponseEntity;
import org.springframework.web.bind.annotation.*;


@RestController //Define that this class exposes some endpoints
@RequestMapping("/reservation") // Base path of all the endpoints in the
class
public class ReservationController {

    private static final Logger LOGGER = LoggerFactory.
getLogger(ReservationController.class);

    @GetMapping("/{id}")
    public ResponseEntity<ReservationDTO> getReservationById(@
PathVariable Long id) {
        LOGGER.info("Obtain information from a reservation with {}",
id);
        ReservationDTO response = new ReservationDTO(1L, "1", "1",
Collections.emptyList(), null);
        return new ResponseEntity<>(response, HttpStatus.OK);
    }
}
```

**LISTING 1.9** Basic definition of one controller with one endpoint.

Several elements in the previous code block include the Spring Boot MVC library. Table 1.5 gives a brief explanation of each one.

**TABLE 1.5** Elements that compose a controller.

| Element | Description |
| --- | --- |
| @RestController | This is specifically designed for building RESTful Web services, making it easier to develop APIs that conform to REST principles. |
| @RequestMapping | This is an annotation that specifies the base URL path for all the endpoints in this controller. |
| @GetMapping | This is an annotation map of HTTP GET requests to the specific URL. |
| @PathVariable | This is an annotation used to extract values from the URI path and assign them to method parameters in a controller. |
| ResponseEntity | This represents the HTTP response, including the status code, headers, and body. |
| HttpStatus[15] | This enum contains a series of constants representing specific HTTP statuses, such as 204 (No Content). |

Each endpoint should return the specific HTTP code representing the result of its execution. For example, when an element is created, the HTTP status code 201 should be returned, indicating to the consumer that a new resource has been successfully created.

**NOTE**

*HTTP status is a standard that all applications should follow to indicate what happens with a request. The responses are grouped into different categories, each with a specific purpose:*

- *Informational (100–199)*
- *Successful (200–299)*
- *Redirection (300–399)*
- *Client error (400–499)*
- *Server error (500–599)*

*To obtain more information about each specific code, check out the Mozilla docs page[16].*

Another recommendation for each endpoint is to include a log to show what the application receives. Of course, try not to use the INFO level on the logs too often because if their tons of logs could by difficult to see what happens on the applications

Additional methods are necessary because the current configuration only supports returning information about a single reservation. This chapter focuses on understanding the core concept of creating and configuring an application, while the whole application structure will be introduced in the next chapter.

**NOTE**

*HTTP defines a set of methods, each representing the intent behind a request. Table 1.6 provides a brief overview of the most relevant available operations.*

[15]https://docs.spring.io/spring-framework/docs/current/javadoc-api/org/springframework/http/HttpStatus.html
[16]https://developer.mozilla.org/en-US/docs/Web/HTTP/Status

**TABLE 1.6** Actions associated with HTTP.

| Action | Description | Example URL |
|---|---|---|
| GET | Retrieve data from the server, which could be one element or a list of elements. | GET /user<br>GET /user/:id |
| POST | Submit data to be processed to a specified resource. | POST /user |
| PUT | Update an existing resource or create a new one if it does not exist. | PUT /user/:id |
| PATCH | Apply partial modifications to a resource. | PATCH /user/:id |
| DELETE | Delete a specified resource. | DELETE / user/:id |

*Consider that in some scenarios, where the volume of information to send on a GET operation is large or the object is complex, some developers use POST as an alternative to GET.*

Let's add all the application methods for creating, updating, and deleting reservation information, as appears in Listing 1.10.

```
package com.twa.flights.api.reservation.controller;

// Other imports

import java.util.Collections;
import java.util.List;

@RestController
@RequestMapping("/reservation")
public class ReservationController {

    private static final Logger LOGGER = LoggerFactory.
getLogger(ReservationController.class);

    // Previous GET operation

    @GetMapping
    public ResponseEntity<List<ReservationDTO>> getReservations() {
        LOGGER.info("Obtain all the reservations");
        List<ReservationDTO> response = Collections.emptyList();
        return new ResponseEntity<>(response, HttpStatus.OK);
    }

    @PostMapping
    public ResponseEntity<ReservationDTO> save(@RequestBody
ReservationDTO reservation) {
        LOGGER.info("Saving new reservation");
        return new ResponseEntity<>(reservation, HttpStatus.CREATED);
    }

    @PutMapping("/{id}")
    public ResponseEntity<ReservationDTO> update(@PathVariable Long id,
@RequestBody ReservationDTO reservation) {
```

```
        LOGGER.info("Updating a reservation with {}", id);
        return new ResponseEntity<>(reservation, HttpStatus.OK);
    }

    @DeleteMapping("/{id}")
    public ResponseEntity<Void> delete(@PathVariable Long id) {
        LOGGER.info("Deleting a reservation with {}", id);
        return new ResponseEntity<>(HttpStatus.OK);
    }
}
```

**LISTING 1.10** New operations on the controller.

As shown in the previous listing, specific annotations correspond to different types of actions, such as @DeleteMapping, @PutMapping, and @PostMapping, making the purpose of each endpoint clear and easy to understand.

Now that a simple application with a defined domain and a set of endpoints is in place, the next step is to validate whether everything functions as expected.

### How to Run the Code

Once the project is created and modified to expose a series of endpoints, the next step involves running the application to verify that everything functions correctly. Various options are available, depending on whether the IDE or command line is preferred; however, the outcome will be the same in both cases.

### Using the IDE

Running the application through the IDE is one of the simplest tasks, as it doesn't require opening a terminal or performing any special steps. This process may vary depending on the IDE used for development. For IntelliJ, opening the main class, ApiReservationApplication, will display two green triangles, as shown in Figure 1.9.

**FIGURE 1.9** Main class to run the application.

Clicking on the green triangles will display various options, as shown in Figure 1.10.

**FIGURE 1.10** Options to execute the application.

If the Run '[application]' option is selected, a terminal will open showing logs similar to those in Listing 1.11.

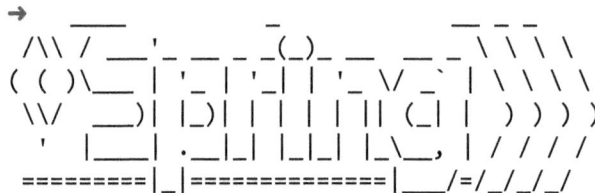

```
   ➜        ___
    /\\ /  ___'_ _ _ _(_)_ __ __ _ \ \ \ \
   ( ( )\___ | '_ | '_| | '_ \/ _` | \ \ \ \
    \\/  ___)| |_)| | | | | || (_| |  ) ) ) )
     '  |____| .__|_| |_|_| |_\__, | / / / /
    =========|_|==============|___/=/_/_/_/

 :: Spring Boot ::                (v3.3.0)

2024-06-12T17:46:21.849-03:00  INFO 178776 --- [api-reservation]
[  restartedMain] c.t.f.a.r.ApiReservationApplication       : Starting
ApiReservationApplication using Java 21.0.2 with PID 178776 (/home/
asacco/Code/api-reservation/target/classes started by asacco in /home/
asacco/Code/api-reservation)
2024-06-12T17:46:21.850-03:00  INFO 178776 --- [api-reservation] [
restartedMain] c.t.f.a.r.ApiReservationApplication       : No active
profile set, falling back to 1 default profile: "default"
2024-06-12T17:46:21.867-03:00  INFO 178776 --- [api-reservation]
[  restartedMain] .e.DevToolsPropertyDefaultsPostProcessor : Devtools
property defaults active! Set 'spring.devtools.add-properties' to
'false' to disable
2024-06-12T17:46:21.868-03:00  INFO 178776 --- [api-reservation] [
restartedMain] .e.DevToolsPropertyDefaultsPostProcessor : For additional
web related logging consider setting the 'logging.level.web' property to
'DEBUG'
2024-06-12T17:46:22.156-03:00  INFO 178776 --- [api-reservation]
[  restartedMain] o.s.b.w.embedded.tomcat.TomcatWebServer  : Tomcat
initialized with port 8090 (http)
```

```
2024-06-12T17:46:22.161-03:00  INFO 178776 --- [api-reservation]
[ restartedMain] o.apache.catalina.core.StandardService  : Starting
service [Tomcat]
2024-06-12T17:46:22.161-03:00  INFO 178776 --- [api-reservation]
[ restartedMain] o.apache.catalina.core.StandardEngine  : Starting
Servlet engine: [Apache Tomcat/10.1.24]
2024-06-12T17:46:22.172-03:00  INFO 178776 --- [api-reservation] [
restartedMain] o.a.c.c.C.[Tomcat].[localhost].[/]      : Initializing
Spring embedded WebApplicationContext
2024-06-12T17:46:22.172-03:00  INFO 178776 --- [api-reservation]
[ restartedMain] w.s.c.ServletWebServerApplicationContext : Root
WebApplicationContext: initialization completed in 304 ms
2024-06-12T17:46:22.279-03:00  INFO 178776 --- [api-reservation] [
restartedMain] o.s.b.d.a.OptionalLiveReloadServer      : LiveReload
server is running on port 35729
2024-06-12T17:46:22.287-03:00  INFO 178776 --- [api-reservation] [
restartedMain] o.s.b.w.embedded.tomcat.TomcatWebServer  : Tomcat started
on port 8080 (http) with context path '/'
2024-06-12T17:46:22.291-03:00  INFO 178776 --- [api-reservation]
[ restartedMain] c.t.f.a.r.ApiReservationApplication    : Started
ApiReservationApplication in 0.556 seconds (process running for 0.813)
```

**LISTING 1.11** The output on running the application.

Once the application is running, the next step is to verify that everything works as expected. There are different ways to send a request to an application, such as `curl`, shown in Listing 1.12.

```
→ ~ curl --location 'localhost:8080/reservation/1'
{"id":1,"itineraryId":"1","searchId":"1","passengers":[],"contact":null}
```

**LISTING 1.12** Curl command to validate whether the application works.

Another alternative involves using tools such as Postman or Insomnia, which offer similar interfaces. In both cases, a request is made to obtain information for a single reservation, but the same can be done with other endpoints—such as DELETE, POST, PUT, and GET—to manage and retrieve all reservations.

## Using the Command Line

It's uncommon for developers to use the command line to execute the application, but in some circumstances, such as failures on the IDE or execution on some machines where the IDE is not installed, this becomes necessary.

To execute the application, run the command shown in Listing 1.13.

```
→ ~ ./mvnw spring-boot:run


  .   ____          _            __ _ _
 /\\ / ___'_ __ _ _(_)_ __  __ _ \ \ \ \
( ( )\___ | '_ | '_| | '_ \/ _` | \ \ \ \
 \\/  ___)| |_)| | | | | || (_| |  ) ) ) )
  '  |____| .__|_| |_|_| |_\__, | / / / /
 =========|_|==============|___/=/_/_/_/
```

```
:: Spring Boot ::                    (v3.3.0)

2024-06-12T17:46:21.849-03:00  INFO 178776 --- [api-reservation]
[ restartedMain] c.t.f.a.r.ApiReservationApplication    : Starting
ApiReservationApplication using Java 21.0.2 with PID 178776 (/home/asacco/
Code/api-reservation/target/classes started by asacco in /home/asacco/Code/
api-reservation)
2024-06-12T17:46:21.850-03:00  INFO 178776 --- [api-reservation] [
restartedMain] c.t.f.a.r.ApiReservationApplication    : No active profile
set, falling back to 1 default profile: "default"
2024-06-12T17:46:21.867-03:00  INFO 178776 --- [api-reservation] [
restartedMain] .e.DevToolsPropertyDefaultsPostProcessor : Devtools property
defaults active! Set 'spring.devtools.add-properties' to 'false' to disable
2024-06-12T17:46:21.868-03:00  INFO 178776 --- [api-reservation] [
restartedMain] .e.DevToolsPropertyDefaultsPostProcessor : For additional web
related logging consider setting the 'logging.level.web' property to 'DEBUG'
2024-06-12T17:46:22.156-03:00  INFO 178776 --- [api-reservation] [
restartedMain] o.s.b.w.embedded.tomcat.TomcatWebServer  : Tomcat initialized
with port 8090 (http)
2024-06-12T17:46:22.161-03:00  INFO 178776 --- [api-reservation] [
restartedMain] o.apache.catalina.core.StandardService   : Starting service
[Tomcat]
......
2024-06-12T17:46:22.291-03:00  INFO 178776 --- [api-reservation]
[ restartedMain] c.t.f.a.r.ApiReservationApplication    : Started
ApiReservationApplication in 0.556 seconds (process running for 0.813)
```

**LISTING 1.13** The command to run the application from the root directory.

After executing the application from the command line, the output should match what is shown in Listing 1.13. The exact requests can then be sent to the endpoints to verify that the application is functioning correctly.

Other commands related to Spring Boot applications can also be executed from the command line, as illustrated in Table 1.7.

**TABLE 1.7** Actions that can be performed from the console with Spring Boot.

| Command | Description |
|---|---|
| mvn spring-boot:build-image | This packages the entire application into an image—similar to a Docker image—that can be deployed across different environments. This topic is explored in more detail in *Chapter 9*. |
| mvn spring-boot:build-info | This generates a file called build-info.properties with all the information about the build process. |
| mvn spring-boot:help | This assists with the use of the command spring-boot. |
| mvn spring-boot:repackage | This command extends the packaging to be executable using java -jar someJar.jar. |
| mvn spring-boot:run | This command runs the application. |

*(Continued)*

*TABLE 1.7* (Continued)

| Command | Description |
|---|---|
| mvn spring-boot:start | This is an alternative method for running the application without locking the console. |
| mvn spring-boot:stop | This command stops the application if it is launched using the start command. |

## Common Problems

During execution, various problems may arise. One of the most common is that another application already allocates the desired port. Spring Boot includes a class called FailureAnalyzer, which analyzes issues during application execution and provides more information about the potential cause of the problem, as shown in Listing 1.14.

```
Error starting ApplicationContext. To display the condition evaluation
report re-run your application with 'debug' enabled.
2024-06-14T11:29:37.579-03:00 ERROR 413844 --- [api-reservation] [
restartedMain] o.s.b.d.LoggingFailureAnalysisReporter   :

***************************
APPLICATION FAILED TO START
***************************

Description:

Web server failed to start. Port 8080 was already in use.

Action:

Identify and stop the process that's listening on port 8080 or configure
this application to listen on another port.
```

*LISTING 1.14* Output of the execution with errors.

Custom exceptions can be created, allowing Spring Boot to interpret the issue and display relevant information on the console.

## BEST PRACTICES

Adopting certain practices during the creation of a new application can help minimize future issues, especially since the application will evolve through different stages, just as it does in real life.

### Reducing Possible Conflicts

Initially, creating an application may seem simple, using the various alternatives offered by Spring Boot. Throughout the application's lifecycle, dependencies can be added directly to the POM file without the need for wizards or tools. This practice might not cause issues initially, but it can lead to significant problems during the build process due to version conflicts between libraries introduced by different dependencies.

Figure 1.11 illustrates a potential conflict between different dependencies, including a transitive JUnit dependency, but utilizing other versions.

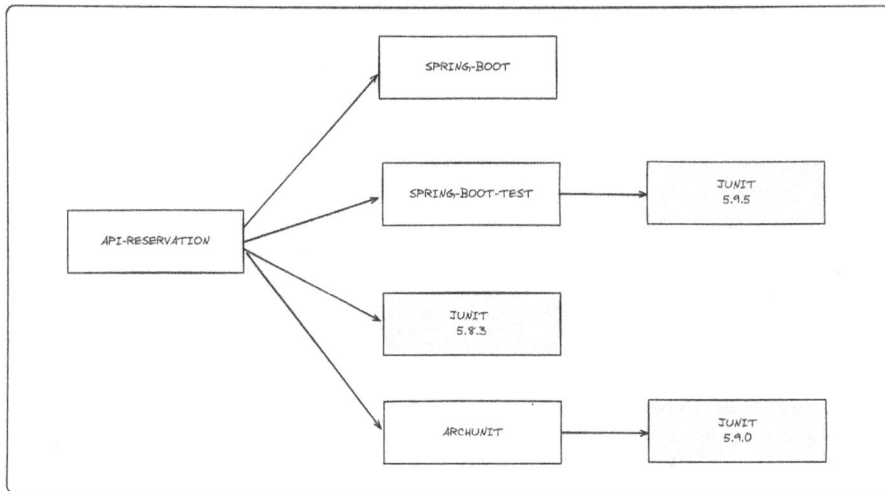

**FIGURE 1.11** Dependencies on a project that could produce conflicts.

To address this issue or restrict the application to specific versions of JDK or Maven, use the Enforcer plugin, supported by both Maven[17] and Gradle[18].

Let's add a plugin like that shown in Listing 1.15 to reduce the chance of having problems with the dependencies on the application throughout the book.

```
<plugin>
   <groupId>org.apache.maven.plugins</groupId>
   <artifactId>maven-enforcer-plugin</artifactId>
   <version>3.0.0-M2</version>
   <executions>
         <execution>
                <id>enforce</id>
                <goals>
                     <goal>enforce</goal>
                </goals>
                <configuration>
                     <rules>
                            <banDuplicatePomDependencyVersions/>
                            <requireMavenVersion>
                                 <version>3.8.3</version>
                                 <message>Invalid Maven version. It
should, at least, be 3.8.3</message>
                            </requireMavenVersion>
                            <requireJavaVersion>
                                 <version>${java.version}</version>
                                 <message>Invalid Java version. It
should, at least, be ${java.version}</message>
```

---

[17]https://maven.apache.org/enforcer/maven-enforcer-plugin/index.html
[18]https://kordamp.org/enforcer-gradle-plugin/#_introduction

```
                        </requireJavaVersion>
                    </rules>
                </configuration>
            </execution>
        </executions>
    </plugin>
```

LISTING 1.15 Plugin to reduce the problems with the project configuration.

When the previous configuration is added to the project, the plugin validates the Maven and Java versions running on the machine and checks for issues with dependencies, such as duplicate definitions or version conflicts.

To validate whether everything works correctly, duplicate any dependency in the `pom.xml` file—such as `spring-boot-test`—and run the command `mvn clean compile`. If successful, the output will resemble Listing 1.16.

```
→  ~ mvn clean install
[INFO] Scanning for projects...
[INFO]
[INFO] -------------------< com.example:api-reservation >--------------------
[INFO] Building api-reservation 0.0.1-SNAPSHOT
[INFO]    from pom.xml
[INFO] --------------------------------[ jar ]---------------------------------
[INFO]
[INFO] --- clean:3.3.2:clean (default-clean) @ api-reservation ---
[INFO] Deleting /home/asacco/Code/api-reservation/target
[INFO]
[INFO] --- enforcer:3.0.0-M2:enforce (enforce) @ api-reservation ---
[WARNING] Rule 0: org.apache.maven.plugins.enforcer.
BanDuplicatePomDependencyVersions failed with message:
Found 1 duplicate dependency declaration in this project:
 - dependencies.dependency[org.springframework.boot:spring-boot-configuration-
processor:jar] ( 2 times )

[INFO] ------------------------------------------------------------------------
[INFO] BUILD FAILURE
[INFO] ------------------------------------------------------------------------
[INFO] Total time:  0.307 s
[INFO] Finished at: 2024-06-12T13:45:24-03:00
[INFO] ------------------------------------------------------------------------
```

LISTING 1.16 Execution of a command to validate the dependencies.

As shown in the execution's output, the plugin throws an exception and provides a clear explanation of the problem, making it relatively simple to identify and fix the issue.

## Formatting the Source Code

The format of the code is a critical aspect of application development because it affects the code's maintainability and reduces the risk that someone will not understand the concept of a particular part of the code.

Most IDEs assist with code formatting according to widely accepted standards, though this support may vary depending on the IDE version, the need for specific plugins, and other factors.

A practical solution is to add a plugin compatible with Maven and Gradle to minimize reliance on IDE-based code formatting.

Let's add a plugin like the one in Listing 1.17 to reduce the chance of having problems with the application code throughout the book.

```
<plugin>
    <groupId>com.diffplug.spotless</groupId>
    <artifactId>spotless-maven-plugin</artifactId>
    <version>2.43.0</version>
    <configuration>
        <java>
            <includes>
                <include>src/main/java/**/*.java</include> <!--
Check application code -->
                <include>src/test/java/**/*.java</include> <!--
Check application tests code -->
            </includes>
            <importOrder /> <!-- standard import order -->
            <removeUnusedImports /> <!-- remove unused imports -->
            <googleJavaFormat>
                <style>AOSP</style> <!-- or GOOGLE (optional) -->
            </googleJavaFormat>
        </java>
    </configuration>
    <executions>
        <execution>
            <goals>
                <goal>check</goal>
                <goal>apply</goal>
            </goals>
        </execution>
    </executions>
</plugin>
```

**LISTING 1.17** Plugin to format the source code.

This plugin enables the specification of parameters, such as ordering or removing imports, on a per-class basis, helping to keep the code clear and easy to understand.

Each time a relevant command—such as compile, clean, build, or install—is executed in the application, the formatter checks the code's format and corrects any formatting issues. To verify that it is functioning correctly, modify any class with incorrect formatting and then run `mvn compile` or another command in the console.

## SUMMARY

Throughout this chapter, the fundamentals of Spring and the key distinctions between it and Spring Boot were introduced. A basic application was created to expose several endpoints, though it currently lacks complex logic. This logic will be incorporated in the following chapter, after exploring the various architectural styles and strategies for organizing logic within an application.

# CHAPTER 2

# CREATING THE DOMAIN OF THE APPLICATION

In the previous chapter, a basic application was created with a set of endpoints. It did not, however, include the core business logic, which is the essential part of any application. Before implementing this logic, it's necessary to understand the various architectural styles employed in platform development. Understanding this provides clarity on the domain structure within the application and contributes to more informed and effective development practices.

Another crucial aspect of every application is establishing structured layers for its internal components and interactions. Without a defined pattern, each application could have its own standard, which would directly impact its maintainability.

Understanding these aspects helps with not only grasping the rationale behind choosing one approach over another within this book but also developing the ability to make strategic decisions regarding key concepts in broader software development contexts.

## INTRODUCTION TO MICROSERVICES

Microservices may appear as a silver bullet to all the problems associated with monoliths, and those who utilize this new paradigm try to build their applications using it from scratch. By not considering the potential issues related to the new paradigm, however, the construction of the new platform can fail. The situation becomes even more complex when working with an existing platform that, aside from some specific issues, generally functions well—under these conditions, the risk of introducing errors increases significantly.

**NOTE**
*Understanding the main differences between these two paradigms is crucial for not only developing new Spring Boot applications but also maintaining and evolving existing ones. Legacy applications may adopt one of these approaches, and any changes introduced can impact the system as a whole; therefore, it is essential to carefully assess the broader implications.*

## Problems Associated with Monoliths

Initially, the monolith was the best option for creating an application that handled multiple functions, as all operations were interconnected as part of the same business. Consequently, the logic and source code of the system resided in a single location, leading to multiple developers working simultaneously and introducing changes that could cause significant conflicts during merges.

Figure 2.1 illustrates a typical monolith architecture, where multiple modules comprise an entire application.

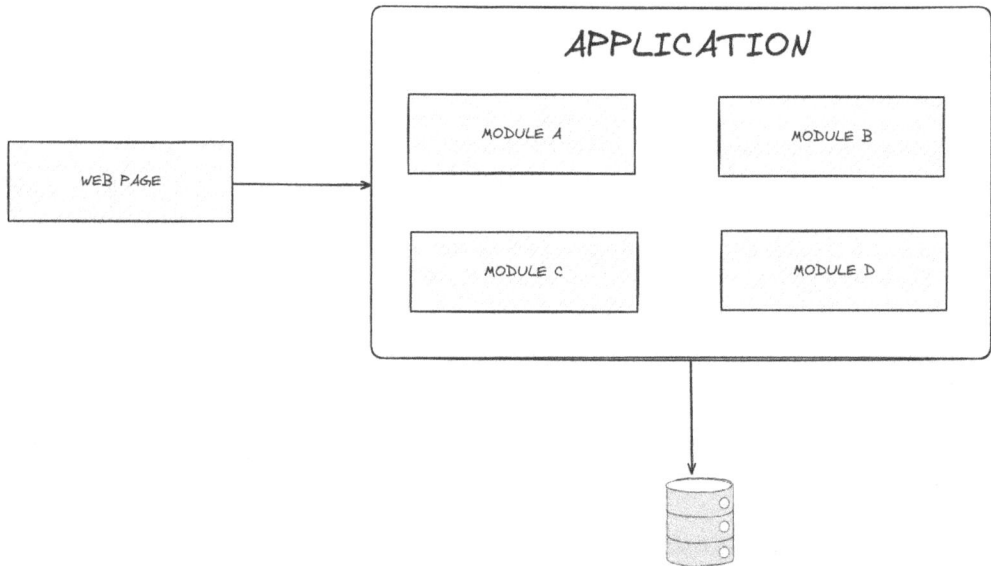

**FIGURE 2.1** Example of the monolith architecture.

Let's examine some key issues associated with monolithic architecture to understand why transitioning to a different architectural paradigm is necessary.

- Poor Flexibility: Implementing changes to the application's language or framework is slow and cumbersome because it requires modifying the entire codebase.
- Development Speed: Progress becomes limited because multiple developers working on the same repository can lead to significant merge conflicts. Additionally, various teams working on the same codebase in large applications can create an overhead in coordinating changes and prioritizing tasks.
- Limited Scalability: Resource usage, such as memory and CPU, is less efficient in an extensive monolithic application than in smaller applications. High traffic to a single endpoint can impact the entire platform. The only available solutions are vertical or horizontal scaling, both of which can substantially raise costs depending on the cloud provider, as they require additional instances or increased resources for a single server.

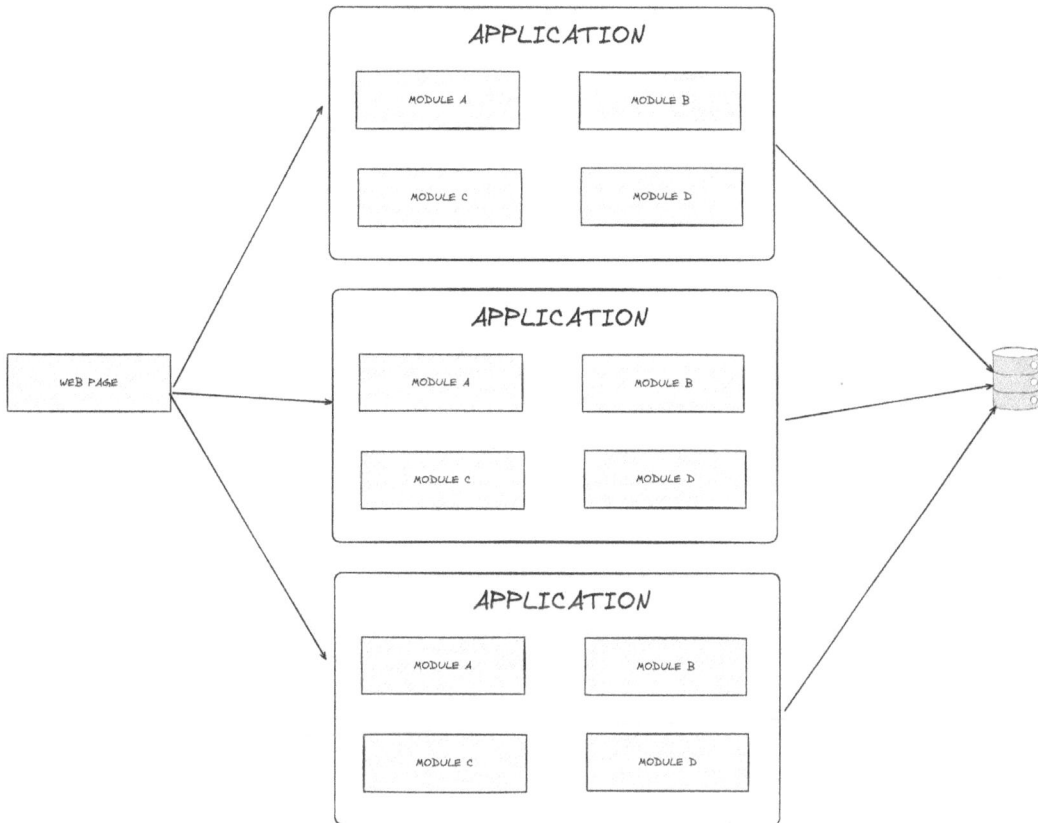

**FIGURE 2.2** An example of the scale of the application.

Figure 2.2 illustrates how multiple application instances share the same database, which can make accessing the information problematic.

The main issue with both types of scaling is the database, which often becomes a bottleneck as all operations attempt to access it for information. Consequently, scaling the infrastructure associated with the database also becomes necessary.

• Poor Reliability: A problem in any part of the application can cause the entire platform to become unstable or go down, impacting all users.

NOTE

*When the first versions of Spring Boot came out, most developers created big applications with tons of endpoints and exposed HTML directly; this approach disappeared when the new paradigm appeared, and most companies migrated their old applications. There are, however, some old applications that some companies, such as banks, still use the old schema for.*

All of these problems directly impact the changes that can be made to the application, affecting its performance and maintainability.

There are many other problems associated with this type of architecture; however, providing detailed information about every kind of architecture is beyond the scope of this book.

## Problems and Solutions Relating to Microservices

Microservices emerged as a solution to many problems with the monolithic paradigm, such as having all the source code in one place and deploying a single, extensive application. Initially, discussions about this paradigm did not garner much interest. When industry experts began documenting its potential and benefits, however, developers began migrating their applications to this new architecture. Influential sources included Chris Richardson's[1] and Martin Fowler's blogs[2].

The idea behind microservices is to reduce complexity by splitting a single application, multiple domains, or multiple operations into small, independent applications, each with a specific responsibility. All operations exhibit high cohesion; for instance, one microservice might handle all functions related to platform users—such as user creation, updating user details, and password resets. In contrast, another microservice could manage the lifecycle of e-commerce orders, interacting with the user-related microservice to retrieve information such as the email address for invoice delivery.

Figure 2.3 illustrates a basic microservices architecture, depicting multiple services interacting to accomplish tasks, each possibly utilizing databases of the same or varying flavors.

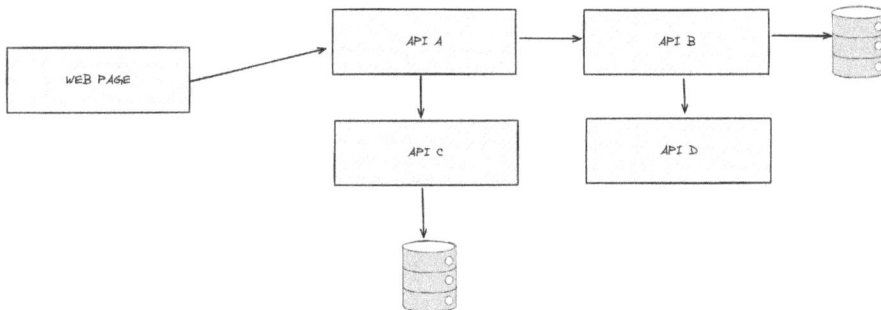

**FIGURE 2.3** An example of a microservices architecture.

Let's explore some major issues associated with a microservices architecture to understand why some companies transitioned to this paradigm:

• Technology: One of the main drawbacks of a monolithic architecture is the difficulty in adopting new technologies or upgrading library versions across the application. In contrast, microservices offer greater flexibility—each service can independently upgrade its libraries or frameworks. This allows for incremental updates, where individual microservices can adopt newer versions at their own pace (e.g., one per week or month), without disrupting

---

[1]https://microservices.io/
[2]https://martinfowler.com/

the rest of the system. This modularity significantly improves maintainability and adaptability.

- Latency: Most of the time, the monolith does not need to interact with other systems or just do it with a database. Hence, the time to complete a request depends, at some point, on the ability to process the request and return the response. Still, microservices need to interact with each other to exchange certain information to complete an operation. In this case, the situation differs from the previous paradigm because communication between different microservices requires the use of the network, which can introduce specific latency in connecting and transferring information.

- Timeout: One critical aspect to consider regarding communication between microservices is that it is not feasible to wait indefinitely for a response from a particular microservice. Consequently, one effective strategy to limit the duration of communication is to implement timeouts. The challenge, however, lies in determining the appropriate timeout for each endpoint. To address this query, it is essential to ascertain the average response time of other microservice endpoints. This information should be utilized to establish the timeout for the invoking microservice. There are many strategies for defining the timeout; one of the most important is to determine the service-level objective (SLO) for each endpoint, so the microservice owner indicates the maximum time each endpoint call takes to return a response.

- Failures: The possibility exists that communication between different microservices fails for various reasons, such as one of the microservices being unhealthy and not responding to requests, exceptions during the processing of requests by the microservices, or network problems. All these kinds of issues affect the platform because, under the previous paradigm, the chance of encountering issues was low, perhaps due to a problem with the connection to the database or a request that produced an exception. With microservices, however, the risk increases due to the need to communicate across multiple services. To address this challenge, various resilience patterns offer different solutions—such as retrying requests or implementing fallback behaviors—which will be explored throughout this book.

- Scaling: Microservices enable the ability to scale only the parts of the platform experiencing increased request volume, resulting in higher CPU or memory usage. It is, however, essential to set restrictions on the maximum and minimum number of instances each microservice can have. Without such limits, if a microservice encounters an issue and scales uncontrollably, it could result in a large number of simultaneous cases, significantly increasing costs.

- Debugging: Microservices introduce additional complexity when debugging specific issues, as having all the source code readily available is often required. Running all microservices locally is typically not feasible due to high resource consumption, such as memory and CPU. To address this challenge, several alternatives exist. One approach is to inspect the platform logs to identify the microservice with the issue and then simulate the scenario using unit or integration tests. Another option is to run only the microservice in question and reproduce the request using the parameters found in the logs to debug the internal behavior of the application.

Finally, depending on the programming language, remote debugging can be performed using an IDE to connect with the application running in specific environments.

- Testing: This topic is relevant to any type of paradigm because it helps developers trust the quality of their changes before deploying them to an environment, thereby avoiding many problems. In the case of microservices, this has more relevance because a microservice with bugs could affect another, so it's important to create more than just unit tests that check whether every single function works fine. Integration tests are necessary to verify that all components function correctly and interact appropriately. Strategies include running the application, making requests, and checking results without manual intervention, as well as mocking specific components, similar to black-box testing.
- Documentation: This is essential for understanding how the platform works and the impact of changes on individual microservices. For example, documentation could include a diagram explaining how a request on one microservice is routed to another to obtain all the necessary information to return an answer.

  Other alternatives include documenting the different flows using tools such as APM, which provide an overview of how microservices interact with actual requests in specific environments. The primary challenge with this approach is determining why one API or microservice interacts with another. Therefore, it must be inferred.

Several important factors must be considered when using microservices, as they offer many benefits but also introduce complexities that can sometimes become problematic.

## Impact on the Developer's Day to Day

Both paradigms present their own set of challenges and solutions. What's most significant, however, is how each paradigm affects developers' daily lives. While benefits such as reduced infrastructure costs are valuable, they don't directly impact developers' daily work.

Let's see some of the critical aspects of both paradigms:

- New Libraries or Languages: In monolithic architectures, the ability to introduce new libraries or languages or perform upgrades is limited because changes affect the entire codebase. This can frustrate developers, as the architecture hinders evolution and may lead to the use of outdated technology over time. In contrast, microservices enable upgrades or the adoption of new technologies in specific microservices, thereby reducing the scope of the changes required and offering greater flexibility for developers.
- Understanding the Source Code: The complexity of a monolithic application can be challenging for developers because the source code may be difficult to navigate, especially when multiple functionalities interact extensively. Imagine troubleshooting a bug in a feature that relies heavily on various interconnected application parts. In contrast, microservices emphasize simplicity within specific domains, making it easier for developers to understand different functionalities and how they interact with each other. This modular approach can simplify development and troubleshooting tasks compared to a monolithic codebase.

- Merging Source Code: As the challenges of monolithic architectures are explored, it is important to consider how merge requests impact developers' work. They may have everything ready to merge into the main branch, only to encounter numerous conflicting changes. The frequency of such conflicts depends on the number of developers working on the same application. From a developer's perspective, this can be frustrating and time-consuming. In contrast, microservices reduce the likelihood of such issues because each service is smaller. Multiple developers are, however, more likely to work simultaneously on specific microservices.
- Finding People to Work on Each Paradigm: One of the significant challenges companies face is finding skilled personnel for their applications. Consider receiving a job offer from a reputable company to work on an older application. This may not be as appealing as the abundance of opportunities to work on microservices or serverless architectures.
- Testing: Testing functionality in a monolithic architecture is straightforward due to access to the entire source code. This enables an understanding of whether new features or fixes will perform adequately in production. Modifying parameters in methods or functions that impact application behavior, however, requires analyzing how these changes affect numerous tests, given the extensive size of the monolith. Additionally, creating specific tests, such as performance tests, lacks precision in monoliths due to the abundance of endpoints, necessitating hours of analysis to simulate realistic scenarios for concurrent requests to each endpoint.
- Monitoring and Alerts: Verifying the application's functionality can be challenging, especially with more extensive applications. In a monolithic architecture, monitoring is particularly demanding as it involves setting up numerous alerts for various reasons, making it unclear which alerts are genuinely impactful. Conversely, receiving an alert from a single service in a microservices setup allows a clearer understanding of its impact on the platform.
- Deployment and Rollback: One significant problem that can occur with the use of a monolith is deploying an unstable version to production, which could impact the entire platform. This issue may also arise with microservices; however, the significant distinction is that monolithic applications require a longer deployment time due to their larger scale. Consequently, if an issue occurs, it is necessary to revert to the prior version, which entails a more protracted execution process.
- Maintainability: If the application does not have the chance to evolve to use new versions of the language or framework, the problems could increase in complexity because of a bug in a library that is solved in a new version. It remains impossible, however, to execute an upgrade. The singular resolution is to seek an alternative approach, such as obtaining the source code of the framework and implementing a corrective measure. An additional concern is that certain languages may not offer extensive support at times, and documentation for specific scenarios may be either absent or limited.

Indeed, the architecture of an application can significantly impact a developer's day-to-day experience and motivation. For instance, if a developer has a brilliant idea to enhance application performance but is constrained by a monolithic architecture that requires extensive modifications across many files, the implementation could take weeks or months. This can lead to frustration among developers who need help with the architecture's limitations, potentially affecting their perception of and motivation to work on the application. Architecture that supports flexibility and modularity, such as microservices, can mitigate these challenges by allowing the more straightforward implementation of innovative ideas without extensive dependencies and modifications.

## DEFINING THE ARCHITECTURE

Organizing an application into distinct parts, each with a specific purpose, is crucial for maintaining simplicity and long-term maintainability. In many cases, the application's structure is defined only when a particular requirement arises, often leading to issues regarding where to place new logic. Questions may emerge, such as whether it belongs in a new component or an existing one, whether a naming convention exists to identify parts responsible for specific tasks, how different elements interact, and where the rules for their intended use are defined.

All these questions, and many others, may arise at the beginning of development; therefore, understanding the available architectures and selecting the most suitable one becomes essential.

### Which Types of Architectures Exist?

The definition of architecture has evolved since 2000, when the first version of Struts[3] appeared; at that time, each company had its own standard, which usually differed between them. Spring Boot was not immune to those problems, but the community of developers took some old ideas about different types and adapted them to use them. The two relevant types of architecture are layers and hexagonal.

### Layers

This type of architecture originated decades ago with the release of the first applications in the 1970s; however, it differs significantly from the format commonly found in modern Spring Boot applications. At that time, applications were split into different parts or layers, each with a specific purpose, but with less complexity than now, because there were fewer things such as certain types of databases or sending events to a queue as there are now.

This architecture is straightforward as it divides the application into distinct layers, similar to layers of a cake, where each layer can only access elements at its level or lower. Architectures of this type evolve from the traditional four-layer architecture (view/presentation, business logic, persistence, and database) to variations with three or five layers. There's no universal standard for the ideal number of layers. Still, a common approach involves three layers, exemplified in Spring Boot by controllers, services, and repositories, with the database conceptually integrated rather than treated as a distinct layer.

---

[3]https://struts.apache.org/

Figure 2.4 illustrates a primary type of layer architecture in which the top layer receives the request and interacts with the layers at the bottom of the image.

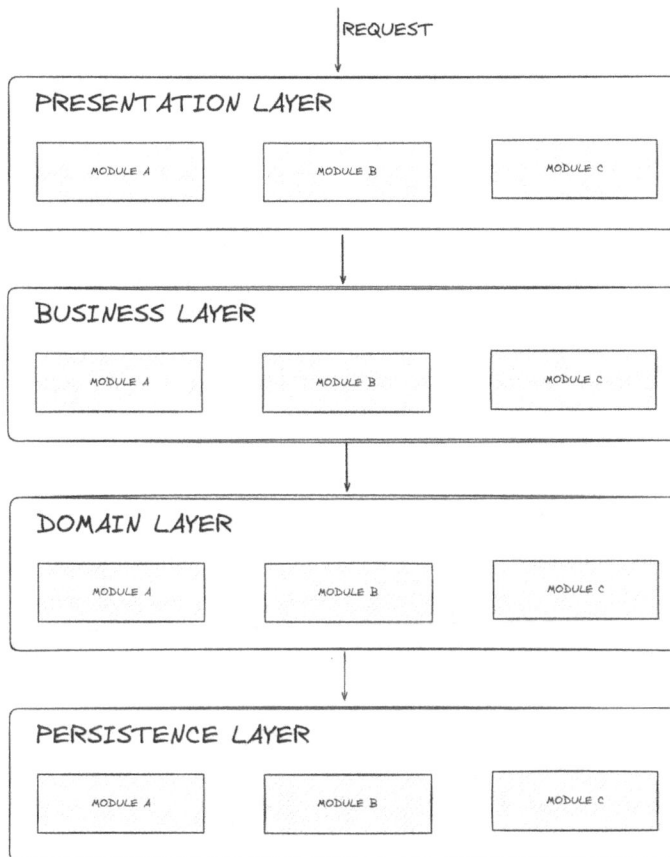

**FIGURE 2.4** An example of layered architecture.

Figure 2.4 shows four distinct layers, each designed with a specific purpose:

- Presentation: This layer provides a user or external application with the interface to communicate with the microservice, perform an action, and return a result, which can be in JSON or HTML.
- Business: This layer contains all the logic related to the application's purpose, such as validations or what the application needs to do after persisting the information.
- Domain: This layer contains the object representing the domain entities and their relationship.
- Persistence: This layer contains all the logic to communicate with an external resource that persists the information. The persistence layer is not directly connected to a database; it could be a file on an FTP server or another method.

Let's see some of the most relevant aspects related to this type of architecture:

- Simplicity: This approach is straightforward to implement due to its precise hierarchical layering. A wealth of resources—including books, articles, and code repositories—demonstrates this structure, offering numerous examples for potential implementations.
- Responsibility: Each layer performs specific tasks, such as accessing the database, communicating with other applications, or validating the information the microservice receives in the request.
- Reusable: The responsibility assigned to each layer enables the reuse of components across different layers for tasks such as accessing a database.
- Maintainability: If each layer has a small part of the logic of the entire microservice, reduce the number of lines of code in each component so that modifications in the code will not affect the whole application. Additionally, creating or modifying tests is straightforward due to the limited number of factors involved.

This approach, however, also brings specific challenges and considerations that must be taken into account:

- Scalability: Depending on the size of the application and the number of components (classes, interfaces, etc.) in the same package, finding or maintaining the application could be challenging.
- Hiding: When the purpose of each component and function is unclear, identifying reusable functionalities can become challenging.

## Hexagonal Architecture

The layered architecture provides developers with a straightforward approach to building applications and separating roles and responsibilities. In 2005, Alistair Cockburn[4] proposed a new alternative that encapsulates or abstracts all external communications with databases or external systems. He introduced the concept of input/output in the architecture to represent interactions with external resources such as databases and external systems.

The primary objective of this type of architecture is to design all business logic in a manner that isolates it from external tools and technologies irrelevant to the application's core functionality.

Figure 2.5 illustrates the most common representation of the hexagonal architecture, but many other variants also exist.

---

[4]https://alistair.cockburn.us/hexagonal-architecture/

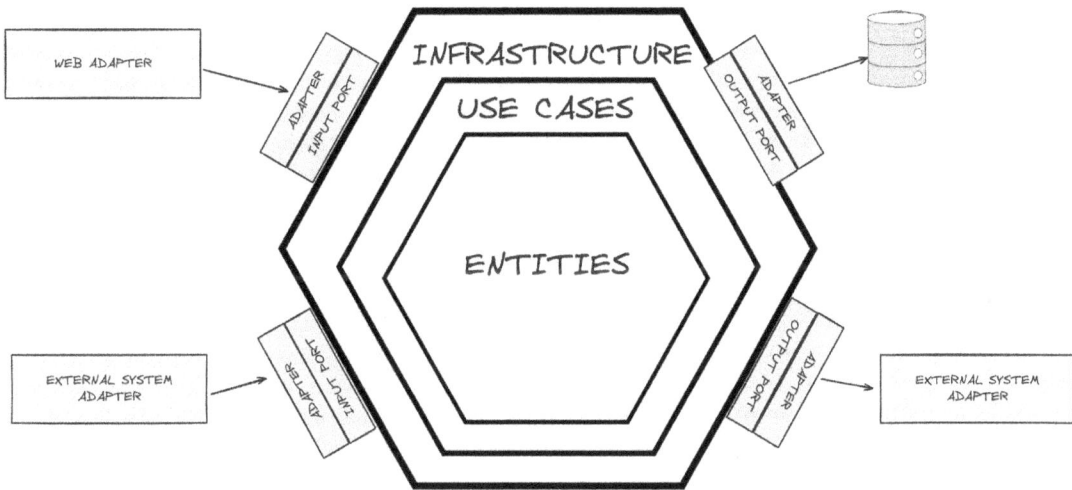

**FIGURE 2.5** An example of hexagonal architecture.

This architecture divides the hexagon into the "driving side" and the "driven side." The "driving side" consists of actors that initiate interactions, such as external systems, Web applications, and mobile applications. On the other side, the "driven side" includes actors that receive requests to provide certain information, such as databases or other external systems.

**NOTE** *There are a lot of variants of the hexagonal architecture, in most cases based on the original idea.*

Figure 2.5 presents various components, each serving a specific purpose. Below are the most relevant ones.

- Infrastructure: This structure includes ports and adapters that connect with external systems or databases using various protocols. Ports are technology-agnostic interfaces that define methods for accessing the application or interacting with other systems. Adapters are implementations of these ports tailored to specific technologies, such as querying a database or handling RESTful API requests.
- Use Cases: This structure forms the system's core, encompassing all the logic related to various scenarios and their interrelationships. Depending on the author, this component may be referred to as the application or domain layer, which combines use cases with the domain component.
- Entities: This structure represents the pure domain of the application, encompassing all the entities and value objects utilized within the application component.

Let's see some of the most relevant aspects of this type of architecture:

- Changeable: This approach introduces a level of abstraction that enables changing the adapters interacting with databases or external systems without impacting other parts of the application. Another important aspect is that the framework can be modified with minimal impact, as the logic for external communication is confined to a single component.
- Pure: The components inside the business or domain parts are pure, so it's simple to understand all the logic.
- Testing: To create specific tests, all the adapters could be modified to include tailored logic.

This approach, however, isn't perfect, as it introduces some challenges and important considerations:

- Standard: This approach is complex because there aren't guidelines for implementing it or knowing which components need to exist in each part of the hexagonal architecture. In most cases, this problem results in applications where the scope of the different parts is unclear or confusing.
- Indirection: It introduces some level of indirection in implementing each adapter port.
- Complexity: Implementing it with specific frameworks can be challenging, as it is easy to make mistakes in identifying what constitutes adapters and ports.

### Which Is the Best Alternative for Each Scenario?

This is an excellent question, as there are many factors to consider when choosing one approach over another. The main things to consider are summarized in the following table.

*TABLE 2.1* Main things to consider when choosing one architecture over another.

| Situation | Layers | Hexagonal |
|---|---|---|
| Experienced team | ✔ | ✔ |
| Something simple | ✔ | ✘ |
| It's essential to decouple the business logic from the rest of the application. | ✔ | ✔ |

Using the information from the previous table, an ADR can be created to document the reasons for choosing layered architecture over hexagonal architecture.

This document enables anyone to understand the reasons behind choosing this approach over others and to review the factors considered during the decision-making process.

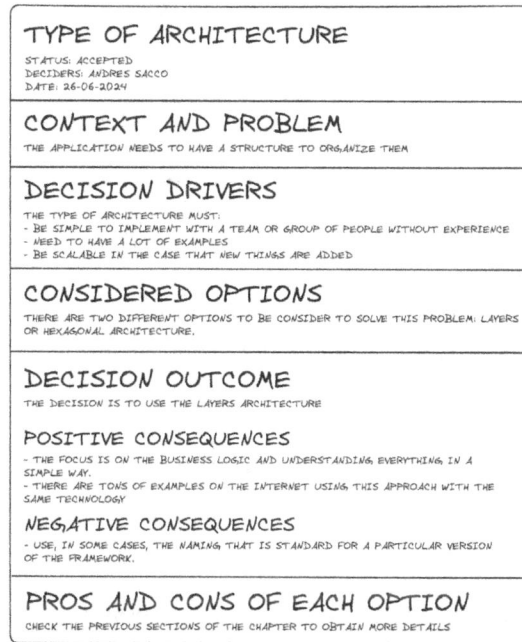

TYPE OF ARCHITECTURE

STATUS: ACCEPTED
DECIDERS: ANDRES SACCO
DATE: 26-06-2024

CONTEXT AND PROBLEM

THE APPLICATION NEEDS TO HAVE A STRUCTURE TO ORGANIZE THEM

DECISION DRIVERS

THE TYPE OF ARCHITECTURE MUST:
- BE SIMPLE TO IMPLEMENT WITH A TEAM OR GROUP OF PEOPLE WITHOUT EXPERIENCE
- NEED TO HAVE A LOT OF EXAMPLES
- BE SCALABLE IN THE CASE THAT NEW THINGS ARE ADDED

CONSIDERED OPTIONS

THERE ARE TWO DIFFERENT OPTIONS TO BE CONSIDER TO SOLVE THIS PROBLEM: LAYERS
OR HEXAGONAL ARCHITECTURE.

DECISION OUTCOME

THE DECISION IS TO USE THE LAYERS ARCHITECTURE

POSITIVE CONSEQUENCES

- THE FOCUS IS ON THE BUSINESS LOGIC AND UNDERSTANDING EVERYTHING IN A
SIMPLE WAY.
- THERE ARE TONS OF EXAMPLES ON THE INTERNET USING THIS APPROACH WITH THE
SAME TECHNOLOGY

NEGATIVE CONSEQUENCES

- USE, IN SOME CASES, THE NAMING THAT IS STANDARD FOR A PARTICULAR VERSION
OF THE FRAMEWORK.

PROS AND CONS OF EACH OPTION

CHECK THE PREVIOUS SECTIONS OF THE CHAPTER TO OBTAIN MORE DETAILS

**FIGURE 2.6** ADR for the decision of which architecture to use.

## How Does a Spring Boot Application Work?

Once a type of architecture has been chosen, it is essential to define the structure of the layers, clarifying the primary responsibility of each. Doing this before developing the application logic helps minimize the risk of encountering issues later that would require refactoring packages or classes.

Figure 2.7 illustrates a possible approach for a Spring Boot application using layered architecture. The application stores information in a database and communicates externally with other microservices to validate specific data.

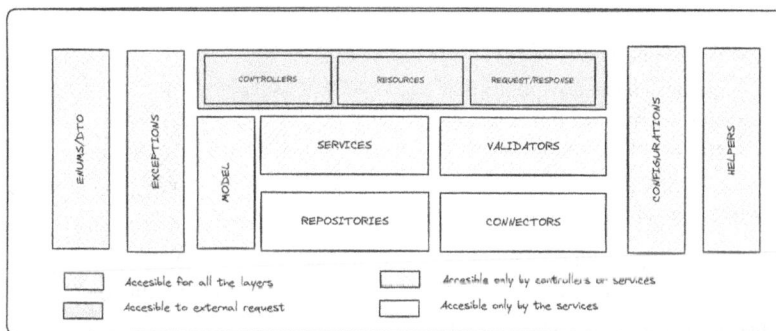

**FIGURE 2.7** A possible approach to layer architecture on Spring Boot.

Table 2.2 provides a detailed explanation of each layer and its components, including the configuration of the connectors.

**TABLE 2.2** Definitions of the layers of the application in this book.

| Layer | Description | Packages | Example(s) |
|---|---|---|---|
| Controllers | This contains all the endpoints of the microservices. | `*.controller` | `UserController` |
| Resources | This contains all documentation about the microservices, such as the definition of the endpoints and Swagger. | `*.controller.documentation` | `UserResources` |
| Request/Response | This layer contains the DTOs used across the different layers. | `*.dto.request`, `*.dto.response` | `UserRequest`, `UserResponse` |
| Services | This contains all the definitions of the services and the implementation. | `*.service`, `*.service.impl` | `IUserService`, `UserService` |
| Validators | This contains all the logic to validate a request for a DTO. | `*.validator` | `UserValidator` |
| Repositories | This layer contains the definition using interfaces and, in some cases, contains the specification to carry out a particular query. | `*.repository`, `*.repository.impl`, `*.specification` | `UserRepository`, `UserSpecification` |
| Connectors | Within this layer, all communications to external microservices or systems are located. | `*.connector` | `UserConnector` |
| Helpers | In this layer are all the classes that help with different things in the entire microservice. | `*.helper` | `UserHelper` |
| Configurations | This contains all the logic to configure different aspects of the microservices (e.g., the format of the response, ports) | `*.configuration` | `DatabaseConfiguration` |
| Exceptions | This contains all the exceptions that each microservice can throw during the execution of a request. | `*.exception` | `ApiException` |
| Model | This particular layer contains all the entities that access the databases. | `*.model` | `User` (no prefix/suffix) |
| Enums | This layer includes all the enums used across the different layers. | `*.enums` | No prefix/suffix. For example FlightType |
| DTO | This layer contains the DTOs used across the different layers. | `*.dto` | `UserDTO` |

This approach serves as a guide to a potential architecture that can be implemented and expanded to include additional layers if needed, such as handling communication with queues or serializing information before persisting it to the database.

**NOTE** *It is recommended to establish a standard for the application layers and validate them using tools such as ArchUnit[5], which will be covered in Chapter 5. This approach helps reduce the time needed to verify that the structure is correct.*

### Implementing the Architecture

Implementing the defined architecture is a key step in building an application, as it often reveals potential issues. These issues may arise during initial development or emerge months after the application's initial release.

Spring Boot provides a set of annotations that help define the role of each layer within the application. These annotations were introduced in the previous chapter when creating controllers to expose endpoints.

**TABLE 2.3** The core annotations on Spring Boot.

| Name | Description |
|------|-------------|
| @Component | This annotation represents a component containing reusable logic that spans multiple parts of the application. It delegates the responsibility of creating and managing all the statuses to Spring Boot. |
| @Service | This annotation indicates that the class contains business logic. It can be seen as a more specific form of the @Component annotation. |
| @Bean | This annotation creates a bean and registers it in the context of Spring. |
| @Repository | This annotation indicates that the class or interface is responsible for database access following the repository or DAO pattern, which will be explained in *Chapter 4.* |
| @ControllerAdvice | Annotations indicate that certain classes are responsible for capturing exceptions and performing specific actions. This allows a global exception handler to apply consistent logic across the application. |
| @ExceptionHandler | This annotation is related to the previous one. It is responsible for capturing one specific exception and taking action. |

Table 2.3 presents only a subset of the available annotations in Spring Boot; additional annotations will be introduced as the book progresses.

### Creating the Application Logic

Let's start adding the application's logic to provide some functionality, keeping the implementation simple. The first thing to add is the persistence layer. Keep in mind that until *Chapter 4,* a database will not be used, so that all information will be stored in memory.

---

[5]https://www.archunit.org/

Before creating the repository, which is responsible for persisting entities in memory or a database, it's necessary to first define the entities themselves. In Chapter 1, only DTOs were created to return or transfer information across different layers. To keep it simple, let's make the model classes with the same attributes and the same name without the prefix DTO. To reduce the number of blocks of code, let's see just one example of this, the `Reservation` class that appears in Listing 2.1.

```
public class Reservation {
    private Long id;
    private String itineraryId;
    private String searchId;
    private List<Passenger> passengers;
    private Contact contact;

    // Setters and Getters of all the attributes

    @Override
    public boolean equals(Object o) {
        if (this == o) return true;
        if (o == null || getClass() != o.getClass()) return false;
        Reservation that = (Reservation) o;
        return Objects.equals(id, that.id) && Objects.
equals(itineraryId, that.itineraryId) && Objects.equals(searchId, that.
searchId) && Objects.equals(passengers, that.passengers) && Objects.
equals(contact, that.contact);
    }

    @Override
    public int hashCode() {
        return Objects.hash(id, itineraryId, searchId, passengers, contact);
    }

    @Override
    public String toString() {
        return "Reservation{" +
                "id=" + id +
                ", itineraryId='" + itineraryId + '\'' +
                ", searchId='" + searchId + '\'' +
                ", passengers=" + passengers +
                ", contact=" + contact +
                '}';
    }
}
```

**LISTING 2.1** Structure of the Reservation entity.

As expected, the remaining classes follow a similar structure; therefore, the book does not include repeated code blocks using the same approach to avoid redundancy.

After creating all of the classes, it is time to make the repository, as shown in Listing 2.2. This simulates an application's persistence in memory.

```java
package com.twa.flights.api.reservation.repository;


import com.twa.flights.api.reservation.model.Passenger;
import com.twa.flights.api.reservation.model.Reservation;
import org.springframework.stereotype.Component;

import java.time.LocalDate;
import java.util.*;

@Component //This annotation replace the @Repository because is not a
real database
public class ReservationRepository {

    static List<Reservation> reservations = new ArrayList<>();

    static {

        Passenger passenger = new Passenger();
        passenger.setFirstName("Andres");
        passenger.setLastName("Sacco");
        passenger.setId(1L);
        passenger.setDocumentType("DNI");
        passenger.setDocumentNumber("12345678");
        passenger.setBirthday(LocalDate.of(1985, 1, 1));

        Contact contact = new Contact();
        contact.setId(1L);
        contact.setEmail("sacco.andres@gmail.com");
        contact.setTelephoneNumber("54911111111");

        Reservation reservation = new Reservation();
        reservation.setId(1L);
        reservation.setPassengers(List.of(passenger));
        reservation.setItineraryId("1");
        reservation.setSearchId("3");
        reservation.setContact(contact);

        reservations.add(reservation);
    }

    public List<Reservation> getReservations() {
        return reservations;
    }

    public Optional<Reservation> getReservationById(Long id) {
        List<Reservation> result = reservations.stream().
filter(reservation -> Objects.equals(reservation.getId(), id))
                .toList();

        Reservation reservation = !result.isEmpty() ? result.get(0) : null;
        return Optional.ofNullable(reservation);
    }
```

```
    public Reservation save(Reservation reservation) {
        reservation.setId((long) (reservations.size() + 1));
        reservations.add(reservation);
        return reservation;
    }

    public Reservation update(Long id, Reservation reservation) {
        List<Reservation> result = reservations.stream().filter(reser ->
reser.getId().equals(id)).toList();
        result.get(0).setId(reservation.getId());
        result.get(0).setItineraryId(reservation.getItineraryId());
        result.get(0).setSearchId(reservation.getSearchId());
        result.get(0).setPassengers(reservation.getPassengers());

        return result.get(0);
    }

    public void delete(Long id) {
        List<Reservation> result = reservations.stream().
filter(reservation -> reservation.getId().equals(id)).toList();

        reservations.remove(result.get(0));
    }
}
```

**LISTING 2.2** Structure the reservation repository to persist the information.

When introducing entity classes, another challenge arises because controllers receive DTOs, while repositories persist entities. At some point, the DTOs used between the controller and the repositories must be transformed into entities. This problem can be addressed with two approaches. The first approach involves creating classes that manually map front-end DTOs to entities and vice versa, although this requires writing and maintaining additional code. The second approach uses a library that handles the mapping automatically with minimal code.

The second approach is the best alternative because it reduces the number of lines of code that need to be maintained and tested; therefore, the next decision is which library is the best alternative. Considering different benchmarks[6] applied to different libraries, the best alternative in terms of performance and community support is MapStruct[7].

To use this library, first add the dependency along with a plugin that dynamically generates the mappings. Listing 2.3 presents the required entries to include in the pom.xml file.

```
<?xml version="1.0" encoding="UTF-8"?>
<project xmlns="http://maven.apache.org/POM/4.0.0" xmlns:xsi="http://www.w3.org/2001/
XMLSchema-instance"
    xsi:schemaLocation="http://maven.apache.org/POM/4.0.0 https://maven.apache.org/xsd/
maven-4.0.0.xsd">
    <modelVersion>4.0.0</modelVersion>
```

---

[6]https://www.baeldung.com/java-performance-mapping-frameworks
[7]https://mapstruct.org/

```xml
<parent>
        <groupId>org.springframework.boot</groupId>
        <artifactId>spring-boot-starter-parent</artifactId>
        <version>3.3.0</version>
        <relativePath/> <!-- lookup parent from repository -->
</parent>
<groupId>com.twa</groupId>
<artifactId>api-reservation</artifactId>
<version>0.0.1-SNAPSHOT</version>
<name>api-reservation</name>
<description>API which manage everything about the reservations</description>
<properties>

        <!-- Other properties →
        <mapstruct.version>1.5.5.Final</mapstruct.version>
<maven-compiler-plugin.version>3.8.1</maven-compiler-plugin.version>

</properties>
<dependencies>

        <!-- Other dependencies →
        <dependency>
                <groupId>org.mapstruct</groupId>
                <artifactId>mapstruct</artifactId>
                <version>${mapstruct.version}</version>
        </dependency>

</dependencies>

<build>
    <plugins>
            <!-- Other plugins →
            <plugin>
                    <groupId>org.apache.maven.plugins</groupId>
                    <artifactId>maven-compiler-plugin</artifactId>
                    <version>${maven-compiler-plugin.version}</version>
                    <configuration>
                            <source>${java.version}</source>
                            <target>${java.version}</target>
                            <annotationProcessorPaths>
                                    <path>
                                            <groupId>org.mapstruct</groupId>
                                            <artifactId>mapstruct-processor</artifactId>
                                            <version>${mapstruct.version}</version>
                                    </path>
                            </annotationProcessorPaths>
                    </configuration>
            </plugin>
    </plugins>
</build>

</project>
```

**LISTING 2.3** Modifications on the POM file to use MapStruct.

Including the dependencies is only the first step, as in some cases, it's necessary to define the mapping rules or equivalences to enable valid transformations between different classes. The next step is to create a series of interfaces that indicate to MapStruct the valid transformation of the classes. Listing 2.4 shows how to define an interface for the mapper to transform one class into another.

```
package com.twa.flights.api.reservation.mapper;

import com.twa.flights.api.reservation.dto.ReservationDTO;
import com.twa.flights.api.reservation.model.Reservation;
import org.mapstruct.Mapper;
import org.springframework.core.convert.converter.Converter;


@Mapper(componentModel = "spring")
public interface ReservationDTOMapper extends Converter<ReservationDTO,
Reservation> {

    @Override
    Reservation convert(ReservationDTO source);

}
```

**LISTING 2.4** Mapper with a valid transformation of classes.

For each mapping, a class must be defined; therefore, it's necessary to create another mapper, as shown in Listing 2.5, to handle the reverse mapping as well.

```
package com.twa.flights.api.reservation.mapper;

import com.twa.flights.api.reservation.dto.ReservationDTO;
import com.twa.flights.api.reservation.model.Reservation;
import org.mapstruct.Mapper;
import org.springframework.core.convert.converter.Converter;

@Mapper(componentModel = "spring")
public interface ReservationMapper extends Converter<Reservation,
ReservationDTO> {

    @Override
    ReservationDTO convert(Reservation source);

}
```

**LISTING 2.5** Another mapper with a valid transformation of classes.

One particular case to consider when creating a mapper is the use of lists, maps, and other types of collections, which means creating a mapper, as in Listing 2.6.

```
package com.twa.flights.api.reservation.mapper;

import com.twa.flights.api.reservation.dto.ReservationDTO;
import com.twa.flights.api.reservation.model.Reservation;
```

```java
import org.mapstruct.Mapper;
import org.springframework.core.convert.converter.Converter;

import java.util.List;


@Mapper(componentModel = "spring")
public interface ReservationsMapper extends Converter<List<Reservation>,
List<ReservationDTO>> {

    @Override
    List<ReservationDTO> convert(List<Reservation> source);


}
```

**LISTING 2.6** Another mapper with a valid transformation of classes.

With the repositories and mappers in place, the next step is to define the service class that contains all the business logic. Listing 2.7 presents the implementation of this service class.

```java
package com.twa.flights.api.reservation.service;

import com.twa.flights.api.reservation.dto.ReservationDTO;
import com.twa.flights.api.reservation.model.Reservation;
import com.twa.flights.api.reservation.repository.ReservationRepository;
import org.springframework.beans.factory.annotation.Autowired;
import org.springframework.core.convert.ConversionService;
import org.springframework.stereotype.Service;

import java.util.List;
import java.util.Objects;
import java.util.Optional;

@Service
public class ReservationService {

    private ReservationRepository repository;

    private ConversionService conversionService;

    @Autowired
    public ReservationService(ReservationRepository repository,
                              ConversionService conversionService) {
        this.repository = repository;
        this.conversionService = conversionService;
    }

    public List<ReservationDTO> getReservations() {
        return  conversionService.convert(repository.getReservations(),
List.class);
    }

    public ReservationDTO getReservationById(Long id) {
        Optional<Reservation> result = repository.
getReservationById(id);
```

```
        if(result.isEmpty()) {
            throw new RuntimeException("Not exist");
        }
        return conversionService.convert(result.get(), ReservationDTO.
class);
    }

    public ReservationDTO save(ReservationDTO reservation) {
        if(Objects.nonNull(reservation.id())) {
            throw new RuntimeException("Duplicate it");
        }

        Reservation transformed = conversionService.convert(reservation,
Reservation.class);
        Reservation result = repository.save(Objects.
requireNonNull(transformed));
        return conversionService.convert(result, ReservationDTO.class);
    }

    public ReservationDTO update(Long id, ReservationDTO reservation) {
        if(getReservationById(id) == null) {
            throw new RuntimeException("Not exist");
        }

        Reservation transformed = conversionService.convert(reservation,
Reservation.class);
        Reservation result = repository.update(id, Objects.
requireNonNull(transformed));
        return conversionService.convert(result, ReservationDTO.class);
    }

    public void delete(Long id) {
        if(getReservationById(id) == null) {
            throw new RuntimeException("Not exist");
        }

        repository.delete(id);
    }
}
```

**LISTING 2.7** Service layer with all the business logic.

One crucial detail in Listing 2.7 is the inclusion of the ConversionService. This class utilizes the mapper created with MapStruct and performs transformations between classes without explicitly specifying which mapper the service should use. Another relevant aspect is using the @Autowired annotation to use the DI provided by Spring to obtain an instance of the classes in the constructor. The last element of the class is using a RuntimeException instead of another type of exception. With this approach, the example can remain simple until the next section, which will explain how to manage and transform the different kinds of exceptions.

**NOTE** *Behind the scenes, the* `ConversionService` *uses the mapper to perform transformations, but it does not use magic. In the folder* `target/generated-sources/annotations`, *there is a package with the same name as the mapper's package—in this case,* `com.twa.` `flights.api.reservation.mapper`. *Inside this package, the concrete implementation classes of the mappers are located. For example, Listing 2.8 shows the implementation of* `ReservationMapper`.

```java
package com.twa.flights.api.reservation.mapper;

import com.twa.flights.api.reservation.dto.ContactDTO;
import com.twa.flights.api.reservation.dto.PassengerDTO;
import com.twa.flights.api.reservation.dto.ReservationDTO;
import com.twa.flights.api.reservation.model.Contact;
import com.twa.flights.api.reservation.model.Passenger;
import com.twa.flights.api.reservation.model.Reservation;
import java.time.LocalDate;
import java.util.ArrayList;
import java.util.List;
import javax.annotation.processing.Generated;
import org.springframework.stereotype.Component;

@Generated(
    value = "org.mapstruct.ap.MappingProcessor",
    date = "2024-06-26T17:18:29-0300",
    comments = "version: 1.5.5.Final, compiler: javac, environment: Java
21.0.2 (GraalVM Community)"
)
@Component
public class ReservationMapperImpl implements ReservationMapper {

    @Override
    public ReservationDTO convert(Reservation source) {
        if ( source == null ) {
            return null;
        }

        Long id = null;
        String itineraryId = null;
        String searchId = null;
        List<PassengerDTO> passengers = null;
        ContactDTO contact = null;

        id = source.getId();
        itineraryId = source.getItineraryId();
        searchId = source.getSearchId();
        passengers = passengerListToPassengerDTOList( source.
getPassengers() );
        contact = contactToContactDTO( source.getContact() );
```

```java
        ReservationDTO reservationDTO = new ReservationDTO( id,
itineraryId, searchId, passengers, contact );

        return reservationDTO;
    }

    protected PassengerDTO passengerToPassengerDTO(Passenger passenger)
{
        if ( passenger == null ) {
            return null;
        }

        Long id = null;
        String firstName = null;
        String lastName = null;
        String documentNumber = null;
        String documentType = null;
        String nationality = null;
        LocalDate birthday = null;

        id = passenger.getId();
        firstName = passenger.getFirstName();
        lastName = passenger.getLastName();
        documentNumber = passenger.getDocumentNumber();
        documentType = passenger.getDocumentType();
        nationality = passenger.getNationality();
        birthday = passenger.getBirthday();

        PassengerDTO passengerDTO = new PassengerDTO( id, firstName,
lastName, documentNumber, documentType, nationality, birthday );

        return passengerDTO;
    }

    protected List<PassengerDTO> passengerListToPassengerDTOList(List<Pa
ssenger> list) {
        if ( list == null ) {
            return null;
        }

        List<PassengerDTO> list1 = new ArrayList<PassengerDTO>( list.
size() );
        for ( Passenger passenger : list ) {
            list1.add( passengerToPassengerDTO( passenger ) );
        }

        return list1;
    }

    protected ContactDTO contactToContactDTO(Contact contact) {
        if ( contact == null ) {
            return null;
        }

        Long id = null;
        String telephoneNumber = null;
        String email = null;
```

```
        id = contact.getId();
        telephoneNumber = contact.getTelephoneNumber();
        email = contact.getEmail();

        ContactDTO contactDTO = new ContactDTO( id, telephoneNumber,
email );

        return contactDTO;
    }
}
```

*LISTING 2.8* Implementation of a mapper.

These implementations are generated during specific commands, such as compiling, building, or running the application. Therefore, whenever modifications are made to the entities or DTOs, it is necessary to execute one of these commands to regenerate the mapper implementations.

The final step involves modifying the controller to use the service and incorporate all the logic defined in this chapter. Listing 2.9 presents the necessary changes to enable the controller to interact with the service.

```
package com.twa.flights.api.reservation.controller;

// Imports

@RestController
@RequestMapping("/reservation")
public class ReservationController {

    private static final Logger LOGGER = LoggerFactory.
getLogger(ReservationController.class);

    private ReservationService service;

    @Autowired
    public ReservationController(ReservationService service) {
        this.service = service;
    }

    @GetMapping("/{id}")
    public ResponseEntity<ReservationDTO> getReservationById(@
PathVariable Long id) {
        LOGGER.info("Obtain information from a reservation with {}", id);
        ReservationDTO response = service.getReservationById(id);
        return new ResponseEntity<>(response, HttpStatus.OK);
    }

    @GetMapping
    public ResponseEntity<List<ReservationDTO>> getReservations() {
        LOGGER.info("Obtain all the reservations");
        List<ReservationDTO> response = service.getReservations();
        return new ResponseEntity<>(response, HttpStatus.OK);
    }
```

```
@PostMapping
public ResponseEntity<ReservationDTO> save(@RequestBody
ReservationDTO reservation) {
    LOGGER.info("Saving new reservation");
    ReservationDTO response = service.save(reservation);
    return new ResponseEntity<>(response, HttpStatus.CREATED);
}

@PutMapping("/{id}")
public ResponseEntity<ReservationDTO> update(@PathVariable Long id,
@RequestBody ReservationDTO reservation) {
    LOGGER.info("Updating a reservation with {}", id);
    ReservationDTO response = service.update(id, reservation);
    return new ResponseEntity<>(response, HttpStatus.OK);
}

@DeleteMapping("/{id}")
public ResponseEntity<Void> delete(@PathVariable Long id) {
    LOGGER.info("Deleting a reservation with {}", id);
    service.delete(id);
    return new ResponseEntity<>(HttpStatus.OK);
}
}
```

**LISTING 2.9** Controller with the modifications.

Let's run the application with all the changes and observe what happens when some requests are made. First, create a reservation using the `curl` command shown in Listing 2.10. Alternatively, Postman can be used to achieve the same result.

```
curl --location 'localhost:8080/reservation' \
--header 'Content-Type: application/json' \
--data-raw '{
    "itineraryId": "5",
    "searchId": "10",
    "passengers": [
        {
            "firstName": "Andres",
            "lastName": "Sacco",
            "documentNumber": "987654321",
            "documentType": "DNI",
            "nationality": null,
            "birthday": "1985-01-01"
        }
    ],
    "contact": {
        "telephoneNumber": "54911111111",
        "email": "sacco.andres@gmail.com"
    }
}'
```

**LISTING 2.10** Curl command to create a new reservation.

After executing the request, if everything works correctly, a response similar to Listing 2.11 will be received.

```
{
    "id": 2,
    "itineraryId": "5",
    "searchId": "10",
    "passengers": [
        {
            "id": null,
            "firstName": "Andres",
            "lastName": "Sacco",
            "documentNumber": "987654321",
            "documentType": "DNI",
            "nationality": null,
            "birthday": "1985-01-01"
        }
    ],
    "contact": {
        "id": null,
        "telephoneNumber": "549111111111",
        "email": "sacco.andres@gmail.com"
    }
}
```

**LISTING 2.11** Response to the execution of the command.

The final step is to verify that the information has been persisted. This can be done by requesting the endpoint to retrieve the data using the command shown in Listing 2.12.

```
curl --location --request GET 'localhost:8080/reservation/2' \
--header 'Content-Type: application/json'
```

**LISTING 2.12** Curl command to get a reservation.

If everything is okay, the result will match Listing 2.11, indicating that the information has been successfully persisted in the application's memory.

## Manage the Exceptions

Most of the time, developers focus on checking the success cases. What happens, though, when something goes wrong in the application? In this case, an exception is thrown when attempting to retrieve information about a reservation that does not exist. Yet, the returned message from the application might not reflect that. To see this in action, make a request, as shown in Listing 2.13, using a nonexistent reservation.

```
curl --location 'localhost:8080/reservation/3' \
--header 'Content-Type: application/json'
```

**LISTING 2.13** Curl command to get a nonexistent reservation.

A response similar to Listing 2.14 will be obtained, containing detailed information about the error and the underlying components the application uses, such as the server.

```
{
    "timestamp": "2024-06-27T13:53:56.876+00:00",
    "status": 500,
    "error": "Internal Server Error",
    "trace": "java.lang.RuntimeException: Not exist\n\tat com.twa.
flights.api.reservation.service.ReservationService.getReservationByI
d(ReservationService.java:36)\n\tat com.twa.flights.api.reservation.
controller.ReservationController.getReservationById(ReservationControll
er.java:30)\n\tat .....",
    "message": "Not exist",
    "path": "/reservation/3"
}
```

**LISTING 2.14** Output of the nonexistent reservation.

This practice is problematic because it exposes sensitive information and fails to provide meaningful clues about the issue with the request or the application. When an application returns information in a clear, readable format, the client making the request can understand the situation and adjust the request accordingly.

By default, the information on Listing 2.14 is created and exposed with a class called `ResponseEntityExceptionHandler`[8] on Spring Boot, which captures all the exceptions and provides the format. Another way to offer a different format is to create a class and override the behavior. First, defining the format of the error message is necessary; although multiple formats exist depending on various factors, Figure 2.8 presents one possible approach to the response.

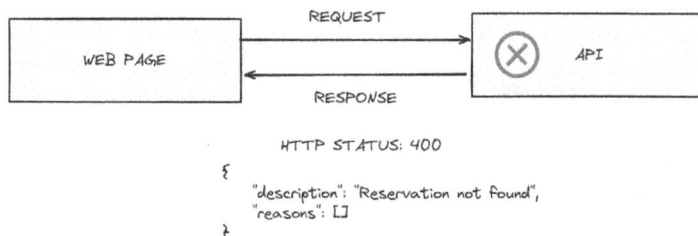

**FIGURE 2.8** Format of the error response.

This approach aims to provide information about the error, a description, and the API that produced the exception, so that a developer can easily understand where the problem lies in an extensive system with multiple applications.

Let's start with creating the components necessary to return a message as it appears in Figure 2.8. Listing 2.15 represents the enumeration of all potential problems that could occur in the application, along with the corresponding HTTP status code to return and some basic information.

---

[8]https://docs.spring.io/spring-framework/docs/current/javadoc-api/org/springframework/web/servlet/mvc/method/annotation/ResponseEntityExceptionHandler.html

```
package com.twa.flights.api.reservation.enums;

import org.springframework.http.HttpStatus;

public enum APIError {
    VALIDATION_ERROR(HttpStatus.BAD_REQUEST, "There are attributes with
wrong values"),
    BAD_FORMAT(HttpStatus.BAD_REQUEST, "The message not have a correct
form"),
    RESERVATION_NOT_FOUND(HttpStatus.NOT_FOUND, "Reservation not
found"),
    RESERVATION_WITH_SAME_ID(HttpStatus.BAD_REQUEST, "There is a
reservation with the same id");

    private final HttpStatus httpStatus;
    private final String message;

    APIError(HttpStatus httpStatus, String message) {
        this.httpStatus = httpStatus;
        this.message = message;
    }

    public HttpStatus getHttpStatus() {
        return httpStatus;
    }

    public String getMessage() {
        return message;
    }
}
```

*LISTING 2.15* Enum with all the information about the different types of errors.

Afterward, creating a custom exception is necessary since using Java's general-purpose exceptions is not considered good practice. Also, the exception in Listing 2.16 will contain all the relevant information about the problem in the application, which will be used to generate the response.

```
package com.twa.flights.api.reservation.exception;

import com.twa.flights.api.reservation.enums.APIError;
import org.springframework.http.HttpStatus;

import java.util.List;

public class TWAException extends RuntimeException {
    private final HttpStatus status;
    private final String description;
    private final List<String> reasons;

    public TWAException(APIError error, List<String> reasons) {
        this.status = error.getHttpStatus();
        this.description = error.getMessage();
        this.reasons = reasons;
    }
```

```
    public TWAException(HttpStatus status, String description,
List<String> reasons) {
        this.status = status;
        this.description = description;
        this.reasons = reasons;
    }

    public HttpStatus getStatus() {
        return status;
    }

    public String getDescription() {
        return description;
    }

    public List<String> getReasons() {
        return reasons;
    }
}
```

**LISTING 2.16** A concrete exception related to the application.

Listing 2.16 shows a list of `reasons`, which is particularly useful when multiple problems or a series of issues occur, and it's essential to provide all relevant information to the client. For instance, this attribute could return details about the validation of all the properties in the DTOs.

Spring Boot does not automatically convert exceptions into a specific message format; instead, it allows throwing particular exceptions within the application, which are then captured and transformed by the handlers. Listing 2.17 shows the class that encapsulates all the information related to a specific exception or issue.

```
package com.twa.flights.api.reservation.dto;

import java.util.List;

public class ErrorDTO {
    private String description;
    private List<String> reasons;

    public ErrorDTO(String description, List<String> reasons) {
        this.description = description;
        this.reasons = reasons;
    }

    public String getDescription() {
        return description;
    }

    public List<String> getReasons() {
        return reasons;
    }
}
```

**LISTING 2.17** Error class to represent the exception in a human format.

After creating all these new classes, the next step is to create a class that extends `ResponseEntityExceptionHandler` to capture the exception defined in Listing 2.16. Listing 2.18 includes the complete logic to catch and transform the exception into a DTO and return the corresponding response.

```
package com.twa.flights.api.reservation.exception;

import com.twa.flights.api.reservation.dto.ErrorDTO;
import com.twa.flights.api.reservation.enums.APIError;
import org.springframework.http.HttpHeaders;
import org.springframework.http.HttpStatus;
import org.springframework.http.HttpStatusCode;
import org.springframework.http.ResponseEntity;
import org.springframework.validation.FieldError;
import org.springframework.web.bind.MethodArgumentNotValidException;
import org.springframework.web.bind.annotation.ExceptionHandler;
import org.springframework.web.bind.annotation.RestControllerAdvice;
import org.springframework.web.context.request.WebRequest;
import org.springframework.web.servlet.mvc.method.annotation.
ResponseEntityExceptionHandler;

import java.util.ArrayList;
import java.util.List;

@RestControllerAdvice
public class APIExceptionHandler extends ResponseEntityExceptionHandler
{

    @ExceptionHandler(TWAException.class)
    public ResponseEntity<ErrorDTO> generalProblem(TWAException e,
WebRequest request) {
        return ResponseEntity.status(e.getStatus()).body(new ErrorDTO(e.
getDescription(), e.getReasons()));
    }
}
```

**LISTING 2.18** Handler to capture the exceptions and transform.

Listing 2.18 shows two different annotations: one is `@RestControllerAdvice`, which tells Spring Boot that this class will handle exceptions occurring throughout the entire application. It is, however, essential to note that the framework will only take action if methods are explicitly created or overridden in this class.

The final step in capturing the problems is to change the exception that the service throws in the different methods from `RuntimeException` to `TWAException`, as shown in Listing 2.19.

```
package com.twa.flights.api.reservation.service;

// Import

@Service
public class ReservationService {
```

```
        //Other logic

    public ReservationDTO getReservationById(Long id) {
        Optional<Reservation> result = repository.
getReservationById(id);
        if(result.isEmpty()) {
            throw new TWAException(APIError.RESERVATION_NOT_FOUND);
        }
        return conversionService.convert(result.get(), ReservationDTO.
class);
    }

    public ReservationDTO save(ReservationDTO reservation) {
        if(Objects.nonNull(reservation.id())) {
            throw new TWAException(APIError.RESERVATION_WITH_SAME_ID);
        }

        Reservation transformed = conversionService.convert(reservation,
Reservation.class);
        Reservation result = repository.save(Objects.
requireNonNull(transformed));
        return conversionService.convert(result, ReservationDTO.class);
    }

    public ReservationDTO update(Long id, ReservationDTO reservation) {
        if(getReservationById(id) == null) {
            throw new TWAException(APIError.RESERVATION_NOT_FOUND);
        }

        Reservation transformed = conversionService.convert(reservation,
Reservation.class);
        Reservation result = repository.update(id, Objects.
requireNonNull(transformed));
        return conversionService.convert(result, ReservationDTO.class);
    }

    public void delete(Long id) {
        if(getReservationById(id) == null) {
            throw new TWAException(APIError.RESERVATION_NOT_FOUND);
        }

        repository.delete(id);
    }
}
```

**LISTING 2.19** The modifications to the service to throw a concrete exception.

Now that all the modifications are complete, it's time to verify the result. Executing the command shown in Listing 2.13 will produce an output similar to Listing 2.20.

```
{
    "description": "Reservation not found",
    "reasons": []
}
```

**LISTING 2.20** Output of a nonexistent reservation.

These modifications reduce the risk of exposing details about the server or programming language used in the application, while also providing clients with valuable information to understand the problem better.

## Add Validators

A common problem when creating an application and sharing information about the different endpoints is that required attributes might be forgotten or sent with incorrect values. Validating all attributes in the controller is one solution, but it often involves writing extensive code that requires ongoing maintenance and testing. Therefore, better alternatives exist.

Another possibility is to use a library that implements the specification JSR-380[9], which provides a series of annotations to check various aspects of a Java bean. For a long time, Hibernate's `Validator` was the only way to validate entities before persisting information into the database. To validate attributes on DTOs, it was necessary to add the dependency and import various classes from Hibernate. The widespread success of this validation mechanism led the Spring Boot maintainers to create a dedicated module called Spring Boot validation.

Spring Boot validation utilizes Hibernate `Validator` behind the scenes, providing an abstraction layer for developers to specify which version of Hibernate `Validator` to include, depending on the framework version in use. Additionally, in the future, Spring could remove its dependency on Hibernate `Validator` and implement its validation code without impacting developers.

Table 2.4 displays some of the most relevant annotations for validating the classes. For a complete list of available annotations, please refer to the specification's Web site[10].

**TABLE 2.4** The core annotations in the JSR-380 specification.

| Name | Description |
| --- | --- |
| @NotNull | This annotation checks that the attribute does not contain a null value. |
| @NotBlank | This annotation only applies to the text attributes and checks that the content of an attribute is different from "" (blank). |
| @NotEmpty | This annotation validates that an attribute is not null or empty. It's valid for `String`, `Collection`, `Map`, and `Array` types. |
| @Min | This annotation checks that a number follows the minimum value rule. |
| @Max | This annotation checks that a number follows the maximum value rule. |
| @Size | This annotation checks that the size of a `String` is between a range with a minimum and maximum length. |
| @Email | This annotation checks whether the value of an attribute contains a value that could be considered an email. |
| @Future | This annotation checks that a date (`Timestamp`, `LocalDate`, or `Date`) contains a value after the date. |
| @Past | This annotation checks that a date (`Timestamp`, `LocalDate`, or `Date`) contains a value before the current date. |

*(Continued)*

[9]https://beanvalidation.org/2.0-jsr380/
[10]https://beanvalidation.org/2.0-jsr380/

*TABLE 2.4* Continued

| Name | Description |
|------|-------------|
| @Negative | This annotation validates that a number is negative. |
| @Positive | This annotation validates that a number is positive. |
| @AssertTrue | This annotation checks whether a boolean attribute contains a true value. |
| @AssertFalse | This annotation checks whether a boolean attribute contains a false value. |

The application's DTOs are modified to validate attributes upon receiving a request. Listing 2.21 shows the validations applied to ReservationDTO:

```
package com.twa.flights.api.reservation.dto;

import jakarta.validation.Valid;
import jakarta.validation.constraints.NotBlank;
import jakarta.validation.constraints.NotEmpty;
import jakarta.validation.constraints.NotNull;

import java.util.List;

public record ReservationDTO(
        Long id,

        @NotBlank(message = "The itineraryId must be defined")
        String itineraryId,

        @NotBlank(message = "The searchId must be defined")
        String searchId,

        @Valid
        @NotEmpty(message = "You need at least one passenger")
        List<PassengerDTO> passengers,

        @Valid
        @NotNull(message = "The contact must be defined")
        ContactDTO contact
){}
```

*LISTING 2.21* ReservationDTO with the validations.

Now, let's add some validations on the passengers to limit some attributes, such as the length of the first and last names, as they appear in Listing 2.22.

```
package com.twa.flights.api.reservation.dto;

import jakarta.validation.constraints.NotBlank;
import jakarta.validation.constraints.NotNull;
import jakarta.validation.constraints.Past;
import jakarta.validation.constraints.Size;
```

```
import java.time.LocalDate;

public record PassengerDTO(
        Long id,
        @NotBlank(message = "firstName is mandatory")
        @Size(min = 2, max = 20, message = "The firstname not have the
correct size")
        String firstName,

        @NotBlank(message = "lastName is mandatory")
        @Size(min = 2, max = 20, message = "The lastName not have the
correct size")
        String lastName,

        @NotBlank(message = "The documentNumber must be defined")
        @Size(min = 2, max = 10, message = "The documentNumber not have the
correct size")
        String documentNumber,

        @NotBlank(message = "The documentType must be defined")
        @Size(min = 3, max = 10, message = "The documentType not have the
correct size")
        String documentType,

        @NotBlank(message = "The nationality must be defined")
        @Size(min = 2, max = 3, message = "The nationality not have the
correct size")
        String nationality,

        @NotNull(message = "The birthday must be defined")
        @Past(message = "birthday need to be a date in the past")
        LocalDate birthday) {
}
```

**LISTING 2.22** PassengerDTO with the validations.

The last entity to add validations is ContactDTO, as shown in Listing 2.23, which is similar to the previous one.

```
package com.twa.flights.api.reservation.dto;

import jakarta.validation.constraints.Email;
import jakarta.validation.constraints.NotBlank;

public record ContactDTO(
        Long id,
        @NotBlank(message = "The telephoneNumber must be defined")
        String telephoneNumber,

        @NotBlank(message = "The email must be defined")
        @Email(message = "The value must be a valid email")
        String email) {
}
```

**LISTING 2.23** ContactDTO with the validations.

With these changes applied only to the DTO, the application will not perform any valida-tion upon receiving a request. It is necessary to add a series of annotations to each endpoint to instruct Spring Boot to validate the request format, as shown in Listing 2.24.

```
package com.twa.flights.api.reservation.controller;

// Previous imports
import org.springframework.validation.annotation.Validated;

import java.util.List;

@Validated
@RestController
@RequestMapping("/reservation")
public class ReservationController {
  //Previous logic

    @PostMapping
    public ResponseEntity<ReservationDTO> save(@RequestBody @Valid
ReservationDTO reservation) {
        //Previous logic
    }

    @PutMapping("/{id}")
    public ResponseEntity<ReservationDTO> update(@PathVariable Long id,
@RequestBody @Valid ReservationDTO reservation) {
        //Previous logic
    }
}
```

**LISTING 2.24** Controller with the annotation to do the validation.

As shown, the annotations `@Validated` and `@Valid` indicate to Spring that the validator needs to be executed to check all the attributes. Annotations can also be added to validate the URL parameters appearing in the delete, update, and find methods.

With all these modifications, the application can be run. Another problem remains, however: the format of the validation issues will appear unclear unless some logic is added to the class that acts as `RestControllerAdvice`. Listing 2.25 includes the logic to transform the validation problems into messages that are easy to understand for everyone.

```
package com.twa.flights.api.reservation.exception;

// Previous imports
import org.springframework.web.bind.MethodArgumentNotValidException;

@RestControllerAdvice
public class APIExceptionHandler extends ResponseEntityExceptionHandler
{

    //Previous logic

    @Override
```

```
    protected ResponseEntity<Object> handleMethodArgumentNotValid(Method
ArgumentNotValidException ex,

HttpHeaders headers, HttpStatusCode status, WebRequest request) {
        List<String> reasons = new ArrayList<>();
        for (FieldError error : ex.getBindingResult().getFieldErrors())
{
            reasons.add(String.format("%s - %s", error.getField(),
error.getDefaultMessage()));
        }
        return ResponseEntity.status(APIError.VALIDATION_ERROR.
getHttpStatus())
                .body(new ErrorDTO(APIError.VALIDATION_ERROR.
getMessage(), reasons));
    }
}
```

**LISTING 2.25** Adding support to handle the problem with the validations.

After introducing all these modifications, the final step is to request confirmation that the validations work correctly, as shown in Listing 2.26.

```
curl --location 'localhost:8080/reservation' \
--header 'Content-Type: application/json' \
--data '{
    "itineraryId": "2",
    "searchId": "2",
    "passengers": [
        {
            "firstName": "",
            "lastName": "Sacco",
            "documentNumber": "987654321",
            "documentType": "DNI",
            "nationality": "ARG",
            "birthday": "2029-01-01"
        }
    ],
    "contact": {
        "telephoneNumber": "54911111111",
        "email": "sacco.andres"
    }
}'
```

**LISTING 2.26** Request with the wrong values.

If everything works correctly, a response similar to Listing 2.27 will be received, describing the issues with the request.

```
{
    "description": "There are attributes with wrong values",
    "reasons": [
        "passengers[0].firstName - The firstname not have the correct
size",
```

```
            "contact.email - The value must be a valid email",
            "passengers[0].firstName - firstName is mandatory",
            "passengers[0].birthday - birthday need to be a date in the past"
    ]
}
```

**LISTING 2.27** Output of the execution of the request.

The application validates attribute formats using built-in annotations; however, complex validations sometimes exceed the capabilities of annotations. In such cases, the specification allows the creation of custom validations through annotations. For example, to validate that each passenger's nationality consists of exactly three alphanumeric characters, a custom validator can be implemented. Listing 2.28 includes the `isValid` method, which contains the logic for this specific validation.

```
package com.twa.flights.api.reservation.validator;

import jakarta.validation.ConstraintValidator;
import jakarta.validation.ConstraintValidatorContext;

public class NationalityFormatValidator implements ConstraintValidator<N
ationalityFormatConstraint, String> {

    @Override
    public void initialize(NationalityFormatConstraint nationality) {
    }

    @Override
    public boolean isValid(String field, ConstraintValidatorContext
constraintValidatorContext) {
        return field != null && field.matches("[A-Z]+") && field.length() == 3;
    }
}
```

**LISTING 2.28** Validator to check the nationality.

The class responsible for the validation is just one part of this approach; the other is defining the annotation and linking this validation class, as in Listing 2.29.

```
package com.twa.flights.api.reservation.validator;

import jakarta.validation.Constraint;
import jakarta.validation.Payload;

import java.lang.annotation.*;

@Documented
@Constraint(validatedBy = NationalityFormatValidator.class)
@Target({ ElementType.METHOD, ElementType.FIELD })
@Retention(RetentionPolicy.RUNTIME)
public @interface NationalityFormatConstraint {
    String message() default "Invalid format of the nationality. Only
three letters are allowed";
```

```
    Class<?>[] groups() default {};

    Class<? extends Payload>[] payload() default {};
}
```

LISTING 2.29 Annotation to execute the validators.

The final step in creating a custom validation is to replace the existing validations on PassengerDTO with the new ones, as shown in Listing 2.30.

```
package com.twa.flights.api.reservation.dto;

//Previous imports
import com.twa.flights.api.reservation.validator.
NationalityFormatConstraint;

public record PassengerDTO(
        //Previous attributtes

        @NationalityFormatConstraint
        String nationality,

        @NotNull(message = "The birthday must be defined")
        @Past(message = "birthday need to be a date in the past")
        LocalDate birthday) {
}
```

LISTING 2.30 PassengerDTO with the new annotation.

Now, it's time to check whether the custom validator works okay, so let's send a request, as in Listing 2.31, with the attribute nationality in the wrong format.

```
curl --location 'localhost:8080/reservation' \
--header 'Content-Type: application/json' \
--data-raw '{
    "itineraryId": "2",
    "searchId": "2",
    "passengers": [
        {
            "firstName": "Andres",
            "lastName": "Sacco",
            "documentNumber": "987654321",
            "documentType": "DNI",
            "nationality": "3",
            "birthday": "2009-01-01"
        }
    ],
    "contact": {
        "telephoneNumber": "54911111111",
        "email": "sacco.andres@gmail.com"
    }
}'
```

LISTING 2.31 curl command with an invalid nationality.

If the custom validator works correctly, the output will appear as shown in Listing 2.32, displaying the message included in the validator.

```
{
    "description": "There are attributes with wrong values",
    "reasons": [
        "passengers[0].nationality - Invalid format of the nationality.
Only three letters are allowed."
    ]
}
```

*LISTING 2.32* Output of the execution of the curl command.

When multiple duplicate validations related to format (such as length or allowed characters) exist, creating a custom validator is recommended to reduce code duplication and improve the application's maintainability.

Validations offer additional capabilities, such as translating error messages into multiple languages. Those aspects, however, are beyond the scope of this book.

## SUMMARY

Defining the scope of an application is crucial to keep it simple and maintainable without problems. For these reasons, microservices are the preferred option over monoliths, and many companies worldwide employ this approach.

Defining a structure within the application clarifies each layer's responsibility and its interactions. With this foundation, tools such as ArchUnit can be used to create basic tests that verify that the application adheres to established standards, thereby minimizing the time required for validation.

# CHAPTER 3

# CONFIGURING BASIC ASPECTS

reating a new application can be a straightforward process. Still, in the microservices ecosystem, only some applications can have duplicate URLs or use the same port, as another application with a different name could have a similar URL, making it difficult for a user to determine which one represents the correct one.

This chapter covers how to modify the application's default configuration, such as the base path, port, and other essential settings. It also explains how to use Spring Boot Actuator to obtain information about the application.

## HOW IS THE APPLICATION CONFIGURED?

Each application comes with a default configuration to minimize the complexity of specifying numerous attributes for execution. To modify any of these default values, Spring Boot offers the option to use either the `application.yml` or `application.properties` file.

### Why Is This Relevant?

There isn't a single answer to this question. If two different microservices need to run on the same machine to identify a bug, however, they cannot use the same port. Therefore, the port of one of the applications must be changed. Another potential issue involves the default application port. If a future version of Spring Boot were to change the default port from 8080 to 9080, this could create inconsistencies with established deployment standards. In such cases, teams would need to justify why new applications deviate from the conventional port 8080, requiring clear communication across the organization to maintain alignment with existing infrastructure practices.

Not all overridden values in the configuration file are meant to be changed; in some cases, a specific value should remain unchanged to ensure consistency if a future version of Spring Boot modifies the default, as seen in the previous port example.

### What Aspects Are Configurable in an Application?

The application must be configured to set several parameters, including the port, base path, and public URLs. Let's start with the basics and then move on to more advanced stuff.

## Port

To change the port of the application, open the application file and make the modification shown in Listing 3.1.

```
spring.application.name=api-reservation
server.port=8090
```

*LISTING 3.1* Application properties with the configuration.

With this port modification, running the application will display a console log confirming that the change was applied, as shown in Listing 3.2.

```
2024-07-22T10:59:21.371-03:00  INFO 53900 --- [api-reservation] [
restartedMain] o.s.b.d.a.OptionalLiveReloadServer      : LiveReload
server is running on port 35729
2024-07-22T10:59:21.379-03:00  INFO 53900 --- [api-reservation] [
restartedMain] o.s.b.w.embedded.tomcat.TomcatWebServer  : Tomcat started
on port 8090 (http) with context path '/'
2024-07-22T10:59:21.382-03:00  INFO 53900 --- [api-reservation]
[ restartedMain] c.t.f.a.r.ApiReservationApplication      : Started
ApiReservationApplication in 0.638 seconds (process running for 0.856)
```

*LISTING 3.2* Output of running the application with the changes.

Spring Boot facilitates the ability to document the application's configuration within a `properties` or YAML file without requiring any alterations to access information from either file. By default, all options for generating a Spring Boot project create an `application.properties` file. To reduce the number of characters to write and keep it simple, however, it could be a good idea to migrate the file to a YAML file.

Considering the simplicity of the YAML file, the rest of the book will use that format with different modifications on the configuration, so let's translate `application.properties` into an `application.yml` file as it appears in Listing 3.3.

```
spring:
  application:
    name: api-reservation

server:
  port: 8090
```

*LISTING 3.3* Application YAML with the same configuration as Listing 3.2.

The use of YAML simplifies understanding where each attribute is in the hierarchy. It's essential to keep in mind that this file format can produce errors if not properly tabulated. Using a tool such as YAMLlint[1] is recommended to validate the format and avoid such issues.

---

[1]https://www.yamllint.com/

NOTE *When creating the YAML file, the* `application.properties` *file should be removed to ensure Spring Boot correctly identifies and applies the intended configuration. This situation usually means that the application uses the* `properties` *file instead of the YAML file.*

It's possible to override the application configuration on any of those files in several ways. To do this, Spring Boot offers a hierarchy of elements to obtain the values of the configuration, as appears in Figure 3.1.

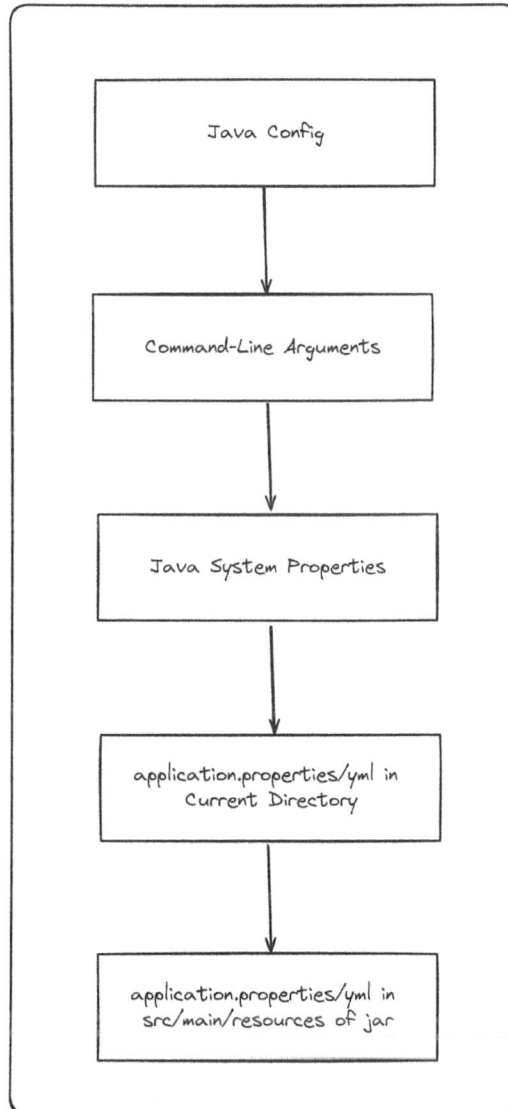

**FIGURE 3.1** Order of loading the configuration of the application.

Another relevant thing to remove from the application is the `static` and `templates` folders, which refer to the place to save all the static resources of the application. All resources related to HTML, CSS, and JavaScript should be placed accordingly if the application exposes a Web page.

## Context-path

The port and application name are not the only customizable elements; settings such as the base path also play a key role in reducing the risk of URL conflicts, not only within a single set of microservices but also with external systems. Figure 3.2 illustrates a possible scenario where some URLs are similar, and the port is one of the most significant aspects that differs between them.

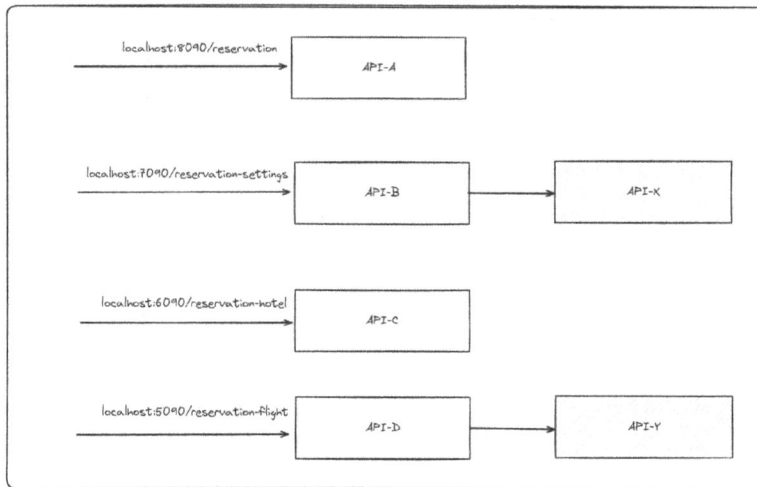

**FIGURE 3.2** Example of different microservices with similar URLs.

A possible solution to this problem is to define a representative URL for each controller, such as `/API/flights/reservation`, which represents the core idea of the application and reduces the risk of confusion. This, however, introduces another problem: When an application contains multiple controllers and the URL needs to be changed, updating it in several locations increases the risk of inconsistencies due to potential oversights. Centralizing such configurations is a better approach to avoid these issues.

To solve these problems, a possible approach is to define the attribute `context-path` in the configuration and specify a URL that represents the concept of the microservices, as shown in Listing 3.4.

```
spring:
  application:
    name: api-reservation

server:
  port: 8090
  servlet:
    context-path: /api/flights/reservation
```

**LISTING 3.4** Definition of the context path.

After introducing the changes on Listing 3.4, the next thing to do is modify the URL that appears on the declaration of the controller, removing the reservation, as shown in Listing 3.5.

```
// Previous imports

@Validated
@RestController
@RequestMapping("/")
public class ReservationController {
    // Previous code

}
```

**LISTING 3.5** Removing the word reservation from the path of the controller.

With these modifications to the application, a request can be submitted to verify that everything is functioning correctly, as shown in Listing 3.6.

```
curl --location --request GET 'localhost:8080/api/flights/reservation/2' \
--header 'Content-Type: application/json'
```

**LISTING 3.6** Curl command to get a reservation.

With any of these modifications that imply changes in the configuration and URL, the application must be restarted before the test.

### Error Pages

Most Web servers include an error Web page to inform the user that something terrible happened during a request. The error page could reveal sensitive information, such as which application server is used behind the scenes, as shown in Figure 3.3.

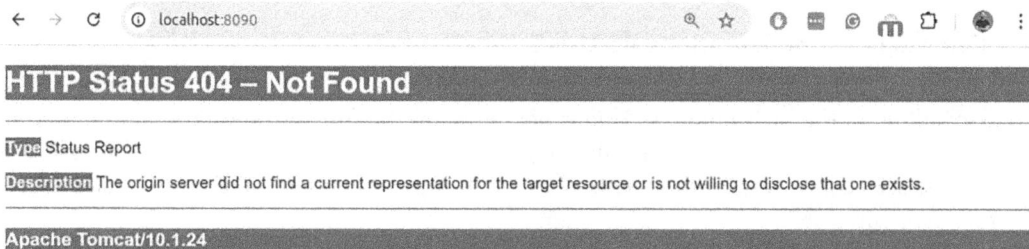

**FIGURE 3.3** Example of an error Web page with details about the server.

If someone discovers one of the platform's URLs and modifies the request to test its behavior, they may uncover the name and version of the Web server being used. This information could expose vulnerabilities and potentially lead to an attack on the platform. To address this issue, the information returned by the Web server in case of an error can be restricted by modifying the include-stacktrace attribute in the configuration, as shown in Listing 3.7.

```
spring:
  application:
    name: api-reservation

server:
  port: 8090

  error:
    include-stacktrace: never

  servlet:
    context-path: /api/flights/reservation
```

**LISTING 3.7** Modification of the configuration to hide the error information.

With this modification, most of the information in Figure 3.3 will disappear and only what is shown in Figure 3.4 will appear.

**FIGURE 3.4** Example of an error Web page without details about the server.

This modification only restricts the information that the Web server returns to the client. If the application itself generates errors containing sensitive data, however—such as attribute validation details—this configuration will not prevent their exposure. The `include-stack-trace` setting does not control application-level error responses, meaning additional measures are needed to secure such information.

### How Can Multiple Configurations Be Used?

One of the most common aspects of an application is using different configurations depending on the environment. This is not the same as showing sensitive information in a development environment where all users of the company have access. Such information may assist in addressing a problem; however, it is imperative to conceal it within a conducive environment.

To address this issue, you can use various configuration files to inform Spring Boot which files to use to execute the application. There is no limit or naming convention for the configuration files, but as it is fairly standard in the industry, most companies use the pattern `application-{environment}.yml`.

Let's create a new file with the name `application-prod.yml` with the same information as on `application.yml`, but instead of using port 8090, change it to 8080 and execute the command that appears in Listing 3.8.

```
→   ~ ./mvnw spring-boot:run -Dspring-boot.run.arguments="--spring.
config.location=classpath:/application-prod.yml"
```

LISTING 3.8 Command to indicate one particular configuration file.

After the execution of this command, the application will operate on port 8080 with the configuration specified in the file.

If an incorrect file name is specified in the command, an error similar to that shown in Listing 3.9 will be displayed on the console.

```
→   ~ ./mvnw spring-boot:run -Dspring-boot.run.arguments="--spring.
config.location=classpath:/application-prodution.yml"

14:00:25.965 [restartedMain] ERROR org.springframework.boot.diagnostics.
LoggingFailureAnalysisReporter --

***************************
APPLICATION FAILED TO START
***************************

Description:

Config data resource 'class path resource [application-production.yml]'
via location 'classpath:/application-production.yml' does not exist

Action:

Check that the value 'classpath:/application-production.yml' is correct,
or prefix it with 'optional:'
```

LISTING 3.9 Command to run the application with the wrong file name.

Utilizing multiple files, each meticulously tailored to specific environments, represents an excellent alternative when diverse configurations are required for distinct environments. Conversely, if a uniform configuration is to be employed across all environments, it is advisable to create a single file.

## WHAT IS AN ACTUATOR?

Each application performs several tasks before it is ready to receive a request. Some are related to connections with a database or external services, such as an FTP check for credentials. Nevertheless, once the application is operational, it is impossible to determine the status of those resources or the internal condition of the application.

An actuator provides a mechanism for applications to expose operational information about their resource status. Depending on the implementation, actuators may also support executing specific actions, such as reloading application components or clearing cache elements. Additionally, metrics can be exported to external monitoring tools, such as Prometheus, without requiring extensive custom code.

## How Does Spring Boot Implement an Actuator?

In the case of Spring Boot, the module actuator provides a mechanism where different existing modules, such as Spring Data and Spring Boot Messaging, can expose certain information without requiring any additional configuration. The focus should be on deciding which information about the application will be exposed to anyone who knows the base URL.

The first step in providing support for the application is adding the dependency on the POM file that which appears in Listing 3.10.

```xml
<?xml version="1.0" encoding="UTF-8"?>
<project xmlns="http://maven.apache.org/POM/4.0.0"
xmlns:xsi="http://www.w3.org/2001/XMLSchema-instance"
         xsi:schemaLocation="http://maven.apache.org/POM/4.0.0
https://maven.apache.org/xsd/maven-4.0.0.xsd">
                <!-- Previous definitions  -->
        <dependencies>
                        <!-- Previous dependencies  -->
            <dependency>
                <groupId>org.springframework.boot</groupId>
                <artifactId>spring-boot-starter-actuator</
artifactId>
            </dependency>
        </dependencies>
    </project>
```

**LISTING 3.10** Spring Boot Actuator dependency.

The next step is to add the configuration to indicate the URL where Spring Boot will expose all the endpoints on the actuator. To accomplish this, modify the `application.yml` file by incorporating the code block shown in Listing 3.11.

```yaml
management:
  endpoints:
    web:
      base-path: /management
      exposure:
        include: "*"
```

**LISTING 3.11** Spring Boot Actuator configuration.

The configuration is straightforward to implement; however, several key considerations should be taken into account. First, defining a custom base path—rather than relying on the default—reduces the risk of exposing sensitive information if an unauthorized party discovers the application's root URL. Second, careful selection of actuator endpoints is necessary. Using * exposes all available actuator endpoints, which may not be advisable in all environments.

After configuring everything, run the application and request as shown in Listing 3.12.

```
→  ~ curl --location 'http://localhost:8090/api/flights/reservation/
management'
```

**LISTING 3.12** Request to obtain information from the actuator.

The execution output shown in Listing 3.12 displays all the available actuator endpoints that can be used. Listing 3.13 has the functionality name and URL of each component on the actuator.

```
{
    "_links": {
        "self": {
            "href": "http://localhost:8090/api/flights/reservation/
management",
            "templated": false
        },
        "beans": {
            "href": "http://localhost:8090/api/flights/reservation/
management/beans",
            "templated": false
        },
        "caches": {
            "href": "http://localhost:8090/api/flights/reservation/
management/caches",
            "templated": false
        },
        "caches-cache": {
            "href": "http://localhost:8090/api/flights/reservation/
management/caches/{cache}",
            "templated": true
        },
        "health": {
            "href": "http://localhost:8090/api/flights/reservation/
management/health",
            "templated": false
        },
        "health-path": {
            "href": "http://localhost:8090/api/flights/reservation/
management/health/{*path}",
            "templated": true
        },
        "info": {
            "href": "http://localhost:8090/api/flights/reservation/
management/info",
            "templated": false
        },
        "conditions": {
            "href": "http://localhost:8090/api/flights/reservation/
management/conditions",
            "templated": false
        },
        "configprops": {
            "href": "http://localhost:8090/api/flights/reservation/
management/configprops",
            "templated": false
        },
        "configprops-prefix": {
            "href": "http://localhost:8090/api/flights/reservation/
management/configprops/{prefix}",
            "templated": true
        },
        "env-toMatch": {
            "href": "http://localhost:8090/api/flights/reservation/
management/env/{toMatch}",
            "templated": true
```

```
        },
        "env": {
            "href": "http://localhost:8090/api/flights/reservation/
management/env",
            "templated": false
        },
        "loggers-name": {
            "href": "http://localhost:8090/api/flights/reservation/
management/loggers/{name}",
            "templated": true
        },
        "loggers": {
            "href": "http://localhost:8090/api/flights/reservation/
management/loggers",
            "templated": false
        },
        "heapdump": {
            "href": "http://localhost:8090/api/flights/reservation/
management/heapdump",
            "templated": false
        },
        "threaddump": {
            "href": "http://localhost:8090/api/flights/reservation/
management/threaddump",
            "templated": false
        },
        "metrics-requiredMetricName": {
            "href": "http://localhost:8090/api/flights/reservation/
management/metrics/{requiredMetricName}",
            "templated": true
        },
        "metrics": {
            "href": "http://localhost:8090/api/flights/reservation/
management/metrics",
            "templated": false
        },
        "sbom-id": {
            "href": "http://localhost:8090/api/flights/reservation/
management/sbom/{id}",
            "templated": true
        },
        "sbom": {
            "href": "http://localhost:8090/api/flights/reservation/
management/sbom",
            "templated": false
        },
        "scheduledtasks": {
            "href": "http://localhost:8090/api/flights/reservation/
management/scheduledtasks",
            "templated": false
        },
        "mappings": {
            "href": "http://localhost:8090/api/flights/reservation/
management/mappings",
            "templated": false
        }
    }
}
```

**LISTING 3.13** Output of the invocation of the base actuator endpoint.

Some endpoints are used frequently, such as `health` or `info` endpoints, while others may be accessed only occasionally.

## What Is the Purpose of Each Endpoint?

The actuator offers a series of endpoints, each with a specific purpose, as listed in Listing 3.13. Table 3.1 gives a detailed description of the most relevant endpoints.

*TABLE 3.1* Description of the most relevant endpoints on the actuator.

| HTTP Method | Path | Description |
|---|---|---|
| GET | /beans | Provide information about all the beans that are loaded on Spring Context. |
| GET | /conditions | Report about the autoconfiguration conditions that passed or failed when creating the different beans. |
| GET | /cache | Give a list of all the caches that are defined in the application. |
| GET | /configprops | Provide information about all the configuration properties with the current values. |
| GET, POST, DELETE | /env | Provide a report with all the properties available on the application. |
| GET | /env/{toMatch} | Describe a single environment property. |
| GET | /health | Return the information about the application's status and validate the status of external resources, such as databases. |
| GET | /heapdump | Return the heap dump of the application. |
| GET | /info | Return the information about the application. Most developers include information such as the application's name and version. |
| GET | /loggers | Produce a list of all the packages with the logger configuration. |
| GET, POST | /loggers/{name} | Return the information about one particular logger and its configuration. |
| GET | /mappings | Return a list of all the HTTP mappings that exist in the application. |
| GET | /metrics | Provide a list of all metrics obtainable from the application. |
| GET | /metrics/{name} | Provide information about a particular metric. |
| GET | /scheduledtasks | Provide a list of the scheduled tasks. |
| GET | /threaddump | Provide a report about all the threads on the application. |

Each time a new Spring Boot module is added to the application, the number of endpoints exposed by the actuator will increase accordingly.

## How Are Endpoints Enabled and Disabled?

In Table 3.1, there are a lot of endpoints with valuable information, and only in some cases is it necessary to expose that information. Considering this situation, Spring Boot offers the option to restrict access to specific endpoints. To do that, let's modify the configuration of the application to expose all the endpoints, excluding some of them, as shown in Listing 3.14.

```
management:
  endpoints:
    web:
      base-path: /api/flights/reservation/management
      exposure:
        include: "*"
      exclude: beans,env,threaddump,heapdump
```

**LISTING 3.14** Spring Boot Actuator configuration with exclusions.

This configuration exposes all available endpoints except those specified in the `exclude` attribute. Any requests to excluded endpoints will generate an exception response, as demonstrated in Listing 3.15. The exclusion mechanism provides granular control over endpoint accessibility while maintaining system transparency for permitted endpoints.

```
→  ~ curl --location 'http://localhost:8090/api/flights/reservation/
management/beans'
{"type":"about:blank","title":"Not Found","status":404,"detail":"No
static resource api/flights/reservation/management/beans.","instance":"/
api/flights/reservation/management/beans"}
```

**LISTING 3.15** Request to exclude the endpoint.

For production environments, explicitly declare enabled endpoints rather than relying on exclusion patterns. This positive security approach minimizes information exposure risks that could occur when adding new application modules without proper exclusion safeguards. Listing 3.16 demonstrates a minimal-exposure configuration that implements this allowlist methodology.

```
management:
  endpoints:
    web:
      base-path: /api/flights/reservation/management
      exposure:
        include: health,info,metrics,cache
```

**LISTING 3.16** Minimal information about the application.

The configuration solely exposes information that can be used to verify the operational status of the application, including specific details regarding the version, the disclosed metrics, and the cache mechanism.

### Using the Actuator Endpoints

The actuator offers a series of different endpoints that provide valuable information not only for developers but also for infrastructure, as some of them, such as the health endpoint, are vital for its operation.

### Info Endpoint

The info endpoint is an excellent way to expose specific information about the application; however, by default, the actuator does not provide any data, as demonstrated when executing a request like the one shown in Listing 3.17.

```
➜  ~ curl --location 'http://localhost:8090/api/flights/reservation/
management/info'
{}
```

**LISTING 3.17** Request to the info endpoint.

In the case of the info endpoint, the actuator has classes that expose information, implementing the `InfoContributor` interface. Table 3.2 presents the most relevant implementations of the interface.

**TABLE 3.2** Implementations of the InfoContributor interface.

| ID | Bean | Usage |
|----|------|-------|
| build | BuildInfoContributor | Exposes information about the build |
| env | EnvironmentInfoContributor | Exposes information about the environment |
| git | GitInfoContributor | Exposes information related to Git |
| java | JavaInfoContributor | Exposes information about the Java version |

The response in Listing 3.17 is empty because, by default, all implementations are disabled. To make them available, each one must be explicitly enabled, as demonstrated in Listing 3.18.

```
management:
 # Previous configuration
  info:
    java:
      enabled: true
    os:
      enabled: true
```

**LISTING 3.18** Enabling part of the info configuration.

Now, executing the request to the info endpoint again will return information about the Java version and the JVM, as shown in Listing 3.19.

```
➜  ~ curl --location 'http://localhost:8090/api/flights/reservation/
management/info'
{
    "java": {
        "version": "21.0.2",
        "vendor": {
            "name": "GraalVM Community",
            "version": "GraalVM CE 21.0.2+13.1"
        },
        "runtime": {
            "name": "OpenJDK Runtime Environment",
            "version": "21.0.2+13-jvmci-23.1-b30"
        },
        "jvm": {
            "name": "OpenJDK 64-Bit Server VM",
            "vendor": "GraalVM Community",
            "version": "21.0.2+13-jvmci-23.1-b30"
        }
```

```
    },
    "os": {
        "name": "Linux",
        "version": "6.5.0-44-generic",
        "arch": "amd64"
    }
}
```

**LISTING 3.19** Request to the info endpoint.

This information is accurate; however, if there is a need to share details about the application's version and other relevant information with consumers, additional configuration or custom endpoints may be required to expose that data securely. The way to do it is to declare the attribute on the root of the application file and enable the env attribute in the same way that is shown in Listing 3.20.

```
management:
 # Previous configuration
 info:
   java:
     enabled: false # Change the value to obtain information about Java
   os:
     enabled: false #Change the value to obtain information about the OS
   env:
     enabled: true

info:
  app:
    name: "@project.artifactId@"
    version: "@project.version@"
  contact:
    email: "sacco.andres@gmail.com"

    slack: "adsacco"
```

**LISTING 3.20** Adding information about the application.

No restriction exists on the information or attribute names that can be included under the info node; in Listing 3.20, only the application's name and version appear, which can be helpful when deploying to an environment without certainty about the running version.

When the application is running and a request is made again, the response will be similar to the one shown in Listing 3.21.

```
→  ~ curl --location 'http://localhost:8090/api/flights/reservation/
management/info'
{
    "app": {
        "name": "api-reservation",
        "version": "0.0.1-SNAPSHOT"
    },
    "contact": {
        "email": "sacco.andres@gmail.com",
        "slack": "adsacco"
    }
}
```

**LISTING 3.21** Request to the info endpoint.

As a recommendation, only expose information about the OS and Java version in a non-productive environment.

## Health Endpoint

Knowing the application's status is crucial for understanding why requests to different endpoints fail or return errors in the response. By default, the actuator offers the health endpoint, which obtains the status of the application that appears on Listing 3.21.

```
→  ~ curl --location 'http://localhost:8090/api/flights/reservation/
management/health'
{
    "status": "UP"

}
```

**LISTING 3.21** Request to obtain information about the health.

In the response, there is one attribute with the status of the application, which in this case has the value UP, but there are some other values, each of which represents the current situation of the application:

- UP: The application is running and can receive requests without problems.
- DOWN: The application is not running, and requests can't be received.
- UNKNOWN: When some part of the application status could be impossible to obtain.
- OUT_OF_SERVICE: The application is unavailable.

The status may not always provide useful information for the service or user; however, the application's configuration can be adjusted to display specific details through a simple modification, as demonstrated in Listing 3.22.

```
management:
 # Previous configuration
 endpoint:
    health:

      show-details: always # The default value is never
```

**LISTING 3.22** Modify the configuration of the health endpoint.

After applying the modifications in Listing 3.22, executing the request again will return information about the disk space and the application's location, as shown in Listing 3.23.

```
→  ~ curl --location 'http://localhost:8090/api/flights/reservation/
management/health'
{
    "status": "UP",
    "components": {
        "diskSpace": {
            "status": "UP",
            "details": {
                "total": 490566533120,
                "free": 205722673152,
                "threshold": 10485760,
```

```
                    "path": "/home/asacco/Code/deguyer/chapter 3/api-
    reservation/.",
                    "exists": true
            }
        },
        "ping": {
            "status": "UP"
        }
    }
}
```

*LISTING 3.23* Request to obtain information about the health.


On the node details, only information about the space on the disk is provided. If, however, the application uses a database such as MongoDB or Cassandra, or a message broker such as RabbitMQ, the status of each component will appear in the same section.

NOTE

*Enabling health checks for external components, such as databases, executes a status query each time the endpoint is accessed.*
*This situation represents a problem because an application with multiple instances and  tool such as Kubernetes[2], or any that makes one request per second to validate the application's status, could affect the database's performance.*
*With this in mind, limit the number of components included in the health validation.*
*Chapter 4 explains how to disable status validation on the database.*

With the appearance of Kubernetes, the concept of liveness shows that the application is running, and readiness means that the application is ready to receive requests. Previously, this functionality was not available in Spring Boot. As this functionality is natively included in Actuator from version 3.0.0, enabling the feature simply requires applying the configuration shown in Listing 3.24. The default implementation eliminates the need for additional dependencies or custom code, streamlining the activation process.

```
management:
 # Previous configuration
 endpoint:
    health:
      show-details: always # The default value is never
      probes:
         enabled: true #The default value is false
```

*LISTING 3.24* Enable the readiness and liveness probes.

Following this modification, two distinct health-related endpoints are now available. Listing 3.25 shows the result of requesting the liveness endpoint.

---

[2]https://kubernetes.io/

```
→  ~ curl --location 'http://localhost:8090/api/flights/reservation/
management/health/liveness'
{
    "status": "UP"

}
```

**LISTING 3.25** Request to the liveness endpoint.

The level of detail pertaining to that endpoint is clearly defined, as the concept is utilized solely for a specific purpose. The alternative endpoint bears similarity; however, instead of denoting "liveness," it is necessary to indicate "readiness."

## Metrics Endpoint

Obtaining information about the application's use is valuable for several reasons, such as detecting possible anomalous behavior or optimizing resource utilization, including CPU and memory. In the context of Spring Boot, endpoint metrics are available, presenting a collection of elements, including the current number of active threads.

To check which metrics are available in the application, request the /metrics endpoint, as shown in Listing 3.26.

```
→  ~ curl --location 'http://localhost:8090/api/flights/reservation/
management/health/metrics'
{
    "names": [
        "application.ready.time",
        "application.started.time",
        "disk.free",
        "disk.total",
        "executor.active",
        "executor.completed",
        "executor.pool.core",
        "executor.pool.max",
        "executor.pool.size",
        "executor.queue.remaining",
        "executor.queued",
        "http.server.requests",
        "http.server.requests.active",
        "jvm.buffer.count",
        "jvm.buffer.memory.used",
        "jvm.buffer.total.capacity",
        "jvm.classes.loaded",
        "jvm.classes.unloaded",
        "jvm.compilation.time",
        "jvm.gc.live.data.size",
        "jvm.gc.max.data.size",
        "jvm.gc.memory.allocated",
        "jvm.gc.memory.promoted",
        "jvm.gc.overhead",
        "jvm.gc.pause",
        "jvm.info",
        "jvm.memory.committed",
        "jvm.memory.max",
        "jvm.memory.usage.after.gc",
```

```
            "jvm.memory.used",
            "jvm.threads.daemon",
            "jvm.threads.live",
            "jvm.threads.peak",
            "jvm.threads.started",
            "jvm.threads.states",
            "logback.events",
            "process.cpu.time",
            "process.cpu.usage",
            "process.files.max",
            "process.files.open",
            "process.start.time",
            "process.uptime",
            "system.cpu.count",
            "system.cpu.usage",
            "system.load.average.1m",
            "tomcat.sessions.active.current",
            "tomcat.sessions.active.max",
            "tomcat.sessions.alive.max",
            "tomcat.sessions.created",
            "tomcat.sessions.expired",
            "tomcat.sessions.rejected"
        ]
}
```

**LISTING 3.26** List of available metrics on the application.

Listing 3.26 exclusively presents the accessible metrics without providing any detailed information. Therefore, if one requires, for instance, the information regarding the request that an individual executes to the application, it is necessary to perform a request similar to that demonstrated in Listing 3.27.

```
➜  ~ curl --location 'http://localhost:8090/api/flights/reservation/
management/health/metrics/http.server.requests'
{
    "name": "http.server.requests",
    "baseUnit": "seconds",
    "measurements": [
        {
            "statistic": "COUNT",
            "value": 20.0
        },
        {
            "statistic": "TOTAL_TIME",
            "value": 0.09346216
        },
        {
            "statistic": "MAX",
            "value": 0.011065125
        }
```

```json
    ],
    "availableTags": [
        {
            "tag": "exception",
            "values": [
                "none"
            ]
        },
        {
            "tag": "method",
            "values": [
                "GET"
            ]
        },
        {
            "tag": "error",
            "values": [
                "none"
            ]
        },
        {
            "tag": "uri",
            "values": [
                "/api/flights/reservation/management/loggers",
                "/api/flights/reservation/management/health",
                "/api/flights/reservation/management/metrics",
                "/api/flights/reservation/management/metrics/
{requiredMetricName}",
                "/**",
                "/api/flights/reservation/management/health/**",
                "/api/flights/reservation/management"
            ]
        },
        {
            "tag": "outcome",
            "values": [
                "CLIENT_ERROR",
                "SUCCESS"
            ]
        },
        {
            "tag": "status",
            "values": [
                "404",
                "200"
            ]
        }
    ]
}
```

**LISTING 3.27** The request that the application receives.

Note that the information in Listing 3.27 is related to the application's current runtime state; therefore, restarting the application will cause all this information to be lost.

### Loggers Endpoint

Loggers represent one of the most valuable features when developing an application. Nonetheless, they enhance the value when the application is deployed in a certain environment, as this is the sole method to acquire insights regarding a particular situation.

The application can have multiple loggers, each covering a specific layer and a particular level (INFO, DEBUG, WARN, FATAL, ERROR, or TRACE). The actuator enables viewing all loggers in the application, as shown in Listing 3.28.

```
➜  ~ curl --location 'http://localhost:8090/api/flights/reservation/
management/health/loggers'
{
    "levels": [
        "OFF",
        "ERROR",
        "WARN",
        "INFO",
        "DEBUG",
        "TRACE"
    ],
    "loggers": {
        "ROOT": {
            "configuredLevel": "INFO",
            "effectiveLevel": "INFO"
        },
        ....
        "com": {
            "effectiveLevel": "INFO"
        },
        "com.twa": {
            "effectiveLevel": "INFO"
        },
        "com.twa.flights": {
            "effectiveLevel": "INFO"
        },
        "com.twa.flights.api": {
            "effectiveLevel": "INFO"
        },
        "com.twa.flights.api.reservation": {
            "effectiveLevel": "INFO"
        },
        .....
    },
    "groups": {
        "web": {
            "members": [
                "org.springframework.core.codec",
                "org.springframework.http",
                "org.springframework.web",
                "org.springframework.boot.actuate.endpoint.web",
```

```
                    "org.springframework.boot.web.servlet.
ServletContextInitializerBeans"
                ]
        },
        "sql": {
            "members": [
                "org.springframework.jdbc.core",
                "org.hibernate.SQL",
                "org.jooq.tools.LoggerListener"
            ]
        }
    }
}
```

**LISTING 3.28** Loggers that exist in the application.

The "ROOT" node contains two attributes: one that indicates the logger level loaded from the application's configuration, and another that shows the level currently in use. Both attributes have the same values, with the idea of using the same logs level since the application starts.

Imagine that an exception appears in the application, but there isn't enough information to solve the problem because the level of the loggers is INFO. A possible solution could change the level of the loggers and deploy the application again, which could, in some cases, take a few minutes. Taking into consideration the problem, Spring Boot offers the possibility to change the level of the logger dynamically, making a POST request to the logger endpoint indicating the level that the application will use, as shown in Listing 3.29.

```
→  ~ curl --location 'http://localhost:8090/api/flights/reservation/
management/loggers/com.twa.flights.api.reservation' \
--header 'Content-Type: application/json' \
--data '{
            "configuredLevel": "DEBUG",
            "effectiveLevel": "DEBUG"

        }'
```

**LISTING 3.29** Modifying the level of the logger.

This modification of the logger's level only applies until the application stops or the value changes again; if either of these situations occurs, the logger will revert to the default value from the configuration.

## Mapping Endpoint

During application development, it is common to send requests to verify the availability of endpoints. Sometimes, these requests fail unexpectedly with a 404 response. A straightforward way to identify the available endpoints is by sending a request to the /mappings endpoint, as shown in Listing 3.30.

```
→  ~ curl --location 'http://localhost:8090/api/flights/reservation/
management/mappings'
{
    "contexts": {
        "api-reservation": {
```

```
        "mappings": {
            "dispatcherServlets": {
                "dispatcherServlet": [
                    ...
                    {
                        "handler": "com.twa.flights.api.reservation.
controller.ReservationController#getReservationById(Long)",
                        "predicate": "{GET [/{id}]}",
                        "details": {
                            "handlerMethod": {
                                "className": "com.twa.flights.api.
reservation.controller.ReservationController",
                                "name": "getReservationById",
                                "descriptor": "(Ljava/lang/Long;)
Lorg/springframework/http/ResponseEntity;"
                            },
                            "requestMappingConditions": {
                                "consumes": [],
                                "headers": [],
                                "methods": [
                                    "GET"
                                ],
                                "params": [],
                                "patterns": [
                                    "/{id}"
                                ],
                                "produces": []
                            }
                        }
                    }
                    ...
                ]
            },
            "servletFilters": [
                ...
            ],
            "servlets": [
                ...
            ]
        }
    }
}
```

*LISTING 3.30* Request to see all the existing mappings.

The response from the endpoint provides details regarding the name of the endpoint, the associated class, and the method that executes the endpoint's logic. It is important to note that the outcomes will not be limited to just the endpoints defined within the application; rather, all existing endpoints, including the actuator, will also be displayed.

## What Are the Steps to Customize the Actuator?

The default functionality provided by each actuator endpoint can cover most requirements; however, in certain situations, it may be necessary to extend an existing endpoint or add new functionality to meet specific needs. Considering this situation, Spring Boot Actuator offers the possibility to do it without needing anything special, just by creating a class that extends a particular interface or abstract class.

## Info Endpoint

This endpoint includes various implementations that deliver detailed information regarding the application's version or the JVM. All of these implement the `InfoContributor` interface, so extending its functionality is relatively straightforward. It creates a class that implements the same interface and puts all the logic inside.

Let's create a new class that extends from `InfoContributor` and provides information about the number of reservations. Listing 3.31 illustrates a possible implementation of the logic to retrieve information about existing reservations.

```
package com.twa.flights.api.reservation.actuator;

import com.twa.flights.api.reservation.repository.ReservationRepository;
import org.springframework.boot.actuate.info.Info;
import org.springframework.boot.actuate.info.InfoContributor;
import org.springframework.stereotype.Component;

import java.util.HashMap;
import java.util.Map;

@Component
public class ReservationCountInfoContributor implements InfoContributor
{

    ReservationRepository repository;

    public ReservationCountInfoContributor(ReservationRepository
repository) {
        this.repository = repository;
    }

    @Override
    public void contribute(Info.Builder builder) {
        long reservationCount = repository.getReservations().size();
        Map<String, Object> reservationMap = new HashMap<>();
        reservationMap.put("amount", reservationCount);
        builder.withDetail("reservation-stats", reservationMap);
    }

}
```

**LISTING 3.31** Class to extend the functionality of the info endpoint.

The next step is to run the application and request the info endpoint to verify that the new node appears in the response, as shown in Listing 3.32.

```
→  ~ curl --location 'http://localhost:8090/api/flights/reservation/
management/info'
{
    "app": {
        "name": "api-reservation",
        "version": "0.0.1-SNAPSHOT"
```

```
    },
    "contact": {
        "email": "sacco.andres@gmail.com",
        "slack": "adsacco"
    },
    "reservation-stats": {
        "amount": 1
    }
}
```

**LISTING 3.32** Request to the info endpoint to check the new attributes.

As shown in the response to Listing 3.32, the information is appended to the existing data. Multiple implementations of InfoContributor can be created without affecting the default behavior.

## Health Endpoint

The health endpoint offers extensive control over the application's different resources, not just internal ones. When the application runs, external resources can be checked. In specific scenarios, however, custom validations must be defined to indicate whether particular parts of the application are functioning correctly or have failed.

In this scenario, functionality can be extended by creating a class that implements the HealthIndicator[3] interface, requiring only the implementation of the health method. Listing 3.33 presents a simple custom health implementation that reports everything as healthy if there are reservations in the application.

```
package com.twa.flights.api.reservation.actuator;

import com.twa.flights.api.reservation.repository.ReservationRepository;
import org.springframework.boot.actuate.health.Health;
import org.springframework.boot.actuate.health.HealthIndicator;
import org.springframework.stereotype.Component;

@Component
public class ReservationHealthIndicator implements HealthIndicator {
    ReservationRepository repository;

    public ReservationHealthIndicator(ReservationRepository repository)
{
        this.repository = repository;
    }
    @Override
    public Health health() {
        if (repository.getReservations().isEmpty()) {
            return Health
                    .down()
                    .withDetail("reason", "There is a problem obtaining
the reservations")
```

---

[3]https://docs.spring.io/spring-boot/api/java/org/springframework/boot/actuate/health/HealthIndicator.html

```
                    .build();
        }
        return Health
                .up()
                .withDetail("reason", "There is not a problem obtaining
the reservations")
                .build();
    }
}
```

**LISTING 3.33** Class to extend the functionality of the health endpoint.

The next step is to check whether the new logic on the health endpoint appears as part of the response, as it does in Listing 3.34.

```
➜  ~ curl --location 'http://localhost:8090/api/flights/reservation/
management/health'
{
    "status": "UP",
    "components": {
        "diskSpace": {
            "status": "UP",
            "details": {
                "total": 490566533120,
                "free": 205244342272,
                "threshold": 10485760,
                "path": "/home/asacco/Code/deguyer/chapter 3/api-
                reservation/.",
                "exists": true
            }
        },
        "ping": {
            "status": "UP"
        },
        "reservation": {
            "status": "UP",
            "details": {
                "reason": "There is not a problem obtaining the
reservations"
            }
        }
    }
}
```

**LISTING 3.34** Request to the health endpoint to check the new attributes.

The logic inside the `health` method depends on the validations or conditions that define when the application is considered healthy.

## Metrics Endpoint

Micrometer[4], a neutral vendor, implements the metric that the application exposes on the default endpoint. Multiple tools, such as Prometheus[5], New Relic[6], and Datadog[7], could consume this information to populate reports or create alerts if they detect anomalous behavior.

Micrometer enables exposing custom metrics beyond the default ones by using the class `MeterRegistry`. It only requires specifying the metric's name and the desired action, such as sum or count.

Let's modify the repository to count the number of times that someone saves a reservation in the application. This means adding the `MeterRegistry` component to the repository and invoking the `counter` method, as shown in Listing 3.35.

```
package com.twa.flights.api.reservation.repository;

import com.twa.flights.api.reservation.model.Contact;
import com.twa.flights.api.reservation.model.Passenger;
import com.twa.flights.api.reservation.model.Reservation;
import io.micrometer.core.instrument.MeterRegistry;
import org.springframework.stereotype.Component;

import java.time.LocalDate;
import java.util.*;

@Component
public class ReservationRepository {

    private final MeterRegistry meterRegistry;

    public ReservationRepository(MeterRegistry meterRegistry) {
        this.meterRegistry = meterRegistry;
    }

    //Previous code

    public Reservation save(Reservation reservation) {
        reservation.setId((long) (reservations.size() + 1));
        reservations.add(reservation);

        meterRegistry.counter("reservation").increment(); //This
increment the metric on each save
        return reservation;
    }

    //Previous code

}
```

LISTING 3.35 Modifications on the repository to save a new metric.

---

[4]https://micrometer.io/
[5]https://prometheus.io/
[6]https://newrelic.com/
[7]https://www.datadoghq.com/

After the modifications on the repository to push the new metric each time that someone saves a reservation, the next thing to do is make multiple requests to that endpoint to populate it with the same information metric. After making different reservations in the application, the final step is to review the new metric, as displayed in Listing 3.36.

```
➜  ~ curl --location 'http://localhost:8090/api/flights/reservation/
management/metrics/reservation'
{
    "name": "reservation",
    "measurements": [
        {
            "statistic": "COUNT",
            "value": 4.0
        }
    ],
    "availableTags": []
}
```

**LISTING 3.36** Request to obtain the custom metric.

The metric indicates the frequency with which the save function was invoked. An empty node is available in Tags; however, it is possible to group the metric based on consistent criteria, such as passenger identification numbers or the date of creation.

## Custom Endpoint

In certain circumstances, the current endpoints may not adequately address the requirements; therefore, it is possible to develop a custom endpoint integral to the actuator. Spring Boot Actuator provides a collection of annotations that must be used to expose the functionality of the newly created endpoint; these annotations are not the standard annotations of Spring Boot MVC, such as @GetMapping, @DeleteMapping, or @PostMapping. Instead of these annotations, the actuator offers @ReadOperation[8], @WriteOperation[9], and @DeleteOperation[10].

To establish and unveil a new endpoint within the actuator, it is necessary to construct a class annotated with @Endpoint, specifying the endpoint's name. Furthermore, within the class, incorporate the operations that this endpoint will authorize, as demonstrated in Listing 3.37.

```
package com.twa.flights.api.reservation.actuator;

import org.springframework.boot.actuate.endpoint.annotation.
DeleteOperation;
import org.springframework.boot.actuate.endpoint.annotation.Endpoint;
import org.springframework.boot.actuate.endpoint.annotation.
ReadOperation;
import org.springframework.boot.actuate.endpoint.annotation.
WriteOperation;
import org.springframework.stereotype.Component;

import java.util.HashMap;
```

---

[8]https://docs.spring.io/spring-boot/api/java/org/springframework/boot/actuate/endpoint/annotation/ReadOperation.html
[9]https://docs.spring.io/spring-boot/api/java/org/springframework/boot/actuate/endpoint/annotation/WriteOperation.html
[10]https://docs.spring.io/spring-boot/api/java/org/springframework/boot/actuate/endpoint/annotation/DeleteOperation.html

```java
import java.util.Map;

@Component
@Endpoint(id="custom", enableByDefault = true)
public class CustomEndpointActuator {

    private final Map<String, String> configuration = new HashMap<>();

    @ReadOperation
    public Map<String, String> getConfiguration() {
        return configuration;
    }

    @WriteOperation
    public Map<String, String> addConfiguration(String key, String value)
{
        configuration.put(key, value);
        return configuration;
    }

    @DeleteOperation
    public void deleteConfiguration(String key) {
        configuration.remove(key);
    }

}
```

**LISTING 3.37** Class that represents the custom endpoint.

To check whether this new endpoint is part of the actuator, just run the application and do a request as a GET operation, as in Listing 3.38.

```
➔  ~ curl --location 'http://localhost:8090/api/flights/reservation/
management/custom'
{}
```

**LISTING 3.38** Request to the custom endpoint.

Let's check whether the write operation works on the custom endpoint, as shown in Listing 3.39.

```
➔  ~ curl --location --request GET 'http://localhost:8090/api/flights/
reservation/management/custom' \
--header 'Content-Type: application/json' \
--data '{
    "key": "tes",
    "value": "asd"
}'

{
    "tes": "asd"
}
```

**LISTING 3.39** Request to add values to the custom endpoint.

If a custom endpoint is needed across multiple applications, consider extracting the logic into a library that can be added to each project. This approach could reduce duplicate code.

## SUMMARY

This chapter covered various aspects of an application, such as changing configurations and obtaining status information, which are crucial when deploying in environments without console access.

Remember, what was covered in this chapter only exposed minimal endpoints in each environment, reducing the risk that someone could misuse the information.

# INTERACTING WITH THE DATABASE

A critical aspect of every system is the use of information, such as validating whether a user exists, obtaining a user's email address to send a notification, or simply saving information about a user. As expected, all data must be stored somewhere, whether in a file or in memory. It can, however, impact the application's performance and the volatility of the information when using memory. Many years ago, this problem was resolved with the introduction of databases, but new problems subsequently emerged, such as how the application could interact with the databases.

This chapter provides a brief overview of various aspects of persistence, the associated problems, and strategies for solving or mitigating them.

## WHAT WAYS EXIST TO PRESERVE INFORMATION?

Applications have evolved significantly since Java Database Connectivity (JDBC) was introduced in JDK 1.1, progressing through object-relational mapping (ORM) to, now, Spring Data, which provides a standard interface for accessing various databases, including both relational and non-relational ones. The most relevant methods for persisting information are shown in Figure 4.1.

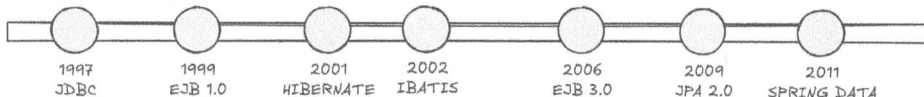

| 1997 | 1999 | 2001 | 2002 | 2006 | 2009 | 2011 |
| JDBC | EJB 1.0 | HIBERNATE | IBATIS | EJB 3.0 | JPA 2.0 | SPRING DATA |

**FIGURE 4.1** History of the different methods of persistence.

Most libraries and methods for interacting with databases remain relevant today, having evolved over the years, and often interoperate with one another. For example, EJB—which stands for Jakarta Enterprise Beans, formerly Enterprise JavaBeans—and JPA—which stands for Jakarta Persistence API, formerly Java Persistence API—are depicted in the figure as separate entities; however, early versions of EJB included all JPA specifications. As JPA gained prominence, EJB 3.0 emerged as two distinct yet interrelated components: EJB and JPA.

## Relational Databases

The persistence of information in relational databases is directly connected to the origins of Java, as all applications used this type of database by the end of the 1990s, regardless of the specific language. Considering this situation, it's not strange to see many libraries persist information into a relational database instead of a non-relational one.

## JDBC

JDBC offers a standardized interface for interacting with a wide range of databases. It enables establishing connections; executing statements to create, drop, or truncate tables; and performing data operations such as SELECT, INSERT, UPDATE, and DELETE. Through JDBC, Java applications can communicate directly with relational databases using SQL commands. Figure 4.2 illustrates all the components of this approach to persisting information.

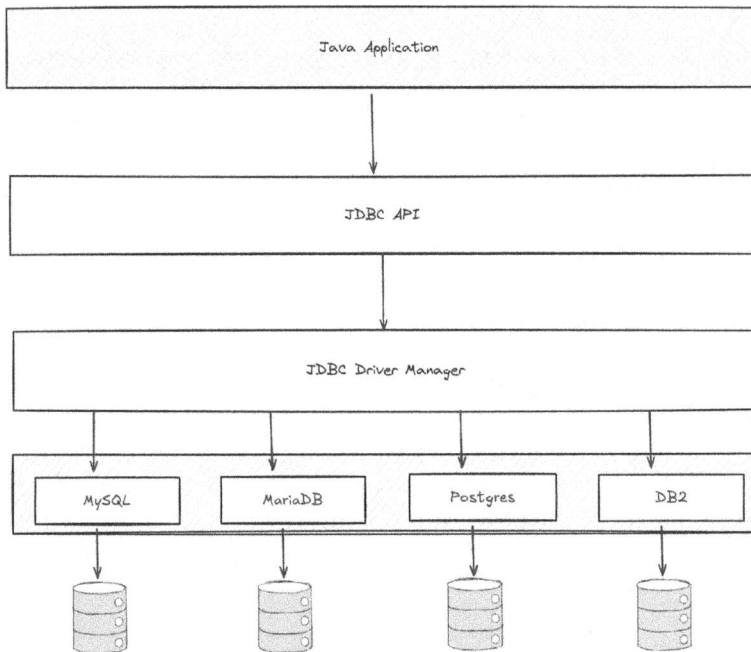

**FIGURE 4.2** Internal structure of JDBC.

As shown in Figure 4.2, JDBC consists of different layers or components, each with a primary responsibility, as follows:

- JDBC API: This layer contains all the interfaces that drivers need to implement, enabling Java developers to interact with databases easily. It is crucial because it allows seamless switching between databases with minimal changes, primarily just swapping the driver and making minor adjustments to the column types.

- JDBC DriverManager: This set of classes connects the drivers and the JDBC API. They handle tasks such as registering and deregistering available databases, obtaining connections to the databases, and managing information related to those connections.
- Drivers: To connect with different databases, JDBC encapsulates the logic needed to interact with each database within a series of drivers. Each driver contains the specific reasoning for a particular database, and in most cases, the companies that develop these databases also create the drivers for various programming languages.

JDBC has undergone continuous evolution since its initial release in 1997, with subsequent versions introducing additional features and addressing performance-related issues. Frameworks such as Spring implement their versions of JDBC, incorporating additional features specific to those frameworks.

## EJB

EJB is a specification for building portable, scalable, and reusable business applications. It streamlines everyday tasks such as security, database access, and message sending across different applications. In early versions of Java, some of these features were available in separate libraries or as primary forms within the JDK. EJB unified these features into a single framework, simplifying development and integration.

One of the most significant differences from the previous approach of using JDBC to access the database is that EJB requires an EJB container, which runs inside an application server such as GlassFish[1], WildFly[2], or Jetty[3].

Since its introduction in 1999, EJB has undergone multiple revisions, each introducing numerous new features, enhancing performance, and addressing bugs from previous versions. In version 3.0, EJB decouples its specification[4] to persist the information, which is then implemented using JPA.

## Ibatis

This library appears as an alternative to the previous solutions. It hides the complexity of accessing the database and transforming the results into a Java object. As a result, all operations remain simple, and complete control is maintained over the specific queries executed against the database.

---

**NOTE**    *This library is a data mapper.*

---

This library has different elements behind the scenes. The most relevant is the Java class, which represents the result of a query, a mapper, and a query to access the database:

---

[1]https://javaee.github.io/glassfish/
[2]https://www.wildfly.org/
[3]https://www.eclipse.org/jetty/
[4]https://www.jcp.org/en/jsr/detail?id=220

- The Java class has certain restrictions: attributes must be defined with setters and getters that match the names of the query results.
- The query must be written using SQL and saved in a single file, typically an XML file, which Ibatis will load to make it accessible to the application.
- The mapper is a predefined class used to invoke the query and transform the result into an object.

This approach enables viewing the queries and sharing them with a DBA in case performance issues are encountered. At the same time, it reduces the complexity of opening and closing communication with the database.

## JPA

The primary difference from the previous alternatives is that JPA is a specification, not a library, that encompasses all the necessary logic to access a database. Since this specification does not include how to perform the operations, the contract must be specified so that all the providers that follow this standard can simply interchange the different implementations.

Figure 4.3 illustrates how JPA operates within an application utilizing a single concrete specification and the existing layers.

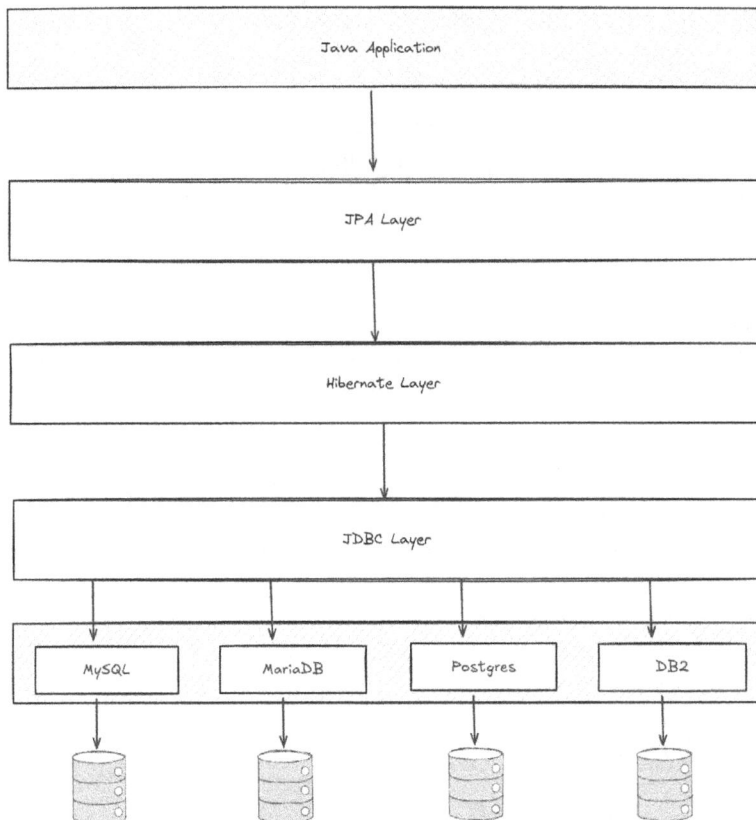

**FIGURE 4.3** Example of the use of JPA.

Using JPA, developers can interact with database information and perform operations such as inserting, updating, deleting, and retrieving data through Java classes representing table structures. To enable these operations, classes must be annotated with metadata that defines essential table attributes, such as table names, column names and sizes, and relationships between tables. These annotations guide the persistence framework in mapping class structures to the corresponding database schema.

JPA offers different methods for querying data. One approach is to use SQL statements directly, similar to JDBC, with classes that assist in constructing the queries. Another approach introduces an abstraction layer, allowing developers to avoid writing the entire query, as the JPA provider dynamically generates the query statements.

Multiple specification implementations exist, some of the most relevant ones being Hibernate[5], EclipseLink[6], Apache OpenJPA[7], and Spring Data JPA[8].

## Non-Relational Databases

In contrast to relational databases, non-relational databases emerge at different times, each with its own rules, structure, and query writing methods, resulting in no standard.

## Native

By default, Java applications access a non-relational database using different drivers, which affects the direct management of communication and the transformation of results. This approach resembles JDBC but lacks a standardized set of classes for database communication.

The primary drawback of this approach is that switching between different databases, such as Redis and MongoDB, necessitates rewriting the entire persistence layer due to differences in class structures and query syntax.

## Custom Libraries

Another alternative is to directly use the drivers of each database and manage the entire lifecycle of the communications, such as Morphia[9] for MongoDB or Hibernate OGM[10], which support databases such as Cassandra, CouchDB, and Redis, but don't have improvements or new features for a long time.

The main problem with custom libraries is that they solve only part of the problem, such as hiding all the mechanisms for communicating with the database. Still, it's impossible to switch between different types, and most of them lack a good level of support or developers.

A unified solution for all databases can be achieved using Spring Data, which supports a broad variety of database systems. The next section will provide more details about this option.

## Both Types of Databases

Both databases offer distinct approaches for persisting and retrieving information, each with its own advantages and disadvantages. When an entire platform relies on multiple types of databases, however, a new set of challenges arises. This situation requires understanding how to

[5]https://hibernate.org/
[6]https://www.eclipse.org/eclipselink/
[7]https://openjpa.apache.org/
[8]https://spring.io/projects/spring-data
[9]https://github.com/MorphiaOrg/morphia
[10]https://hibernate.org/ogm/

operate and manage each database type, as well as configuring the application to handle their differences effectively. As a result, the complexity of development, maintenance, and operations increases significantly.

Another potential problem is that if a database is initially chosen but later found to be unsuitable for various reasons, it may require rewriting the entire persistence layer and making numerous changes.

Considering all these problems, Spring created a module called Spring Data in 2011. This module handles database access, minimizing the number of classes or annotations that require changes when switching databases. It provides a set of interfaces called repositories that implement Create, Retrieve, Update, Delete (CRUD) operations, as well as other operations, such as counting or checking for the existence of an element. For operations not supported by these repositories, custom implementations can be created, although doing so may reduce the level of abstraction.

Standard repositories typically include the most common database operations. The most relevant are `CrudRepository`[11], which provides basic operations for all entities, and `PagingAndSortingRepository`[12], which contains logic for retrieving information from a database using pagination and sorting criteria. Most databases use these repositories by default, but others have their own. Figure 4.4 shows the hierarchy of Spring Data's existing repositories and examples of different non-relational databases.

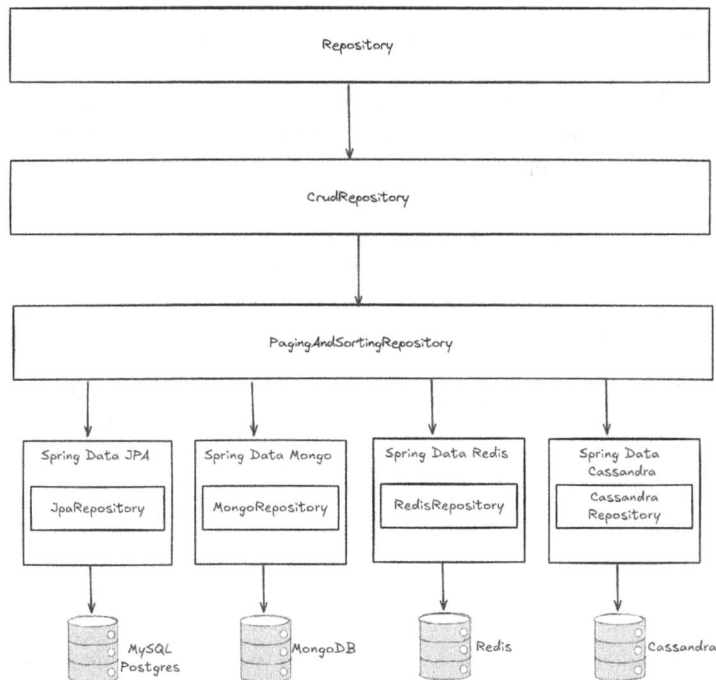

**FIGURE 4.4** Structure of repositories depending on the database.

[11]https://docs.spring.io/spring-data/commons/docs/current/api/org/springframework/data/repository/CrudRepository.html
[12]https://docs.spring.io/spring-data/commons/docs/current/api/org/springframework/data/repository/PagingAndSortingRepository.html

As shown in Figure 4.4, Spring Data has support for MongoDB[13], Redis[14], Cassandra[15], and all relational databases using JPA. There is also support for a long list of non-relational databases, such as Neo4j[16], Elasticsearch[17], and Couchbase[18].

NOTE *This book focuses on persistence using Spring Data with JPA, MongoDB, and Redis. The other databases are outside the book's scope, but they have a similar approach for use within the Spring Boot application.*

Spring Data consists of various module groups, some applicable to all databases and others specific to certain types of databases. Let's explore some of the most relevant modules:

• General Modules:

  • Spring Data Commons: Provides a metadata model for persisting Java classes in a specific database using repository interfaces, which will be covered in the next section.
  • Spring Data REST: Built on top of Spring Data modules, this module facilitates the creation of RESTful APIs by exposing repositories associated with entities directly as REST endpoints.

• Specific Modules:

  • Spring Data JPA: Offers a JPA implementation using repositories, often interfaces supporting all CRUD operations. A custom repository with specific logic for database access can be created if necessary.
  • Spring Data JDBC: Provides database access implementation using JDBC with repositories without the additional capabilities offered by JPA, such as lazy-loading and caching.
  • Spring Data MongoDB: This enables executing all operations on a MongoDB database using repositories or `MongoTemplate`, an alternative way to perform CRUD operations.
  • Spring Data Redis: This library enables access to a Redis database, allowing the storage of simple values or more complex objects. It also supports using Redis with a Sentinel mechanism, which monitors and exposes a highly available service.
  • Others: Spring Data supports many other modules, one per database.

The source code for all Spring Data projects is available for download on Spring's GitHub repository[19].

---

[13]https://www.mongodb.com/
[14]https://redis.io/
[15]https://cassandra.apache.org/
[16]https://neo4j.com/
[17]https://www.elastic.co/
[18]https://www.couchbase.com/
[19]https://github.com/spring-projects?q=data&type=all&language=&sort=

## Which Is the Best Alternative for Each Scenario?

The discussion about which is the best alternative—considering the different types of databases that exist, which in most cases do not share much in common, such as architecture, commands, or the types of information they support—is fascinating. Sometimes, an application starts using a specific database, and for various reasons, developers discover that it is not the best option. Therefore, it is essential to consider the impact of modifying the database, along with other critical factors.

Table 4.1 provides a brief overview of the comparison between using specific solutions and general ones, such as Spring Data.

**TABLE 4.1** Main things to consider when choosing a type of persistence.

| Feature | Specific | General |
|---|:---:|:---:|
| Well documented. | ✓ | ✓ |
| A significant number of users used it. | ✓ | ✓ |
| Support for multiple databases. | ✓ | ✓ |
| It is simple to change between different databases. | ✗ | ✓ |
| Hides the complexity of the database. | ✗ | ✓ |

As illustrated in Figure 4.5, synthesizing all arguments into a single document is best achieved by creating an ADR, which clearly outlines the rationale behind the chosen database access model.

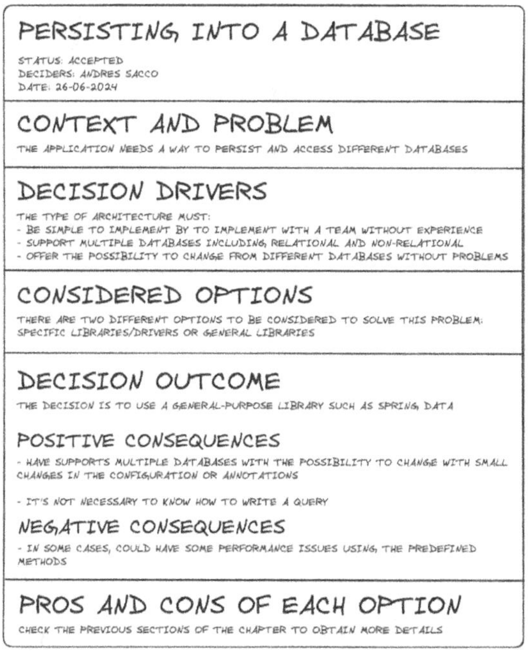

**PERSISTING INTO A DATABASE**

STATUS: ACCEPTED
DECIDERS: ANDRES SACCO
DATE: 26-06-2024

**CONTEXT AND PROBLEM**

THE APPLICATION NEEDS A WAY TO PERSIST AND ACCESS DIFFERENT DATABASES

**DECISION DRIVERS**

THE TYPE OF ARCHITECTURE MUST:
- BE SIMPLE TO IMPLEMENT BY TO IMPLEMENT WITH A TEAM WITHOUT EXPERIENCE
- SUPPORT MULTIPLE DATABASES INCLUDING RELATIONAL AND NON-RELATIONAL
- OFFER THE POSSIBILITY TO CHANGE FROM DIFFERENT DATABASES WITHOUT PROBLEMS

**CONSIDERED OPTIONS**

THERE ARE TWO DIFFERENT OPTIONS TO BE CONSIDERED TO SOLVE THIS PROBLEM:
SPECIFIC LIBRARIES/DRIVERS OR GENERAL LIBRARIES

**DECISION OUTCOME**

THE DECISION IS TO USE A GENERAL-PURPOSE LIBRARY SUCH AS SPRING DATA

**POSITIVE CONSEQUENCES**

- HAVE SUPPORTS MULTIPLE DATABASES WITH THE POSSIBILITY TO CHANGE WITH SMALL
CHANGES IN THE CONFIGURATION OR ANNOTATIONS

- IT'S NOT NECESSARY TO KNOW HOW TO WRITE A QUERY

**NEGATIVE CONSEQUENCES**

- IN SOME CASES, COULD HAVE SOME PERFORMANCE ISSUES USING THE PREDEFINED
METHODS

**PROS AND CONS OF EACH OPTION**

CHECK THE PREVIOUS SECTIONS OF THE CHAPTER TO OBTAIN MORE DETAILS

**FIGURE 4.5** ADR about the decision of which database model to use.

This document enables readers to understand the rationale behind selecting this approach over others and to review the factors considered during the decision-making process.

## PERSISTING THE INFORMATION

Two core concepts exist for persisting information in Spring Data: object mapping, which transforms a query's response into an object, and repositories, which contain various methods for executing database operations.

### Object Mapping

Object mapping is responsible for creating objects, accessing properties, and establishing mappings. The process involves creating a new object using the class's public constructor and populating all its exposed properties. To do this, Spring Data obtains the list of persistence entities in the application context and generates a factory class that implements the interface `ObjectInstantiator`[20] at runtime to create a new instance of the entity class, as appears in Figure 4.6.

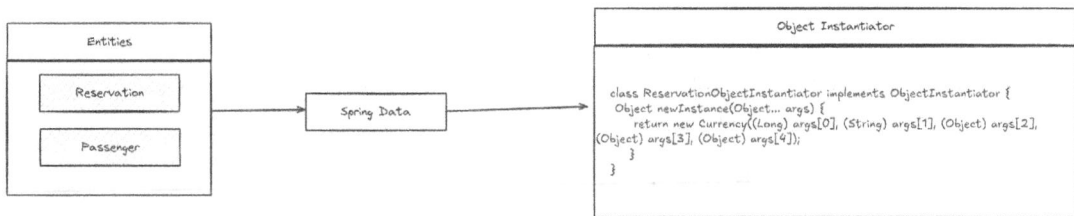

**FIGURE 4.6** Transformation of the different entities into an ObjectInstantiator.

The approach in Figure 4.6 for creating a new class instance using the constructor depends on whether the default constructor is overridden; if only the default constructor is present, the generator will instead create a method to invoke the various attribute setters for mapping.

_____
**NOTE**
*Object mapping refers to the process by which Spring Data converts the entities defined with JPA annotations, or with module-specific annotations for non-relational databases, into the format of the query results.*

Last but not least, there are some rules that entities must follow:

• The class representing an entity needs to be public, not private or static; inner classes are valid.
• Each entity is required to have at least one public constructor. It is possible to override the constructor or rely on the default one. If multiple public constructors are defined, however, the primary constructor that Spring Data should use must be marked with the `@Persis-tenceConstructor` annotation.
• The attributes must have public setter and getter methods.

---
[20]https://docs.spring.io/spring-data/commons/docs/2.1.16.RELEASE/api/org/springframework/data/convert/ClassGeneratingEntityInstantiator.ObjectInstantiator.html

Failure to follow these rules may cause an exception to be thrown during application execution.

## Repositories

Repositories serve as the abstraction Spring Data uses to interact with various databases, significantly reducing the amount of code within the application. For those familiar with older frameworks or libraries for database access, the large and complex DAO classes responsible for managing database interactions and result mapping come to mind. These classes were often challenging to follow. In contrast, as shown in Listing 4.1, Spring Data repositories are simple interfaces that extend other interfaces with no embedded logic. All the complex operations happen behind the scenes.

```
package com.twa.flights.api.reservation.repository;

import org.springframework.data.repository.CrudRepository;
import org.springframework.stereotype.Repository;

import com.twa.flights.api.reservation.model.Reservation;

@Repository
public interface ReservationRepository extends
CrudRepository<Reservation, Long> {

}
```

**LISTING 4.1** Repository to access the database.

Spring Data provides a range of repositories, all of which are implemented as interfaces. These interfaces can be extended by specifying the entity and its ID type, enabling the framework to generate all the necessary database access logic at runtime. In the specific case of Listing 4.1, the repository extends from `CrudRepository`, which provides methods for executing CRUD operations in the database. Some of these operations are illustrated in Figure 4.7.

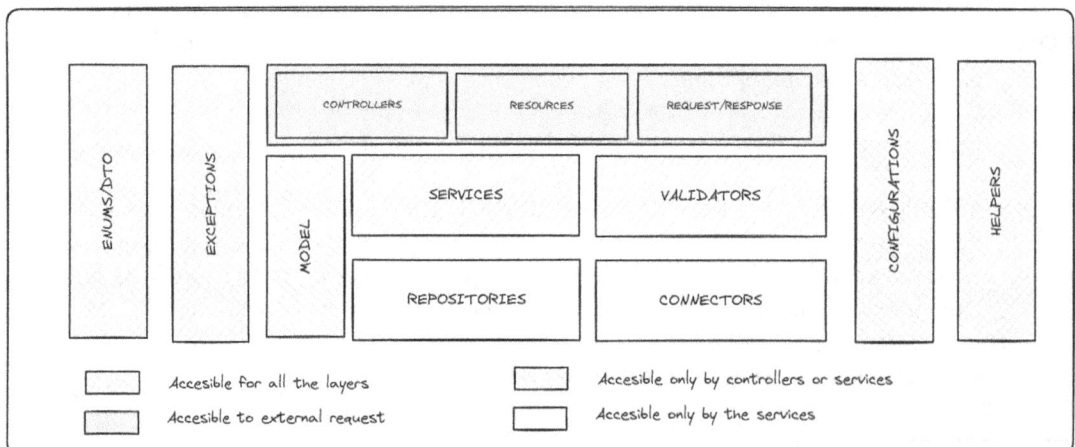

**FIGURE 4.7** Example of the hierarchy of repositories.

Other interfaces include `PagingAndSortingRepository`, which extends from `CrudRepository`, `JpaRepository`, and `MongoRepository`. Each of these interfaces is designed for a specific type of database, whereas `CrudRepository` and `PagingAndSortingRepository` are generic interfaces that can be used with any database.

## Automatic Queries

As explained in the previous section, Spring Data provides a set of predefined methods for common operations, such as `findById` and `deleteById`, where it is only necessary to specify the type of ID for a particular entity and annotate one of its attributes with `@Id`. In some cases, these methods suffice for specific applications; however, there are many scenarios where defining a query is required without writing the complete query statement.

In these scenarios, Spring Data facilitates the enhancement of predefined repository functionality through the use of naming conventions or automatic queries. It allows the definition of a method within the repository utilizing established keywords, such as `findBy` or `existsBy`, followed by the designation of the field in which a search is desired within the table. Spring will throw an exception if the specified attribute does not exist in the table. Additional keywords allow the creation of various queries by combining different attributes, limiting the number of results, or ordering them in specific ways. The query structure is divided into two parts: the first part defines the subject of the query, specifying the type of operation to execute, while the second part consists of the predicates, which are the attributes used in the filter, order, or distinct clauses. To see the structure of this method, look at Figure 4.8.

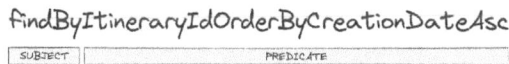

findByItineraryIdOrderByCreationDateAsc

| SUBJECT | PREDICATE |

**FIGURE 4.8** Structure of the methods.

Listing 4.2 shows some examples of additional queries in `ReservationRepository`. Different attributes filter these queries and order the results.

```
package com.twa.flights.api.reservation.repository;

import org.springframework.data.repository.CrudRepository;
import org.springframework.stereotype.Repository;

import com.twa.flights.api.reservation.model.Reservation;

@Repository
public interface ReservationRepository extends CrudRepository<Reservation,
Long> {
    // General queries
    List<Reservation> findByItineraryId(String itineraryId);
    List<Reservation> findByItineraryIdAndSearchId(String itineraryId,
String searchId);

    // Order queries
    List<Reservation> findByItineraryIdOrderByIdAsc(String itineraryId);
    List<Reservation> findByItineraryIdOrderByIdDesc(String itineraryId);
}
```

**LISTING 4.2** Examples of custom queries that find and order the results.

Table 4.2 presents the most relevant subject keywords. Certain databases might not support some of these keywords.

**TABLE 4.2** Query subject keywords.

| Keyword | Description |
|---|---|
| findBy... / readBy... getBy... / queryBy... searchBy... | These keywords are generally associated with select queries and return an element or a set of elements, which can be a `Collection` or `Streamable` subtype. |
| countBy... | Returns the number of elements that match the query. |
| existBy... | Returns a boolean value, with `true` indicating that something matches the query. |
| deleteBy... / removeBy... | Removes a set of elements that match the query but return nothing. |
| ...First\<number>... / ...Top\<number>... | These keywords limit certain aspects of the queries, such as the number of elements to retrieve or exclude. |
| ...Distinct... | This keyword ignores duplicate elements in the result. |

Table 4.3 displays certain predicate keywords and their corresponding database keywords. For a more comprehensive list of keywords, refer to the official Spring Data documentation.

**TABLE 4.3** Query predicate keywords.

| Keyword | Expressions |
|---|---|
| LIKE | Like |
| IS_NULL | Null or IsNull |
| LESS_THAN | LessThan |
| GREATER_THAN | GreaterThan |
| BETWEEN | Between or IsBetween |
| AND | And |
| OR | Or |
| AFTER | After or IsAfter |
| BEFORE | Before or IsBefore |
| STARTING_WITH | StartingWith or IsStartingWith |
| ENDING_WITH | EndingWith or IsEndingWith |

Last but not least, another category of predicate words modifies the results, provides order, or ignores part of them. Table 4.4 shows the most relevant of these modifiers.

*TABLE 4.4* Query predicate modifier keywords.

| Keyword | Description |
|---|---|
| IgnoreCase<br>IgnoringCase | Used with a predicate keyword to perform a case-insensitive comparison. |
| AllIgnoreCase<br>AllIgnoringCase | Ignore the case for all suitable properties. |
| OrderBy... | Specify the attribute and the direction in which to order the results. |

This approach offers numerous possibilities for creating queries without prior knowledge of a specific database.

## Manual Queries

The second method for creating queries to access the database follows a traditional approach. It involves writing the query explicitly, using a syntax similar to SQL or the specific query language of the target database, and associating it with a method defined in the repository interface. Let's modify the previous repository to include some queries for different attributes, such as those that appear in Listing 4.3.

```java
package com.twa.flights.api.reservation.repository;

import org.springframework.data.repository.CrudRepository;
import org.springframework.data.repository.query.Param;
import org.springframework.stereotype.Repository;
import org.springframework.data.jpa.repository.Query;

import com.twa.flights.api.reservation.model.Reservation;

import java.util.List;

@Repository
public interface ReservationRepository extends
CrudRepository<Reservation, Long> {
    // Other queries

    // Manual query
    @Query("SELECT r FROM Reservation r where r.itineraryId =
:itineraryId")
    List<Reservation> retrieveByItineraryId(@Param("itineraryId") String
itineraryId);

    @Query("SELECT r FROM Reservation r where r.itineraryId = :itineraryId
and r.searchId = :searchId")
    List<Reservation>  retrieveByItineraryIdAndSearchId(@Param("itineraryId")
String itineraryId, @Param("searchId") String searchId);
}
```

*LISTING 4.3* Examples of manual queries.

Here are some suggestions for using this approach instead of named queries or the automatic query generation:

- Declare queries as constants at the top of the interface to maintain clarity and ensure that method declarations are easily understood.
- Externalize all queries into a `properties` file and import them dynamically into each repository. This approach, however, requires careful organization to manage which file contains the queries for each repository.
- Alternatively, use a dedicated class to hold all the queries for a specific repository. This method is beneficial when dealing with numerous or lengthy queries, as it keeps the repository focused on methods while organizing queries separately.

Each approach offers its advantages and disadvantages, making the optimal choice dependent on the specific requirements.

## How Can Information Be Persisted Within a Relational Database?

Now, the functionality of all the standard components of Spring Data should be clear. These components can then be put into practice using a relational database—MySQL is used as the reference in this book. Any relational database can be used, however, as one of the key advantages of JPA is the ability to switch databases by simply updating the driver, without requiring changes to the rest of the application code.

## Configuration

The first step to use Spring Data in the application is to add the dependencies related to JPA and the driver of the database, as shown in Listing 4.4.

```
<dependency>

        <groupId>com.mysql</groupId>
        <artifactId>mysql-connector-j</artifactId>
</dependency>

<dependency>
        <groupId>org.springframework.boot</groupId>
        <artifactId>spring-boot-starter-data-jpa</artifactId>
</dependency>
```

**LISTING 4.4** Dependencies to add in the POM file.

Note that it's not always necessary to specify the version of the database driver, as the parent POM for Spring Boot has defined a version for most standard drivers. In certain situations, however, the database version might not be compatible with the driver version. In such cases, it is necessary to explicitly define the version, as demonstrated in Listing 4.4.

**NOTE** *Appendix D provides detailed instructions on installing and configuring the database. Using Docker to run the database is recommended, however, to save time and avoid manual configuration.*

The next step is to introduce the information about the database, username, and password in `application.yml`, as appears in Listing 4.5.

```
spring:
  datasource:
    driver-class-name: com.mysql.cj.jdbc.Driver
    url: jdbc:mysql://localhost:3310/flights_reservation
    username: root
    password: muppet
  jpa:
    show-sql: true # Shows the information about the queries that are
executed
    generate-ddl: false
    hibernate:
      ddl-auto: validate # Validate the entities with the model in the
database
```

**LISTING 4.5** Modifications to the configuration of the application.

In the current configuration, the application can run without throwing any exceptions. Once the entities are modified and repositories are introduced to interact with the database, however, specific issues may arise.

## Annotations

In Spring Data JPA, a vast set of annotations is available to represent various aspects, including the type of columns, relationships between different entities, and many other details. Review some of the most relevant ones in Table 4.5.

**TABLE 4.5** Annotations to use in JPA entities.

| Annotation | Description |
|---|---|
| @Table | Use this annotation to specify that one class is a table and could have a different name in the database; for example, the class has the name Reservation, but in the database, it is called reser. |
| @Entity | This annotation indicates that a class is an entity equivalent to a table in a database. |
| @Id | This attribute represents the primary key of an entity. |
| @GeneratedValue | This annotation is related to @Id because that's how our application will generate the value. The following sections will discuss different strategies. |
| @Column | Use this annotation to indicate that one particular attribute has certain restrictions, such as length, whether it accepts null, and the column's name in the table. |
| @Enumerated | This annotation indicates that the element is an enumeration with a list of possible values, which in the database are defined as either a number corresponding to the position of the value or a string corresponding to the enumeration value. |
| @Transient | Indicates that one attribute of an entity needs to be ignored to validate with the database. |
| @Order | This annotation defines the order of some elements in a collection. |

Let's modify the application's entities to use the different annotations in Table 4.5, as appears in the `Reservation` in Listing 4.6.

```
package com.twa.flights.api.reservation.model;

import jakarta.persistence.Column;
import jakarta.persistence.Entity;
import jakarta.persistence.Id;
import jakarta.persistence.Table;

import java.util.List;
import java.util.Objects;

@Entity
@Table(name = "reservation") //Only use this annotation if the name is
different
public class Reservation {

    @Id
    private Long id;

    @Column(name = "itinerary_id", nullable = false, length = 50)
    private String itineraryId;

    @Column(name = "search_id", nullable = false, length = 50)
    private String searchId;

    private List<Passenger> passengers;
    private Contact contact;

    // Setters and Getters
}
```

**LISTING 4.6** Modifications on the Reservation class.

The annotation `@Table` is optional; include it if the table's name does not match the class's. A possible approach to improve the quality of the application is to replicate the DTO classes' validations in the entity to prevent an error from being saved into the database. Still, in this case, the entities will only use the JPA annotations to keep the code simple.

Let's replicate the changes in the `Passenger` class, which has a vast number of attributes with different types, as shown in Listing 4.7.

```
package com.twa.flights.api.reservation.model;

import jakarta.persistence.Column;
import jakarta.persistence.Entity;
import jakarta.persistence.Id;
import jakarta.persistence.Table;
import java.time.LocalDate;
import java.util.Objects;

@Entity
@Table(name = "passenger") //Only use this annotation if the name is
different
```

```
public class Passenger{

    @Id
    private Long id;

    @Column(name = "first_name", nullable = false, length = 10)
    private String firstName;

    @Column(name = "last_name", nullable = false, length = 10)
    private String lastName;

    @Column(name = "document_number", nullable = false, length = 10)
    private String documentNumber;

    @Column(name = "document_type", nullable = false, length = 10)
    private String documentType;

    @Column(name = "nationality", nullable = false, length = 3)
    private String nationality;

    @Column(name = "birthday", nullable = false)
    private LocalDate birthday;

    // Setters and Getters
}
```

**LISTING 4.7** Modifications on the Passenger class.

At the end, introduce the same modifications into the Contact class, as shown in Listing 4.8.

```
package com.twa.flights.api.reservation.model;

import jakarta.persistence.Column;
import jakarta.persistence.Entity;
import jakarta.persistence.Id;
import jakarta.persistence.Table;

import java.util.Objects;

@Entity
@Table(name = "contact") //Only use this annotation if the name is
different
public class Contact {
    @Id
    private Long id;

    @Column(name = "telephone_number", nullable = false, length = 30)
    private String telephoneNumber;

    @Column(name = "email", nullable = false, length = 30)
    private String email;

    // Setters and Getters
}
```

**LISTING 4.8** Modifications on the Contact class.

With these modifications, the application will fail if run without additional adjustments. It's necessary to include several critical aspects, such as defining relationships between entities and specifying attribute generation strategies. The following sections will cover these required modifications.

### Primary Key and Generators

After selecting an entity's primary key, the next step is to define the strategy for generating its value. To achieve this, the attribute designated as the primary key must include the @ GeneratedValue annotation, specifying the strategy for value generation. JPA will then handle the automatic generation of this value prior to persisting the entity.

There are multiple ways to indicate to JPA which strategy to use to generate a value; let's see the most relevant ones:

- GenerationType.SEQUENCE: Define a numeric sequence in the database so that JPA can call it to obtain the following number to insert before persisting information in the table. The main advantage of using a sequence is that it can be applied to any column across different tables, though it is typically used for specific purposes.
- GenerationType.IDENTITY: Some databases do not support the definition of a SEQUENCE, so they offer an alternative: a special column with an auto-incremented value. This column automatically checks for and uses the next available value, functioning similarly to a SEQUENCE.
- GenerationType.TABLE: This approach is an alternative for databases that do not support SEQUENCE, such as MySQL versions 5.7 or earlier. It involves creating a table in the schema with one row per entity that requires an ID to be generated. This table tracks the next available value for each entity.
- GenerationType.AUTO: This strategy automatically selects the most appropriate ID generation method based on the database. It's possible to specify the strategy with the annotation @GeneratedValue(strategy = GenerationType.AUTO) or simply use @ GeneratedValue(), as both indicate the same strategy.

---

**NOTE** *As a suggestion, always specify the value of the generation, as something could change and affect the entire application between different versions of Spring Data or JPA.*

---

Let's modify the Reservation entity to use the IDENTITY strategy to generate the ID.

```
package com.twa.flights.api.reservation.model;

import jakarta.persistence.*;

import java.util.Objects;

@Entity
@Table(name = "reservation") //Only use this annotation if the name is
different
public class Reservation {
```

```
@Id
@GeneratedValue(strategy = GenerationType.IDENTITY)
private Long id;

// Attributes, Setters, and Getters
}
```

**LISTING 4.9** Add logic to generate the ID of the Reservation.

To ensure consistent behavior, apply the exact same changes to the other entities. Otherwise, persistence of those elements will fail since Spring Data expects the ID value to be provided.

## Type of Relationships

In JPA, different annotations specify the types of relationships between entities. These relationships can be unidirectional—allowing access to information from only one side (for example, knowing a country's currency without the reverse)—or bidirectional—enabling navigation between both entities from either side.

Here are the types of relationships between entities in detail:

- @ManyToOne: This is a relationship in which many entities reference a single entity. For example, many countries might share the same currency. Spring Data uses a foreign key in one table to join with another table.
- @OneToOne: This is a less common relationship. It indicates that one table has a foreign key associated with a single row in another table without the ability to reference multiple rows.
- @ManyToMany: This is a complex relationship. Traditionally, it requires an intermediate table that holds the primary keys of both related tables. In JPA, however, these three tables are treated as two entities, with the JPA implementation managing the query generation and abstracting the underlying database details.

Let's modify the `Reservation` entity to indicate the relationship with `Passengers` and `Contact`, as shown in Listing 4.10.

```
package com.twa.flights.api.reservation.model;

import jakarta.persistence.*;

import java.util.Objects;

@Entity
@Table(name = "reservation") //Only use this annotation if the name is
different
public class Reservation {

    @OneToMany(cascade = CascadeType.ALL)
    @JoinColumn(name = "reservation_id")
    private List<Passenger> passengers;
```

```
@OneToOne(cascade = CascadeType.ALL)
@JoinColumn(name = "reservation_id")
private Contact contact;

// Attributes, Setters, and Getters
}
```

**LISTING 4.10** Relationship between the different entities.

Listing 4.10 shows that the entity relationship includes an attribute called `CascadeType`; this attribute defines whether database operations performed on one entity, such as `Reservation`, will cascade and affect related entities as well.

### Lazy and Eager Loading

JPA provides a mechanism to minimize the data held in memory until needed. This is done by adding a `fetch` property to the annotation that defines the relationship between entities. The `fetch` property has two possible values:

- `FetchType.LAZY`: This value signifies that JPA does not need to fetch the relationship information until the `get` method for the attribute is called. Behind the scenes, Hibernate uses a proxy for the attribute representing the relationship, which knows the query to execute when fetching the data. This approach uses less memory and provides faster initial loading. If the relationship information is frequently accessed, however, the query's cost can increase, leading to longer retrieval times.
- `FetchType.EAGER`: This value indicates that JPA will fetch all the information of the related entity when executing the query. While this approach reduces the initialization time by ensuring all associated data is available in memory, it may increase the query execution time and negatively impact application performance.

Let's modify the `Reservation` entity to indicate the relationship with `Passengers`. As appears in Listing 4.11, the `Contact` does not need to load all the information when executing the query.

```
package com.twa.flights.api.reservation.model;

import jakarta.persistence.*;

import java.util.Objects;

@Entity
@Table(name = "reservation") //Only use this annotation if the name is
different
public class Reservation {

    @OneToMany(fetch = FetchType.LAZY, cascade = CascadeType.ALL)
    @JoinColumn(name = "reservation_id")
    private List<Passenger> passengers;
```

```
@OneToOne(fetch = FetchType.LAZY, cascade = CascadeType.ALL)
@JoinColumn(name = "reservation_id")
private Contact contact;

// Attributes, Setters, and Getters
}
```

*LISTING 4.11* Add the restriction not to obtain all the information by default.

Always specify which strategy to use for loading information from the application's relationship. The default value changed from EAGER to LAZY in different versions of JPA, resulting in numerous problems in other applications. Specifying the strategy explicitly minimizes the risk that something will go wrong.

## Repositories

Repositories represent one of the final changes needed to enable database access in the application. As shown in Listing 4.2, the modifications involve defining interfaces that extend Spring Data repository interfaces. It's essential, however, to remove any previous versions beforehand, as having multiple classes or interfaces with the same name will cause conflicts.

**NOTE**

*Spring Data offers a way to encapsulate query logic through the use of classes known as specifications. These classes implement the* Specification *interface[21], enabling the encapsulation of custom query criteria in a reusable and composable manner—without the need to create an entirely separate repository implementation.*

This approach ensures maintenance is limited to interfaces representing the database access layer, guaranteeing that interaction with the database occurs solely through these interfaces.

Let's see a possible specification implementation using the Reservation entity to find the searchId, as shown in Listing 4.12.

```
package com.twa.flights.api.reservation.specification;

import com.twa.flights.api.reservation.model.Reservation;
import jakarta.persistence.criteria.CriteriaBuilder;
import jakarta.persistence.criteria.CriteriaQuery;
import jakarta.persistence.criteria.Predicate;
import jakarta.persistence.criteria.Root;
import org.springframework.data.jpa.domain.Specification;

import java.util.ArrayList;
import java.util.List;

public class ReservationSpecification implements
Specification<Reservation> {

    Reservation entity;
```

---

[21]https://docs.spring.io/spring-data/jpa/reference/jpa/specifications.html

```
    public ReservationSpecification(Reservation entity) {
        this.entity = entity;
    }

    @Override
    public Predicate toPredicate(Root<Reservation> root,
CriteriaQuery<?> query, CriteriaBuilder builder) {

        //create a new predicate list
        List<Predicate> predicates = new ArrayList<>();

        CriteriaQuery<Reservation> cq = builder.createQuery(Reservation.
class);

        // It's needed to define the main entity
        Root<Reservation> reservation = cq.from(Reservation.class);

        // Define all the conditions of the query
        Predicate codePredicate = builder.equal(reservation.
get("searchId"), entity.getSearchId());

        predicates.add(codePredicate);

        return builder.and(predicates.toArray(new Predicate[0]));
    }
}
```

**LISTING 4.12** Reservation specification.

This specification can be passed into the different methods that exist in the default implementation of the `ReservationRepository`.

After modifying the repository, the next step is to alter the service. For some methods, their names change, such as `delete`, which is now `deleteById`. Listing 4.13 offers a clear and thorough reference for all the necessary updates in `ReservationService`. It outlines each modification step by step to ensure a smooth and reliable transition while implementing the required changes.

```
// Previous imports and package

@Service
public class ReservationService {
    // Previous constructor and attributes

    public List<ReservationDTO> getReservations() {
        return  conversionService.convert(repository.findAll(), List.
class);
    }

    public ReservationDTO getReservationById(Long id) {
        Optional<Reservation> result = repository.findById(id);
        if(result.isEmpty()) {
            throw new TWAException(APIError.RESERVATION_NOT_FOUND);
        }
        return conversionService.convert(result.get(), ReservationDTO.
class);
    }
```

```
    // Save method without changes

    public ReservationDTO update(Long id, ReservationDTO reservation) {
        if(getReservationById(id) == null) {
            throw new TWAException(APIError.RESERVATION_NOT_FOUND);
        }

        Reservation transformed = conversionService.convert(reservation,
Reservation.class);
        Reservation result = repository.save(Objects.
requireNonNull(transformed));
        return conversionService.convert(result, ReservationDTO.class);
    }

    public void delete(Long id) {
        if(getReservationById(id) == null) {
            throw new TWAException(APIError.RESERVATION_NOT_FOUND);
        }

        repository.deleteById(id);
    }
}
```

**LISTING 4.13** Reservation service with changes to use the repository.

After completing all the modifications, the final step is to ensure everything functions as expected. This can be done by running the relational database using any preferred method and loading all the scripts available in the GitHub repository.

The initial step involves retrieving all existing reservations from the database. If the process executes correctly, the result will be similar to that shown in Listing 4.14.

```
➜  ~ curl --location 'http://localhost:8090/api/flights/reservation'
[]
```

**LISTING 4.14** Request to check the information in the database.

The next step is to create a reservation, as described in the previous chapter, but with the correct values for all the attributes listed in Listing 4.15.

```
➜  ~ curl --location 'http://localhost:8090/api/flights/reservation/' \
--header 'Content-Type: application/json' \
--data-raw '{
    "itineraryId": "2",
    "searchId": "2",
    "passengers": [
        {
            "firstName": "Andres",
            "lastName": "Sacco",
            "documentNumber": "987654321",
            "documentType": "DNI",
            "nationality": "ARG",
            "birthday": "1985-01-01"
        }
    ],
```

```
    "contact": {
        "telephoneNumber": "54911111111",
        "email": "sacco.andres@gmail.com"
    }
}'

{
    "id": 1,
    "itineraryId": "2",
    "searchId": "2",
    "passengers": [
        {
            "id": 1,
            "firstName": "Andres",
            "lastName": "Sacco",
            "documentNumber": "987654321",
            "documentType": "DNI",
            "nationality": "ARG",
            "birthday": "1985-01-01"
        }
    ],
    "contact": {
        "id": 1,
        "telephoneNumber": "54911111111",
        "email": "sacco.andres@gmail.com"
    }
}
```

**LISTING 4.15** Request to create a new reservation.

To understand what happens behind the scenes, check the console output, which displays all the queries executed by the application to retrieve the information, shown in Listing 4.16, when creating a new reservation.

```
2024-08-05T15:29:23.492-03:00  INFO 282458 --- [api-reservation] [nio-
8090-exec-1] c.t.f.a.r.c.ReservationController    : Saving new
reservation
Hibernate: insert into contact (email,telephone_number) values (?,?)
Hibernate: insert into reservation (reservation_id,itinerary_id,search_
id) values (?,?,?)
Hibernate: insert into passenger (birthday,document_number,document_
type,first_name,last_name,nationality) values (?,?,?,?,?,?)
Hibernate: update passenger set reservation_id=? where id=?
```

**LISTING 4.16** Logs of the request to create a new reservation.

To omit this information from the console or hide it, modify the show-sql attribute to false.

## How Can Information Be Persisted in a Non-Relational Database?

When creating an application, it may be necessary to store information in a specific format that could evolve. While a relational database might seem like the best choice, non-relational databases offer the flexibility to modify the structure of "tables" easily and save complex objects while allowing for complex queries.

The evolution and stability of some non-relational databases allow for excellent performance with large amounts of data. Certain features available in relational databases, such as preventing duplicate information, however, might be compromised.

*Appendix E contains detailed information on installing and configuring various databases. Using Docker, however, is a recommended alternative to simplify the process and save time on configuration.*

## MongoDB

MongoDB is a popular non-relational database that stores data in JSON-like format. JSON consists of key-value pairs, but it differs from traditional key-value databases. A document store, such as MongoDB, enables the storage of complex documents and the execution of various queries.

The structure of a non-relational database, such as MongoDB, is similar to that of a relational database. For example, both types share the concept of a database. Table 4.6 provides a comparison between relational databases and MongoDB.

As observed, working with a non-relational database brings several advantages. Certain concepts and operations, however, can still be found in traditional relational databases.

**TABLE 4.6** Comparison between two types of databases.

| Relational Databases | MongoDB |
|---|---|
| Database | Database |
| Table | Collection |
| Row | Document |
| Column | Field |

*Remove everything not connected to MongoDB, including all dependencies related to JPA/ MySQL and annotations on entities associated with relational databases, including the specifications. The repositories and the logic for accessing information in the services should be kept, however.*

### Configuration

The first step to use Spring Data in the application is to add the dependencies related to MongoDB without including the driver of the database, as appears in Listing 4.16.

```
<dependency>
    <groupId>org.springframework.boot</groupId>
    <artifactId>spring-boot-starter-data-mongodb</artifactId>
</dependency>
```

**LISTING 4.16** Dependencies connected to MongoDB.

The next step is to introduce the information about the database, username, and password in `application.yml`, as appears in Listing 4.17.

```
spring:
 data:
   mongodb:
     uri: "mongodb://root:rootpassword@localhost:27017/flights_
reservation?authSource=admin"
```

**LISTING 4.17** Modifications to the configuration of the application.

With these minor changes, the application supports MongoDB. To enable access and operation with the database, the entities must be modified, and the repositories updated accordingly.

### Annotations

In Spring Data MongoDB, a variety of annotations can be applied to entities. Some of the most relevant annotations are summarized in Table 4.7.

**TABLE 4.7** Annotations to use in MongoDB entities.

| Annotation | Description |
| --- | --- |
| @Document | A domain object needs to be persisted in MongoDB. |
| @Indexed | A specific field that should be indexed to enhance search performance. |
| @Id | An attribute that contains the collection identifier. |
| @Transient | An annotation to ignore a particular field during the persistence process. |
| @IndexDirection | An annotation to specify the direction of the index: DESCENDING or ASCENDING. |
| @Field | An annotation to explicitly indicate the attribute name in the database, similar to @Column in JPA. |
| @DBRef | This annotation connects multiple collections, similar to @OneToMany or @ManyToMany in JPA. |

When referencing another entity using @DBRef in Spring Data MongoDB, modifications to the referenced object are not automatically persisted. Unlike JPA, MongoDB does not support cascade operations by default. To achieve similar behavior, the persistence logic must be implemented manually.

Considering these annotations, introduce some minor modifications to the Reservation entity to persist all the information without using the @DBRef annotation, as illustrated in Listing 4.18.

```
package com.twa.flights.api.reservation.model;

import org.springframework.data.annotation.Id;
import org.springframework.data.mongodb.core.mapping.Document;
import org.springframework.data.mongodb.core.mapping.Field;
```

```
import java.util.List;
import java.util.Objects;
import java.util.UUID;

@Document("reservation")
public class Reservation {

    @Id
    private String id = UUID.randomUUID().toString();

    @Field(value = "itinerary_id")
    private String itineraryId;

    @Field(value = "search_id")
    private String searchId;

    private List<Passenger> passengers;

    private Contact contact;

    // Setters and Getters
}
```

**LISTING 4.18** Modifications on the Reservation class.

By default, MongoDB provides a mechanism to generate IDs like a relational database, so the best way to develop a unique value is by using the class UUID. This class generates a random value considering various aspects, such as time. The attribute ID changes from Long to String to ensure the attribute's value is saved correctly.

Let's replicate the changes in the Passenger class, which has many attributes of different types, as in Listing 4.19.

```
package com.twa.flights.api.reservation.model;

import org.springframework.data.mongodb.core.mapping.Field;

import java.time.LocalDate;
import java.util.Objects;

public class Passenger {

    @Field(value = "first_name")
    private String firstName;

    @Field(value = "last_name")
    private String lastName;

    @Field(value = "document_number")
    private String documentNumber;

    @Field(value = "document_type")
    private String documentType;
```

```
@Field(value = "nationality")
private String nationality;

@Field(value = "birthday")
private LocalDate birthday;

// Setters and Getters
}
```

**LISTING 4.19** Modifications on the Passenger class.

One consideration regarding this entity is that it does not contain the annotation `@Document`, unlike the previous entity. The idea is to save the entire document and have only one identification for all the reservations.

At the end, introduce the same modifications into the `Contact` class, as in Listing 4.20.

```
package com.twa.flights.api.reservation.model;

import org.springframework.data.mongodb.core.mapping.Field;

import java.util.Objects;

public class Contact {

    @Field(value = "telephone_number")
    private String telephoneNumber;

    @Field(value = "email")
    private String email;

    // Setters and Getters
}
```

**LISTING 4.20** Modifications on the Contact class.

Considering that the `Contact` and `Passenger` entities will be part of the `Reservation` and not have an ID, remove the DTO with the same name as the field ID. With all these modifications in place, the entity and application configuration is complete. One final adjustment remains, however: updating the repositories.

### Repositories

Spring Data aims to simplify repositories across different database types by requiring only a change in the extended interface. For MongoDB, this means extending the `MongoRepository` interface. Let's modify the previous repository version, removing the manual queries. The repository with the changes needs to be similar to Listing 4.21.

```
package com.twa.flights.api.reservation.repository;

import org.springframework.data.mongodb.repository.MongoRepository;
import org.springframework.stereotype.Repository;
```

```java
import com.twa.flights.api.reservation.model.Reservation;

import java.util.List;

@Repository
public interface ReservationRepository extends
MongoRepository<Reservation, String> {

    // General queries
    List<Reservation> findByItineraryId(String itineraryId);
    List<Reservation> findByItineraryIdAndSearchId(String itineraryId,
String searchId);

    // Order queries
    List<Reservation> findByItineraryIdOrderByIdAsc(String itineraryId);
    List<Reservation> findByItineraryIdOrderByIdDesc(String itineraryId);

}
```

**LISTING 4.21** Modifications on the ReservationRepository.

As shown in Listing 4.21, named queries or automatically generated queries remain unchanged, as each database type dynamically generates the appropriate queries.

Once all the modifications are complete, the final step involves verifying that everything functions as expected. This can be done by executing the exact requests shown in Listings 4.14 and 4.15, using the same parameters. If successful, information about a specific reservation will be retrieved, as demonstrated in Listing 4.22.

```
→  ~ curl --location 'http://localhost:8090/api/flights/reservation/66b
191d0078f3e4b80447069'
{
    "id": "66b191d0078f3e4b80447069",
    "itineraryId": "2",
    "searchId": "2",
    "passengers": [
        {
            "firstName": "Andres",
            "lastName": "Sacco",
            "documentNumber": "987654321",
            "documentType": "DNI",
            "nationality": "ARG",
            "birthday": "1985-01-01"
        }
    ],
    "contact": {
        "telephoneNumber": "54911111111",
        "email": "sacco.andres@gmail.com"
    }
}
```

**LISTING 4.22** Request to obtain a reservation.

As shown, switching from one database to another is relatively straightforward for the application.

## Redis

Salvatore Sanfilippo created Redis in 2009 to address a scalability issue with a Web analyzer at his company. One of the key attributes of this database is its high performance. Redis is a lightweight store capable of saving various types of information.

Let's delve deeper into its most relevant attributes:

- Supports key/value pairs with a maximum size of 512 MB
- Supports various data types, including `String`, `Hash`, `List`, `Set`, `Sorted Set`, and complex data objects in JSON format

Spring Data Redis aims to simplify database interactions, much like the JPA version, by providing a set of classes and components for easy interaction. Specifically, it includes the following elements:

- Driver: Handles interactions with the database to execute operations.
- `RedisConnection` / `RedisConnectionFactory`: Manages communication with the driver, transforming operations and exceptions to resemble JPA repositories.
- Entities: Represent and contain the data intended for persistence in the database. This approach promotes consistency across various Spring Data implementations (such as JPA, Redis, and Cassandra), though it's also possible to persist simple strings or use DTOs instead.
- Serializers: Facilitate the persistence and retrieval of data in various formats. For example, objects can be transformed into strings and compressed to save space, which is particularly useful when dealing with many rows. This is beneficial, considering that some cloud providers, such as AWS, charge based on the memory used by Redis.

**NOTE**

*Remove everything not connected to Redis, including all JPA/MySQL/MongoDB dependencies and annotations on entities associated with other databases, including the specifications. The repositories and the logic for accessing information in the services, however, should be kept.*

The structure of a non-relational database such as Redis differs significantly from that of other relational, and even non-relational, databases. Some concepts do not have an equivalence; let's see Table 4.8.

*TABLE 4.8* Comparison between two types of databases.

| Relational databases | Redis |
|---|---|
| Database | Database |
| Table | Does not exist equivalent on this database |
| Row | Key-value pair |
| Column | Does n<br>Not exist equivalent on this database |

As expected, the method of saving information in this type of database differs from others, and features such as TTL are offered where data expires after a specific period.

## Configuration

The first step to use Spring Data in the application is to add the dependencies related to Redis without including the driver of the database, as shown in Listing 4.23.

```
<dependency>
   <groupId>org.springframework.boot</groupId>
   <artifactId>spring-boot-starter-data-redis</artifactId>
</dependency>
```

**LISTING 4.23** Dependencies connected with Redis.

The next step is to introduce the information about the database, username, and password in `application.yml`, as shown in Listing 4.24.

```
spring:
 data:
    redis:
      database: 0
      host: localhost
      port: 6379
      timeout: 2000 #Connection timed out
```

**LISTING 4.24** Modifications to the configuration of the application.

The last aspect of the configuration is to declare how the application will save the information into the database. Remember that Redis has a limited number of formats for saving data, which is the main difference from other types of databases. To do this, it's necessary to define a configuration of `RedisTemplate`, which is similar to `EntityManager` on JPA, with a format to save the information. Listing 4.25 shows the class that contains all the configurations with a key serializer and a value serializer.

```
package com.twa.flights.api.reservation.configuration;

import org.springframework.context.annotation.Bean;
import org.springframework.context.annotation.Configuration;
import org.springframework.data.redis.connection.RedisConnectionFactory;
import org.springframework.data.redis.connection.lettuce.
LettuceConnectionFactory;
import org.springframework.data.redis.core.RedisTemplate;
import org.springframework.data.redis.repository.configuration.
EnableRedisRepositories;
import org.springframework.data.redis.serializer.
GenericJackson2JsonRedisSerializer;
import org.springframework.data.redis.serializer.StringRedisSerializer;

@Configuration
@EnableRedisRepositories // This annotation enables the Redis
repositories
public class RedisConfiguration {
```

```
    @Bean
    public RedisConnectionFactory redisConnectionFactory() {
        return new LettuceConnectionFactory();
    }

    @Bean
    public RedisTemplate<String, Object> redisTemplate(RedisConnectionFa
ctory redisConnectionFactory) {
        RedisTemplate<String, Object> template = new RedisTemplate<>();
        template.setConnectionFactory(redisConnectionFactory);
        template.setKeySerializer(new StringRedisSerializer());
        template.setValueSerializer(new
GenericJackson2JsonRedisSerializer());
        return template;
    }

}
```

**LISTING 4.25** Configuration of the serializers.

In the case of the value serializer—which by default converts an object into JSON for storage in the database—it performs the inverse operation when reading data. In earlier versions of Spring Data, this serializer was not included by default and had to be explicitly defined.

With these minor adjustments, the application can be configured to support Redis. To run and access the database correctly, however, the entities must be modified and the repositories updated accordingly.

### Annotations

In Spring Data Redis, a set of annotations can be applied to various entities. Some of the most relevant annotations are summarized in Table 4.9.

**TABLE 4.9** Annotations to use in Redis entities.

| Annotation | Description |
| --- | --- |
| @RedisHash | A domain object needs to be persisted in Redis. |
| @Indexed | A specific field that should be indexed to enhance search performance. |
| @Id | An attribute that contains the collection identifier. |

The number of annotations is limited compared to JPA or MongoDB, which reduces the amount of modifications needed on the entity. The necessary changes are applied to the Reservation entity, shown in Listing 4.26.

```
package com.twa.flights.api.reservation.model;

import org.springframework.data.annotation.Id;
import org.springframework.data.redis.core.RedisHash;

import java.util.List;
import java.util.Objects;
import java.util.UUID;
```

```
@RedisHash("reservation")
public class Reservation {

    @Id
    private String id = UUID.randomUUID().toString();

    private String itineraryId;

    private String searchId;

    private List<Passenger> passengers;

    private Contact contact;

    // Setters and Getters
}
```

**LISTING 4.26** Modifications on the Reservation class.

As shown in the previous listing, the approach to converting the `id` attribute into a string is the same as the one used in the MongoDB section. Repeat the same modifications as in that section, removing the `id` attribute from the `Passenger` and `Contact` entities and the DTO.

The other classes, `Passenger` and `Contact`, do not need to include any annotation because they are part of the same database row.

### Repositories

As previously discussed, modifying the repositories involves some small changes to ensure the correct interface is used. When working with Redis, the same interfaces used for JPA can be applied. Therefore, the previous version of the repository can be updated by removing the manual queries. The repository with the changes needs to be similar to Listing 4.27.

```
package com.twa.flights.api.reservation.repository;

import org.springframework.data.repository.CrudRepository;
import org.springframework.stereotype.Repository;

import com.twa.flights.api.reservation.model.Reservation;

import java.util.List;

@Repository
public interface ReservationRepository extends
CrudRepository<Reservation, String> {

    // General queries
    List<Reservation> findByItineraryId(String itineraryId);
    List<Reservation> findByItineraryIdAndSearchId(String itineraryId,
String searchId);

    // Order queries
    List<Reservation> findByItineraryIdOrderByIdAsc(String itineraryId);
    List<Reservation> findByItineraryIdOrderByIdDesc(String itineraryId);
}
```

**LISTING 4.27** Modifications on ReservationRepository.

After completing all the modifications, the final step is to confirm that everything functions as intended. This can be done by executing the exact requests shown in Listings 4.14 and 4.15 using the same parameters. If the application is working correctly, it will return the details of a specific reservation, as illustrated in Listing 4.28.

```
➜  ~ curl --location 'http://localhost:8090/api/flights/
reservation/03fba51e-927a-4c53-adb8-c2fce59ef46c
{
    "id": "03fba51e-927a-4c53-adb8-c2fce59ef46c",
    "itineraryId": "2",
    "searchId": "2",
    "passengers": [
        {
            "firstName": "Andres",
            "lastName": "Sacco",
            "documentNumber": "987654321",
            "documentType": "DNI",
            "nationality": "ARG",
            "birthday": "1985-01-01"
        }
    ],
    "contact": {
        "telephoneNumber": "549111111111",
        "email": "sacco.andres@gmail.com"
    }
}
```

**LISTING 4.28** Request to obtain a reservation.

As shown, switching from one database to another involves specific changes and the addition of classes responsible for converting data before saving it or after retrieving it from the database.

This database will help implement cache mechanisms and reduce the number of requests to other microservices. The next chapter will explore this topic in greater detail.

## VERSIONING THE CHANGES

Databases undergo modifications over time. Some tables appear to save specific information, and in other situations, someone needs to add or remove a column from a table. In most cases, these modifications are part of the informal communication between the developers and the DBA or the person who runs a script in one particular environment.

Some companies use tools such as Jira[22] or Notion[23] to create tickets that track database changes and identify who requested them. At some point, however, any chosen solution must also allow visibility into the database's state at a specific point in time. For example, when recreating a database for testing or running an application locally, it may be necessary to restore the database structure to a specific version. In such cases, relying on a DBA to provide a backup can be problematic—backups might be outdated or no longer available. Another common challenge

---

[22]https://www.atlassian.com/software/jira
[23]https://www.notion.so

arises when trying to determine which queries were executed on a particular day. This typically requires checking with the DBA and hoping that a ticket exists in one of those tools that captures the relevant details.

One way to address these challenges is by versioning database changes using simple SQL scripts. Each script contains a set of modifications to one or more tables, allowing for consistent tracking and application of changes. This approach allows the database to be recreated from scratch, starting at version zero and progressing to a specific version, on any environment, including a local machine. Additionally, each script can include metadata, such as the author and the purpose of the changes, which improves traceability and collaboration. Figure 4.9 illustrates how the database evolves, with scripts responsible for both structural changes and data modifications.

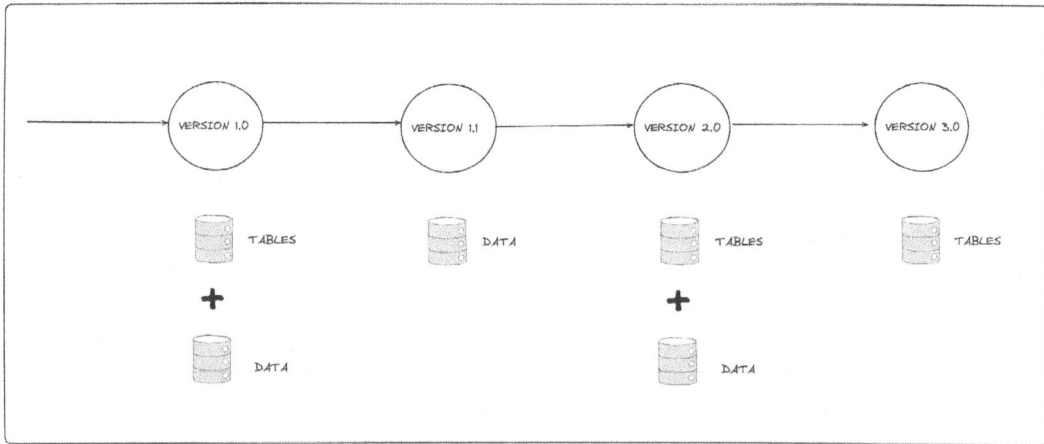

**FIGURE 4.9** Evolution of the database.

The different tools that exist do more or less the same thing behind the scenes: They define a set of scripts that correspond to a specific version of the database, and all the scripts reside in one file, where the name of the file has some vital information, such as the version name and a brief description of the main reason for the change. With the information on each file, the different tools verify whether the file has been applied, searching the tables created to track all changes made to a database.

When the tool validates the database's status and checks each file, it will execute the script if it does not exist. If something goes wrong during the script's execution, the tool reverts the changes to the previous version, much like a transaction where all changes must be approved before being committed.

There are some common suggestions regardless of which tool is used:

- Create one file with all the changes that have something in common. It's not a good practice to create multiple files containing just one SQL query or script because it's difficult to see the entire impact of the modifications on the database.
- Suppose a mistake is made and a script is executed against the database. In that case, the recommended approach is to either roll back the changes or create a new script file containing the necessary corrections. Existing files should never be modified, as most tools

compute a hash for each script to ensure its integrity. Altering a file after it has been executed will result in a validation failure during the subsequent tool execution.

- Define a structure or pattern name for all the scripts and configure the tool with that pattern.
- Always run all scripts with the tool, as it will perform a rollback in the event of a catastrophic failure.

## Which Tools Exist to Do It?

Most tools or libraries for versioning database changes are language-agnostic, meaning they are compatible with various programming languages and frameworks used in applications; they all provide the capability to execute operations seamlessly via the command line. Another way to run the different tools is to use Docker images with a volume that contains all the necessary changes, thereby reducing the risk of issues related to configuration or meeting the minimum requirements.

**NOTE**

*There is no standard regarding where all the files need to be placed. As a recommendation, however, try to always keep them in one Git repository to track all the changes or modifications that the scripts may undergo.*

*Suppose the scripts are stored in the same repository as the application, and their execution is delegated to the application itself. In that case, it is advisable to create a dedicated database user with limited privileges. This restriction helps minimize potential damage in the event of issues with the scripts—for instance, if a script includes a* TRUNCATE *or* DROP *statement that affects all tables, the consequences could be severe. Limiting access rights serves as a protective measure against such scenarios.*

This section introduces the tools Flyway[24] and Liquibase[25], which support Spring Boot, but there are many others that could be used. These tools simplify the application's configuration by adding a dependency with minimal modifications to `application.yml`.

## Flyway

Flyway is a tool that manages versioning of database changes. It supports execution via the command line across multiple operating systems and can also be integrated directly into Java applications using Maven or Gradle, which support many frameworks such as Spring Boot and Quarkus[26].

This tool offers two different editions: Community and Teams. The main differences between these editions lie in the number of features they offer. For example, the Teams edition provides:

- A mechanism to undo changes in a database, with the ability to specify the order in which a certain number of scripts are undone.
- A method to preview changes before they are applied to the database, enabling verification of script correctness.
- The possibility of storing scripts on AWS or GCP.

---

[24]https://www.red-gate.com/products/flyway/community/
[25]https://www.liquibase.com/
[26]https://quarkus.io/

The tool provides a default naming structure to identify different types of operations, though this pattern can be customized. Each file name must have four parts: the first part indicates the type of operation, the second specifies the version, the third offers a brief description, and the last part is the suffix.

Lastly, Flyway offers a series of helpful commands, such as `validate` to check whether all the scripts have been executed correctly and `clean` to remove all information from the schema.

## Liquibase

Like the previous tool, Liquibase can be used on operating systems and Java projects that utilize Maven or Gradle, which leverage frameworks such as Spring Boot or Quarkus behind the scenes. Additionally, it supports integration with various CI/CD tools, such as GitHub Actions[27] and Jenkins[28], and provides detailed documentation on how to use it with these platforms.

This tool offers two different editions: Open-Source and Pro. The main differences between these editions lie in the number of features they offer. For example, the Pro edition provides:

• A UI that provides reports and monitors the execution of changes.
• Detection of potentially malicious scripts, with notifications sent to alert the appropriate users or systems.
• The ability to roll back a single change or a set of changes introduced to the database.

This tool allows the registration of all scripts to be executed in a single file, with the flexibility to assign arbitrary names to each script without adhering to a specific naming convention. Unlike other tools, the execution order is determined by the order in which the files are included, rather than being based on their names.

Finally, the tool provides the option to "tag" the current state of the database, allowing rollback to that specific point in the future if needed. Additionally, if there is any uncertainty about a script, the `validate` feature can be used to verify that everything is correct and consistent before applying changes.

## Which Is the Best Alternative for Each Scenario?

The discussion about the best tool for versioning changes is extensive, with numerous articles and comments available on various forums. Most tools have the same features, but the difference lies in their versatility or the ease with which specific processes can be accomplished. Table 4.10 summarizes the most relevant features of the different tools.

_____

[27]https://docs.liquibase.com/workflows/liquibase-community/setup-github-actions-workflow.html
[28]https://docs.liquibase.com/workflows/liquibase-community/using-the-jenkins-pipeline-stage-with-spinnaker.html

*TABLE 4.10* The main things to consider when choosing one versioning option over another.

| Feature | Flyway | Liquibase |
|---|:---:|:---:|
| Well documented | ✔ | ✔ |
| Has a fantastic community of users | ✔ | ✔ |
| Supports multiple formats to describe the migration | ✘ | ✔ |
| Has a set of functions to extend the basic functionality | ✘ | ✔ |
| Has support for tools such as Maven, Gradle, and CI/CD | ✔ | ✔ |
| Performance to execute the scripts | ✔ | ✘ |
| Supports a significant number of databases, including relational and non-relational | ✘ | ✔ |

As evident, the two database versioning alternatives present significant differences. To consolidate all arguments into a single document, creating an ADR, as depicted in Figure 4.10, is considered a good approach.

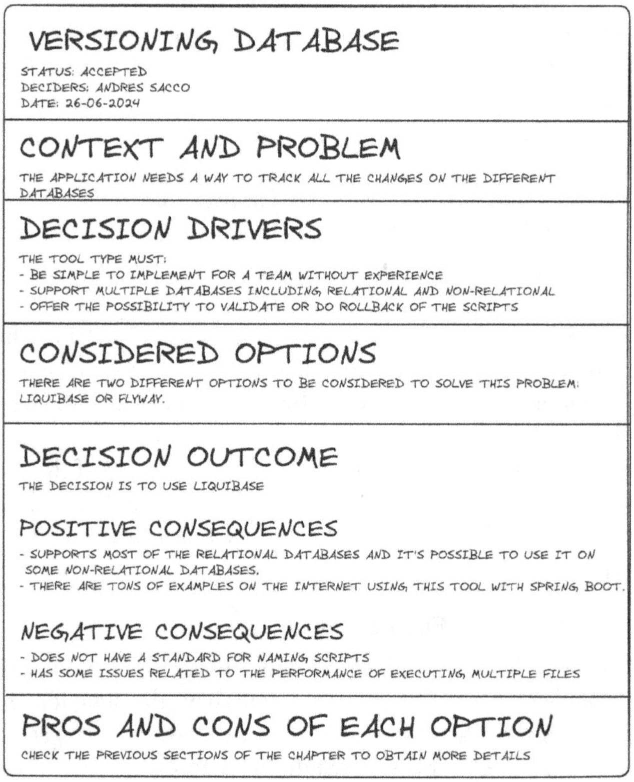

**VERSIONING DATABASE**

STATUS: ACCEPTED
DECIDERS: ANDRES SACCO
DATE: 26-06-2024

**CONTEXT AND PROBLEM**

THE APPLICATION NEEDS A WAY TO TRACK ALL THE CHANGES ON THE DIFFERENT DATABASES

**DECISION DRIVERS**

THE TOOL TYPE MUST:
- BE SIMPLE TO IMPLEMENT FOR A TEAM WITHOUT EXPERIENCE
- SUPPORT MULTIPLE DATABASES INCLUDING RELATIONAL AND NON-RELATIONAL
- OFFER THE POSSIBILITY TO VALIDATE OR DO ROLLBACK OF THE SCRIPTS

**CONSIDERED OPTIONS**

THERE ARE TWO DIFFERENT OPTIONS TO BE CONSIDERED TO SOLVE THIS PROBLEM: LIQUIBASE OR FLYWAY.

**DECISION OUTCOME**

THE DECISION IS TO USE LIQUIBASE

**POSITIVE CONSEQUENCES**

- SUPPORTS MOST OF THE RELATIONAL DATABASES AND IT'S POSSIBLE TO USE IT ON SOME NON-RELATIONAL DATABASES.
- THERE ARE TONS OF EXAMPLES ON THE INTERNET USING THIS TOOL WITH SPRING BOOT.

**NEGATIVE CONSEQUENCES**

- DOES NOT HAVE A STANDARD FOR NAMING SCRIPTS
- HAS SOME ISSUES RELATED TO THE PERFORMANCE OF EXECUTING MULTIPLE FILES

**PROS AND CONS OF EACH OPTION**

CHECK THE PREVIOUS SECTIONS OF THE CHAPTER TO OBTAIN MORE DETAILS

*FIGURE 4.10* ADR about the decision of which method of versioning to implement.

This document enables any reader to understand the reasons behind choosing this approach over others and to review the factors considered during the decision-making process.

### How Can It Be Implemented on a Spring Boot Application?

The first step to using Liquibase in the application is to add the dependency without specifying any version, as shown in Listing 4.29.

```
<dependency>
        <groupId>org.liquibase</groupId>
        <artifactId>liquibase-core</artifactId>
</dependency>
```
**LISTING 4.29** Dependencies to add in the POM file.

The following step is to add the route to indicate where the main file, which contains the list of all the necessary scripts to execute, appears in Listing 4.30.

```
spring:
  #Previous configuration of the file on a relational database
  liquibase:
    change-log: classpath:db/changelog/db.changelog-root.xml
```
**LISTING 4.30** Configuration to execute the versioning of the changes.

An excellent way to organize Liquibase components is to create two separate folders: one called changelog, which contains the organization or order of execution for the other scripts, and another folder with all the scripts. In the changelog folder, create a file with the name db.changelog-root.xml with the content of Listing 4.31.

```
<?xml version="1.0" encoding="UTF-8"?>
<databaseChangeLog
        xmlns="http://www.liquibase.org/xml/ns/dbchangelog"
        xmlns:xsi="http://www.w3.org/2001/XMLSchema-instance"
        xmlns:pro="http://www.liquibase.org/xml/ns/pro"
        xsi:schemaLocation="http://www.liquibase.org/xml/ns/dbchangelog
     http://www.liquibase.org/xml/ns/dbchangelog/dbchangelog-4.1.xsd
     http://www.liquibase.org/xml/ns/pro
     http://www.liquibase.org/xml/ns/pro/liquibase-pro-4.1.xsd">

    <include file="db/migrations/V1.0__init_database.sql"/>
    <include file="db/migrations/V1.1__insert_rows.sql"/>
</databaseChangeLog>
```
**LISTING 4.31** Files to execute on Liquibase.

As demonstrated in Listing 4.31, two distinct files reside within a folder named migrations in the project's resources folder. These files are duplicates, also appearing in the scripts folder located in the root directory of the GitHub repository. Just copy and paste both files into the migrations directory, and at the top of each file, include the comments that are shown in Listing 4.32.

```
--liquibase formatted sql

--changeset reservation:1
```

***LISTING 4.32*** Header of each Liquibase script.

This header indicates that the file contains elements usable by Liquibase in SQL format. The second line means that the user of this modification is `reservation`, and the version is `1`.

When the modifications are made in the correct order, a log similar to Listing 4.33 will appear on the console.

```
2024-08-05T23:07:55.096-03:00  INFO 325109 --- [api-reservation] [
restartedMain] liquibase.executor                  : Changelog
query completed.
2024-08-05T23:07:55.099-03:00  INFO 325109 --- [api-reservation] [
restartedMain] liquibase.executor                  : Changelog
query completed.
2024-08-05T23:07:55.102-03:00  INFO 325109 --- [api-reservation] [
restartedMain] liquibase.executor                  : Changelog
query completed.
2024-08-05T23:07:55.106-03:00  INFO 325109 --- [api-reservation] [
restartedMain] liquibase.executor                  : Changelog
query completed.
2024-08-05T23:07:55.107-03:00  INFO 325109 --- [api-reservation] [
restartedMain] liquibase.executor                  : Changelog
query completed.
2024-08-05T23:07:55.109-03:00  INFO 325109 --- [api-reservation] [
restartedMain] liquibase.lockservice               : Successfully
acquired change log lock
2024-08-05T23:07:55.118-03:00  INFO 325109 --- [api-reservation]
[  restartedMain] liquibase.changelog                : Creating
database history table with name: flights_reservation.DATABASECHANGELOG
2024-08-05T23:07:55.132-03:00  INFO 325109 --- [api-reservation] [
restartedMain] liquibase.executor                  : Changelog
query completed.
2024-08-05T23:07:55.134-03:00  INFO 325109 --- [api-reservation] [
restartedMain] liquibase.changelog                 : Reading from
flights_reservation.DATABASECHANGELOG
2024-08-05T23:07:55.135-03:00  INFO 325109 --- [api-reservation] [
restartedMain] liquibase.executor                  : Changelog
query completed.
2024-08-05T23:07:55.137-03:00  INFO 325109 --- [api-reservation] [
restartedMain] liquibase.executor                  : Changelog
query completed.
Running Changeset: db/migrations/V1.0__init_database.sql::1::reservation
2024-08-05T23:07:55.261-03:00  INFO 325109 --- [api-reservation] [
restartedMain] liquibase.changelog                 : Custom SQL
executed
2024-08-05T23:07:55.261-03:00  INFO 325109 --- [api-reservation] [
restartedMain] liquibase.changelog                 : ChangeSet db/
migrations/V1.0__init_database.sql::1::reservation ran successfully in 109ms
```

```
2024-08-05T23:07:55.263-03:00  INFO 325109 --- [api-reservation] [
restartedMain] liquibase.executor                    : Changelog
query completed.
2024-08-05T23:07:55.264-03:00  INFO 325109 --- [api-reservation] [
restartedMain] liquibase.executor                    : Changelog
query completed.
Running Changeset: db/migrations/V1.1__insert_rows.sql::2::reservation
2024-08-05T23:07:55.271-03:00  INFO 325109 --- [api-reservation] [
restartedMain] liquibase.changelog                   : Custom SQL
executed
2024-08-05T23:07:55.273-03:00  INFO 325109 --- [api-reservation] [
restartedMain] liquibase.changelog                   : ChangeSet db/
migrations/V1.1__insert_rows.sql::2::reservation ran successfully in 6ms
2024-08-05T23:07:55.275-03:00  INFO 325109 --- [api-reservation] [
restartedMain] liquibase.executor                    : Changelog
query completed.
2024-08-05T23:07:55.277-03:00  INFO 325109 --- [api-reservation] [
restartedMain] liquibase                             : Update command
completed successfully.
2024-08-05T23:07:55.278-03:00  INFO 325109 --- [api-reservation] [
restartedMain] liquibase.executor                    : Changelog
query completed.
2024-08-05T23:07:55.280-03:00  INFO 325109 --- [api-reservation] [
restartedMain] liquibase.lockservice                 : Successfully
released change log lock
2024-08-05T23:07:55.321-03:00  INFO 325109 --- [api-reservation] [
restartedMain] o.hibernate.jpa.internal.util.LogHelper  : HHH000204:
Processing PersistenceUnitInfo [name: default]
2024-08-05T23:07:55.348-03:00  INFO 325109 --- [api-reservation] [
restartedMain] org.hibernate.Version                 : HHH000412:
Hibernate ORM core version 6.5.2.Final

2024-08-05T23:07:56.487-03:00  INFO 325109 --- [api-reservation]
[ restartedMain] c.t.f.a.r.ApiReservationApplication    : Started
ApiReservationApplication in 12.578 seconds (process running for 12.806)
2024-08-05T23:07:56.917-03:00  INFO 325109 --- [api-reservation] [on(3)-
127.0.0.1] o.a.c.c.C.[.[./api/flights/reservation] : Initializing Spring
DispatcherServlet 'dispatcherServlet'
2024-08-05T23:07:56.917-03:00  INFO 325109 --- [api-reservation] [on(3)-
127.0.0.1] o.s.web.servlet.DispatcherServlet      : Initializing
Servlet 'dispatcherServlet'
2024-08-05T23:07:56.917-03:00  INFO 325109 --- [api-reservation]
[on(3)-127.0.0.1] o.s.web.servlet.DispatcherServlet      : Completed
initialization in 0 ms
```

**LISTING 4.33** Logs of executing the application with Liquibase.

These changes help mitigate potential issues, reducing the risk of critical failures. Control over the specific queries executed against the database remains limited, however. In the event of an error within the SQL script, the changes will not be applied, and the execution will be automatically rolled back.

## SUMMARY

The persistence layer is a fundamental part of any system or application, making the selection of the appropriate approach critical. Documenting the decision using an ADR helps clarify the chosen library or framework for saving and retrieving data, including the alternatives that were evaluated.

Spring Data offers flexibility by enabling the integration of various database types with minimal changes. Its repository abstraction simplifies data access, reducing the amount of boilerplate code developers need to write.

When working with relational databases, however, it is essential to manage schema changes over time. Tools such as Flyway and Liquibase allow version-controlled, automated database migrations, helping to maintain consistency and traceability.

The next chapter will focus on testing various components of an application, including techniques for evaluating query performance in a relational database context.

# CHAPTER 5

# COMMUNICATION WITH EXTERNAL SERVICES

Sometimes, applications only need to communicate with a database to persist or process that information without interacting with any other component. This scenario seems great, but in most cases, applications must interact with others to obtain specific information or delegate tasks, such as sending a notification or processing a payment.

This chapter explains how communication occurs between applications to retrieve specific information, taking into account factors such as errors and timeouts, as well as strategies to limit the number of requests for data that changes infrequently.

## WHAT DOES COMMUNICATION BETWEEN APPLICATIONS MEAN?

Communication between two or more applications means the transfer of information to do something specific with a specific result. For example, in some cases, the application that generates the request could or could not wait until it has the result. Figure 5.1 illustrates a basic communication flow between two distinct applications.

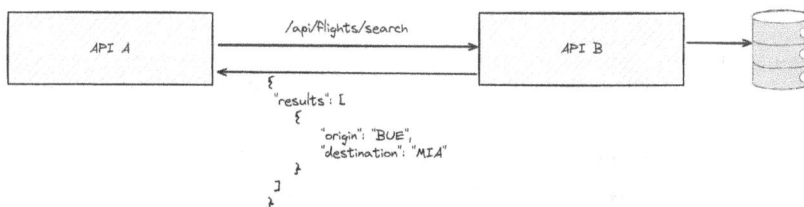

**FIGURE 5.1** Communication between different applications.

During this communication, certain aspects must be taken into account, such as the response time. Since one application cannot wait indefinitely for a reply, it is essential to set time limits to prevent delays that could impact other parts of the platform.

### Which Components Are Connected with Communication?

At a high level, communication can be viewed as the interaction between two applications or components through a channel. Thinking in this way is an abstraction, however, because behind the scenes, many things contribute to the communication. Figure 5.2 illustrates the structure of both the request and the response, highlighting the key elements that must be considered during communication.

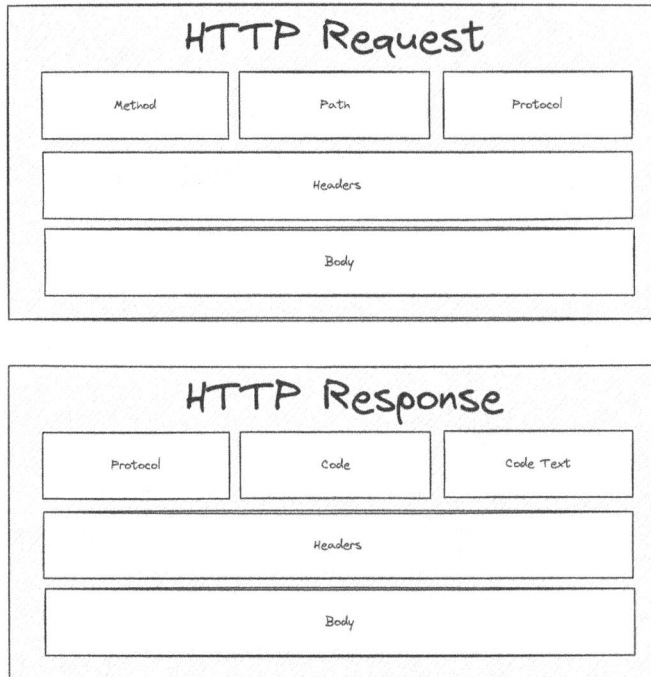

**FIGURE 5.2** Elements of the request/response.

Table 5.1 explains the various communication elements.

**TABLE 5.1** Components of a request/response.

| Keyword | Description |
|---|---|
| HTTP Method | This indicates the type of operation being performed: GET, POST, PATCH, DELETE, or PUT. |
| Path | This means the URL considers the host, port, and path to access one resource. |
| Body | For complex data, this section transmits structured information, typically in a standardized format, such as JSON. |
| Param | These are appended to the URL/path as key-value pairs. |
| Headers | Additional metadata can be included here, such as `content-type` (body format) and `accept-encoding` (compression support). |
| Code (HTTP Status) | Successful operations return HTTP status codes from the 2xx family (e.g., 200 OK, 201 Created). |
| Code Text (HTTP Status) | This attribute provides a human-readable explanation of the response code. |
| Protocol | This specifies the body's data format (e.g., JSON, XML), with more examples covered in the following section. |

This component is used for most communication scenarios, but only in specific cases where the response contains content.

## Which Protocols Exist?

The protocol for communication between different applications is critical because it defines the format for exchanging messages. If some applications understand the format, the communication will succeed.

Protocols have evolved since the days when most applications relied on Simple Object Access Protocol (SOAP) as the standard. Now, new formats, such as GraphQL and gRPC, are supported by Spring Boot.

## SOAP

SOAP is a lightweight XML-based protocol for exchanging information with applications that support it. This protocol supports multiple languages and was one of the first methods for exchanging information between applications using a standard format.

Listing 5.1 shows how to execute a request to obtain information about one specific object of an entity.

```
POST /webservice HTTP/1.1
Host: www.example.com
Content-Type: text/xml; charset=utf-8
Content-Length: length
SOAPAction: "http://www.example.com/GetCity"

<?xml version="1.0"?>
<soap:Envelope xmlns:soap="http://schemas.xmlsoap.org/soap/envelope/">
  <soap:Body>
    <GetCityRequest xmlns="http://www.example.com/">
      <CityId>123</CityId>
    </GetCityRequest>
  </soap:Body>
</soap:Envelope>
```

**LISTING 5.1** SOAP Request.

As shown in Listing 5.1, XML requires a significant amount of information to retrieve data. This is one of the reasons why the protocol has declined in popularity compared to other options.

Now, let's look at the response in Listing 5.2 associated with the previous request; the format of the response is an object that represents another object.

```
HTTP/1.1 200 OK
Content-Type: text/xml; charset=utf-8
Content-Length: length

<?xml version="1.0"?>
<soap:Envelope xmlns:soap="http://schemas.xmlsoap.org/soap/envelope/">
  <soap:Body>
    <GetCityResponse xmlns="http://www.example.com/">
      <City>
        <Id>123</Id>
        <Name>Buenos Aires</Name>
        <Code>BUE</Code>
```

```
          </City>
        </GetCityResponse>
      </soap:Body>
    </soap:Envelope>
```

LISTING 5.2 SOAP Response.

Until now, most legacy systems and large companies have used this protocol because the cost associated with migrating to a new protocol, such as Representational State Transfer (REST), includes a lot of time and changes to the application, with the risk of something going wrong during this process.

## REST

The REST protocol appears as an alternative to the previous one but does not directly relate to microservices; many applications used this protocol before the new architecture paradigm emerged.

The protocol utilizes JSON to exchange information, simplifying the complexity of requests and responses with a human-readable format. Another difference arises when retrieving information about a specific entity—only the entity's ID needs to be sent, without the need to construct a full object as required in the SOAP example shown in Listing 5.1.

Let's look at Listing 5.3, a simple request to obtain the information using this protocol.

```
GET /city/123 HTTP/1.1
Host: www.example.com
Accept: application/json
```

LISTING 5.3 REST Request.

Listing 5.3 shows how the HTTP method specifies the intended action—for example, GET to retrieve information, PUT to update data, and DELETE to remove an entity. This represents a key difference from the previous protocol, where the HTTP method was always POST regardless of the operation, due to the need to send a complex object.

Let's examine a possible response to the request in Listing 5.3 in JSON format, similar to Listing 5.4.

```
HTTP/1.1 200 OK
Content-Type: application/json

{
  "id": 123,
  "name": "Buenos Aires",
  "code": "BUE"
}
```

LISTING 5.4 REST Response.

The request and response in this protocol are straightforward, and numerous online tools are available to generate language-specific objects directly from JSON. This reduces the time it takes for the classes to parse the response in the application.

## gRPC

This is an open-source communication architecture initially sponsored by Google. The primary concept is to utilize a remote procedure call (RPC) model, where communication between applications takes place on the same machine through the exchange of information.

One significant difference between gRPC and other implementations of RPC is that the former utilizes HTTP/2 to transport information and Protocol Buffers as a language for exchanging information, thereby reducing the message size.

Many companies, such as Netflix and Cisco, utilize this communication mechanism because it's supported in multiple languages and features various libraries that provide support; however, the implementation is not straightforward.

## GraphQL

One of the main problems that appears in all of the previous approaches to exchanging information is that the responses always have the same format. One client may not need all the information that one endpoint provides, or it may require information that exists in two different endpoints of the same API. This situation leads to wasted resources by transferring unnecessary data. For example, if a company provides both a mobile and a desktop application, and the mobile version displays only a subset of the available information, sending the entire response becomes inefficient—especially when much of it won't be used.

This communication method resolves many of the shortcomings of earlier approaches by allowing the application to specify only the required attributes, thereby minimizing the response size to include just the information necessary for a specific task.

The request format, as shown in Listing 5.5, includes an attribute called `"query"`. In this structure, the names of the desired attributes must be specified, much like selecting fields in a database query.

```
POST /graphql HTTP/1.1
Host: www.example.com
Content-Type: application/json

{
  "query": "{ city(id: \"123\") { id, name, code } }"
}
```

**LISTING 5.5** GraphQL Request.

Listing 5.6 shows the response as a simple JSON object that includes all the information requested by the application.

```
HTTP/1.1 200 OK
Content-Type: application/json

{
    "data": {
        "id": 123,
        "name": "Buenos Aires",
        "code": "BUE"
    }
}
```

**LISTING 5.6** GraphQL Response.

This approach improves on REST by providing a response that is both simple to read and flexible enough to request specific attributes as needed.

## Which Types of Communication Exist?

There are various types of communication between different applications, each with different approaches. For instance, synchronous communication involves waiting for the entire response, whereas asynchronous communication allows sending a message without waiting for a response.

## Synchronous

Initially, all communication between applications occurred synchronously, which meant opening a channel, making a request, and waiting for a response. This process sometimes took a considerable amount of time. Figure 5.3 illustrates this type of communication.

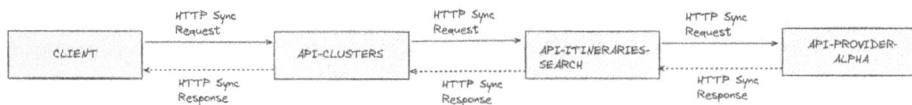

FIGURE 5.3 Synchronous communication.

NOTE  *All of the protocols listed in the previous JSON can be applied without issues.*

Several aspects must be considered when adopting this approach. When a communication channel is established between two applications, data is only transmitted once the provider generates a response. This means that resources, such as CPU and memory, are consumed while waiting at various points in the process. Additionally, there is a risk of message loss in the event of communication failure, unless a retry strategy is implemented.

This approach isn't all bad; it's simple to implement, and most companies use it on their platform. At the same time, each application knows which other applications use its information, and the flow of the communication is sequential, so drawing the interaction between the different components is simple. This approach sometimes complements asynchronous communication to interact with the UI.

## Asynchronous

As the system's complexity grows, there are better options than the waiting required with synchronous communication. Consider a scenario where a user completes the checkout process on a popular e-commerce site and clicks the Buy button. The user waits only for confirmation that the operation was successful, and a few minutes later, they receive an email with the purchase details. In this case, the Web page does not need to remain open while the application sends the email; it is sufficient to confirm that the payment was successful, after which all subsequent actions can be handled asynchronously.

Figure 5.4 presents an example of this type of communication, based on the case study used in this book.

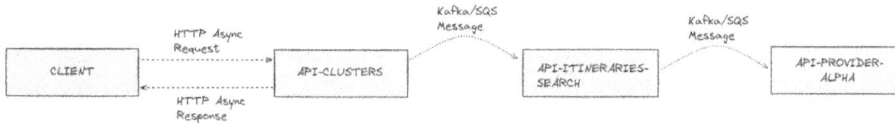

**FIGURE 5.4** - Synchronous communication.

This approach presents several advantages, notably the capacity to adjust the flow with minimal complications, as the application, in its role as the producer, transmits a message to a queue utilized by multiple other applications. The message format, in most instances, is JSON, which can be validated through various tools to ensure the integrity of the message structure.

> **NOTE**
>
> *There is a variant of this type of communication called reactive communication, which takes the same approach as synchronous communication. Instead of waiting until it has all the information to return a response, however, the idea is to return the information in chunks as it becomes available, thereby reducing the time that the channel remains inactive.*

Different tools implement the asynchronous communication mechanism, such as Apache Kafka, Apache Pulsar, AWS SQS, RabbitMQ, and ActiveMQ. Each has its pros and cons, depending on the maintenance costs and the skills required to configure and administer it.

## Which Is the Best Option for Each Scenario?

The discussion about the best option needs to be divided into two parts. The first part concerns the choice between synchronous and asynchronous communication, based on a set of considerations outlined in Table 5.2.

**TABLE 5.2** Main things to consider when choosing an option.

| Feature | Synchronous | Asynchronous |
|---|---|---|
| There is a big community of companies and developers. | ✓ | ✓ |
| There is plenty of documentation and best practices. | ✓ | ✓ |
| It's simple to implement with a team with little experience. | ✓ | ✗ |
| It works well for a complex process with many steps. | ✗ | ✓ |
| There is a cost associated with the use, such as maintaining a tool. | ✓ | ✗ |

Significant differences exist between the two options for communication between applications. A good idea is to create an ADR to synthesize all the arguments in one document, as shown in Figure 5.5.

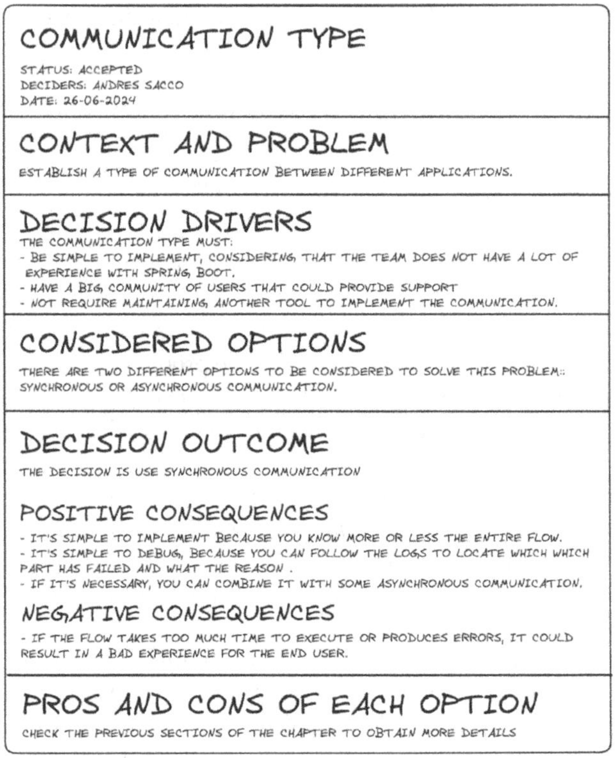

COMMUNICATION TYPE

STATUS: ACCEPTED
DECIDERS: ANDRES SACCO
DATE: 26-06-2024

CONTEXT AND PROBLEM

ESTABLISH A TYPE OF COMMUNICATION BETWEEN DIFFERENT APPLICATIONS.

DECISION DRIVERS

THE COMMUNICATION TYPE MUST:
- BE SIMPLE TO IMPLEMENT, CONSIDERING THAT THE TEAM DOES NOT HAVE A LOT OF EXPERIENCE WITH SPRING BOOT.
- HAVE A BIG COMMUNITY OF USERS THAT COULD PROVIDE SUPPORT
- NOT REQUIRE MAINTAINING ANOTHER TOOL TO IMPLEMENT THE COMMUNICATION.

CONSIDERED OPTIONS

THERE ARE TWO DIFFERENT OPTIONS TO BE CONSIDERED TO SOLVE THIS PROBLEM:
SYNCHRONOUS OR ASYNCHRONOUS COMMUNICATION.

DECISION OUTCOME

THE DECISION IS USE SYNCHRONOUS COMMUNICATION

POSITIVE CONSEQUENCES

- IT'S SIMPLE TO IMPLEMENT BECAUSE YOU KNOW MORE OR LESS THE ENTIRE FLOW.
- IT'S SIMPLE TO DEBUG, BECAUSE YOU CAN FOLLOW THE LOGS TO LOCATE WHICH WHICH PART HAS FAILED AND WHAT THE REASON .
- IF IT'S NECESSARY, YOU CAN COMBINE IT WITH SOME ASYNCHRONOUS COMMUNICATION.

NEGATIVE CONSEQUENCES

- IF THE FLOW TAKES TOO MUCH TIME TO EXECUTE OR PRODUCES ERRORS, IT COULD RESULT IN A BAD EXPERIENCE FOR THE END USER.

PROS AND CONS OF EACH OPTION

CHECK THE PREVIOUS SECTIONS OF THE CHAPTER TO OBTAIN MORE DETAILS

**FIGURE 5.5** ADR about the decision of which communication to use.

After selecting the type of communication, the next step is to define its format. This can be complex, considering the numerous options, but Table 5.3 summarizes the most relevant points.

**TABLE 5.3** Main things to consider when choosing a format option.

| Feature | SOAP | REST | gPRC | GraphQL |
|---|---|---|---|---|
| There is a big community of users and companies that use it. | ✓ | ✓ | ✗ | ✗ |
| It's simple to implement for inexperienced developer teams. | ✓ | ✓ | ✗ | ✗ |
| The network is optimized to handle a large number of responses. | ✗ | ✗ | ✓ | ✓ |
| There is support for multiple libraries. | ✗ | ✓ | ✗ | ✓ |
| It has a slight learning curve. | ✓ | ✓ | ✗ | ✗ |

Often, more than one solution is required to tackle all problems; in most cases, companies choose to use multiple approaches, such as REST with GraphQL. Let's create an ADR to synthesize all the arguments in one document, as shown in Figure 5.6.

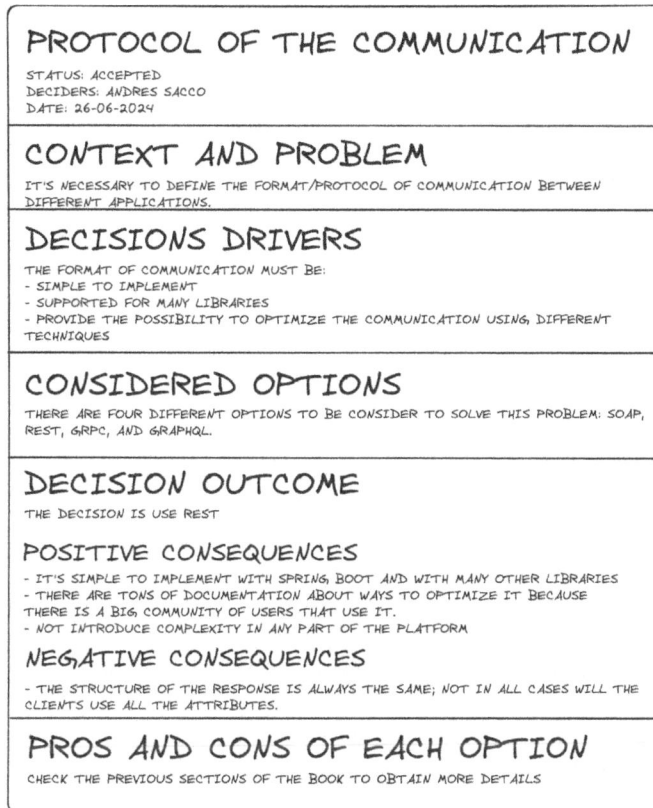

```
PROTOCOL OF THE COMMUNICATION

STATUS: ACCEPTED
DECIDERS: ANDRES SACCO
DATE: 26-06-2024

CONTEXT AND PROBLEM

IT'S NECESSARY TO DEFINE THE FORMAT/PROTOCOL OF COMMUNICATION BETWEEN
DIFFERENT APPLICATIONS.

DECISIONS DRIVERS

THE FORMAT OF COMMUNICATION MUST BE:
- SIMPLE TO IMPLEMENT
- SUPPORTED FOR MANY LIBRARIES
- PROVIDE THE POSSIBILITY TO OPTIMIZE THE COMMUNICATION USING DIFFERENT
TECHNIQUES

CONSIDERED OPTIONS

THERE ARE FOUR DIFFERENT OPTIONS TO BE CONSIDER TO SOLVE THIS PROBLEM: SOAP,
REST, GRPC, AND GRAPHQL.

DECISION OUTCOME

THE DECISION IS USE REST

POSITIVE CONSEQUENCES

- IT'S SIMPLE TO IMPLEMENT WITH SPRING BOOT AND WITH MANY OTHER LIBRARIES
- THERE ARE TONS OF DOCUMENTATION ABOUT WAYS TO OPTIMIZE IT BECAUSE
THERE IS A BIG COMMUNITY OF USERS THAT USE IT.
- NOT INTRODUCE COMPLEXITY IN ANY PART OF THE PLATFORM

NEGATIVE CONSEQUENCES

- THE STRUCTURE OF THE RESPONSE IS ALWAYS THE SAME; NOT IN ALL CASES WILL THE
CLIENTS USE ALL THE ATTRIBUTES.

PROS AND CONS OF EACH OPTION

CHECK THE PREVIOUS SECTIONS OF THE BOOK TO OBTAIN MORE DETAILS
```

**FIGURE 5.6** ADR about the decision of the communication format.

Once the type and format of communication for the application have been decided, the next step is to implement them within the application.

## HOW TO IMPLEMENT COMMUNICATION IN SPRING BOOT

Implementing communication in a Spring Boot application is straightforward because multiple implementations share the same concept, thus simplifying the number of modifications required.

The book's repository includes a file named `docker-compose.yml` located in the `docker/platform` directory, which must be executed. This file contains all the platform applications, such as those shown in Listing 5.7.

```
version: '3.1'
services:
  api-catalog:
    image: adschosen/api-catalog:1.0.0
    container_name: api-catalog
    ports:
     - 6070:6070
    restart: always
```

```
    links:
      - api-catalog-db

  api-catalog-db:
    container_name: api-catalog-db
    image: mysql:5.7
    restart: always
    environment:
      MYSQL_DATABASE: 'flights_catalog'
      MYSQL_ROOT_PASSWORD: 'muppet'
    ports:
      - 3310:3306

# Other services

  api-reservation-db:
    container_name: api-reservation-db
    image: mysql:8.2.0
    restart: always
    environment:
      MYSQL_DATABASE: 'flights_reservation'
      MYSQL_ROOT_PASSWORD: 'muppet'
    ports:
      - 3312:3306
```

**LISTING 5.7** Docker Compose file with all the microservices.

After running `docker-compose.yml`, a request should be made to verify that everything is working correctly, as shown in Listing 5.8.

```
→  ~ curl --location
'http://localhost:4070/api/flights/clusters/itineraries?from=BUE%2CMIA&to
=MIA%2CBUE&departure=2025-09-29%2C2025-10-03&adults=1&children=1&infants
=1&amount=10'

{
    "id": "TWA_g=2024-08-20T20:39:04.846776_f=BUE,MIA_t=MIA,BUE_d=2025-
09-29,2025-10-03_a=1_c=1_i=1",
    "pagination": {
        "offset": 0,
        "limit": 10,
        "total": 4
    },
    "itineraries": [
      //Too many elements in the array
    ]
}
```

**LISTING 5.8** Curl to validate the microservices.

Once validation is complete, modifications to the application can be made to obtain or validate specific information.

---

**NOTE** *Microservices are not mocks that always return the same data; they include a certain level of logic to perform searches and calculate prices, providing a more realistic scenario for practice.*

### How Can Communication Be Carried Out?

Communication within the application requires several modifications, and various approaches can be taken to address these changes. One option is to create classes that represent communication with other microservices, including all necessary details such as the URL, port, and host. This approach, however, has drawbacks since the host or port can vary across different environments. Embedding long URLs directly in Java classes is not ideal, making this method suitable mainly for local development and testing, but not recommended for applications that require deployment across multiple environments.

Another option is to put all the information in the `application.yml` and load it into different classes. The modifications on the configuration files look as in Listing 5.9.

```
http-connector:
  hosts:
    api-catalog:
      host: "localhost"
      port: 6070
      endpoints:
        country-by-id:
          url: "/api/flights/catalog/country/{nationality}"
```

*LISTING 5.9* Configuration of the endpoints.

The configuration shown in Listing 5.9 allows defining additional endpoints and is designed to be extensible, enabling the inclusion of more communication properties as needed. After that, the next step is to create a class that represents the last part of the configuration, which contains the path or URL of each endpoint, as shown in Listing 5.10.

```
package com.twa.flights.api.reservation.connector.configuration;

public class EndpointConfiguration {

    private String url;
    //Setters and getters
}
```

*LISTING 5.10* Class that contains the URL.

The next step is to create a class containing all the information about the host, port, and URL of one particular microservice, as shown in Listing 5.11.

```
package com.twa.flights.api.reservation.connector.configuration;

import java.util.HashMap;

public class HostConfiguration {

    private String host;
    private int port;
    private HashMap<String, EndpointConfiguration> endpoints;

    //Setters and getters
}
```

*LISTING 5.11* Class that represents the node of the HTTP configuration of one microservice.

The final step is to create a class that loads all configurations from various microservices and their associated endpoints, as shown in Listing 5.12.

```
package com.twa.flights.api.reservation.connector.configuration;

import org.springframework.boot.context.properties.
ConfigurationProperties;
import org.springframework.context.annotation.Configuration;

import java.util.HashMap;

@Configuration
@ConfigurationProperties(prefix = "http-connector")
public class HttpConnectorConfiguration {

    private HashMap<String, HostConfiguration> hosts;

    //Setters and getters
}
```

**LISTING 5.12** Class that represents the node of all the HTTP configurations.

After all these modifications, the URL, host, and ports can be changed across different environments. Running the application, however, will not produce any effect until additional changes are made, such as selecting the client to be used for communication.

## Client

In the communication between different applications, especially synchronous communication, the choice of client is crucial. It should be straightforward to implement, offering features such as transforming responses into objects and the ability to set timeouts to prevent waiting indefinitely.

Spring Boot has expanded the possibilities of communication across different versions by simplifying certain aspects and providing more opportunities for specific tasks, such as asynchronous communication. Table 5.4 shows some of the most relevant options.

**TABLE 5.4** Main HTTP clients to use on Spring Boot.

| Client | Type | Description |
| --- | --- | --- |
| RestTemplate[1] | Synchronous | This client was the first and most popular on Spring Boot, but it is gradually being deprecated in favor of WebClient, especially for reactive applications. |
| WebClient[2] | Synchronous Asynchronous | This client is an alternative to the previous one, providing support beyond synchronous communication; it can be used asynchronously with minimal modifications. Spring recommends using this client instead of RestTemplate as RestTemplate will be deprecated. |

*(Continued)*

[1]https://docs.spring.io/spring-framework/docs/current/javadoc-api/org/springframework/web/client/RestTemplate.html
[2]https://docs.spring.io/spring-framework/reference/web/webflux-webclient.html

**TABLE 5.4** Continued

| Client | Type | Description |
|---|---|---|
| OpenFeign[3] | Synchronous | This client conceals the implementation of communication, accomplishing most tasks through configuration, and creates an interface that functions similarly to the repositories for persistence. |
| OkHttpClient[4] | Synchronous | This is a third-party library that can be integrated with Spring Boot with some modifications. Some developers use it because it has good performance. |
| Apache HttpClient[5] | Synchronous | This is another third-party library that provides most of the standard communication features. Different aspects of the request and response can be configured. |

Table 5.4 presents multiple options, most of which emphasize one approach over others. To implement asynchronous communication using reactive programming, significant code changes are required. Taking this into account, and following Spring's recommendation to use WebClient, the following section demonstrates how to exchange information between microservices using that client.

The first step is to add support to the WebClient application, which is part of the WebFlux dependency in Spring Boot. Let's add it to the POM file with the information about the `artifactId` and `groupId`, which is shown in Listing 5.13.

```
<dependency>
    <groupId>org.springframework.boot</groupId>
    <artifactId>spring-boot-starter-webflux</artifactId>
</dependency>
```

**LISTING 5.13** Dependency to add support to WebClient.

A good practice after that is to create an abstract class that encapsulates all the logic to configure the WebClient for a particular endpoint, helping reduce duplicate code when multiple endpoints need to be consumed. Listing 5.14 demonstrates how to build the WebClient, including setting the request and response formats in the headers.

```
package com.twa.flights.api.reservation.connector;

import
com.twa.flights.api.reservation.connector.configuration.
EndpointConfiguration;
import com.twa.flights.api.reservation.connector.configuration.
HostConfiguration;

import org.springframework.http.HttpHeaders;
import org.springframework.http.MediaType;
import org.springframework.http.client.reactive.
ReactorClientHttpConnector;
import org.springframework.web.reactive.function.client.WebClient;
import reactor.netty.http.client.HttpClient;
```

---

[3]https://github.com/OpenFeign/feign
[4]https://square.github.io/okhttp/
[5]https://hc.apache.org/httpcomponents-client-4.5.x/index.html

```
public abstract class TWAConnector {

    protected WebClient getConnector(HostConfiguration hostConfiguration,
EndpointConfiguration endpointConfiguration) {
        HttpClient httpClient = HttpClient.create();

        return WebClient.builder()
                .baseUrl("http://" + hostConfiguration.getHost() + ":" +
hostConfiguration.getPort())
                .defaultHeader(HttpHeaders.CONTENT_TYPE, MediaType.
APPLICATION_JSON_VALUE)
                .defaultHeader(HttpHeaders.ACCEPT, MediaType.
APPLICATION_JSON_VALUE)
                .clientConnector(new ReactorClientHttpConnector(httpClie
nt)).build();
    }
}
```

**LISTING 5.14** Generic connector to reuse in all the applications.

The next step involves defining a class that models the output returned by the microservice when the application executes a request to retrieve information. This class is a simple DTO and resembles the example shown in Listing 5.15.

```
package com.twa.flights.api.reservation.connector.response;

public class CountryDTO {
    private String name;
    private String code;
    //Setters and getters
}
```

**LISTING 5.15** Class that represents the response of the API.

Let's create a concrete connector that requests the api-catalog and transforms the response into a specific object, as in Listing 5.16.

```
package com.twa.flights.api.reservation.connector;

import com.twa.flights.api.reservation.connector.configuration.
EndpointConfiguration;
import com.twa.flights.api.reservation.connector.configuration.
HostConfiguration;
import com.twa.flights.api.reservation.connector.configuration.
HttpConnectorConfiguration;
import com.twa.flights.api.reservation.connector.response.CountryDTO;
import org.slf4j.Logger;
import org.slf4j.LoggerFactory;
import org.springframework.beans.factory.annotation.Autowired;
import org.springframework.stereotype.Component;

@Component
public class CatalogConnector extends TWAConnector {
```

```
    private static final Logger LOGGER = LoggerFactory.
getLogger(CatalogConnector.class);

    private final String HOST = "api-catalog";
    private final String ENDPOINT = "country-by-id";

    private HttpConnectorConfiguration configuration;

    @Autowired
    public CatalogConnector(HttpConnectorConfiguration configuration) {
        this.configuration = configuration;
    }

    public CountryDTO getCountry(String code) {
        LOGGER.info("calling to api-catalog");

        HostConfiguration hostConfiguration = configuration.getHosts().
get(HOST);
        EndpointConfiguration endpointConfiguration = hostConfiguration.
getEndpoints().get(ENDPOINT);

        String url = UriComponentsBuilder.fromUriString(endpointConfiguration.
getUrl())
                    .buildAndExpand(Collections.singletonMap("nationality",
code))
                    .toUriString();

        return getConnector(hostConfiguration, endpointConfiguration).get()
                    .uri(url).retrieve().bodyToMono(CountryDTO.class).share()
                    .block();
    }
}
```

**LISTING 5.16** Catalog connector reusing part of the default connector.

The next step is to create a service that provides access to the connector, following best practices, so that no one outside the service can access a repository or a connector directly. Listing 5.17 shows a simple service that only has one method.

```
package com.twa.flights.api.reservation.service;

import com.twa.flights.api.reservation.connector.CatalogConnector;
import com.twa.flights.api.reservation.connector.response.CountryDTO;
import org.springframework.beans.factory.annotation.Autowired;
import org.springframework.stereotype.Service;

@Service
public class CatalogService {

    private CatalogConnector connector;

    @Autowired
    public CatalogService(CatalogConnector connector) {
        this.connector = connector;
    }
```

```
    public CountryDTO getCountryByCode(String code) {
        return connector.getCountry(code);
    }
}
```

**LISTING 5.17** Catalog service to use the connector.

The next step is to introduce the modifications into `ReservationService` to make the request that is shown in Listing 5.18.

```
package com.twa.flights.api.reservation.service;

//Previous imports
@Service
public class ReservationService {

    //Previous code
    private CatalogService catalogService;

    public ReservationDTO save(ReservationDTO reservation) {
        if(Objects.nonNull(reservation.id())) {
            throw new TWAException(APIError.RESERVATION_WITH_SAME_ID);
        }

        validateWithExternalServices(reservation);
        //Previous code
    }

    private void validateWithExternalServices(ReservationDTO reservation)
{
        if (reservation.passengers() != null) {
            for (PassengerDTO passenger : reservation.passengers()) {
                catalogService.getCountryByCode(passenger.
nationality());
            }
        }
    }
}
```

**LISTING 5.18** Modifications on ReservationService.

One required change in `NationalityFormatValidator` is to adjust the field length from 3 to 2. After making this modification, the application can be run, and a `curl` request similar to the one shown in Listing 5.19 can be executed to verify the behavior.

```
➜  ~ curl --location 'http://localhost:8090/api/flights/reservation/' \
--header 'Content-Type: application/json' \
--data-raw '{
    "itineraryId": "2",
    "searchId": "2",
    "passengers": [
        {
            "firstName": "Andres",
```

```
            "lastName": "Sacco",
            "documentNumber": "987654321",
            "documentType": "DNI",
            "nationality": "AR",
            "birthday": "1985-01-01"
        }
    ],
    "contact": {
        "telephoneNumber": "54911111111",
        "email": "sacco.andres@gmail.com"
    }
}
```

*LISTING 5.19* curl to check that everything works.

If everything works correctly, a new reservation with an ID will be received. To verify, check the application's console to see whether the logs match those shown in Listing 5.20.

```
2024-08-23T15:07:59.193-03:00  INFO 247150 --- [api-reservation] [nio-
8090-exec-2] c.t.f.a.r.c.ReservationController        : Saving new
reservation
2024-08-23T15:07:59.193-03:00  INFO 247150 --- [api-reservation] [nio-
8090-exec-2] c.t.f.a.r.connector.CatalogConnector     : calling to api-
catalog
```

*LISTING 5.20* Output of the curl command.

The logger's level can be changed to DEBUG to obtain more detailed information about the communication.

> **NOTE** *The source code for this chapter includes another connector that checks whether the search IDs are valid. Since its implementation is relatively similar to what has already been presented, however, it is not included in this section. Feel free to download it and check the implementation.*

## Timeouts

Communication between different applications can sometimes have a varying duration and impact a platform's overall behavior. A good practice is to define how long the application will wait to receive a response—this is called a timeout. Once this time elapses, the communication stops, and an exception is thrown.

There are different timeouts, each of them for a specific purpose:

• Connection Timeout: Refers to the maximum time the client waits to communicate with another service.
• Read Timeout: The maximum time the client waits to read the response data after establishing the communication.

• Response Timeout: This term can be used for the same purpose as the previous time-out; however, in some contexts, it refers to the maximum time it takes to obtain all responses.

Let's modify the configuration file to include the different timeouts, considering that the endpoints could have different values. Listing 5.21 provides a default value for the timeout and overrides the values on some hosts.

```
http-connector:
  defaultConfig: &commonDefaultConfig
    connectionTimeout: 5000
    readTimeout: 5000
    responseTimeout: 5000

  hosts:
    api-catalog:
      host: "localhost"
      port: 6070
      defaultConfig: &hostDefaultConfig
        <<: *commonDefaultConfig
        responseTimeout: 2000
      endpoints:
        country-by-id:
          <<: *hostDefaultConfig
          url: "/api/flights/catalog/country/{nationality}"
          connectionTimeout: 4000
```
LISTING 5.21 Configuration of the endpoints, including the timeouts.

The next step is to modify the EndpointConfiguration class to include the new attributes, as shown in Listing 5.22.

```
package com.twa.flights.api.reservation.connector.configuration;

public class EndpointConfiguration {

    private String url;
    private int readTimeout;
    private int responseTimeout;
    private int connectionTimeout;

  //Setters and getters
}
```
LISTING 5.22 Modifications to load the different timeouts.

The last modification involves changes to the generic connector, specifically to the generation of HttpClient, which includes adding the different timeouts listed in Listing 5.23.

```
package com.twa.flights.api.reservation.connector;

//Other imports

import io.netty.channel.ChannelOption;
```

```
import io.netty.handler.timeout.ReadTimeoutHandler;
import io.netty.handler.timeout.WriteTimeoutHandler;
import org.springframework.http.client.reactive.
ReactorClientHttpConnector;
import reactor.netty.http.client.HttpClient;
import java.util.concurrent.TimeUnit;

public abstract class TWAConnector {

    protected WebClient getConnector(HostConfiguration hostConfiguration,
EndpointConfiguration endpointConfiguration) {
        HttpClient httpClient = HttpClient.create()
                .option(ChannelOption.CONNECT_TIMEOUT_MILLIS,
                        Math.toIntExact(endpointConfiguration.
getConnectionTimeout()))
                .doOnConnected(conn -> conn
                        .addHandler(
                                new ReadTimeoutHandler(endpointConfigurat
ion.getReadTimeout(), TimeUnit.MILLISECONDS))
                        .addHandler(new WriteTimeoutHandler(endpointConfi
guration.getResponseTimeout(),
                                TimeUnit.MILLISECONDS)));
        //Previous code
    }
}
```

**LISTING 5.23** Modifications to use the timeouts.

With these modifications, the application defines the number of milliseconds that it waits for a response from another application. To verify the changes, modify the TimeUnit in Listing 5.23 from MILLISECONDS to NANOSECONDS and execute the same curl command shown in Listing 5.19. If everything works correctly, an exception similar to the one in Listing 5.24 will appear on the console.

```
2024-08-26T14:43:07.910-03:00  INFO 448646 --- [api-reservation] [nio-
8090-exec-1] c.t.f.a.r.connector.CatalogConnector     : calling to api-
catalog
2024-08-26T14:43:08.115-03:00  WARN 448646 --- [api-reservation] [or-
http-epoll-2] r.netty.http.client.HttpClientConnect    : [17981639-1,
L:/127.0.0.1:38944 - R:localhost/127.0.0.1:6070] The connection observed
an error

io.netty.handler.timeout.ReadTimeoutException: null

2024-08-26T14:43:08.124-03:00 ERROR 448646 --- [api-reservation] [nio-
8090-exec-1] o.a.c.c.C.[.[.[.[dispatcherServlet]      : Servlet.
service() for servlet [dispatcherServlet] in context with path [/api/
flights/reservation] threw exception [Request processing failed: org.
springframework.web.reactive.function.client.WebClientRequestException]
with root cause

io.netty.handler.timeout.ReadTimeoutException: null
```

**LISTING 5.24** Output of the execution of the request.

After the test, revert the changes to use milliseconds as the unit of timeouts.

## Errors

Problems during communication are common in all applications and can occur for various reasons, such as issues in other applications, timeouts, or network errors. One possible approach to tackle this problem is to transform the exception into something else. First, though, let's check what the exception looks like. We'll make the same request that appears in Listing 5.19 but change the nationality to AA and make the request. An error like the one shown in Listing 5.25 will be displayed.

```
{
    "timestamp": "2024-08-23T18:20:45.184+00:00",
    "status": 500,
    "error": "Internal Server Error",
    "trace": "org.springframework.web.reactive.function.client.We
bClientResponseException$NotFound: 404 Not Found from GET http://
localhost:6070/api/flights/catalog/country/AA\n\tat org.springframework.
web.reactive.function.client.WebClientResponseException.create(WebCli
entResponseException.java:310)\n\tSuppressed: The stacktrace has been
enhanced by Reactor, refer to additional information below: \nError
has been observed at the following site(s):\n\t*__checkpoint ⇢ 404
NOT_FOUND from GET http://localhost:6070/api/flights/catalog/country/AA
[DefaultWebClient]
\n",
    "message": "404 Not Found from GET http://localhost:6070/api/flights/
catalog/country/AA",
    "path": "/api/flights/reservation/"
}
```

*LISTING 5.25* Output of a request with a non-existent nationality.

To handle this problem effectively, WebClient offers a method called `status`, which can be used to specify which HTTP status codes should be intercepted and processed. There are two ways to do it: Specify one HTTP status, such as 201, or indicate an entire family of statuses, such as 2xx. In Listing 5.26, `CatalogConnector` captures the different families of problems, logs the problem, and throws another exception. A new value that represents COUNTRY_NOT_FOUND can be added to the APIError.

```
package com.twa.flights.api.reservation.connector;

//Previous imports
import com.twa.flights.api.reservation.enums.APIError;
import org.springframework.http.HttpStatusCode;

public class CatalogConnector extends TWAConnector {

    public CountryDTO getCountry(String code) {
        //Previous code
        return getConnector(hostConfiguration, endpointConfiguration).get()
                .uri(url).retrieve()
                .onStatus(HttpStatusCode::is4xxClientError, response ->
{
                LOGGER.error("Error to obtain the data with this
code {}", code);
```

```
                        return Mono.error(new TWAException(APIError.COUNTRY_
NOT_FOUND)));
                })
                .onStatus(HttpStatusCode::is5xxServerError, response ->
{
                    LOGGER.error("Error to obtain the data with this
code {}", code);
                    return Mono.error(new TWAException(APIError.COUNTRY_
NOT_FOUND)));
                })
                .bodyToMono(CountryDTO.class).share()
                .block();
    }
}
```

**LISTING 5.26** Modifications to the connector.

These simple modifications help mitigate the issue of exceptions. To observe how this works, the same request from the beginning of this section can be made again, and a response similar to Listing 5.27 will be returned.

```
{
    "description": "The country does not exist",
    "reasons": []
}
```

**LISTING 5.27** Output of the exception with a transformation.

Transforming the errors into something else reduces the impact of exposing critical information about the communication between different services. At the same time, it provides the client with some information about the problem, which it can use to change something in the request.

## HOW TO REDUCE THE IMPACT OF ERRORS

Errors are common in all applications and platforms; some result from a logic error, while others are caused by many requests that affect the resources the application has assigned. With this in mind, there are different ways to deal with the situation. The most common approach is to do nothing; if something fails, capture or throw an exception, and then stop executing that flow. There is nothing wrong with this approach, but imagine if a customer went to the Web site of a popular retailer to purchase a product, or a travel agency to buy a flight, and nothing appeared on the Web page; the most common situation if this happens is the customer will go to another Web site, resulting in the loss of business for the company.

Another option is to add some mechanism to mitigate the impact of that problem or have a default behavior, which is where the idea of having a resilient platform comes in.

### What Is Resilience?

Resilience refers to an application or platform's capability to keep functioning correctly despite failures in other applications or unexpected conditions during communication. This concept has gained importance with the rise of distributed systems. Previously, applications were typically monolithic, with a single point of failure often limited to the database or an external system. Today, however, numerous communications occur every second between different applications, significantly increasing the risk of issues such as network failures, hardware problems, or software bugs.

Naturally, there isn't a single, straightforward solution for all scenarios in a distributed system; instead, there is a collection of patterns, each addressing a specific aspect of the problem. Before diving deeper, it's helpful to review which libraries provide support for these patterns.

### How Can Resilience Be Implemented?

Many libraries implement most of the patterns associated with resilience. Not all of them support using them with Spring Boot in a straightforward manner, however, which is what often drives choosing one over another. Let's look at the most relevant options in Table 5.5:

*TABLE 5.5* Main HTTP clients to use on Spring Boot.

| Library | Description |
| --- | --- |
| Hystrix[6] | Netflix developed this library, and it was one of the first to provide support for most of the resilience patterns. It hasn't, however, had a new version since 2018, so using it is not recommended. |
| Resillence4j[7] | This library is an alternative to Hystrix. It's a lightweight library that supports not only integration with Spring Boot but also usage with Micronaut. |
| Bucket4j[8] | This is a simple library for implementing Rate Limit, one of the resilience patterns, but it does not support any other pattern. |
| Vert.x[9] | This library supports only the Circuit Breaker pattern, another key resilience mechanism. It functions well when building applications with Vert.x as the framework. |
| Sentinel[10] | This library provides support for various resilience patterns in an agnostic way, making it compatible with different libraries or frameworks. It can also be integrated into applications that use Spring Cloud or AspectJ. |
| Failsafe[11] | This library supports all the resilience patterns; however, to use it with Spring Boot and WebClient, a custom code block must be introduced, as native support is only provided for Retrofit and OkHttp. |

Considering all the possible options, the decision seems simple. The idea is to use a single library that supports all the resilience patterns, with some native support for applications that use Spring Boot and have a large developer community. Considering all these aspects, the winner is Resilience4j because it is similar to Hystrix, a library that was trendy at the beginning of the microservices era and has a lot of useful functionality.

To add support to the application, the first thing to do is add the dependency to the POM file, as shown in Listing 5.27.

---

[6]https://github.com/Netflix/Hystrix
[7]https://resilience4j.readme.io/
[8]https://github.com/bucket4j/bucket4j
[9]https://vertx.io/
[10]https://github.com/alibaba/Sentinel
[11]https://github.com/failsafe-lib/failsafe

```
<dependency>
    <groupId>io.github.resilience4j</groupId>
    <artifactId>resilience4j-spring-boot3</artifactId>
    <version>2.1.0</version>
</dependency>
```

*LISTING 5.27* Resilience4j dependency.

**NOTE** *It's important to note that the dependency name differs when using it in a project based on Spring Boot 2.x.x.*

With this modification, the application is ready to support the patterns introduced in the following section.

## Patterns

Different patterns are associated with resilience, and they all tackle some specific problem. Combining some of them, such as Circuit Breaker with Fallback, to create a better solution is recommended in some instances.

Let's see each of the most relevant resilience patterns and how to implement them with Resillience4j.

## Circuit Breaker

Imagine a request is sent to a microservice that has an issue. For a period, every request from the application received the same error response. In this scenario, continuing to send requests despite knowing the microservice is down only wastes resources and delays recovery, so it's better to stop or limit requests until the service issues are resolved.

To solve this problem of communication between applications, there exists the pattern Circuit Breaker, which is responsible for collecting the exceptions on problems during communication. After some errors occur, the circuit breaker does not send requests to other applications for a period. After that period, the circuit breaker opens the communication and resends some requests to the different applications.

This pattern has three different statuses:

- OPEN: This status indicates a situation where a large number of errors have occurred, causing the application to halt any communication with a specific application or endpoint.
- CLOSE: This status is the default and represents when everything is okay in the application communication.
- HALF_OPEN: This status represents when there are some errors in the communication, and the circuit is OPEN. After a specific period, it attempts to execute a request to validate that everything is working, and then closes the circuit and sends all the requests.

Implementing this on Spring Boot with Resilience4j is not complex because most of the changes are related to the configuration of the circuit breaker, as shown in Listing 5.28.

```
resilience4j.circuitbreaker:
  configs:
    default:
```

```
        # % of error to enable the Circuit Breaker
        failure-rate-threshold: 50

        # Which strategy will use to count the errors
        sliding-window-type: count_based
        sliding-window-size: 5

        #Configuration about how is the transition between different states
        automatic-transition-from-open-to-half-open-enabled: true
        wait-duration-in-open-state: 10s
        permitted-number-of-calls-in-half-open-state: 1

        #Ignoring the Health of the other API
        register-health-indicator: false

        # Which exceptions will be considered to enable or disable
        record-exceptions:
          - java.lang.RutimeException
          - java.lang.InterruptedException
          - io.netty.handler.timeout.ReadTimeoutException
          - org.springframework.web.reactive.function.client.
WebClientRequestException
    #Configuration for each host or endpoint
    backends:
      catalog:
        baseConfig: default
```

**LISTING 5.28** Circuit breaker configuration.

Listing 5.28 shows the parameters required to configure the pattern. The most important ones include the threshold that enables or disables the circuit and the exceptions that the application considers relevant for counting errors. It is necessary to configure the circuit to transition automatically to the half-open state; otherwise, this transition must be handled manually somewhere in the code under specific conditions.

The next step in using this pattern is to indicate where it will be used in the application. In this case, the circuit will work on `CatalogConnector` using the annotation `@CircuitBreaker` with the name of the circuit breaker that appears in the `application.yml`, as in Listing 5.29.

```java
package com.twa.flights.api.reservation.connector;

//Previous imports
import io.github.resilience4j.circuitbreaker.annotation.CircuitBreaker;

@Component
public class CatalogConnector extends TWAConnector {

    //Previous logic

    @CircuitBreaker(name = "catalog")
    public CountryDTO getCountry(String code) {
      //Previous logic
    }
}
```

**LISTING 5.29** Circuit breaker on a method.

To test whether this approach works, run the application and attempt to stop the API before creating any reservations. After halting the API, executing the same request multiple times will result in an exception, as shown in Listing 5.30.

```
{
    "timestamp": "2024-08-28T16:47:54.818+00:00",
    "status": 500,
    "error": "Internal Server Error",
    "trace": "io.github.resilience4j.circuitbreaker.
CallNotPermittedException: CircuitBreaker 'catalog' is OPEN and does
not permit further calls\n\tat io.github.resilience4j.circuitbreaker.
CallNotPermittedException.createCallNotPermittedException(CallNotPermitt
edException.java:
    ...../java.lang.Thread.run(Thread.java:1583)\n",
    "message": "CircuitBreaker 'catalog' is OPEN and does not permit
further calls",
    "path": "/api/flights/reservation/"
}
```

**LISTING 5.30** Circuit breaker exception.

The exception displays the status of the circuit breaker, raising the question of why the other microservices do not execute the request. It's not a good idea, however, to expose all of this information in the response. Instead, capture this type of exception in an exception handler and transform it into something else.

One final comment about this pattern: Adding the Resilience4j dependency to the application causes Spring Boot to include several actuator endpoints related to the supported patterns automatically. For the circuit breaker, for instance, the status of each instance can be retrieved by sending a request to the URL, as shown in Listing 5.31.

```
→  ~ curl --location 'http://localhost:8090/api/flights/reservation/
management/circuitbreakers'
  {
      "circuitBreakers": {
          "catalog": {
              "failureRate": "-1.0%",
              "slowCallRate": "-1.0%",
              "failureRateThreshold": "50.0%",
              "slowCallRateThreshold": "100.0%",
              "bufferedCalls": 0,
              "failedCalls": 0,
              "slowCalls": 0,
              "slowFailedCalls": 0,
              "notPermittedCalls": 0,
              "state": "HALF_OPEN"
          }
      }
  }
```

**LISTING 5.31** Status of all the circuit breakers on the application.

Consider excluding this endpoint in production environments for security reasons.

## Fallback

Exceptions are common during communication between different applications, but not all have the same level of priority. For instance, in an e-commerce scenario, if the service responsible for applying price markups fails, the Web site may display incorrect prices, leading potential customers to abandon the purchase and turn to a competitor. This would be considered a high-priority exception. To address this issue, a default behavior can be configured using the Fallback pattern, allowing the application to continue functioning in a degraded but controlled state.

To define the default behavior, create a method that accepts the same parameters as the original method, plus a `RuntimeException`, which can be handled or ignored. After implementing this method, configure the circuit breaker to use it as the default fallback, as shown in Listing 5.32.

```
package com.twa.flights.api.reservation.connector;

//Previous imports

@Component
public class CatalogConnector extends TWAConnector {

    //Previous logic

   @CircuitBreaker(name = "catalog", fallbackMethod =
"fallbackGetCountry")
    public CountryDTO getCountry(String code) {
      //Previous logic
    }

   private CountryDTO fallbackGetCountry(String code, RuntimeException
exception) {
        LOGGER.info("using fallback method for errors on api-catalog");

        CountryDTO country = new CountryDTO();
        country.setCode(code);
        country.setName("DEFAULT");

        return country;
    }
}
```

*LISTING 5.32* Fallback method.

The Fallback method's logic can be customized to whatever behavior is deemed most appropriate for the situation. In Listing 5.32, a mock response is returned along with a log indicating that an issue has occurred. To verify these changes, simply run the application and make the request again while the `api-catalog` is down; the console will display output similar to Listing 5.33.

```
2024-08-28T14:26:18.851-03:00  INFO 120046 --- [api-reservation] [nio-8090-
exec-2] c.t.f.a.r.connector.CatalogConnector      : calling to api-catalog
```

*LISTING 5.33* Logs of the execution.

Another option is to throw another exception that represents something for the client that tries to request the API.

## Bulkhead

This pattern draws inspiration from ship design, where a problem in one section of a part can quickly be resolved to prevent a catastrophic event from occurring throughout the entire ship.

The concept behind microservices is that resource-intensive parts of an application can be isolated and have their operations limited independently, allowing for effective management and control of resource consumption. Some examples of approaches that developers frequently use are thread pools and connection pools, which aim to minimize the impact on the database or application by limiting the number of operations that can run in parallel.

Configuring this pattern is straightforward; it requires specifying the maximum number of operations allowed to run concurrently, as demonstrated in Listing 5.34.

```
resilience4j.bulkhead:
  configs:
    default:
      maxConcurrentCalls: 1
  instances:
    catalog:
      maxConcurrentCalls: 1
```

**LISTING 5.34** Bulkhead configuration.

The next step is to add the annotation that enables support for this pattern. Suppose the target application experiences issues or has limits on the number of requests it can handle. In that case, this pattern can be combined with Circuit Breaker and Fallback, as illustrated in Listing 5.35.

```
package com.twa.flights.api.reservation.connector;

//Previous imports
import io.github.resilience4j.bulkhead.annotation.Bulkhead;

@Component
public class CatalogConnector extends TWAConnector {

    //Previous logic
    @Bulkhead(name = "catalog", fallbackMethod = "fallbackGetCountry")
    @CircuitBreaker(name = "catalog", fallbackMethod =
"fallbackGetCountry")
    public CountryDTO getCountry(String code) {
      //Previous logic
    }

    //Previous logic
}
```

**LISTING 5.35** Bulkhead logic.

In this case, run the application and make sure that api-catalog is working before making any request. Executing the same request multiple times to create a reservation will generate logs similar to those shown in Listing 5.36.

```
2024-08-28T15:28:53.276-03:00  INFO 129952 --- [api-reservation] [nio-
8090-exec-9] c.t.f.a.r.connector.CatalogConnector    : using fallback
method for errors on api-catalog
```

*LISTING 5.36* Logs of the execution.

Spring Boot provides an actuator endpoint that allows access to information about a specific bulkhead, helping to understand the application's state at a given moment, as shown in Listing 5.37.

```
→  ~ curl --location 'http://localhost:8090/api/flights/reservation/
management/bulkheads/catalog'
{
    "bulkheadEvents": [
        {
            "bulkheadName": "catalog",
            "type": "CALL_PERMITTED",
            "creationTime": "2024-08-28T15:28:53.127631843-
03:00[America/Argentina/Buenos_Aires]"
        },
        {
            "bulkheadName": "catalog",
            "type": "CALL_FINISHED",
            "creationTime": "2024-08-28T15:28:53.276864593-
03:00[America/Argentina/Buenos_Aires]"
        }
    ]
}
```

*LISTING 5.37* Situation of the bulkhead.

This pattern can be used independently or in combination with others, as demonstrated in the example. It is recommended to always declare a Fallback method to convert the issue into a manageable form for the application, such as throwing a different exception.

## Rate Limit

Suppose an endpoint is expected to handle a high volume of simultaneous requests due to resource-intensive operations, such as heavy CPU or memory usage. In that case, it becomes necessary to limit the number of requests it receives. This can be achieved by implementing the Rate Limit pattern, which restricts the number of requests allowed either concurrently or within a defined time frame.

The configuration of this pattern is relatively simple. It is necessary to specify the number of requests to be supported and the duration of this validation, as illustrated in Listing 5.38.

```
resilience4j.ratelimiter:
  configs:
    default:
      register-health-indicator: false # Not include the request to the
health
      timeout-duration: 1000ms
      limit-refresh-period: 10s #How many seconds count the number of
requests
      limit-for-period: 2 #Number of requests to the same endpoint
```

```
#Configuration for each host or endpoint
instances:
  reservation:
    baseConfig: default
```

**LISTING 5.38** Rate Limit configuration.

The next step is to enable this mechanism in certain parts of the application. In this case, a good idea would be to implement this limit in the controller layer, as shown in Listing 5.39.

```java
package com.twa.flights.api.reservation.controller;

//Previous imports
import io.github.resilience4j.ratelimiter.annotation.RateLimiter;

@Validated
@RestController
@RequestMapping("/")
public class ReservationController {

    //Previous logic

    @GetMapping("/{id}")
    @RateLimiter(name = "reservation", fallbackMethod =
"fallbackGetReservationById")
    public ResponseEntity<ReservationDTO> getReservationById(@
PathVariable Long id) {
    //Previous logic
    }

  private ResponseEntity<ReservationDTO>
fallbackGetReservationById(Long id, RuntimeException exception) {
        LOGGER.info("Exceed the number of request to this endpoint");
        return new ResponseEntity<>(null, HttpStatus.TOO_MANY_REQUESTS);
    }
}
```

**LISTING 5.39** Rate Limit with the Fallback method.

Listing 5.39 illustrates a Fallback method associated with the Rate Limit mechanism, which throws an exception and returns a meaningful response to the client, such as an appropriate HTTP status code. When multiple requests are made to the endpoint to retrieve information about a specific reservation, the logs will reflect entries similar to those shown in Listing 5.40.

```
2024-08-28T14:48:43.808-03:00  INFO 123729 --- [api-reservation] [nio-
8090-exec-8] c.t.f.a.r.c.ReservationController        : Exceed the
number of requests to this endpoint
```

**LISTING 5.40** Logs of the execution.

As with other patterns, Spring Boot provides an endpoint on the actuator to check which rate limiters are registered in the application, as shown in Listing 5.41.

```
➜  ~ curl --location 'http://localhost:8090/api/flights/reservation/
management/ratelimiters'
{
    "rateLimiters": [
        "reservation"
    ]
}
```

*LISTING 5.41* Status of all the rate limiters on the application.

This pattern serves as a practical solution when a specific resource struggles to handle complex operations. It is not advisable to apply it across all endpoints in the application, however.

### What Is the Best Scenario for Using Each of the Patterns?

A common error when individuals reference patterns is employing them excessively. It is advisable to utilize these patterns solely in situations where their necessity is evident, such as in external communications with other microservices. Implementing Circuit Breaker may prove beneficial; however, it is not applicable in every scenario. A default behavior can be established if exceptions arise.

The same situation applies to Rate Limit; its application across all endpoints of the application may adversely impact numerous other applications that utilize these endpoints. It is advisable to implement Rate Limit solely on critical endpoints that influence all applications.

## HOW CAN THE IMPACT OF THE REQUEST BE REDUCED?

On a distributed system, the number of requests increases significantly compared with an old and giant monolith, where most of the communications occur internally. The information that crosses the network, in many cases, such as a catalog with data on countries, cities, and airports, is typically static and does not change frequently. All information that travels across the network adds some delay to the execution time of a process. Additionally, with certain cloud providers, data transfer can increase monthly costs. Therefore, it's essential to implement mechanisms that reduce the number of requests or minimize the size of the data transmitted over the network.

### Methods to Minimize the Impact

Multiple options exist to minimize the information that crosses the network; some help reduce the number of requests between different applications, such as using the cache mechanism, while others involve reducing the response size by compressing or removing attributes.

These mechanisms do not serve as a singular solution for all issues; one may choose to combine several or utilize just one. The decision depends on the user, as each option has its advantages and disadvantages, some of which involve higher memory or CPU usage.

The following section presents some of the most common solutions to mitigate these problems. There are others, but covering them all falls outside the scope of this book.

## Cache

The use of cache is common; there are many implementations of this mechanism, and most of them are connected to the front end, such as downloading CSS or JavaScript files only when they are modified, which reduces the time it takes to load a Web page.

It's possible to apply the same concept to applications, especially for static information about countries, cities, and many other things that do not change frequently. There are at least two different strategies for implementing cache in an application: one involves using the application's memory, and the other consists of delegating the responsibility to an external tool, such as Redis.

### In Memory

Saving information in the application's memory is one of the most common approaches to solving the problem of making multiple requests with the same parameters to other applications. At the same time, it's essential to consider that by depending on the number of elements, their size, and how long each component remains in memory, resource consumption may increase. When used properly, however, this impact is generally minimal.

The first step in providing support for using cache in the application is to add the dependencies shown in Listing 5.42.

```
<dependency>
    <groupId>org.springframework.boot</groupId>
    <artifactId>spring-boot-starter-cache</artifactId>
</dependency>

<dependency>
    <groupId>com.github.ben-manes.caffeine</groupId>
    <artifactId>caffeine</artifactId>
</dependency>
```

*LISTING 5.42* Dependencies to add to the POM file.

The next step is to define the cache configuration, including the duration and the number of elements to save. Refreshing the cache after a specified period can also be configured, as shown in Listing 5.43.

```
cache:
  configuration:
    CATALOG_COUNTRY:
      refreshAfterWriteTime: 5 #MINUTES
      expireAfterWriteTime: 10 #MINUTES
      maxSize: 180
```

*LISTING 5.43* Cache configuration on application.yml.

The approach in Listing 5.43 allows creating different cache configurations based on criteria such as host or endpoint, since it functions like a map.

After that, it's time to create a class that represents the attributes of the configurations that appear in Listing 5.44.

```
package com.twa.flights.api.reservation.configuration.settings;

import java.util.Objects;

public class CacheSettings {

    private Integer refreshAfterWriteTime;
    private Integer expireAfterWriteTime;
    private Integer maxSize;

    private static final Integer DEFAULT_REFRESH_AFTER = 10; //Refresh time
    private static final Integer DEFAULT_EXPIRE_AFTER = 15; //Expiration time
    private static final Integer DEFAULT_MAX_SIZE = 180; //Number of elements

    public static final CacheSettings DEFAULT_CACHE_SETTINGS =
            new CacheSettings(DEFAULT_REFRESH_AFTER,
            DEFAULT_EXPIRE_AFTER, DEFAULT_MAX_SIZE);

    public CacheSettings() {
    }

    public CacheSettings(Integer refreshAfterWriteTime, Integer
expireAfterWriteTime, Integer maxSize) {
        this.refreshAfterWriteTime = refreshAfterWriteTime;
        this.expireAfterWriteTime = expireAfterWriteTime;
        this.maxSize = maxSize;
    }

    public boolean areValid() {
        return expireAfterWriteTime > refreshAfterWriteTime;
    }

    //Setters and getters
}
```

**LISTING 5.44** Class that represents the configuration of one cache.

The previous class included a set of attributes with default values, designed so that if no specific configuration is created for an endpoint or host, this default can be used to prevent the application from failing.

Let's create a class that loads all the information on the node `cache` from `application.yml` to use in the application as it appears in Listing 5.45.

```
package com.twa.flights.api.reservation.configuration.settings;

import org.springframework.boot.context.properties.
ConfigurationProperties;
import org.springframework.context.annotation.Configuration;

import java.util.Map;
@Configuration
@ConfigurationProperties("cache")
public class CacheConfiguration {
    private Map<String, CacheSettings> configuration;
```

```
    public CacheSettings getCacheSettings(final String cacheName) {
        return configuration.getOrDefault(cacheName, CacheSettings.
DEFAULT_CACHE_SETTINGS);
    }

    //Setters and getters
}
```

**LISTING 5.45** Class to load the configuration.

The primary purpose of caching is to define the various caches used within the application and specify their configuration, including duration. One way to achieve this is by creating a class that enables caching with the @EnableCaching[12] annotation. Inside this class, a bean must be defined to configure the CacheManager[13], which is how Spring Boot manages all cache-related settings. Listing 5.46 presents the complete configuration details.

```
package com.twa.flights.api.reservation.configuration;

import java.util.List;
import java.util.concurrent.TimeUnit;
import java.util.function.Function;

import com.github.benmanes.caffeine.cache.Caffeine;
import com.twa.flights.api.reservation.configuration.settings.
CacheConfiguration;
import com.twa.flights.api.reservation.configuration.settings.
CacheSettings;
import com.twa.flights.api.reservation.connector.CatalogConnector;
import org.springframework.beans.factory.annotation.Autowired;
import org.springframework.cache.CacheManager;
import org.springframework.cache.annotation.EnableCaching;
import org.springframework.cache.caffeine.CaffeineCache;
import org.springframework.cache.support.SimpleCacheManager;
import org.springframework.context.annotation.Bean;
import org.springframework.context.annotation.Configuration;


@Configuration
@EnableCaching
public class CacheManagerConfiguration {

    public static final String CATALOG_COUNTRY = "CATALOG_COUNTRY";

    private final CacheConfiguration cacheConfiguration;

    private final CatalogConnector catalogConnector;

    @Autowired
    public CacheManagerConfiguration(final CacheConfiguration
cacheConfiguration,
```

---

[12]https://docs.spring.io/spring-framework/docs/current/javadoc-api/org/springframework/cache/annotation/EnableCaching.html
[13]https://docs.spring.io/spring-framework/docs/current/javadoc-api/org/springframework/cache/CacheManager.html

```
                                             final CatalogConnector
catalogConnector) {
        this.cacheConfiguration = cacheConfiguration;
        this.catalogConnector = catalogConnector;
    }

    //Define a bean with all the caches, and which is the method
responsible for obtaining the value if not exist in the cache
    @Bean
    public CacheManager cacheManager() {
        CacheSettings cacheCitySettings = cacheConfiguration.
getCacheSettings(CATALOG_COUNTRY);

        SimpleCacheManager simpleCacheManager = new
SimpleCacheManager();
        simpleCacheManager.setCaches(List.of(buildCaffeineCache(CATALOG_
COUNTRY, cacheCitySettings, catalogConnector::getCountry)));

        return simpleCacheManager;
    }


    //Define the size, duration, and behaviour of the cache
    public static CaffeineCache buildCaffeineCache(String cacheName,
CacheSettings settings,
                                        Function<String,
Object> serviceCall) {

        return new CaffeineCache(cacheName,
                Caffeine.newBuilder().refreshAfterWrite(settings.
getRefreshAfterWriteTime(), TimeUnit.MINUTES)
                        .expireAfterWrite(settings.
getExpireAfterWriteTime(), TimeUnit.MINUTES)
                        .maximumSize(settings.getMaxSize()).build(key ->
serviceCall.apply(key.toString()))));
    }
}
```

**LISTING 5.46** Class responsible for the cache mechanism.

NOTE *Since Spring Boot 2.x.x, the default implementation of the cache mechanism in memory is Caffeine, which has an excellent performance for saving information in memory.*

The final step in this series of modifications to the application is to specify which method in the application will utilize the cache. In the case of Spring Boot, there is an annotation called @ Cacheable, which works like an interceptor checking whether or not the values exist in cache; in the case that the value exists, return the information from the memory, but in the case that there is no value, the application will execute the logic inside the method to obtain the information and save it into cache before returning the value. The modifications in Listing 5.47 show the use of the @Cacheable annotation.
```
package com.twa.flights.api.reservation.service;
```

```
//Previous imports
import com.twa.flights.api.reservation.configuration.
CacheManagerConfiguration;
import org.springframework.cache.annotation.Cacheable;

@Service
public class CatalogService {

    // Existing logic

  @Cacheable(cacheNames = CacheManagerConfiguration.CATALOG_COUNTRY,
unless = "#result == null")
    public CountryDTO getCountryByCode(String code) {
        return connector.getCountry(code);
    }
}
```

**LISTING 5.47** Enabling support for cache in the connector.

After completing all these modifications, run the application and perform multiple reservation creation operations. Then, check the logs in the Docker container for api-catalog; if everything works correctly, only the log shown in Listing 5.48 will appear.

```
2024-08-27 15:14:15 2024-08-27 18:14:15.127   INFO 1 --- [qtp792782299-
18] c.t.f.a.c.controller.CatalogController   : Obtain all the
information about the country with code AR
```

**LISTING 5.48** Log of api-catalog.

One last note about this approach: If the application is stopped or another instance of the same application is started, the cached information will not be retained in either case. The cache will populate it with the requests it receives and not share the information with other applications or instances.

### Distributed

Another alternative to using a cache mechanism across different instances of the same or other applications is to store the information in a central location that everyone can access. The solution in this case involves using a database such as Redis, which allows specifying the TTL for stored elements.

The first step is adding an image of Redis to docker-compose.yml to save the information of the cache that appears in Listing 5.49.

```
api-reservation-cache-db:
    container_name: api-reservation-cache-db
    image: redis:alpine
    restart: always
    ports:
      - 6081:6379
```

**LISTING 5.49** New service in the Docker Compose file.

The next step involves adding Redis support to the application using the appropriate driver, since the information will be serialized before being saved. The two required dependencies for the POM file are the same as those shown in Listing 5.50.

```
<dependency>
        <groupId>org.springframework.boot</groupId>
        <artifactId>spring-boot-starter-data-redis</artifactId>
</dependency>

<dependency>
        <groupId>redis.clients</groupId>
        <artifactId>jedis</artifactId>
</dependency>
```

**LISTING 5.50** Dependencies to add to the POM file.

After including the dependencies, it's relevant to include in the configuration file the information about Redis, such as the host and port, as shown in Listing 5.51.

```
redis:
  remote-cache:
    host: localhost
    port: 6081
```

**LISTING 5.51** Configuration of Redis in application.yml.

It's time to create a class that represents the configuration of Redis, as in Listing 5.52.

```
package com.twa.flights.api.reservation.configuration.settings;

public class RedisSettings {

    private String host;
    private int port;

    //Setters and getters
}
```

**LISTING 5.52** Class to load the settings of Redis.

One of the key aspects of this approach is loading and configuring `RedisTemplate` to execute database operations, as shown in Listing 5.53.

```
package com.twa.flights.api.reservation.configuration;

import com.twa.flights.api.reservation.configuration.settings.
RedisSettings;
import com.twa.flights.api.reservation.connector.response.CountryDTO;
import org.springframework.boot.context.properties.
ConfigurationProperties;
import org.springframework.context.annotation.Bean;
import org.springframework.context.annotation.Configuration;
import org.springframework.data.redis.connection.
RedisStandaloneConfiguration;
```

```
import org.springframework.data.redis.connection.jedis.
JedisConnectionFactory;
import org.springframework.data.redis.core.RedisTemplate;

import java.util.Map;

@Configuration
@ConfigurationProperties
public class RedisConfiguration {

    private Map<String, RedisSettings> redis;

    @Bean
    public JedisConnectionFactory catalogJedisConnectionFactory() {
        RedisSettings settings = redis.get("remote-cache");
        RedisStandaloneConfiguration redisStandaloneConfiguration = new Re
disStandaloneConfiguration(settings.getHost(),
                settings.getPort());
        return new JedisConnectionFactory(redisStandaloneConfiguration);
    }

    @Bean
    public RedisTemplate<String, CountryDTO> catalogRedisTemplate() {
        RedisTemplate<String, CountryDTO> redisTemplate = new
RedisTemplate<>();
        redisTemplate.setConnectionFactory(catalogJedisConnectionFacto
ry());

        return redisTemplate;
    }

    //Setters and getters
}
```

**LISTING 5.53** Configuration of RedisTemplate.

There are multiple ways to save the information in a database. In the case of Redis, as other applications may use different languages for the saved information, it is a good idea to save it as JSON. To provide flexibility in how information is saved, Redis offers a serializer.

Listing 5.54 contains the default code to use a serializer to save different objects.

```
package com.twa.flights.api.reservation.serializer;

import java.io.IOException;

import org.slf4j.Logger;
import org.slf4j.LoggerFactory;

import com.fasterxml.jackson.databind.DeserializationFeature;
import com.fasterxml.jackson.databind.MapperFeature;
import com.fasterxml.jackson.databind.ObjectMapper;
import com.fasterxml.jackson.databind.PropertyNamingStrategy;
import com.fasterxml.jackson.datatype.jsr310.JavaTimeModule;
```

```
public class JsonSerializer {
    private static final Logger LOGGER = LoggerFactory.
getLogger(JsonSerializer.class);
    private static final ObjectMapper OBJECT_MAPPER;

    private JsonSerializer() {
        // just to avoid create instances
    }

    static {
        OBJECT_MAPPER = new ObjectMapper().configure(MapperFeature.USE_
GETTERS_AS_SETTERS, false)
                    .configure(DeserializationFeature.FAIL_ON_UNKNOWN_
PROPERTIES, false)
                    .setPropertyNamingStrategy(PropertyNamingStrategy.SNAKE_
CASE).registerModule(new JavaTimeModule());
    }

    public static byte[] serialize(Object object) {
        byte[] compressedJson = null;
        try {
            compressedJson = OBJECT_MAPPER.writeValueAsString(object).
getBytes();
        } catch (IOException e) {
            LOGGER.error("Error serializing object: {}",
e.getMessage());
        }
        return compressedJson;
    }

    public static <T> T deserialize(byte[] raw, Class<T> reference) {
        if (raw == null)
            return null;

        T object = null;
        try {
            object = OBJECT_MAPPER.readValue(raw, reference);
        } catch (IOException e) {
            LOGGER.error("Can't deserialize object: {}",
e.getMessage());
        }
        return object;
    }
}
```

**LISTING 5.54** General serializer to transform an object.

Listing 5.54 contains generic code without reference to any specific class; therefore, to use it, another serializer must be defined that applies the logic from GeneralSerializer, as demonstrated in Listing 5.55.

```
package com.twa.flights.api.reservation.serializer;

import com.twa.flights.api.reservation.connector.response.CountryDTO;
import org.springframework.data.redis.serializer.RedisSerializer;
```

```
import org.springframework.stereotype.Service;
@Service
public class CountrySerializer implements RedisSerializer<CountryDTO> {

    @Override
    public byte[] serialize(CountryDTO clusterSearch) {
        return JsonSerializer.serialize(clusterSearch);
    }

    @Override
    public CountryDTO deserialize(byte[] bytes) {
        return JsonSerializer.deserialize(bytes, CountryDTO.class);
    }
}
```

**LISTING 5.55** Country serializer to transform the information.

The final modification step involves updating the `CacheManager` code to switch from using in-memory storage to Redis, specifically configuring the serializer to store data in the database. Listing 5.56 demonstrates how to modify the previous configuration, taking into account the use of Redis.

```
package com.twa.flights.api.reservation.configuration;

import java.time.Duration;
import java.util.List;
import java.util.Objects;
import java.util.concurrent.TimeUnit;
import java.util.function.Function;

import com.github.benmanes.caffeine.cache.Caffeine;
import com.twa.flights.api.reservation.configuration.settings.
CacheConfiguration;
import com.twa.flights.api.reservation.configuration.settings.
CacheSettings;
import com.twa.flights.api.reservation.connector.CatalogConnector;
import com.twa.flights.api.reservation.serializer.CountrySerializer;
import org.springframework.beans.factory.annotation.Autowired;
import org.springframework.cache.CacheManager;
import org.springframework.cache.annotation.EnableCaching;
import org.springframework.cache.caffeine.CaffeineCache;
import org.springframework.cache.support.SimpleCacheManager;
import org.springframework.context.annotation.Bean;
import org.springframework.context.annotation.Configuration;
import org.springframework.data.redis.cache.RedisCacheConfiguration;
import org.springframework.data.redis.cache.RedisCacheManager;
import org.springframework.data.redis.connection.jedis.
JedisConnectionFactory;
import org.springframework.data.redis.serializer.
RedisSerializationContext;
import org.springframework.data.redis.serializer.StringRedisSerializer;
```

```java
@Configuration
@EnableCaching
public class CacheManagerConfiguration {

    public static final String CATALOG_COUNTRY = "CATALOG_COUNTRY";

    private final CacheConfiguration cacheConfiguration;

    private final JedisConnectionFactory catalogJedisConnectionFactory;

    private final CountrySerializer countrySerializer;

    @Autowired
    public CacheManagerConfiguration(final CacheConfiguration
cacheConfiguration,
                                     final JedisConnectionFactory
catalogJedisConnectionFactory,
                                     final CountrySerializer
countrySerializer) {
        this.cacheConfiguration = cacheConfiguration;
        this.catalogJedisConnectionFactory =
catalogJedisConnectionFactory;
        this.countrySerializer = countrySerializer;
    }

    @Bean
    public CacheManager cacheManager() {
        SimpleCacheManager simpleCacheManager = new
SimpleCacheManager();
        simpleCacheManager.setCaches(List.of(Objects.requireNonNull(Redi
sCacheManager.builder(catalogJedisConnectionFactory)
                .cacheDefaults(redisCacheConfiguration()).build().
getCache(CATALOG_COUNTRY))));

        return simpleCacheManager;
    }

    private RedisCacheConfiguration redisCacheConfiguration() {
        CacheSettings cacheCitySettings = cacheConfiguration.
getCacheSettings(CATALOG_COUNTRY);
        return RedisCacheConfiguration.defaultCacheConfig()
                .serializeKeysWith(
                        RedisSerializationContext.SerializationPair.
fromSerializer(new StringRedisSerializer()))
                .serializeValuesWith(RedisSerializationContext.
SerializationPair.fromSerializer(countrySerializer))
                .entryTtl(Duration.ofMinutes(cacheCitySettings.
getExpireAfterWriteTime())));
    }
}
```

**LISTING 5.56** Modifications to the Cache Manager.

Run the application with the modification, execute the request multiple times to create reservations, and check the logs to verify whether a request is present in the API. After that, stop the application and repeat the process. If everything works fine, the log appearing on the console is the same as in Listing 5.57, without any reference to a request to the API.

```
2024-08-29T14:42:55.713-03:00  INFO 223754 --- [api-reservation] [nio-
8090-exec-3] c.t.f.a.r.c.ReservationController      : Saving new
reservation
```

**LISTING 5.57** Logs of the execution of the flow.

This mechanism serves as a good option for saving information across different applications and reducing the number of requests. It does, however, introduce a potential point of failure and a source of latency that can affect the endpoint's response time.

## Compression

The information in a response has a specific size, whether it is big or small. The main problem is not the size; it's the number of requests that one API response with that size produces, because there is some cost associated with the transference of information. This depends exclusively on each cloud provider. Sometimes, the data takes longer to cross the network if it's too long.

One possible approach to addressing the issue with a response's size is to compress it in cases where the client exclusively requests the information in a compressed format. Let's see an example of this problem related to the case study of this book. An entire search flow is around 116.69 KB without any compression, but the same flow applying compression reduces to 27.05 KB. Imagine the same situation but with hundreds of requests per second; the difference is even more evident.

> **NOTE** *Keep in mind that compression and decompression can increase CPU usage. The CPU percentage depends on the response size and the number of simultaneous requests.*

Compressing the response requires adding support to react responding with a gzip format Spring Boot provides a simple way to do this, adding support for the configuration, as shown in Listing 5.58.

```
server:
    #Other configurations
    compression:
        enabled: true
        min-response-size: 2048
        mime-types: application/json,application/xml,text/html,text/
xml,text/plain
```

**LISTING 5.58** Add support to compress the response.

With a slight modification to Listing 5.58, all clients who request compressed information will receive it in that format. The primary benefit is to modify the application's connector to request compressed details from other applications. Including a header on the WebClient is all that's needed, as shown in Listing 5.59.

```
//Previous code

public abstract class TWAConnector {

    protected WebClient getConnector(HostConfiguration hostConfiguration,
EndpointConfiguration endpointConfiguration) {
```

```
    //Previous code
    return WebClient.builder()
                .baseUrl("http://" + hostConfiguration.getHost() + ":" +
hostConfiguration.getPort())
                .defaultHeader(HttpHeaders.CONTENT_TYPE, MediaType.
APPLICATION_JSON_VALUE)
                .defaultHeader(HttpHeaders.ACCEPT, MediaType.
APPLICATION_JSON_VALUE)
                .defaultHeader(HttpHeaders.ACCEPT_ENCODING, "gzip") //
Accept compress response
                .clientConnector(new ReactorClientHttpConnector(httpClie
nt)).build();
    }
}
```

**LISTING 5.59** Requiring a compressed response on the communication.

The final step is to verify that everything works correctly by simply requesting the reservation information, using the header to indicate the application's response format. Listing 5.60 presents the `curl` command used to save the response into a file, allowing verification that the format differs from a standard JSON format.

```
➜  ~ curl --location 'http://localhost:8090/api/flights/reservation/1'
--header 'Accept-Encoding: gzip' > file.txt
```

**LISTING 5.60** curl command to check the compression.

Opening the file reveals content similar to that shown in Listing 5.61.

```
\8B\00\00\00\00\00\00\FFL\8E?o\83@f\8Bg\F5hhS+E\8AX\DAnQs\B8\E1\A4\
FB\83\EÈ"\BE{}Q\8Bby\F1\CF\EF\D9\EFf\80F'\D8x\8A\97Vf(\A1\80D\F5\B8\8D\
A6D\FEJ1As\B9\FD\DB~LL⊃#Q\BD\FB!R\A9ð}\A2\D6A\D0\F4\EC\C8s7\BB\9E\A2,\
EA\E3\EBKux.\D5\C3\F2k\99\B2\E7ƅ=\B2\AD\E1%\DF\FE8
\EBM\E4q\C0T}\ACvOJ\D6\EFt\F0\8C\9A\A1˙1Y\9A\C6\E0i{Yj\F5Wr\8B+4\E5\84{\
BCg\BBf\B8\D7\C1\C1\BA\FE\00\00\FF\FF\00$\D1P\00\00
```

**LISTING 5.61** Content of the file with the response of the endpoint.

Most tools, such as Insomnia and Postman, automatically detect compressed responses and decompress them, so the response will never appear in an unreadable format.

## Remove Empty Values

Another option to reduce the information transfer across the network is to exclude all the null attributes from the response. This option has some considerations. The clients need to be supported so that the reaction can be dynamic and so that all the attributes appear only in some cases.

Listing 5.62 presents the class that creates it, along with the configuration required to exclude null values from the response.

```java
package com.twa.flights.api.reservation.configuration;

import java.util.List;

import org.springframework.context.annotation.Configuration;
import org.springframework.http.converter.HttpMessageConverter;
import org.springframework.http.converter.json.
MappingJackson2HttpMessageConverter;
import org.springframework.web.servlet.config.annotation.WebMvcConfigurer;

import com.fasterxml.jackson.annotation.JsonInclude.Include;
import com.fasterxml.jackson.databind.DeserializationFeature;
import com.fasterxml.jackson.databind.ObjectMapper;

@Configuration
public class WebConfiguration implements WebMvcConfigurer {

    @Override
    public void configureMessageConverters(List<HttpMessageConverter<?>>
converters) {
        for (HttpMessageConverter<?> converter : converters) {
            if (converter instanceof MappingJackson2HttpMessageConverter
messageConverter) {
                ObjectMapper objectIdMapper = messageConverter.
getObjectMapper();
                objectIdMapper.configure(DeserializationFeature.FAIL_ON_
UNKNOWN_PROPERTIES, false);
                objectIdMapper.setSerializationInclusion(Include.NON_
NULL);
            }
        }
    }
}
```

**LISTING 5.62** Remove null attributes on the response.

Afterward, to verify whether the code functions correctly, some attributes in the database can be set to null before making a request. A possible response is shown in Listing 5.63.

```
➜  ~ curl --location --request GET 'http://localhost:8090/api/flights/
reservation/5' \
--header 'Content-Type: application/json'

{
    "id": 5,
    "itineraryId": "69c18158-e28b-48b5-85ab-174b40035b40",
    "searchId": "TWA_g=2024-08-23T17:50:52.236303_f=BUE,MIA_t=MIA,BUE_
d=2024-09-29,2024-10-03_a=1_c=1_i=1",
    "passengers": [
        {
            "id": 4,
            "firstName": "Andres",
```

```
            "lastName": "Sacco",
            "nationality": "ARG",
            "birthday": "1985-01-01"
        }
    ],
    "contact": {
        "id": 5
    }
}
```

**LISTING 5.63** Curl command to check the removal of null values.

This approach reduces information use by a small amount, but the reduction in the number of requests is considerable.

## SUMMARY

Communication is crucial in applications, especially microservices, so ensure it is done well. All applications must consider errors and define timeouts for each endpoint to reduce the risk that problems in one particular endpoint could affect a request from another application at some point.

One key point in communication is reducing latency. Options exist, such as using different cache mechanisms, compressing the response, or removing null values. Each option has its pros and cons that must be considered carefully, as they impact the application's performance.

# TESTING DIFFERENT ASPECTS

Creating an application is a complex process that involves analyzing requirements, defining endpoints, and determining which other applications need to be invoked to complete a particular flow. This process involves communicating with many people to resolve doubts or make an agreement about the request/response of the different endpoints.

All of these processes require time to complete. Initially, manually running the applications and making requests to the different endpoints can be an effective way to verify that everything works correctly. To improve quality and reduce the risk of critical issues in any environment, however, the best approach is to create tests that can be executed with a simple command. This chapter presents various types of testing designed to help verify different aspects of the application before deployment.

## WHAT DOES TESTING APPLICATIONS INVOLVE?

Creating tests involves multiple steps, such as determining which cases or scenarios require coverage or validation. It is important to consider situations beyond the happy path, where everything works smoothly. Scenarios in which various issues could impact the application must be considered.

Testing on an application should involve the minimum possible manual intervention to validate that everything is okay, proving that anyone can execute the test locally or in a pipeline where it's not necessarily connected to any external service. With this in mind, it is essential to ensure that the test functions correctly in terms of any communication involving another service, regardless of the type of test being conducted.

Another relevant aspect is ensuring that each test uses a unique set of data to reduce the possibility of conflict with other scenarios; this is especially useful in integration or end-to-end tests, where one test could affect the context of another.

## WHICH KINDS OF TESTS EXIST?

One topic that generates different opinions is the type of test to employ, as many people use the different terms interchangeably, such as unit tests to describe integration tests. This creates various challenges, including the complexity of creating each test scenario, the time required for team members to develop the tests, and the risk of not covering all possible scenarios, which increases the likelihood of critical issues occurring in production.

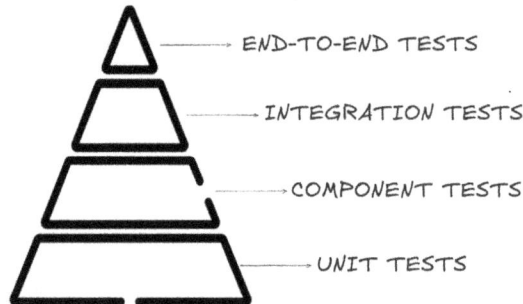

FIGURE 6.1 Types of testing.

The pyramid in Figure 6.1 illustrates four different layers or types of tests; in some cases, integration and component tests are considered the same layer. The debate over the boundary between component and integration tests is a longstanding one. Opinions vary depending on the programming language used in the application, but for this book, both concepts are treated as equivalent.

The following sections explain how to create different types of tests for an application without going into an in-depth explanation of each kind. To reduce the complexity and execution time of running multiple tests, the application includes different profiles in the POM file, with each profile executing a specific set of tests.

## Unit Tests

Unit tests, shown at the bottom of Figure 6.1, are the foundational type of tests. These tests help verify or validate the application's behavior in scenarios where other tests may not be feasible or would require more complex setups. In the case of Java, the debate over which library to use for testing has been settled for many years, with JUnit as the default testing framework, supported by Mockito. Additionally, Spring Boot includes both dependencies by default within a Spring Boot test, so explicit inclusion in the application is not necessary. It is only required to ensure that the POM file contains the dependency shown in Listing 6.1.

```
<dependency>
   <groupId>org.springframework.boot</groupId>
   <artifactId>spring-boot-starter-test</artifactId>
   <scope>test</scope>
</dependency>
```

LISTING 6.1 Spring Boot tests dependency.

Suppose it is necessary to include the dependencies explicitly, either to use a different version or for other reasons. This can be done as shown in Listing 6.2. It is, however, essential to consider adding exclusions for the dependencies included in `spring-boot-starter-test`.

```
<dependencies>
    <!-- Other dependencies -->

    <!-- JUnit 5 -->
    <dependency>
        <groupId>org.junit.jupiter</groupId>
        <artifactId>junit-jupiter-api</artifactId>
        <version>5.10.0</version>
        <scope>test</scope>
    </dependency>
    <dependency>
        <groupId>org.junit.jupiter</groupId>
        <artifactId>junit-jupiter-engine</artifactId>
        <version>5.10.0</version>
        <scope>test</scope>
    </dependency>

    <!-- Mockito -->
    <dependency>
        <groupId>org.mockito</groupId>
        <artifactId>mockito-core</artifactId>
        <version>5.4.0</version>
        <scope>test</scope>
    </dependency>

    <!-- Mockito with JUnit 5 Integration -->
    <dependency>
        <groupId>org.mockito</groupId>
        <artifactId>mockito-junit-jupiter</artifactId>
        <version>5.4.0</version>
        <scope>test</scope>
    </dependency>
</dependencies>
```

**LISTING 6.2** Explicit declaration of the dependencies to write tests.

Knowing the basic annotations for using JUnit, as listed in Table 6.1, is required before writing automated tests.

**TABLE 6.1** Annotations on JUnit.

| Annotation | Description |
| --- | --- |
| @Test | Annotates a method as a JUnit test method. The process should have a public scope and a void return type. |
| @BeforeEach | Marks a method to run before every test method. It is useful for setting up test fixtures. The @Before method of a superclass is run before the current class. |
| @AfterEach | Marks a method to be run after every test method. It is useful for tearing down test fixtures. The @After method of a superclass is run before the current class. |

*(Continued)*

**TABLE 6.1** Continued

| Annotation | Description |
|---|---|
| @Disabled | Marks a method to be ignored during test runs. This helps avoid the need to comment on half-baked test methods. |
| @BeforeAll | Annotates a method to run before any test method is run. The process is run only once for a test case and can be used to provide class-level setup work. |
| @AfterAll | Annotates a method to run after all the test methods are run. This can be useful for performing any cleanups at a class level. |
| @ExtendWith | Specifies the class and extends the test methods for another class. |

Many others exist on JUnit, but covering them all is beyond the scope of this book. A simple example of this type of test using JUnit is what appears in Listing 6.3.

```
import org.junit.jupiter.api.Test;

import static org.junit.jupiter.api.Assertions.assertFalse;
import static org.junit.jupiter.api.Assertions.assertTrue;

public class StringUtilsTest {
    @Test
    public void shouldReturnTrueWithNull() {
        assertTrue(StringUtils.isEmpty(null));
    }
}
```

**LISTING 6.3** Example of unit tests.

Another relevant aspect before writing a unit test is knowing the most appropriate methods in the Mockito library, which are shown in Table 6.2.

**TABLE 6.2** Mockito methods.

| Method | Description |
|---|---|
| mock | This method creates a mock for a specific class, enabling the interception of all invocations and the modification of the class's behavior as required. |
| verify | This method helps verify whether a particular mock was invoked with specific parameters, which is crucial for ensuring the logic functions correctly. |
| any | This method specifies that the mock should adopt a new behavior whenever it receives a value. |
| doThrow | This method can trigger an exception when the mock is invoked under certain conditions. |
| when / given | This method allows defining the condition under which the mock invocation should be executed. |

*The objective of this section is not to explain how to create tests using JUnit or Mockito; instead, it aims to provide a brief introduction to the importance of creating unit tests and to compare them with other types, such as integration tests, which play a crucial role in verifying whether all components function correctly.*

After including the dependencies in the unit tests, the next step is to declare a class that contains all the scenarios to validate, such as mocking all external communication with other services. Let's, for example, test `CatalogService`, which interacts with `CatalogConnector`. The scope of the unit test is only to check that all the logic inside that class works, assuming that someone creates a test for the connector. An example of this test is shown in Listing 6.4.

```
package com.twa.flights.api.reservation.service;

import com.twa.flights.api.reservation.connector.CatalogConnector;
import com.twa.flights.api.reservation.connector.response.CountryDTO;
import org.junit.jupiter.api.BeforeEach;
import org.junit.jupiter.api.Test;
import org.mockito.InjectMocks;
import org.mockito.Mock;
import org.mockito.MockitoAnnotations;

import static org.mockito.Mockito.*;
import static org.junit.jupiter.api.Assertions.*;

class CatalogServiceTest {

    @Mock
    private CatalogConnector catalogConnector;

    @InjectMocks
    private CatalogService catalogService;

    @BeforeEach
    void setUp() {
        MockitoAnnotations.openMocks(this);
    }

    @Test
    void should_return_information_for_a_country() {
        // Arrange
        String countryCode = "US";
        CountryDTO country = new CountryDTO();
        country.setCode(countryCode);
        country.setName("United States");

        when(catalogConnector.getCountry(countryCode)).
thenReturn(country);

        // Act
        CountryDTO result - catalogService.
getCountryByCode(countryCode);
```

```
        // Assert
        assertNotNull(result);
        assertEquals(countryCode, result.getCode());
        assertEquals("United States", result.getName());

        // Verify that the connector's getCountry method was called once
        verify(catalogConnector, times(1)).getCountry(countryCode);
    }

    //Other test cases
}
```

**LISTING 6.4** Service tests to check whether the business logic works.

The test example in Listing 6.4 mocks all external communication, proving a default behavior in the sentence that starts with the keyword when and verifying the invocation of that mock at the end of the test. Another point to note about the previous code block is that the test is split into different sections to understand the relevance of the code lines, such as which are responsible for setting the context and which are responsible for validating the results.

**NOTE**
*A critical aspect of this type of test is to avoid starting the application under any circumstances. Doing so would turn the test into an integration test, as multiple components become involved in the application's execution. Unit tests should remain simple, minimizing the number of elements required for their execution.*

Another example of a test is the controller, which may be considered optional, as integration tests can provide similar coverage. If there is logic within this layer, however, it is advisable to include a few targeted tests, such as those shown in Listing 6.5.

```
package com.twa.flights.api.reservation.controller;

import com.twa.flights.api.reservation.service.ReservationService;
import com.twa.flights.api.reservation.dto.ReservationDTO;
import org.junit.jupiter.api.BeforeEach;
import org.junit.jupiter.api.Test;
import org.mockito.InjectMocks;
import org.mockito.Mock;
import org.mockito.MockitoAnnotations;
import org.springframework.http.HttpStatus;
import org.springframework.http.ResponseEntity;

import java.util.ArrayList;
import java.util.List;

import static org.junit.jupiter.api.Assertions.*;
import static org.mockito.Mockito.*;

class ReservationControllerTest {

    @Mock
    private ReservationService reservationService;
```

```
    @InjectMocks
    private ReservationController reservationController;

    @BeforeEach
    void setUp() {
        MockitoAnnotations.openMocks(this);
    }

    @Test
    void should_get_reservation_that_exist() {
        // Arrange
        Long reservationId = 1L;
        ReservationDTO reservation = new ReservationDTO(reservationId,
null, null, null, null);

        when(reservationService.getReservationById(reservationId)).
thenReturn(reservation);

        // Act
        ResponseEntity<ReservationDTO> response = reservationController.
getReservationById(reservationId);

        // Assert
        assertNotNull(response);
        assertEquals(HttpStatus.OK, response.getStatusCode());
        assertNotNull(response.getBody());
        assertEquals(reservationId, response.getBody().id());

        // Verify that the service's getReservationById method was
called once
        verify(reservationService, times(1)).getReservationById(reservat
ionId);
    }
}
```

**LISTING 6.5** Controller tests to check whether everything works.

The last step of this process is running all the tests using the Maven command, as shown in Listing 6.6.

```
➜   ~ mvn test
[INFO] Scanning for projects...
[INFO]
[INFO] ----------------------< com.twa:api-reservation >----------------
[INFO] Building api-reservation 0.0.1-SNAPSHOT
[INFO]   from pom.xml
[INFO] --------------------------------[ jar ]--------------------------
......

[INFO] ---------------------------------------------------------
[INFO]  T E S T S
[INFO] ---------------------------------------------------------
......
[INFO] Tests run: 2, Failures: 0, Errors: 0, Skipped: 0, Time elapsed:
0.509 s -- in com.twa.flights.api.reservation.service.ClusterServiceTest
```

```
[INFO] Running com.twa.flights.api.reservation.service.CatalogServiceTest
[INFO] Tests run: 2, Failures: 0, Errors: 0, Skipped: 0, Time elapsed:
0.023 s -- in com.twa.flights.api.reservation.service.CatalogServiceTest
[INFO] Running com.twa.flights.api.reservation.controller.
ReservationControllerTest
[INFO] Tests run: 5, Failures: 0, Errors: 0, Skipped: 0, Time
elapsed: 0.042 s -- in com.twa.flights.api.reservation.controller.
ReservationControllerTest
[INFO]
[INFO] Results:
[INFO]
[INFO] Tests run: 9, Failures: 0, Errors: 0, Skipped: 0
[INFO]
[INFO] -----------------------------------------------------------------
[INFO] BUILD SUCCESS
[INFO] -----------------------------------------------------------------
[INFO] Total time:  2.997 s
[INFO] Finished at: 2024-09-18T11:24:04-03:00
[INFO] -----------------------------------------------------------------
```

**LISTING 6.6** Execution of the tests.

Consider using this type of test to validate the layers that contain a certain level of logic, excluding layers such as exceptions and models, which typically contain simple logic.

**NOTE** *Many other tests can be created to validate different parts of the application's logic. The purpose of this chapter, however, is not to present all possible scenarios, but rather to demonstrate the basics of each type of test.*

## Integration Tests

Integration tests are the second step of the pyramid, which is responsible for validating the interaction of all application components, excluding communication with external elements such as databases or other microservices, at least in the actual implementation of those components.

The discussion about which is the best option, considering the different types of frameworks and libraries in the world of integration testing, is complex because there are so many. Some are extremely well documented, while others lack basic documentation on how to use them and have limited user communities, which can pose challenges if issues arise during the creation of these tests. Some libraries have resolved this by ensuring they have plenty of documentation and encouraging an active community: Spring Boot, Karate[1], and REST Assured[2].

Table 6.3 provides a brief overview of the features to consider when selecting the best option.

---

[1]https://karatelabs.github.io/karate/
[2]https://rest-assured.io/

**TABLE 6.3** Main things to consider when choosing an option.

| Feature | Spring Boot | Karate | REST Assured |
|---|:---:|:---:|:---:|
| Well documented | ✔ | ✔ | ✔ |
| A significant number of users use it | ✔ | ✔ | ✔ |
| Possibility to combine use with other tools | ✘ | ✔ | ✘ |
| Helps with creating different types of tests | ✘ | ✔ | ✔ |
| Library or framework agnostic | ✘ | ✔ | ✔ |

There are notable differences between Karate and REST Assured. Overall, Karate is the best because it allows combining other tools, such as Gatling[3] to create performance tests or Playwright[4] to carry out tests on the UI.

### How Are Integration Tests Created?

Karate is a simple library that minimizes the complexity involved in adding support to an application. The first step is to add the dependencies to the POM file, as shown in Listing 6.7.

```
<dependencies>

        <! -- Other dependencies -->

    <dependency>
        <groupId>com.intuit.karate</groupId>
        <artifactId>karate-junit5</artifactId>
        <version>1.4.1</version>
        <scope>test</scope>
    </dependency>
</dependencies>

<! -- Other definitions -->

<profiles>
    <profile>
        <id>IT</id>
        <build>
            <plugins>
                <plugin>
                    <groupId>org.apache.maven.plugins</groupId>
                    <artifactId>maven-surefire-plugin</
artifactId>
                    <version>3.1.2</version>
                    <configuration>
                        <includes>

    <include>**/ApiITTest.java</include>
                        </includes>
```

---

[3]https://gatling.io/
[4]https://playwright.dev/

```
                                    <argLine>-Dfile.encoding=UTF-8</
argLine>
                                    <argLine>-
XX:+EnableDynamicAgentLoading</argLine>
                                </configuration>
                            </plugin>
                        </plugins>
                </build>
        </profile>
</profile>
```

*LISTING 6.7* Adding Karate dependencies.

The new profile includes the Maven Surefire dependency, which enables exporting execution results in multiple formats. Karate considers this output when generating its reports.

**NOTE**
*As a best practice, all of the previous tests should be placed inside a package named* unit, *which allows different types of tests to be grouped into separate folders. This helps reduce the complexity of understanding the scope of each file.*

The next step is to create a file named `karate-config.js`, located in `src/test/resources`, with the content shown in Listing 6.8. This file contains all information related to the configuration of the tests, including the base path for executing the various tests. Different configurations can be maintained depending on the environment, if preferred.

```
function fn() {
    let env = karate.env; // get system property 'karate.env'
    karate.log('karate.env system property was:', env);
    if (!env) {
        env = 'dev';
    }
    const config = {
        env: env,
        AppUrl: '/api/flights/reservation' //The URL of the API
    };
    if (env === 'dev') {
        config.AppUrl = 'http://127.0.0.1:8090' + config.AppUrl //The
entire URL with the host
    } else if (env === 'e2e') {
        config.AppUrl = 'http://127.0.0.1:8090' + config.AppUrl
    }
    return config;
}
```

*LISTING 6.8* Karate configuration.

As shown in Listing 6.8, the file defines a variable called `AppUrl`, which can be reused across all tests. This helps avoid writing the full path each time a request needs to be executed.

As a good practice, the `application.yml` file used by the application should be copied into `src/test/resources`, with minor adjustments to limit the information exposed by the actuator and keep the tests simple. The changes are related to the level of detail of the `info` endpoint, which is shown in Listing 6.9.

```
# Previous configuration

management:

  # Previous configuration
  endpoint:
    health:
      show-details: never
      probes:
        enabled: false

# Previous configuration
```

**LISTING 6.9** application.yml with the modifications.

After creating the configuration, the next step is to create a Karate test using Gherkin. To do this, let's create a file called `health.feature` and place it in `src/test/java/com/twa/flights/api/reservation/integration/actuator/` with the content that appears in Listing 6.10.

```
Feature: Health of Spring Boot
  Background:
    * url AppUrl #Load from the configuration
    * def health_response_ok = read('./response/health_response.json')

  Scenario: Obtain information about whether the application is healthy
or not
    Given path 'management/health' #The URL to make the request
    When method GET #HTTP method to execute
    Then status 200 #HTTP Status of the response
    And match response == health_response_ok
```

**LISTING 6.10** First Karate test.

As shown in the text, following the word `Feature`, this file contains a test that verifies whether the actuator's health endpoint functions correctly. The structure may appear unusual, as it differs from conventional test declarations such as those in JUnit. Table 6.4 explains the meaning of each relevant keyword in Gherkin.

**TABLE 6.4** Gherkin's most relevant keywords.

| Keyword | Description |
| --- | --- |
| Feature | This keyword provides a high-level description of the various scenarios. |
| Background | This typically indicates that something needs to be done before executing one or more tests. Placing all the variables used across scenarios in a central location is considered a good practice. |
| Scenario | This keyword is used to represent a specific test or scenario to be validated. |
| Given | This describes the initial context or preconditions for the scenario. It is the starting point of the test. |
| When | This specifies the action or event that triggers the behavior in the scenario. |
| Then | This describes the expected outcome or result of the action performed in the When step. |

***TABLE 6.4*** Continued

| Keyword | Description |
|---------|-------------|
| And | This is used to concatenate multiple `Given`, `When`, or `Then` steps in a scenario. |
| def | This word is used when declaring a variable. |
| match | This is responsible for validating something in the response. It is possible to validate the entire response or just a single attribute. |

The previous table covers all the relevant keywords, but in Listing 6.10, there is the word `read`, which is not one of the Karate keywords. This term refers to a feature that Karate provides to simplify everyday tasks, such as reading files, writing files, printing a string, or logging information, but there are many other functions available.

Considering the existence of these functions, it is a good idea to include the expected result in the tests because while the JSON could be short, in some cases, it could have hundreds of lines. With this in mind, create a file called `health_response.json` located in `src/test/resources/com/twa/flights/api/reservation/integration/actuator/response/` with the response content that appears in Listing 6.11.

```
{"status": "UP"}
```

***LISTING 6.11*** Response file.

Let's create another test to validate whether the `info` endpoint works fine. To do this, create a file called `health.feature` in the exact location of the previous tests with the content that appears in Listing 6.12.

```
Feature: Info of Spring Boot
  Background:
    * url AppUrl
    * def info_response_ok = read('./response/info_response.json')

  Scenario: Obtain information about the application
    Given path 'management/info'
    When method GET
    Then status 200
    And match response == info_response_ok
```

***LISTING 6.12*** Test to validate the info endpoint.

Both tests are similar and straightforward to replicate with other endpoints if necessary. Let's create a file called `info_response.json` located in the same place as the previous response with the response content that appears in Listing 6.13.

```
{
  "app": {
    "name": #notnull,
    "version": #notnull
  },
```

```
  "contact": {
    "email": "sacco.andres@gmail.com",
    "slack": "adsacco"
  },
  "reservation-stats": {
    "amount": #notnull
  }
}
```

**LISTING 6.13** info response.

As shown in Listing 6.13, some unusual values appear that are not part of the standard JSON format but are specific to Karate. These values represent dynamic content or fields where exact validation is not necessary. This approach is beneficial in scenarios such as creating new entities in a database, where IDs may vary, or when fields include timestamps for creation, updates, or other operations. Table 6.5 highlights the most relevant of these wildcards.

**TABLE 6.5** Karate wildcards.

| Wildcard | Description |
| --- | --- |
| #notnull | Ensures the field is not null |
| #null | Ensures the field is null |
| #string | Ensures the field is a string |
| #number | Ensures the field is a number |
| #boolean | Ensures the field is a boolean |
| #array | Ensures the field is an array |
| #object | Ensures the field is an object |
| #present | Ensures the field is present in the response |
| #ignore | Ignores the field entirely in the validation |

After the tests are created, a class must be defined to locate and execute all Karate tests. This class is relatively simple, as it specifies that the Spring Boot application should be launched before running all Karate tests, using the profile that enables them. The code appears similar to Listing 6.14.

```
package com.twa.flights.api.reservation.integration;

import com.intuit.karate.junit5.Karate;
import org.springframework.boot.test.context.SpringBootTest;
import org.springframework.context.annotation.Profile;

@Profile(value = "IT")
@SpringBootTest(webEnvironment = SpringBootTest.WebEnvironment.DEFINED_
PORT)
class ApiITTest {
```

```
@Karate.Test
Karate runAllTests() {
    return Karate.run().tags("~@ignore").relativeTo(getClass());
}
}
```

**LISTING 6.14** Karate execution of the tests.

The final step of this process is to run all the tests to verify that everything works correctly. To do this, just run the Maven command to execute the test with the IT profile that appears in Listing 6.15. Before running the tests, it is essential to ensure that all services defined in the Docker Compose file—such as databases and microservices—are up and running.

```
➜  ~ mvn test -P IT
…..
2024-09-18T18:13:00.098-03:00  INFO 223183 --- [api-reservation]
[           main] com.intuit.karate                          : karate.env
system property was: null
2024-09-18T18:13:00.205-03:00  INFO 223183 --- [api-reservation] [nio-
8090-exec-1] o.a.c.c.C.[.[.[/api/flights/reservation] : Initializing
Spring DispatcherServlet 'dispatcherServlet'
2024-09-18T18:13:00.205-03:00  INFO 223183 --- [api-reservation] [nio-
8090-exec-1] o.s.web.servlet.DispatcherServlet         : Initializing
Servlet 'dispatcherServlet'
2024-09-18T18:13:00.206-03:00  INFO 223183 --- [api-reservation] [nio-
8090-exec-1] o.s.web.servlet.DispatcherServlet         : Completed
initialization in 1 ms
---------------------------------------------------------
feature:
classpath:com/twa/flights/api/reservation/integration/actuator/health.
feature
scenarios:  1 | passed:  1 | failed:  0 | time: 0.2019
---------------------------------------------------------

2024-09-18T18:13:00.537-03:00  INFO 223183 --- [api-reservation]
[           main] com.intuit.karate                          : karate.env
system property was: null
---------------------------------------------------------
feature:
classpath:com/twa/flights/api/reservation/integration/actuator/info.
feature
scenarios:  1 | passed:  1 | failed:  0 | time: 0.0155
---------------------------------------------------------

Karate version: 1.4.1
=========================================================
elapsed:   1.08 | threads:    1 | thread time: 0.22
features:     2 | skipped:    0 | efficiency: 0.20
scenarios:    2 | passed:     2 | failed: 0
=========================================================

HTML report: (paste into browser to view) | Karate version: 1.4.1
file:///home/asacco/Code/deguyer/deguyer-spring-boot-microservices/
chapter-6/api-reservation/target/karate-reports/karate-summary.html
=========================================================
```

```
[INFO] Tests run: 2, Failures: 0, Errors: 0, Skipped: 0, Time elapsed:
14.85 s -- in com.twa.flights.api.reservation.integration.ApiITTest
[INFO]
[INFO] Results:
[INFO]
[INFO] Tests run: 2, Failures: 0, Errors: 0, Skipped: 0
[INFO]
[INFO] -------------------------------------------------------------
```

*LISTING 6.15* Result of the execution of the Karate tests.

The output shown in Listing 6.15 provides basic information about the test execution. In the case of Karate, however, a complete Web page with more detailed information is generated and can be accessed via the location indicated in the execution result under the name `HTML Report`.

The report contains valuable information, including the number of tests and their results, as well as the time it takes to complete each file, as shown in Figure 6.2.

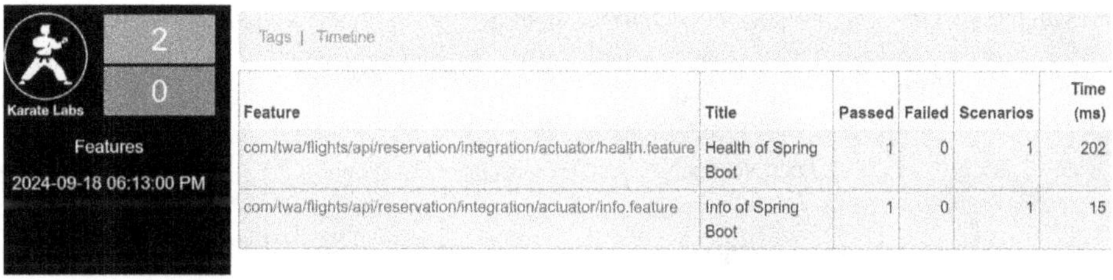

*FIGURE 6.2* Result of the execution of the integration tests.

If each file contains several scenarios with some failed tests, an effective way to view the details of each test is by clicking on any of the files to display the test step details. These details include information about which specific steps passed or failed, as illustrated in Figure 6.3.

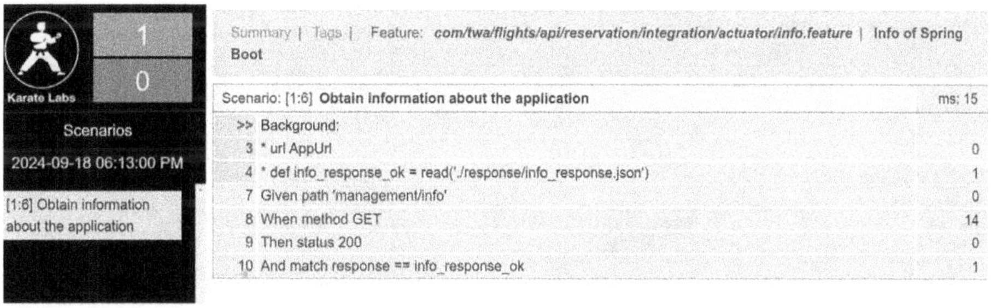

*FIGURE 6.3* Details about the execution of the different files.

For more detailed information about execution times, Karate provides a timeline feature that visually represents the entire test execution.

## What Are the Ways to Interact with a Database?

One of the most common situations during the creation of integration tests involves interacting with a database. Using a real database from an existing environment can be risky, however, as tests might inadvertently alter its data. In the past, to tackle this problem, some developers used

H2[5], a database in-memory solution with limited functionality, which is vendor-agnostic; however, it produces errors because some functionalities or data types only exist in that database.

To tackle these problems, a good idea is to use Docker with a library called Testcontainers[6]. This lightweight, open-source library enables running containers within your application and reusing test cases. It supports various testing frameworks, such as different versions of JUnit and Spock, and can be used in both Java and Kotlin projects.

The containers can be databases or other services required by the application. For instance, when interaction with specific AWS services is needed, the `LocalStack` image can be used. Testcontainers provides a set of modules that simplify the process of running and configuring these containers. For example, modules[7] exist for the most popular databases and message queues.

The first step in running a database exclusively for integration tests is to add the Testcontainers dependency, as shown in Listing 6.16.

```
<dependency>
    <groupId>org.testcontainers</groupId>
    <artifactId>junit-jupiter</artifactId>
    <version>1.19.7</version>
    <scope>test</scope>
</dependency>
```

**LISTING 6.16** Add a Testcontainers dependency.

The next step is to modify the class responsible for executing all the Karate tests to support Testcontainers, as shown in Listing 6.17.

```
package com.twa.flights.api.reservation.integration;

//Previous imports

import org.testcontainers.containers.DockerComposeContainer;
import org.testcontainers.containers.wait.strategy.Wait;
import org.testcontainers.junit.jupiter.Testcontainers;

import java.io.File;

@Testcontainers
@Profile(value = "IT")
@SpringBootTest(webEnvironment = SpringBootTest.WebEnvironment.DEFINED_
PORT)
class ApiITTest {

    static DockerComposeContainer dockerComposeContainer = new
DockerComposeContainer(
            new File("src/test/resources/docker/docker-compose.yml"))
            .waitingFor("api-reservation-db",
                    Wait.forLogMessage(".*MySQL init process done. Ready
for start up.*\\n", 1))
            .withLocalCompose(true);
```

---

[5]https://www.h2database.com/html/main.html
[6]https://testcontainers.com/
[7]https://testcontainers.com/modules/

```
@BeforeAll
static void setUp() {
    dockerComposeContainer.start();
}

@AfterAll
static void tearDown() {
    dockerComposeContainer.stop();
}

//Previous code
}
```

**LISTING 6.17** Modifications to the main Karate class.

The modifications include the use of the annotation `@Testcontainers` in the class to indicate that some containers may be executed in the class. Additionally, a variable containing the URL of a Docker Compose file is declared, and two different methods are part of the JUnit specification: one to start the containers and another to stop them.

**NOTE** *Multiple ways exist to declare and use containers within a Java class; however, Docker Compose reduces the complexity by allowing verification of file functionality locally via the command line.*

After the modifications in the class that launched the tests, the next step is to create a Docker Compose file inside the folder `src/test/resources/docker/`, as shown in Listing 6.18.

```
version: '3.1'
services:
  api-reservation-db:
    image: mysql:8.2.0
    restart: always
    environment:
      MYSQL_DATABASE: 'flights_reservation'
      MYSQL_ROOT_PASSWORD: 'muppet'
    ports:
      - 3312:3306
```

**LISTING 6.18** Docker file to run the database.

The container configuration is similar to the one shown in the `docker-compose.yml` file used throughout the chapters of this book. Still, with some modification, the `container_name` attributes can be used because Testcontainers does not support this feature.

With all these modifications, it's time to create a simple test that retrieves the information of one reservation from the database, as shown in Listing 6.19.

```
Feature: Get Reservation by ID endpoint
  Background:
    * url AppUrl
    * def get_response_ok = read('./response/get_response.json')

  Scenario: Obtain the information about one reservation
    Given path '/1'
```

```
When method GET
Then status 200
And match response == get_response_ok
```

**LISTING 6.19** Test to obtain information about one particular reservation.

Before running the tests, the next step is to define the file containing the endpoint's response with the duplicate content, as in Listing 6.20.

```
{
  "id": 1,
  "itineraryId": "2",
  "searchId": "2",
  "passengers": [
    {
      "id": 1,
      "firstName": "Andres",
      "lastName": "Sacco",
      "documentNumber": "987654321",
      "documentType": "DNI",
      "nationality": "ARG",
      "birthday": "1985-01-01"
    }
  ],
  "contact": {
    "id": 1,
    "telephoneNumber": "54911111111",
    "email": "sacco.andres@gmail.com"
  }
}
```

**LISTING 6.20** Response of the endpoint.

After configuring and creating the test, it's time to run it and verify that everything works as expected. First, stop all the containers on your machine that are connected to this book, and then run the tests as they appear in Listing 6.21.

```
➜  ~ mvn test -P IT
…..
14:26:05.879 [main] INFO org.testcontainers.images.PullPolicy -- Image
pull policy will be performed by: DefaultPullPolicy()
14:26:05.880 [main] INFO org.testcontainers.utility.
ImageNameSubstitutor -- Image name substitution will be
performed by: DefaultImageNameSubstitutor (composite of
'ConfigurationFileImageNameSubstitutor' and 'PrefixingImageNameSubstitutor')
14:26:06.003 [main] INFO org.testcontainers.dockerclient.
DockerClientProviderStrategy -- Loaded org.testcontainers.dockerclient.
UnixSocketClientProviderStrategy from ~/.testcontainers.properties, will
try it first
14:26:06.144 [main] INFO org.testcontainers.dockerclient.
DockerClientProviderStrategy -- Found Docker environment with Docker
accessed via Unix socket (/home/asacco/.docker/desktop/docker.sock)
14:26:06.145 [main] INFO org.testcontainers.DockerClientFactory --
Docker host IP address is localhost
```

```
14:26:06.154 [main] INFO org.testcontainers.DockerClientFactory --
Connected to docker:
  Server Version: 23.0.5
  API Version: 1.42
  Operating System: Docker Desktop
  Total Memory: 9962 MB
14:26:06.155 [main] INFO org.testcontainers.utility.RyukResourceReaper
-- Ryuk started - will monitor and terminate Testcontainers containers
on JVM exit
14:26:06.155 [main] INFO org.testcontainers.DockerClientFactory --
Checking the system...
14:26:06.155 [main] INFO org.testcontainers.DockerClientFactory -- ✓□
Docker server version should be at least 1.6.0
14:26:06.172 [main] INFO tc.testcontainers/ryuk:0.6.0 -- Creating
container for image: testcontainers/ryuk:0.6.0
14:26:06.718 [main] INFO tc.testcontainers/ryuk:0.6.0
-- Container testcontainers/ryuk:0.6.0 is starting:
edebfa92476450c74bc77a3a827f6267e1cb46e55f21c983b797d25647b777c4
14:26:06.928 [main] INFO tc.testcontainers/ryuk:0.6.0 -- Container
testcontainers/ryuk:0.6.0 started in PT0.75614281S
14:26:06.932 [main] INFO org.testcontainers.containers.ComposeDelegate
-- Preemptively checking local images for 'mysql:8.2.0', referenced via a
compose file or transitive Dockerfile. If not available, it will be pulled.
14:26:06.933 [main] INFO tc.docker-compose -- Local Docker Compose is
running command: up -d
14:26:06.959 [Thread-6] INFO tc.docker-compose --  Network gnhqbnrfqfae_
default  Creating
14:26:06.987 [Thread-6] INFO tc.docker-compose --  Network gnhqbnrfqfae_
default  Created
14:26:06.987 [Thread-6] INFO tc.docker-compose --  Container
gnhqbnrfqfae-api-reservation-db-1  Creating
14:26:07.018 [Thread-6] INFO tc.docker-compose --  Container
gnhqbnrfqfae-api-reservation-db-1  Created
14:26:07.021 [Thread-6] INFO tc.docker-compose --  Container
gnhqbnrfqfae-api-reservation-db-1  Starting
14:26:07.234 [Thread-6] INFO tc.docker-compose --  Container
gnhqbnrfqfae-api-reservation-db-1  Started
14:26:07.236 [main] INFO tc.docker-compose -- Docker Compose has finished
running
14:26:13.047 [main] INFO org.springframework.boot.devtools.restart.
RestartApplicationListener -- Restart disabled due to context in which
it is running
…
[INFO] Tests run: 3, Failures: 0, Errors: 0, Skipped: 0, Time elapsed:
25.41 s -- in com.twa.flights.api.reservation.integration.ApiITTest
[INFO]
[INFO] Results:
[INFO]
[INFO] Tests run: 3, Failures: 0, Errors: 0, Skipped: 0
[INFO]
[INFO] -----------------------------------------------------------------
[INFO] BUILD SUCCESS
[INFO] -----------------------------------------------------------------
```

**LISTING 6.21** Output of the execution.

As shown in the execution output, the container names and startup processes are specified before running the various scenarios. After the execution, the containers are stopped. At the beginning, however, a strange container called `ryuk` appears, which is responsible for managing all the test containers.

Consider Testcontainers not only for databases but also for cloud services, such as AWS, that use `LocalStack`[8] or a tool connected to event-driven systems such as Apache Kafka[9].

## How to Simulate External Communications

The application interacts with a database and other microservices through specific endpoints, exchanging requests and responses. Therefore, a tool or library is needed that can return mocks with a certain level of behavior, such as validating the parameters sent by the other API. There are many tools to tackle this problem, but the most relevant are WireMock[10], Microcks[11], and Hoverfly[12]. Table 6.4 provides a brief overview of the features to consider when selecting the best option.

*TABLE 6.4* Main things to consider when choosing an option.

| Feature | Hoverfly | Microcks | WireMock |
|---|---|---|---|
| It is well documented. | ✔ | ✔ | ✔ |
| A significant number of users use it. | ✘ | ✘ | ✔ |
| It's simple to write a mock. | ✔ | ✘ | ✔ |
| It's language agnostic. | ✘ | ✔ | ✔ |
| It supports multiple protocols. | ✘ | ✔ | ✔ |
| It has some kind of UI to configure the mocks. | ✘ | ✔ | ✔ |

WireMock appears to be the best, considering the comparison in the previous table, but Microcks is also one to keep in mind, because the number of features and users is increasing.

The first step is to modify the previous Docker Compose to include the image of WireMock with a simple configuration, which in this case uses the same port that the `api-catalog` uses, 6070. Listing 6.22 shows the modifications to introduce in the file.

```
version: '3.1'
services:
  # Previous definitions
  api-catalog:
    image: wiremock/wiremock:2.32.0
    ports:
      - 6070:8080
```

---

[8]https://github.com/localstack/localstack
[9]https://kafka.apache.org/
[10]https://wiremock.org/
[11]https://github.com/microcks/microcks
[12]https://github.com/SpectoLabs/hoverfly

```
  volumes:
    - ./wiremock:/home/wiremock
  restart: always
```

**LISTING 6.22** Modifications to Docker Compose to support WireMock.

The next step involves creating a test for making reservations, which is structured similarly to the earlier test designed to verify the actuator endpoints. Listing 6.23 shows the final result of the test.

```
Feature: Get Reservation by Id endpoint
  Background:
    * url AppUrl
    * def save_request_ok = read('./request/save_request.json')
    * def save_response_ok = read('./response/save_response.json')

  Scenario: Obtain the information about one reservation
    Given path '/'
    And request save_request_ok
    When method POST
    Then status 201
    And match response == save_response_ok
```

**LISTING 6.23** Test to validate that the creation of reservations works.

As shown in Listing 6.23, there are two separate files related to the request and response of this test. Listing 6.24 contains the request content that serves as the basis for creating a reservation.

```
{
  "itineraryId": "2",
  "searchId": "2",
  "passengers": [
    {
      "firstName": "Andres",
      "lastName": "Sacco",
      "documentNumber": "987654321",
      "documentType": "DNI",
      "nationality": "AR",
      "birthday": "1985-01-01"
    }
  ],
  "contact": {
    "telephoneNumber": "54911111111",
    "email": "sacco.andres@gmail.com"
  }
}
```

**LISTING 6.24** Request to create a reservation.

On the other hand, Listing 6.25 contains the response content with a #notnull attribute because the database dynamically generates the ID, so it's impossible to know what the next value is.

```
{
  "id": #notnull,
  "itineraryId": "2",
  "searchId": "2",
  "passengers": [
    {
      "id": #notnull,
      "firstName": "Andres",
      "lastName": "Sacco",
      "documentNumber": "987654321",
      "documentType": "DNI",
      "nationality": "AR",
      "birthday": "1985-01-01"
    }
  ],
  "contact": {
    "id": #notnull,
    "telephoneNumber": "54911111111",
    "email": "sacco.andres@gmail.com"
  }
}
```

**LISTING 6.25** Response to create a reservation.

A test has been created to validate certain functionality and includes support for using WireMock. Some details, however, must be defined before executing the tests. WireMock enables predefined responses to be returned when specific requests are received, but this behavior must be configured explicitly. To achieve this, a file named `response-AR.json` should be created at the following location: `src/test/resources/docker/wiremock/__files/api-catalog/response/`. The content shown in Listing 6.26 represents a valid response for a request to `api-catalog`.

```
{
  "name": "Argentina",
  "code": "AR",
  "continent": {
    "name": "South America",
    "code": "SA"
  }
}
```

**LISTING 6.26** Response to a specific request to api-catalog.

The response for a specific request to `api-catalog` has been defined, but it is also necessary to specify which request will trigger this mocked response. WireMock enables the creation of a JSON file that contains all the mappings. Each mapping corresponds to a specific mock, where the parameters, headers, and HTTP method that activate the mock can be specified.

Let's create a file called `operation-success.json` at this location: `src/test/resources/docker/wire mock/mappings/API/`. This file contains all the mappings to activate different mocks. Listing 6.27 includes a single mapping that corresponds to the file specified in Listing 6.26.

```
{
  "mappings": [
    {
      "priority": 1,
      "request": {
        "method": "GET",
        "urlPath": "/api/flights/catalog/country/AR",
        "headers": {
          "Content-Type": {
            "equalTo": "application/json"
          }
        }
      },
      "response": {
        "status": 200,
        "headers": {
          "Content-Type": "application/json"
        },
        "bodyFileName": "api-catalog/response/response-AR.json"
      }
    }
  ]
}
```

**LISTING 6.27** Mappings that use WireMock to return a specific response.

The content in Listing 6.27 has the structure of a list of mappings. The priority of each mapping can be specified, allowing a mock to be defined for particular cases with high priority and a default fallback with low priority. WireMock attempts to find a mapping that matches a given request; when multiple mappings qualify, the one with the highest priority is selected.

In the `response` section of the mappings, it is possible to include the entire JSON that WireMock should return. When the response contains many lines, however, maintaining the file and adding new mappings can become challenging. To address this, the response can be moved to an external file that is referenced in the `mappings` section, as shown in Listing 6.27.

Now, imagine a scenario where none of the defined mappings match the incoming request; in that case, it's possible to configure the system to return a 404 Not Found response. A good idea is to create another file called `operation-error.json` in the exact location as the previous one to represent this idea in the same way that appears in Listing 6.28.

```
{
  "mappings": [
    {
      "priority": 1,
      "request": {
        "method": "GET",
        "urlPattern": "/api/flights/catalog/country/[A-Z]{2}",
        "headers": {
          "Content-Type": {
            "equalTo": "application/json"
          }
        }
      },
```

```
        "response": {
          "status": 404,
          "headers": {
            "Content-Type": "application/json"
          }
        }
      }
    ]
  }
```

**LISTING 6.28** Default response in the case that no mapping exists.

Listing 6.28 is similar in structure and purpose to the previous listing. There is, however, a slight difference in the URL because in Listing 6.27, there is the attribute `urlPath` with a specific string, but in Listing 6.28, there is the attribute `urlPattern` with a regex; this is because WireMock offers the possibility to define mappings using a regex without need to specify all the possible situations. In this case, the mapping defined for any request that contains two letters in uppercase will return a 404 error.

The final step of this process is to run the tests to validate that everything works correctly. Listing 6.29 shows the command to run and the output of the execution.

```
→   ~ mvn test -P IT
.....
[INFO] Tests run: 4, Failures: 0, Errors: 0, Skipped: 0, Time elapsed:
26.52 s -- in com.twa.flights.api.reservation.integration.ApiITTest
[INFO]
[INFO] Results:
[INFO]
[INFO] Tests run: 4, Failures: 0, Errors: 0, Skipped: 0
[INFO]
[INFO] ------------------------------------------------------------
[INFO] BUILD SUCCESS
[INFO] ------------------------------------------------------------
.....
```

**LISTING 6.29** Result of the execution of the tests.

The response to the execution confirms that the mapping functions correctly. A good idea is to create different scenarios, so that all situations are checked, not just successes.

## Performance Tests

This type of test is used to detect possible problems in the application using different strategies. Some of these tests validate the entire behavior of the application, sending a considerable number of requests. Others attempt to validate a small part of the application to detect possible database access problems, such as queries with incorrect format.

---

**NOTE** *Gatling introduces another level of complexity to creating tests because it requires knowing the basics of Scala, so this book will not include creating this type of test.*

## How Can Only the Queries Be Checked?

In 2021, QuickPerf was introduced—a library that enables performance analysis of specific sections of an application, considering various factors such as JVM usage or the number of queries executed by a code block. This library is compatible with multiple versions of JUnit and supports frameworks such as Spring Boot, Quarkus, and MicroProfile.

One of its key advantages is identifying potential excessive resource usage in specific code blocks without requiring the creation of numerous new tests. Adding annotations to validate the behavior of methods allows the reuse of the integration tests previously created with Testcontainers earlier in the chapter.

Let's begin by adding the necessary dependencies to our POM file, as shown in Listing 6.30, to check whether some queries work.

```
<dependencies>
   <!-- QuickPerf dependencies -->
   <dependency>
         <groupId>org.quickperf</groupId>
         <artifactId>quick-perf-junit5</artifactId>
         <version>1.1.0</version>
         <scope>test</scope>
   </dependency>
   <dependency>
         <groupId>org.quickperf</groupId>
         <artifactId>quick-perf-springboot2-sql-starter</artifactId>
         <version>1.1.0</version>
         <scope>test</scope>
   </dependency>
   <!-- End of QuickPerf dependencies -->
</dependencies>


<profiles>
   <profile>
         <id>PE</id>
         <build>
               <plugins>
                     <plugin>
                           <groupId>org.apache.maven.plugins</groupId>
                           <artifactId>maven-surefire-plugin</artifactId>
                           <version>${maven.surefire.version}</version>
                           <configuration>
                                 <excludes>
                                       <exclude>**/unit/**Test.java</exclude>
                                       <exclude>**/architecture/**Test.java</exclude>
                                       <exclude>**/integration/**Test.java</exclude>
                                 </excludes>
                                 <argLine>-Dfile.encoding=UTF-8</argLine>
```

```
                                        <argLine>-
XX:+EnableDynamicAgentLoading</argLine>
                                    </configuration>
                            </plugin>
                    </plugins>
            </build>
    </profile>
</profiles>
```

**LISTING 6.30** Inclusion of new dependencies to check performance.

After including the dependencies, the next step is to create tests to validate the behavior of one method of `ReservationRepository`. To do this, let's make a class reusing part of the logic of the previous type of tests to run and stop the containers, and add the logic to validate the `find-ById` method. Listing 6.31 illustrates how this class appears with all its logic included.

```java
package com.twa.flights.api.reservation.performance;

import com.twa.flights.api.reservation.model.Reservation;
import com.twa.flights.api.reservation.repository.ReservationRepository;
import org.junit.jupiter.api.AfterAll;
import org.junit.jupiter.api.BeforeAll;
import org.junit.jupiter.api.Test;
import org.springframework.beans.factory.annotation.Autowired;
import org.springframework.boot.test.context.SpringBootTest;
import org.springframework.context.annotation.Import;
import org.testcontainers.containers.DockerComposeContainer;
import org.testcontainers.containers.wait.strategy.Wait;
import org.testcontainers.junit.jupiter.Testcontainers;
import org.quickperf.junit5.QuickPerfTest;
import org.quickperf.spring.sql.QuickPerfSqlConfig;
import org.quickperf.sql.annotation.*;

import java.io.File;
import java.util.Optional;

import static org.junit.jupiter.api.Assertions.*;

@Import(QuickPerfSqlConfig.class)
@QuickPerfTest
@Testcontainers
@SpringBootTest(webEnvironment = SpringBootTest.WebEnvironment.DEFINED_
PORT)
class ReservationRepositoryPerformanceTest {

    @Autowired
    ReservationRepository repository;

    static DockerComposeContainer dockerComposeContainer = new
DockerComposeContainer(
            new File("src/test/resources/docker/docker-compose.yml"))
            .waitingFor("api-reservation-db",
                    Wait.forLogMessage(".*MySQL init process done. Ready
for start up.*\\n", 1))
            .withLocalCompose(true);
```

```
    @BeforeAll
    static void setUp() {
        dockerComposeContainer.start();
    }

    @AfterAll
    static void tearDown() {
        dockerComposeContainer.stop();
    }

    @Test
    @ExpectSelect(1) // Validate the number of queries that are executed
    @ExpectMaxQueryExecutionTime(thresholdInMilliSeconds = 2) // This
checks the duration of the execution of the query
    void should_get_a_reservation() {
        Optional<Reservation> entity = repository.findById(1L);

        assertAll(
                () -> assertTrue(entity.isPresent()),
                () -> assertEquals("2", entity.get().getItineraryId()));
    }
}
```

**LISTING 6.31** Class to validate the performance.

The previous class shows that, when omitting all the logic related to the containers, only minor modifications remain, resembling standard unit tests. The first change involves annotating the entire class with `@QuickPerfTest`, signaling that certain tests within the class will need to validate specific criteria and include the necessary library configuration. By default, it uses the configuration provided in the `QuickPerfSqlConfig` class, though this class can be extended to customize the values. The final adjustment specifies the number of database operations to be tracked. In the previous example, a select operation was monitored, but it is also possible to track the number of insert, delete, or update operations executed.

Other annotations appear on each method to validate the number of operations it executes. Table 6.5 lists the most relevant annotations, each accompanied by a brief description.

**TABLE 6.5** Relevant annotations of QuickPerf.

| Annotation | Description |
| --- | --- |
| @ProfileConnection | This will reveal all the operations that occur during the connection to the database. |
| @ExpectSelect<br>@ExpectInsert<br>@ExpectDelete<br>@ExpectUpdate | This will monitor and count the number of queries executed by a specific type. |
| @ExpectMaxSelect  @ExpectMaxInsert<br>@ExpectMaxDelete<br>@ExpectMaxUpdate | This will verify that the number of executed statements does not exceed a specified limit. |

*(Continued)*

*TABLE 6.5* Continued

| Annotation | Description |
|---|---|
| @ExpectMaxQueryExecutionTime | The expected execution time for the query can be specified. |
| @ExpectSelectedColumn<br>@ExpectUpdateColumn | This annotation verifies the number of columns involved in the query. |
| @DisableSameSelects | This checks whether the same query is being executed two or more times. |

When running the tests, everything will continue to work as described previously. Ensuring correct functionality, however, requires carefully verifying the test results and outputs. Let's modify the value of the @ExpectedSelect annotation to 2 and rerun the test. If everything is set up correctly, you'll see an error message in the console similar to Listing 6.32.

```
➜  ~ mvn test -P PE
…..
[PERF] You may think that <2> select statements were sent to the
database
        But there is in fact <1>...

[JDBC QUERY EXECUTION (executeQuery, executeBatch, ...)]
   Time:1, Success:True, Type:Prepared, Batch:False, QuerySize:1,
BatchSize:0, Query:["
    select
          r1_0.id,
          r1_0.reservation_id,
          r1_0.itinerary_id,
          r1_0.search_id
    from
          reservation r1_0
    where
          r1_0.id=?"], Params:[(1)]
...
```

*LISTING 6.32* Result of the execution of tests.

This message indicates that the following query was executed only once, meaning the assertion specified by the annotation is incorrect. Remember that the annotation checks only the number of queries executed, not the number of rows affected.

Another functional annotation for detecting potential issues is @AnalyzeSql, which provides detailed metrics about the query execution. Let's update the previous example to include this annotation, as shown in Listing 6.33.

```
    @Test
    @ExpectSelect(1) // Validate the number of queries that are executed
    @ExpectMaxQueryExecutionTime(thresholdInMilliSeconds = 2) // This
checks the duration of the execution of the query
    @AnalyzeSql
    void should_get_a_reservation() {
        Optional<Reservation> entity = repository.findById(1L);
```

```
          assertAll(
                  () -> assertTrue(entity.isPresent()),
                  () -> assertEquals("2", entity.get().getItineraryId()));
    }
```

*LISTING 6.33* Modifications to analyze the query.

Rerunning the same test will still succeed, but this time all the analysis details will be displayed in the console, as shown in Listing 6.34.

```
→  ~ mvn test -P PE
.....
[QUICK PERF] SQL ANALYSIS
                                      *  *  *  *  *
SQL EXECUTIONS: 1
MAX TIME: 2 ms
                                   *  *  *  *  *
SELECT: 1
                                   *  *  *  *  *
QUERY
   Time:2, Success:True, Type:Prepared, Batch:False, QuerySize:1,
BatchSize:0, Query:["
   select
       r1_0.id,
       r1_0.reservation_id,
       r1_0.itinerary_id,
       r1_0.search_id
   from
       reservation r1_0
   where
       r1_0.id=?"], Params:[(1)]
...
```

*LISTING 6.34* Result of the execution of tests.

As expected, this solution is limited to relational databases. In the case of non-relational databases, however, it is still possible to analyze potential issues within the service or controller layers that access the repository by using QuickPerf's JVM-related annotations. For instance, annotations such as `@MeasureHeapAllocation` and `@HeapSize(value = 1, unit = AllocationUnit.GIGA_BYTE)` make it possible to monitor the memory usage of specific methods, offering insight into how much memory is consumed during their execution.

## Other Types

The previous types of tests are the most relevant and are shared by different companies. While not all organizations use the same libraries or tools mentioned in this chapter, other approaches exist to enhance development practices by analyzing the code from different perspectives, such as evaluating test effectiveness or validating the project structure.

For all of the types of tests discussed in this section, the comparison between libraries is straightforward since, at the time of writing, each scenario has a single widely adopted option.

Other types of testing, such as documentation, will be covered in the corresponding chapters that tackle that topic.

## Architecture Tests

One of the biggest challenges when starting to create multiple microservices within a team or company is maintaining a consistent application structure. Not all developers may be familiar with the correct naming conventions for packages or the location of specific classes, such as controllers or repositories, that are required to access the database properly. One example is the use of annotations that are not recommended, such as using `RequestMapping` on the different methods of the controllers. Instead, use `GetMapping`, `PostMapping`, and others that represent the various actions on an endpoint.

To tackle this problem, most companies define the structure of the packages and the names of the different files in the API. This, however, only partially mitigates the problem, as manual validations are still required, resulting in a time-consuming process. There is a risk that someone may not review all the files, and the application may not adhere to the standard.

Considering all these problems, there is a library called ArchUnit[13] that could help automate this work. The library is open source and enables defining rules as unit tests. It uses a declarative approach to specify rules that determine the initial scope for analysis, covering methods, fields, and classes.

The first step to using the library is adding the dependencies that appear in Listing 6.35.

```xml
<?xml version="1.0" encoding="UTF-8"?>
<project xmlns="http://maven.apache.org/POM/4.0.0"
   xmlns:xsi="http://www.w3.org/2001/XMLSchema-instance"
         xsi:schemaLocation="http://maven.apache.org/POM/4.0.0  https://
maven.apache.org/xsd/maven-4.0.0.xsd">
        <properties>
                              <!-- Other properties -->
           <archunit-junit5.version>1.2.1</archunit-junit5.version>
        </properties>
        <dependencies>
             <!-- Other configurations →
           <dependency>
                  <groupId>com.tngtech.archunit</groupId>
                  <artifactId>archunit-junit5</artifactId>
                  <version>${archunit-junit5.version}</version>
                  <scope>test</scope>
           </dependency>

           <dependency>
                  <groupId>com.tngtech.archunit</groupId>
                  <artifactId>archunit-junit5-api</artifactId>
                  <version>${archunit-junit5.version}</version>
                  <scope>test</scope>
           </dependency>
        </dependencies>
     </project>
```

**LISTING 6.35** POM configuration of the architecture tests.

---

[13]https://www.archunit.org/

After including the dependencies necessary to create the architecture rules, let's define a simple rule that validates that all the variables related to the logger have one particular name and must be static, final, and private. Listing 6.36 shows the class that contains the definition of this test.

```
package com.twa.flights.api.reservation.architecture.general;

import com.tngtech.archunit.core.importer.ImportOption;
import com.tngtech.archunit.junit.AnalyzeClasses;
import com.tngtech.archunit.junit.ArchTest;
import com.tngtech.archunit.lang.ArchRule;
import org.slf4j.Logger;

import static com.tngtech.archunit.lang.syntax.ArchRuleDefinition.*;

@AnalyzeClasses(packages = "com.twa.flights.api", importOptions =
ImportOption.DoNotIncludeTests.class) //1
class GeneralCodingRulesTest {

    @ArchTest //2
    static final ArchRule loggersShouldBePrivateStaticAndFinal = fields().
that().haveRawType(Logger.class).should()
            .bePrivate().andShould().beStatic().andShould().beFinal().
andShould().haveName("LOGGER")
            .because("Logger variables should be private, static and
final, and it should be named as LOGGER"); //3

}
```

**LISTING 6.36** Rule to validate the name of the attributes.

Listing 6.36 has some significant differences from the standard unit tests; most of the them connected with the annotations and how to define the test. Each block of code is broken down here:

1. The first thing to do is to use the annotation @AnalyzeClasses to indicate the scope (packages) to analyze. The attribute importOptions of the annotation can be used to include or exclude test classes.
2. This annotation must be used on a field or method to indicate to ArchUnit that a rule to validate exists inside.
3. This is the test with all the conditions to validate.

It is a good practice not to define multiple times the suffix of the classes or the package names using a class that contains all this information as a constant, as shown in Listing 6.37.

```
package com.twa.flights.api.reservation.architecture.general;

public class ArchitectureConstants {

    // Suffixes
    public static final String CONTROLLER_SUFFIX = "Controller";
```

```
    // Packages
    public static final String CONTROLLER_PACKAGE = "..controller..";

    // Explanations
    public static final String ANNOTATED_EXPLANATION = "Classes in %s
package should be annotated with %s";
    public static final String NAMING_EXPLANATION = "Classes in %s package
should be named with %s suffix";

    // Package to scan
    public static final String DEFAULT_PACKAGE = "com.twa.flights.api";

    private ArchitectureConstants() {

    }

    public static String namingExplanation(String packageName, String suffix) {
        return String.format(NAMING_EXPLANATION, packageName, suffix);
    }
}
```

**LISTING 6.37** Definition of the constants across all the tests.

After defining the constants, let's create a test that validates that the controllers' constructors must all be public without any anonymous classes—Listing 6.38 shows how this rule looks to validate it.

```
package com.twa.flights.api.reservation.architecture.layer;

import static com.tngtech.archunit.lang.syntax.ArchRuleDefinition.methods;

import static com.tngtech.archunit.lang.syntax.ArchRuleDefinition.
constructors;
import static com.twa.flights.api.reservation.architecture.general.
ArchitectureConstants.*;

import com.tngtech.archunit.core.importer.ImportOption;
import com.tngtech.archunit.junit.AnalyzeClasses;
import com.tngtech.archunit.junit.ArchTest;
import com.tngtech.archunit.lang.ArchRule;

@AnalyzeClasses(packages = DEFAULT_PACKAGE, importOptions = ImportOption.
DoNotIncludeTests.class)
public class ControllerRulesTest {

    @ArchTest
    static final ArchRule publicConstructorsAreOnlyAllowed = constructors()
            .that().areDeclaredInClassesThat().resideInAPackage(CONTROLLER_
PACKAGE).and()
            .areDeclaredInClassesThat().areNotAnonymousClasses().should().
bePublic()
            .because("Public constructors are only allowed in " +
CONTROLLER_PACKAGE);
}
```

**LISTING 6.38** Validate that the constructors are only public.

This is just one example of what to validate; let's see another example:

- Annotations: It is possible to define which annotations on a method or class are valid using the method that "should" be combined with "and." In cases where there are many annotations, the opposite approach can be used—defining only the valid annotations. Listing 6.39 shows how to validate that the methods in the controller use the @RequestMapping annotation.

```
@ArchTest
    static final ArchRule publicMethodsShouldBeProperlyAnnotated = methods().
that().areDeclaredInClassesThat()
            .resideInAPackage(CONTROLLER_PACKAGE).and().arePublic().
should().notBeAnnotatedWith(RequestMapping.class)
            .andShould().notBeAnnotatedWith(ResponseBody.class)
            .because("Controller endpoints should not be annotated with @
RequestMapping or @ResponseBody");
```

**LISTING 6.39** Rule to validate the use of annotations.

Another example of the same rule is Listing 6.40, which validates the use of correct annotations in class definitions for a controller.

```
@ArchTest
    static final ArchRule classesShouldBeAnnotated = classes().that().
resideInAPackage(CONTROLLER_PACKAGE)
            .should().beAnnotatedWith(RestController.class).orShould()
            .beAnnotatedWith(Controller.class)
            .because(String.format(ANNOTATED_EXPLANATION, CONTROLLER_
SUFFIX, "@RestController"));
```

**LISTING 6.40** Rule to validate the annotations on the class.

- Return: Another common problem is validating that certain layers or methods are returned, such as the controller, where all methods must return a ResponseEntity class. Listing 6.41 shows how this can be done.

```
@ArchTest
    static final ArchRule methodsShouldReturnResponseEntity =
            methods().that().arePublic()
                .and().areDeclaredInClassesThat()
                .resideInAPackage(CONTROLLER_PACKAGE)
                .should().haveRawReturnType(ResponseEntity.class)
                .because("Controller endpoints should return a
ResponseEntity object");
```

**LISTING 6.41** Rule to validate the response of a method.

- Naming: Another common problem is the naming of different classes or interfaces, which must follow a standard by using a prefix or suffix. Listing 6.42 is a common example of the rule for validating the names of controller classes.

```
@ArchTest
   static final ArchRule classesInControllerShouldBeNamedProperly =
classes()
             .that().resideInAPackage(CONTROLLER_PACKAGE)
             .should().haveSimpleNameEndingWith(CONTROLLER_SUFFIX)
             .because(namingExplanation(CONTROLLER_PACKAGE, CONTROLLER_
SUFFIX));
```

**LISTING 6.42** Rule to validate the name of the class.

**NOTE** *Other rules can also be defined in ArchUnit, such as restricting access between layers—for instance, allowing only services to access connectors. The official documentation provides some examples of the definitions of different types of architecture, such as layers[14] or hexagonal[15].*

Defining all possible scenarios and rules is beyond the scope of the book.

After defining the different rules, running all of them just requires executing the command mvn test. If everything is configured correctly, information about the executed regulations will be displayed, as shown in Listing 6.43.

```
→  ~ mvn test
......
[INFO] Running com.twa.flights.api.reservation.architecture.general.
GeneralCodingRulesTest
13:36:56.593 [main] INFO com.tngtech.archunit.core.PluginLoader -- Detected
Java version 21.0.2
[ERROR] Tests run: 1, Failures: 1, Errors: 0, Skipped: 0, Time elapsed:
0.698 s <<< FAILURE! -- in com.twa.flights.api.reservation.architecture.
general.GeneralCodingRulesTest
[ERROR] GeneralCodingRulesTest.loggersShouldBePrivateStaticAndFinal -- Time
elapsed: 0.694 s <<< FAILURE!
java.lang.AssertionError:
Architecture Violation [Priority: MEDIUM] - Rule 'fields that have raw type
org.slf4j.Logger should be private and should be static and should be final
and should have name 'LOGGER', because Logger variables should be private,
static and final, and it should be named as LOGGER' was violated (1 times):
Field <com.twa.flights.api.reservation.service.ClusterService.LOGGER> does
not have modifier STATIC in (ClusterService.java:0)
        at com.tngtech.archunit.lang.ArchRule$Assertions.
assertNoViolation(ArchRule.java:94)
        at com.tngtech.archunit.lang.ArchRule$Assertions.check(ArchRule.
java:86)
        at com.tngtech.archunit.lang.ArchRule$Factory$SimpleArchRule.
check(ArchRule.java:165)
        at com.tngtech.archunit.junit.internal.ArchUnitTestDescriptor$ArchU
nitRuleDescriptor.execute(ArchUnitTestDescriptor.java:166)
        at com.tngtech.archunit.junit.internal.ArchUnitTestDescriptor$ArchU
nitRuleDescriptor.execute(ArchUnitTestDescriptor.java:149)
        at java.base/java.util.ArrayList.forEach(ArrayList.java:1596)
        at java.base/java.util.ArrayList.forEach(ArrayList.java:1596)

[INFO] Running com.twa.flights.api.reservation.architecture.layer.
ControllerRulesTest
```

---

[14]https://www.archunit.org/userguide/html/000_Index.html#_layer_checks
[15]https://www.archunit.org/userguide/html/000_Index.html#_onion_architecture

```
[INFO] Tests run: 5, Failures: 0, Errors: 0, Skipped: 0, Time elapsed:
0.016 s -- in com.twa.flights.api.reservation.architecture.layer.
ControllerRulesTest
[INFO]
[INFO] Results:
[INFO]
[ERROR] Failures:
[ERROR]   Architecture Violation [Priority: MEDIUM] - Rule 'fields that have
raw type org.slf4j.Logger should be private and should be static and should
be final and should have name 'LOGGER', because Logger variables should be
private, static and final, and it should be named as LOGGER' was violated (1
times):
Field <com.twa.flights.api.reservation.service.ClusterService.LOGGER> does
not have modifier STATIC in (ClusterService.java:0)
[INFO]
[ERROR] Tests run: 6, Failures: 1, Errors: 0, Skipped: 0
......
```

**LISTING 6.43** Command to execute the architecture tests.

The output of the test's execution, which appears in Listing 6.44, refers to a class that does not follow the standard for defining variables.

Initially, everything appears well structured, with numerous rules established to prevent the creation of files that deviate from the standard. Over time, however, a new challenge tends to emerge: replicating those rules across multiple projects. This process introduces the risk of omissions or inconsistencies. When new laws are introduced, someone must manually propagate them to every repository, increasing the likelihood of errors or incomplete enforcement.

Considering the problems mentioned in the previous paragraph, Societe Generale[16] developed a plugin that enables the creation of a simple library containing all the rules, which can then be imported into all projects to reduce duplicated code. Since the purpose of this chapter is only to introduce different types of tests, migrating the rules to use that plugin is beyond its scope.

## Mutation Tests

When creating tests for an application, tools such as Sonar are commonly used to evaluate code coverage and identify potentially untested sections of code. The assumption that a method is adequately tested simply because multiple tests cover it is flawed. For instance, having numerous tests that lack assertions, or merely verifying that a method's response is not null without inspecting the attributes of the returned object, does not guarantee the correctness or effectiveness of the test suite.

Let's see a simple example of tests that pass and increase the code coverage but have some problems, such as not checking anything. Listing 6.44 is a simple example of a possible tests.

```
@Test
  void should_return_information_for_a_country() {
      // Arrange
      String countryCode = "US";
      CountryDTO country = new CountryDTO();
      country.setCode(countryCode);
      country.setName("United States");

      when(catalogConnector.getCountry(countryCode)).thenReturn(country);
```

---

[16]https://github.com/societe-generale/arch-unit-maven-plugin

```
    // Act
    CountryDTO result = catalogService.getCountryByCode(countryCode);

    // Assert
    assertNotNull(result);
}
```

LISTING 6.44 Example of tests.

The previous example illustrates a simple test where validation of all response attributes is omitted. Thus, if someone introduces changes affecting the methods' response, no one will detect the problems.

Mutation tests attempt to introduce modifications to the source code, known as mutations, which involve removing code blocks, duplicating code, or altering conditions. The idea behind this type of test is to avoid writing any new code in the application; instead, it uses the existing tests to validate the effectiveness of the implemented code.

Mutation tests involve running the unit tests before introducing any modifications to check whether all of them pass. After that, the library introduces some changes to the code and reruns the same tests to detect which of them pass again. If some of the tests pass, they are ineffective in checking the results of the methods' invocation.

In Java, performing mutation tests typically involves using a library called pitest[17], which must be included in the POM file, as shown in Listing 6.45.

```
<?xml version="1.0" encoding="UTF-8"?>
<project xmlns="http://maven.apache.org/POM/4.0.0"
    xmlns:xsi="http://www.w3.org/2001/XMLSchema-instance"
        xsi:schemaLocation="http://maven.apache.org/POM/4.0.0  https://maven.apache.org/
xsd/maven-4.0.0.xsd">
        <properties>
                        <!-- Other properties -->
                <pitest-maven.version>1.7.6</pitest-maven.version>
                <pitest-junit5-plugin.version>0.15</pitest-junit5-plugin.version>
        </properties>
        <!-- Other configurations →
        <profiles>
                <profile>
                        <id>M
    T</id>
                        <build>
                            <plugins>
                                <plugin>
                                    <groupId>org.pitest</groupId>
                                    <artifactId>pitest-maven</artifactId>
                                    <version>${pitest-maven.version}</version>

                                    <configuration>
                                        <outputFormats>
                                            <outputFormat>HTML</
outputFormat>
                                            <outputFormat>XML</
outputFormat>
                                        </outputFormats>
                                        <targetClasses>
                                            <param>com.twa.flights.
api.reservation.*</param>
                                        </targetClasses>
```

[17]https://pitest.org/

```
                                                    <targetTests>
                                                        <param>com.twa.flights.
api.reservation.*</param>
                                                    </targetTests>
                                                </configuration>
                                                <dependencies>
                                                    <dependency>
                                                        <groupId>org.pitest</
groupId>
<artifactId>pitest-junit5-plugin</artifactId>
                                                        <version>${pitest-
junit5-plugin.version}</version>
                                                    </dependency>
                                                </dependencies>
                                            </plugin>
                                        </plugins>
                                    </build>
                                </profile>
                            </profiles>
                        </project>
```

**LISTING 6.45** POM configuration of the mutation tests.

Listing 6.45 contains configurations such as the report format, which allows checking the execution status. Readable formats include XML and HTML. Another relevant part is the package declaration, which allows for modifying the source code; it is also where the tests that need to be executed after introducing the modifications are located.

**NOTE** *Some versions of pitest present compatibility issues with JUnit 5 when executing tests; therefore, explicit inclusion of the* `pitest-junit5-plugin` *dependency is required to ensure proper support.*

After introducing the modifications, the next step is just to run a command to validate the effectiveness of the tests, as shown in Listing 6.46.

```
➜  ~ mvn clean package org.pitest:pitest-maven:mutationCoverage -P MT

[INFO] --- pitest:1.7.6:mutationCoverage (default-cli) @ api-reservation
---

. . . .

3:34:11 PM PIT >> INFO : Calculated coverage in 1 seconds.
3:34:11 PM PIT >> INFO : Incremental analysis reduced number of mutations
by 0
3:34:11 PM PIT >> INFO : Created  30 mutation test units
-3:34:19 PM PIT >> INFO : Completed in 9 seconds
===========================================================================
- Mutators
===========================================================================
> org.pitest.mutationtest.engine.gregor.mutators.returns.
PrimitiveReturnsMutator
>> Generated 8 Killed 0 (0%)


. . . .


---------------------------------------------------------------------------
```

```
================================================================
- Timings
================================================================
> pre-scan for mutations : < 1 second
> scan classpath : < 1 second
> coverage and dependency analysis : 1 seconds
> build mutation tests : < 1 second
> run mutation analysis : 7 seconds
----------------------------------------------------------------
> Total  : 9 seconds
----------------------------------------------------------------

================================================================
- Statistics
================================================================
>> Line Coverage: 52/524 (10%)
>> Generated 188 mutations Killed 14 (7%)
>> Mutations with no coverage 174. Test strength 100%
>> Ran 16 tests (0.09 tests per mutation)
Enhanced functionality available at https://www.arcmutate.com/
[INFO] ----------------------------------------------------------
[INFO] BUILD SUCCESS
[INFO] ----------------------------------------------------------
```

**LISTING 6.46** Command to execute the mutation tests.

After the test is executed, as shown in Listing 6.46—which includes extensive details about the execution of various mutations—two options are available: either analyze all the logs in the console (which is not recommended due to the time it takes to locate a specific class) or access the `pit-reports` directory inside the target folder, which provides an HTML report offering a different perspective on the execution. Figure 6.4 summarizes the execution of the mutation tests.

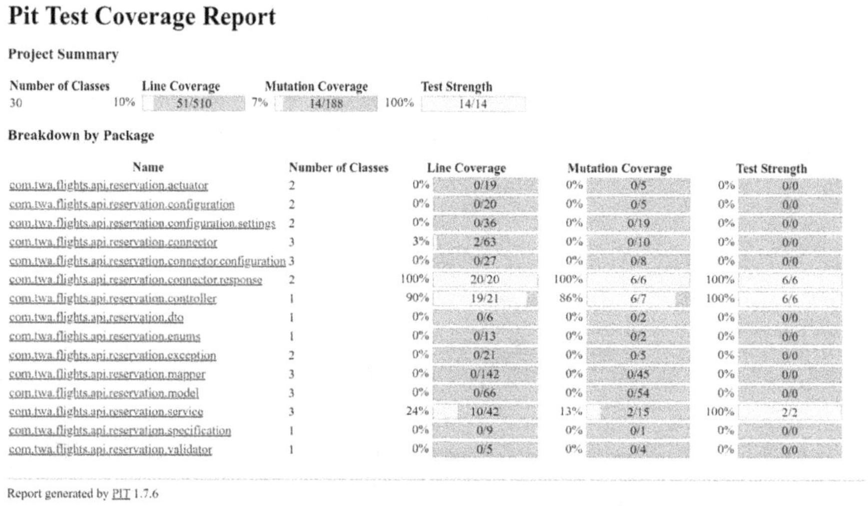

## Pit Test Coverage Report

**Project Summary**

| Number of Classes | Line Coverage | Mutation Coverage | Test Strength |
|---|---|---|---|
| 30 | 10% 51/510 | 7% 14/188 | 100% 14/14 |

**Breakdown by Package**

| Name | Number of Classes | Line Coverage | | Mutation Coverage | | Test Strength | |
|---|---|---|---|---|---|---|---|
| com.twa.flights.api.reservation.actuator | 2 | 0% | 0/19 | 0% | 0/5 | 0% | 0/0 |
| com.twa.flights.api.reservation.configuration | 2 | 0% | 0/20 | 0% | 0/5 | 0% | 0/0 |
| com.twa.flights.api.reservation.configuration.settings | 2 | 0% | 0/36 | 0% | 0/19 | 0% | 0/0 |
| com.twa.flights.api.reservation.connector | 3 | 3% | 2/63 | 0% | 0/10 | 0% | 0/0 |
| com.twa.flights.api.reservation.connector.configuration | 3 | 0% | 0/27 | 0% | 0/8 | 0% | 0/0 |
| com.twa.flights.api.reservation.connector.response | 2 | 100% | 20/20 | 100% | 6/6 | 100% | 6/6 |
| com.twa.flights.api.reservation.controller | 1 | 90% | 19/21 | 86% | 6/7 | 100% | 6/6 |
| com.twa.flights.api.reservation.dto | 1 | 0% | 0/6 | 0% | 0/2 | 0% | 0/0 |
| com.twa.flights.api.reservation.enums | 1 | 0% | 0/13 | 0% | 0/2 | 0% | 0/0 |
| com.twa.flights.api.reservation.exception | 2 | 0% | 0/21 | 0% | 0/5 | 0% | 0/0 |
| com.twa.flights.api.reservation.mapper | 3 | 0% | 0/142 | 0% | 0/45 | 0% | 0/0 |
| com.twa.flights.api.reservation.model | 3 | 0% | 0/66 | 0% | 0/54 | 0% | 0/0 |
| com.twa.flights.api.reservation.service | 3 | 24% | 10/42 | 13% | 2/15 | 100% | 2/2 |
| com.twa.flights.api.reservation.specification | 1 | 0% | 0/9 | 0% | 0/1 | 0% | 0/0 |
| com.twa.flights.api.reservation.validator | 1 | 0% | 0/5 | 0% | 0/4 | 0% | 0/0 |

Report generated by PIT 1.7.6

**FIGURE 6.4** Result of the execution of the mutation tests.

By opening a specific class within any package, it is possible to view detailed information about the mutators used in the tests. The results are illustrated in Figure 6.5.

**CatalogService.java**

**Mutations**

**Active mutators**

- CONDITIONALS_BOUNDARY
- EMPTY_RETURNS
- FALSE_RETURNS
- INCREMENTS
- INVERT_NEGS
- MATH
- NEGATE_CONDITIONALS
- NULL_RETURNS
- PRIMITIVE_RETURNS
- TRUE_RETURNS
- VOID_METHOD_CALLS

**Tests examined**

- com.twa.flights.api.reservation.service.CatalogServiceTest.[engine:junit-jupiter]/[class:com.twa.flights.api.reservation.service.CatalogServiceTest] [method:should_return_information_for_a_country()] (2 ms)
- com.twa.flights.api.reservation.architecture.general.GeneralCodingRulesTest.[engine:archunit]/[class:com.twa.flights.api.reservation.architecture.general.GeneralCodingRulesTest] [field:loggersShouldBePrivateStaticAndFinal] (20 ms)
- com.twa.flights.api.reservation.service.CatalogServiceTest.[engine:junit-jupiter]/[class:com.twa.flights.api.reservation.service.CatalogServiceTest] [method:should_not_return_information_for_a_country()] (2 ms)

Report generated by PIT 1.7.6

**FIGURE 6.5** Result of the execution of the mutation on one class.

One way to optimize the execution of these mutation tests is to limit the scope of the classes or methods being analyzed. This can be achieved by configuring pitest to specify the packages or classes to be excluded, as shown in Listing 6.47.

```
<plugin>
  <groupId>org.pitest</groupId>
  <artifactId>pitest-maven</artifactId>
  <version>${pitest-maven.version}</version>

  <configuration>
      <!-- Other configurations -->
      <excludedMethods>
            <excludedMethod>convert</excludedMethod>
      </excludedMethods>
      <excludedClasses>
<excludedClass>com.twa.flights.api.reservation.repository.*</excludedClass>
<excludedClass>com.twa.flights.api.reservation.dto.*</excludedClass>
<excludedClass>com.twa.flights.api.reservation.enums.*</excludedClass>
      </excludedClasses>
  </configuration>
</plugin>
```

**LISTING 6.47** Excluding methods and classes from the mutation.

Another alternative to optimizing the execution of mutation tests is to use incremental analysis. The first time, it takes more time to generate the reports. In the following executions, it detects which files have changed and makes modifications to the source code that are affected by the changes or the configuration of the POM file. The way to do it is to add an extra parameter to the execution, as shown in Listing 6.48.

```
→   ~ mvn clean package org.pitest:pitest-maven:mutationCoverage
-DwithHistory -P MT
```

**LISTING 6.48** Command to execute the mutation tests with history.

There are some considerations with the use of this type of test:

• Consumes Resources: This type of test involves utilizing numerous resources, such as CPU and memory, to generate mutations in the source code and run the test multiple times with different source code.
• Run in a Pipeline: Consider running this type of test in a separate pipeline or on demand because validating multiple classes takes considerable time.
• Scope: One of the biggest challenges lies in failing to narrow the scope of what to test in order to be effective. Including all tests and classes can lead to the issues described earlier. A more effective approach involves limiting the scope to only the classes or methods considered most critical to the application.
• Black box: This type of test is limited to the code developed within the application itself. When relying heavily on external libraries, it becomes impractical to validate or modify their internal logic through such tests.

## Which Is the Best Option for Each Scenario?

There are multiple scenarios in which all the different tests help mitigate or reduce the risks of introducing environmental problems. Still, it is only sometimes possible to use all of them. Table 6.6 suggests when it is recommended to implement the different tests.

**TABLE 6.6** Scenarios to implement the different types of tests.

| Situation | Unit | Integration | Performance | Mutation | Architecture |
|---|---|---|---|---|---|
| Simple to implement. | ✓ | ✗ | ✗ | ✓ | ✓ |
| Increase the quality quickly to detect problems with legacy code. | ✗ | ✓ | ✓ | ✓ | ✗ |
| Incremental validations. | ✓ | ✓ | ✓ | ✓ | ✓ |
| A team without a lot of experience. | ✓ | ✓ | ✓ | ✗ | ✗ |
| Reuse part of the work from a previous step. | ✗ | ✗ | ✓ | ✓ | ✓ |
| Detect problems with the interaction with other components. | ✗ | ✓ | ✓ | ✗ | ✗ |
| Send metrics to some tools such as Sonar. | ✓ | ✓ | ✗ | ✓ | ✗ |

There are many other scenarios and considerations to consider when deciding to use or implement a particular type of test. It is recommended to proceed step by step, implementing a test at a time and allowing the team or organization to build experience with each one before moving on to the next.

NOTE *If the scope of each type of test is not clearly understood, an interactive article on Martin Fowler's blog[18] explains each type of test graphically and provides some advice.*

## SUMMARY

This chapter examined various technologies and types of testing designed to minimize the risk of failures in production or other environments. Understanding the priority and purpose of each test type can be time-consuming and initially frustrating, often requiring many hours to implement even a simple feature.

One advantage of using tools such as Karate is the ability to delegate the creation of test skeletons to individuals beyond the development or QA team; for instance, business analysts can also contribute to this process.

Testing is a crucial component of application development. Attempting to implement all test types without sufficient experience can lead to numerous challenges, however. A more effective approach is to introduce them gradually, starting with unit and integration tests, followed by performance tests, and then extending to additional types as familiarity grows.

---

[18]https://martinfowler.com/articles/microservice-testing/

# CHAPTER 7

# DOCUMENTING THE ENDPOINTS

Application documentation is one of the most relevant aspects to prevent issues related to task responsibility. In many cases, companies invest hours in writing complex documents that detail the entire execution flow of a particular operation, yet overlook a critical element: the description of various endpoints, including the URL, request, and response. This information is essential for developers or other companies that intend to integrate with the application.

This chapter explains how to document the application's endpoints to provide valuable information for others. It also describes how this documentation can serve as input for tools such as Postman or Insomnia. Finally, it presents methods to validate whether the documentation adheres to a recognized standard.

## WHAT DOES DOCUMENTING MICROSERVICES MEAN?

Documenting anything shortens the time it takes for people to understand it. In the case of microservices, however, this may be different because there are numerous aspects to consider, such as the types of attributes and which values are valid or invalid.

Documenting microservices can take more or less time depending on when it is done. For example, if the documentation co-occurs with creating different endpoints, it takes less time. On the other hand, if someone tries to document an application with ten or more endpoints, it may take longer. This situation often arises when some legacy applications attempt to adopt new approaches.

### Which Options Exist to Do It?

There isn't just one option. Not all options are suitable for every case, but knowing they exist is essential. Not all of them are tools; in some cases, they are specifications that some tools implement.

### OpenAPI

OpenAPI is a specification that provides a standard way to describe HTTP APIs simply. It allows for the information of one API to be exposed on a Web page where users can check the details and execute requests.

The specification offers the possibility of documenting endpoints and requests/responses, adding some authentication mechanism and examples, and many other things. Another feature is the possibility of autogenerating and autoupdating the documentation from the application, reducing the risk that the documentation will not be updated.

Many tools or libraries exist to implement this specification, but the most relevant are:

- Swagger (UI, Editor, Codegen)[1]: This offers an interactive UI for exploring APIs, a specification editor, and tools for generating code.
- Springdoc (for Spring Boot)[2]: This automatically generates OpenAPI documentation using Spring annotations, minimizing the manual effort.
- Redoc[3]: This is a sleek and responsive OpenAPI documentation renderer.

## AsyncAPI

This is an open standard for documenting event-driven APIs. The idea behind it is similar to OpenAPI, but it focuses on illustrating how applications consume or produce events using messaging tools such as Kafka, RabbitMQ, AMQP, or AWS SQS.

In the same way, OpenAPI allows adding some examples and a Web page to trigger an event. Many tools or libraries exist to implement this specification, but the most relevant are:

- AsyncAPI Generator[4]: Assists in generating documentation and code from AsyncAPI specifications
- AsyncAPI Studio[5] and Playground: Interactive tools for designing and visualizing event-driven APIs

## Conventional Tools

Conventional tools do not follow a standard to document the application, so at some point, the company or team must decide on one. There could be disagreement about the standard to use.

This approach has additional problems, such as requiring a lot of manual work to keep the documentation updated.

Implementing it requires many tools, each offering different features, so knowing which ones exist is essential:

- Slate[6], Docusaurus[7], and MkDocs[8]: These static site generators help organize and publish API documentation.
- Confluence[9], Notion[10], and Wiki: These are valuable internal API documentation tools.
- Postman[11]: It's possible to create API documentation from request collections and offer mock APIs.

---

[1]https://editor.swagger.io/

[2]https://springdoc.org/

[3]https://redocly.com/docs/redoc

[4]https://github.com/asyncapi/generator

[5]https://studio.asyncapi.com/

[6]https://github.com/slatedocs/slate

[7]https://docusaurus.io/

[8]https://www.mkdocs.org/

[9]https://www.atlassian.com/en/software/confluence

[10]https://www.notion.com/

[11]https://www.postman.com/

## What Is the Best Way to Do It?

The decision on how to document an application's different endpoints could be difficult for someone who has never done it before or when multiple people have different preferences. To help decide which solution would be best, compare the different tools in Table 7.1.

**TABLE 7.1** Main things to consider when choosing an option.

| Feature | OpenAPI | AsyncAPI | Conventional Tools |
|---|---|---|---|
| Provides the possibility of automated generation. | ✓ | ✓ | ✗ |
| Syncs with the application without any assistance. | ✓ | ✓ | ✗ |
| There is a big community of companies and developers. | ✓ | ✓ | ✗ |
| Has tons of documentation and best practices. | ✓ | ✗ | ✗ |
| It's ideal for documenting REST APIs. | ✓ | ✗ | ✓ |
| It's ideal for documenting event-driven APIs. | ✗ | ✓ | ✓ |

All of the options have significant differences. Therefore, as depicted in Figure 7.1, creating an ADR to synthesize all the arguments into one document is a good idea.

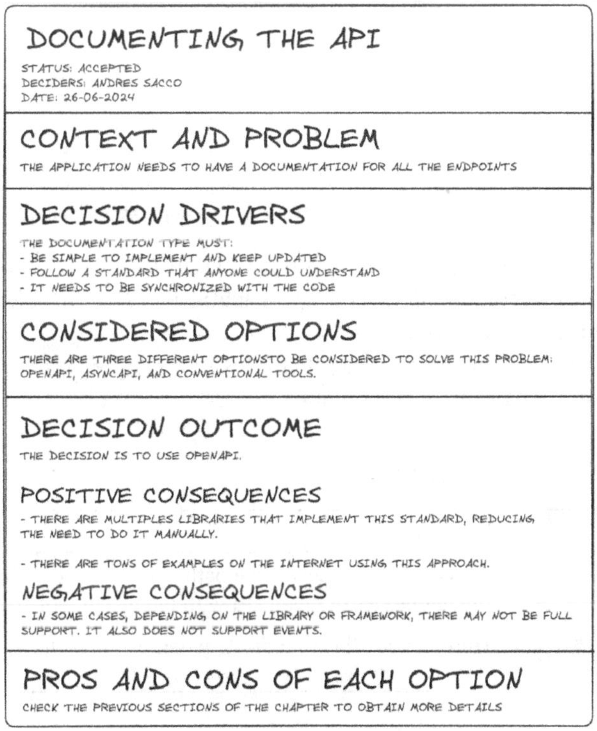

**DOCUMENTING THE API**

STATUS: ACCEPTED
DECIDERS: ANDRES SACCO
DATE: 26-06-2024

**CONTEXT AND PROBLEM**

THE APPLICATION NEEDS TO HAVE A DOCUMENTATION FOR ALL THE ENDPOINTS

**DECISION DRIVERS**

THE DOCUMENTATION TYPE MUST:
- BE SIMPLE TO IMPLEMENT AND KEEP UPDATED
- FOLLOW A STANDARD THAT ANYONE COULD UNDERSTAND
- IT NEEDS TO BE SYNCHRONIZED WITH THE CODE

**CONSIDERED OPTIONS**

THERE ARE THREE DIFFERENT OPTIONS TO BE CONSIDERED TO SOLVE THIS PROBLEM: OPENAPI, ASYNCAPI, AND CONVENTIONAL TOOLS.

**DECISION OUTCOME**

THE DECISION IS TO USE OPENAPI.

**POSITIVE CONSEQUENCES**

- THERE ARE MULTIPLES LIBRARIES THAT IMPLEMENT THIS STANDARD, REDUCING THE NEED TO DO IT MANUALLY.

- THERE ARE TONS OF EXAMPLES ON THE INTERNET USING THIS APPROACH.

**NEGATIVE CONSEQUENCES**

- IN SOME CASES, DEPENDING ON THE LIBRARY OR FRAMEWORK, THERE MAY NOT BE FULL SUPPORT. IT ALSO DOES NOT SUPPORT EVENTS.

**PROS AND CONS OF EACH OPTION**

CHECK THE PREVIOUS SECTIONS OF THE CHAPTER TO OBTAIN MORE DETAILS

**FIGURE 7.1** ADR about the decision of which documentation method to use.

As shown in the previous figure, the decision is to use a library or tool that produces OpenAPI documentation while offering a visual interface for viewing and interfacing.

## HOW ARE THE ENDPOINTS ON THE APPLICATION DOCUMENTED?

After checking the different options for documenting the endpoints in an application and deciding which is best, it's time to implement them in the microservice. In this chapter, we will add support for using OpenAPI 3.

The first thing to do is add the dependencies connected with OpenAPI, as shown in Listing 7.1.

```
<dependency>
  <groupId>org.springdoc</groupId>
  <artifactId>springdoc-openapi-starter-webmvc-ui</artifactId>
  <version>2.1.0</version>
</dependency>
```

*LISTING 7.1* Springdoc dependency.

Other dependencies related to implementing OpenAPI, such as Springfox, which only supports a previous version of the documentation standard, should be considered. Many libraries offer varying levels of documentation or integration with Spring Boot, so it is advisable to avoid those with limited support or outdated features.

The next step involves adding the configuration for the endpoints that expose the documentation. These settings must be included in the `application.yml` file, as shown in Listing 7.2.

```
springdoc:

  api-docs:
    path: "/documentation/api-docs"
  swagger-ui:
    path: "/documentation/swagger-ui"
```

*LISTING 7.2* Springdoc configuration in application.yml.

The definition in Listing 7.2 is optional, but standardizing how all company microservices expose information is recommended. This approach reduces the likelihood of spending excessive time locating the correct URL.

In Table 7.2, let's explain some of the attributes that can be configured on the application related to the generation of the documentation and expose a Web UI to view the information in a friendly way.

*TABLE 7.2* Relevant attributes to configure.

| Attribute | Description |
| --- | --- |
| springdoc.api-docs. path | This attribute indicates the path where the documentation is located in all the definitions of OpenAPI without any kind of UI. |
| springdoc.api-docs. enabled | Here, it's possible to indicate whether the endpoint is enabled. |

*(Continued)*

*TABLE 7.2* Continued

| Attribute | Description |
|---|---|
| `springdoc.`<br>`packages-to-scan` | These are the packages that are considered part of the application documentation. |
| `springdoc.`<br>`paths-to-exclude` | This indicates which paths the documentation will not consider as part of the documentation. |
| `springdoc.`<br>`show-actuator` | This indicates whether the application exposes all the endpoints connected with the actuator in the documentation. |
| `springdoc.swagger-ui.`<br>`path` | This attribute indicates the path where the documentation is located in all the definitions of OpenAPI with a UI. |
| `springdoc.swagger-ui.`<br>`enabled` | Here, it's possible to indicate whether the Web UI is enabled. |

Many other attributes can be configured in OpenAPI, but only some are relevant to the scope of this book. The official Web site of Springdoc has an extensive list of characteristics with full explanations[12].

After introducing these simple changes, it's possible to run the application in the same way and make a request to *http://localhost:8090/api/flights/reservation/documentation/swagger-ui* to obtain the duplicate content that appears in Figure 7.2, which contains all the application's endpoints.

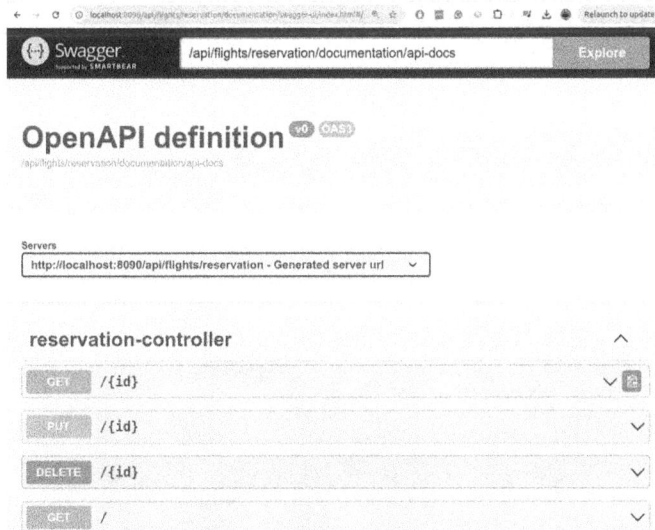

*FIGURE 7.2* Access to the UI with the documentation.

Documentation is essential—it should include the description, required parameters, and many other details. A microservice should include at least some documentation.

---

[12]https://springdoc.org/#properties

In many cases, this type of documentation is not helpful because it is not possible to import it into another tool, such as Postman, Insomnia, or Backstage. These tools need a document in YML or JSON format; this is the actual format of OpenAPI, but to be more user-friendly, the library offers a UI.

To obtain the document's actual format, make a request to `http://localhost:8090/api/flights/reservation/documentation/api-docs`. This will return a document like the one in Listing 7.3.

```
{
  "openapi": "3.0.1",
  "info": {
    "title": "OpenAPI definition",
    "version": "v0"
  },
  "servers": [
    {
      "url": "http://localhost:8090/api/flights/reservation",
      "description": "Generated server url"
    }
  ],
  "paths": {
    "/{id}": {
      "get": {
        "tags": [
          "reservation-controller"
        ],
        "operationId": "getReservationById",
        "parameters": [
          {
            "name": "id",
            "in": "path",
            "required": true,
            "schema": {
              "type": "integer",
              "format": "int64"
            }
          }
        ],
        "responses": {
          "200": {
            "description": "OK",
            "content": {
              "*/*": {
                "schema": {
                  "$ref": "#/components/schemas/ReservationDTO"
                }
              }
            }
          }
        }
      }
    }
    //Other endpoints of the application
  },
```

```
  "components": {
    "schemas": {
      "ContactDTO": {
        "required": [
          "email",
          "telephoneNumber"
        ]
      //Other information
      }
    }
  }
}
```

**LISTING 7.3** api-docs definition of the endpoints.

The microservice's documentation allows sharing information with other people or companies to reduce or mitigate the problems associated with using the different endpoints. It also, however, introduces the problem of needing more information about the correct use of each endpoint. The following section provides more information about how to tackle this problem.

## Documenting the Different Endpoints

Essential documentation with a simple UI is a considerable step, but it does not give anything that can be shown to or shared with others who want to use a microservice. If the documentation doesn't offer relevant information, users will request different parameters as they will not know which are required or what the correct formats for the attributes are.

Let's reduce this problem by introducing valuable information about each endpoint. First, to keep the controller and not have many lines of code related to the documentation, a possible approach is to create an interface containing all the controller method definitions, as in Listing 7.4.

```
package com.twa.flights.api.reservation.controller.resource;

import com.twa.flights.api.reservation.dto.ReservationDTO;
import io.github.resilience4j.ratelimiter.annotation.RateLimiter;
import jakarta.validation.Valid;
import org.springframework.http.ResponseEntity;
import org.springframework.web.bind.annotation.*;

import java.util.List;

public interface ReservationResource {

    @GetMapping("/{id}")
    @RateLimiter(name = "reservation", fallbackMethod =
"fallbackGetReservationById")
    ResponseEntity<ReservationDTO> getReservationById(@PathVariable Long
id);

    @GetMapping
    ResponseEntity<List<ReservationDTO>> getReservations();
```

```
    @PostMapping
    ResponseEntity<ReservationDTO> save(@RequestBody @Valid
ReservationDTO reservation);

    @PutMapping("/{id}")
    ResponseEntity<ReservationDTO> update(
            @PathVariable Long id, @RequestBody @Valid ReservationDTO
reservation);

    @DeleteMapping("/{id}")
    ResponseEntity<Void> delete(@PathVariable Long id);
}
```

**LISTING 7.4** Interface to reduce the complexity of the controller.

The definition of the different methods in Listing 7.4 reduces the number of lines of code that appear on the controller, which looks similar to Listing 7.5.

```
package com.twa.flights.api.reservation.controller;

import com.twa.flights.api.reservation.controller.resource.
ReservationResource;
//Previous imports

@Validated
@RestController
@RequestMapping("/")
public class ReservationController implements ReservationResource {
    //Previous logic
}
```

**LISTING 7.5** Interface to reduce the complexity of the controller.

The controller's code is annotation agnostic and straightforward because it is in charge of the interface, which is vital, as you will see at the end of this section. Let's introduce details to the documentation, as in Listing 7.6, which shows how to use another annotation connected with the dependencies that have been part of the project since the beginning of this section.

```
package com.twa.flights.api.reservation.controller.resource;

import io.swagger.v3.oas.annotations.Operation;
import io.swagger.v3.oas.annotations.tags.Tag;

// Previous imports

@Tag(name = "Reservation", description = "Operations about the
reservations")
public interface ReservationResource {

    @Operation(summary = "Get a reservation by ID", description =
"Fetches a reservation by its unique ID")
    @GetMapping("/{id}")
```

```
    @RateLimiter(name = "reservation", fallbackMethod =
"fallbackGetReservationById")
    ResponseEntity<ReservationDTO> getReservationById(@PathVariable Long
id);
}
```

**LISTING 7.6** First steps in the documentation of the different endpoints.

The two annotations, `@Tag` and `@Operation`, provide different capabilities. The first allows operations to be grouped across multiple controllers, enabling the categorization of endpoints, while the second is used to describe the purpose of each individual endpoint.

There are not just two annotations to provide information on the API; there is a set of different annotations, each incrementing the endpoint data. Table 7.3 shows the most relevant annotations, which cover various scenarios, such as the definition of the response and the types of content each endpoint has.

**TABLE 7.3** Relevant annotations in OpenAPI.

| Annotation | Description |
|---|---|
| `@Tag` | This annotation is a way to group different endpoints that have some level of connection. |
| `@Operation` | This annotation defines a single API operation or endpoint, including details such as a summary and description. |
| `@ApiResponses` | This annotation contains the list of possible responses that the API could return in different situations. It's necessary to use the following annotation to provide all the information. |
| `@ApiResponse` | Using this annotation, it's possible to indicate the different HTTP codes with a problem description. This is especially useful in cases in which the microservices return vague information about errors. |
| `@Parameter` | This annotation represents all the parameters that the endpoint receives on the URL. |
| `@RequestBody` | This annotation describes the request body of an operation, including the content type and the schema. |
| `@Schema` | This annotation explains the response's schema, such as DTOs. It can be used in combination with `@RequestBody` or `@ApiResponse`. |
| `@Content` | This defines the media type of the request or response and can be combined with `@RequestBody` or `@ApiResponse`. |
| `@Header` | This annotation explains some particular headers that the application needs to receive and the proposal. |
| `@Hidden` | It's possible to hide the endpoints to expose the information using this annotation. |

After understanding all the possible annotations and their scope or responsibility, it's time to modify `ReservationResource` to include them. Listing 7.7 shows the modifications related to the response type and the parameter in an endpoint.

```java
package com.twa.flights.api.reservation.controller.resource;

import io.swagger.v3.oas.annotations.Operation;
import io.swagger.v3.oas.annotations.responses.ApiResponse;
import io.swagger.v3.oas.annotations.responses.ApiResponses;
import io.swagger.v3.oas.annotations.Parameter;
import io.swagger.v3.oas.annotations.tags.Tag;

// Previous imports

@Tag(name = "Reservation", description = "Operations about the
reservations")
public interface ReservationResource {

    @Operation(summary = "Get a reservation by ID", description =
"Fetches a reservation by its unique ID")
    @ApiResponses(value = {
        @ApiResponse(responseCode = "200", description = "Reservation
found successfully", content = {@Content(mediaType = "application/json",
schema = @Schema(implementation = ReservationDTO.class))}),
        @ApiResponse(responseCode = "404", description = "Reservation
not found", content = {@Content(mediaType = "application/json", schema =
@Schema(implementation = ErrorDTO.class))}),
        @ApiResponse(responseCode = "429", description = "Rate limit
exceeded", content = {@Content(mediaType = "application/json", schema =
@Schema(implementation = ErrorDTO.class))})})
    @Parameter(name = "id", description = "ID of the reservation to
fetch", required = true)
    @GetMapping("/{id}")
    @RateLimiter(name = "reservation", fallbackMethod =
"fallbackGetReservationById")
    ResponseEntity<ReservationDTO> getReservationById(@PathVariable Long
id);
    //Other methods
}
```

*LISTING 7.7* Adding annotations to document an endpoint

The modifications are simple to include in the documentation, and many details about the different response codes can be included. Let's do the same process on another endpoint to see how other annotations, such as ResponseBody, look, as in Listing 7.8.

```java
package com.twa.flights.api.reservation.controller.resource;

import io.swagger.v3.oas.annotations.parameters.RequestBody;

// Previous imports

@Tag(name = "Reservation", description = "Operations about the
reservations")
public interface ReservationResource {

    @Operation(summary = "Save a new reservation", description = "Creates
a new reservation")
```

```
    @ApiResponses(value = {
            @ApiResponse(responseCode = "201", description =
"Reservation created successfully", content = {@Content(mediaType =
"application/json", schema = @Schema(implementation = ReservationDTO.
class))}),
            @ApiResponse(responseCode = "400", description = "Invalid
reservation data", content = {@Content(mediaType = "application/json",
schema = @Schema(implementation = ErrorDTO.class))})
    })
    @RequestBody(description = "Details of the reservation to create",
required = true,
            content = @Content(schema = @Schema(implementation =
ReservationDTO.class)))
    @PostMapping
    ResponseEntity<ReservationDTO> save(@RequestBody @Valid
ReservationDTO reservation);
    //Other methods
}
```

**LISTING 7.8** Add documentation to another endpoint.

After all these modifications, the next step is to run the application to check how the documentation appears. Enter the following URL: `http://localhost:8090/api/flights/reservation/documentation`. This will display a Web page similar to Figure 7.3.

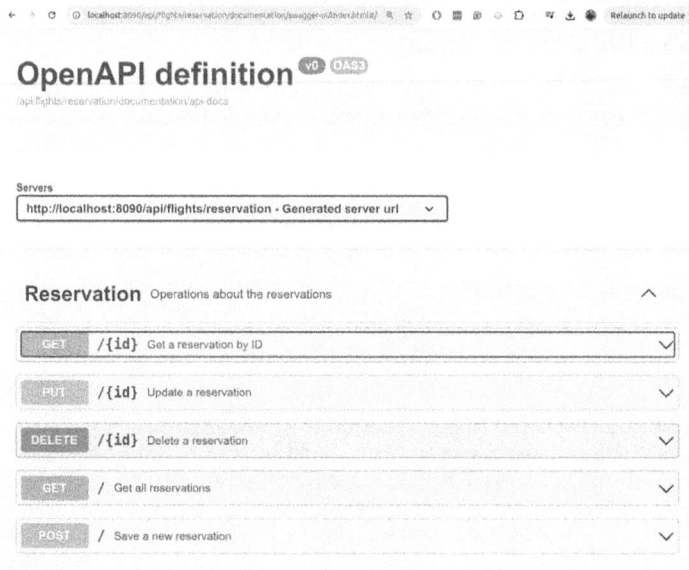

**FIGURE 7.3** Access to the UI with the documentation and descriptions.

Each endpoint can display all the information about the method and object that must be sent in the case of PUT/POST. This interface also allows users to execute requests to the API, like the one shown in Figure 7.4.

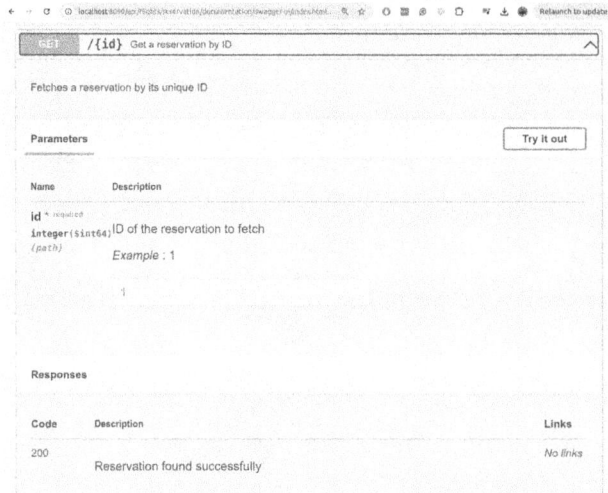

**FIGURE 7.4** Full description of an endpoint.

Documentation is an excellent way to distribute information to many other teams. Still, it's necessary to consider that some endpoints that manage sensitive information need security mechanisms to reduce the possibility of a significant security issue.

## Adding Examples to the Documentation

One of the main problems when accessing an application's documentation is discovering the possible values for each attribute. This situation often requires numerous requests to an endpoint or emailing several people to find the correct values. While the solution may seem obvious, it is not always the case for developers. If examples of each attribute or endpoint are included in the documentation, these issues can be significantly reduced.

Let's modify the previous documentation to add examples that create a reservation in the endpoint. To do that, it's necessary to use the annotation @ExampleObject, which appears in Listing 7.9 and contains JSON representing a valid request.

```
//Other annotations
@ApiResponses(value = {
        @ApiResponse(responseCode = "201", description =
"Reservation created successfully", content = {@Content(mediaType =
"application/json", schema = @Schema(implementation = ReservationDTO.
class), examples = {
                @ExampleObject(name = "Successful response",
                        value = "{\"id\": 6,\"itineraryId\":\"2\",\"
searchId\":\"2\",\"passengers\":[{\"firstName\":\"Andres\",\"lastName\":\
"Sacco\",\"documentNumber\":\"987654321\",\"documentType\":\"DNI\",\"nat
ionality\":\"AR\",\"birthday\":\"1985-01-01\"}],\"contact\":{\"telephone
Number\":\"54911111111\",\"email\":\"sacco.andres@gmail.com\"}}")
        })}),
        @ApiResponse(responseCode = "400", description = "Invalid
reservation data", content = {@Content(mediaType = "application/json",
schema = @Schema(implementation = ErrorDTO.class))})
    })
```

```
    ResponseEntity<ReservationDTO> save(@RequestBody @Valid
ReservationDTO reservation);
```

**LISTING 7.9** Add examples to the response.

Let's do the same but in another endpoint, and instead of having all the JSON together, let's add some breaklines, as shown in Listing 7.10.

```
    //Other annotations
    @RequestBody(description = "Details of the reservation to create",
required = true,
            content = @Content(mediaType = "application/json",
                    schema = @Schema(implementation = ReservationDTO.
class),
                    examples = {
                            @ExampleObject(name = "Valid reservation
request",
                                    value = "{\n" +
                                        "   \"itineraryId\":
\"2\",\n" +
                                        "   \"searchId\": \"2\",\n" +
                                        "   \"passengers\": [\n" +
                                        "     {\n" +
                                        "       \"firstName\":
\"Andres\",\n" +
                                        "       \"lastName\":
\"Sacco\",\n" +
                                        "       \"documentNumber\":
\"987654321\",\n" +
                                        "       \"documentType\":
\"DNI\",\n" +
                                        "       \"nationality\":
\"AR\",\n" +
                                        "       \"birthday\": \"1985-
01-01\"\n" +
                                        "     }\n" +
                                        "   ],\n" +
                                        "   \"contact\": {\n" +
                                        "     \"telephoneNumber\":
\"54911111111\",\n" +
                                        "     \"email\": \"sacco.
andres@gmail.com\"\n" +
                                        "   }\n" +
                                        "}"),
                            @ExampleObject(name = "Invalid reservation
request",
                                    value = "{\n" +
                                        "   \"itineraryId\":
\"3\",\n" +
                                        "   \"searchId\": \"4\",\n" +
                                        "   \"passengers\": [\n" +
                                        "     {\n" +
                                        "       \"firstName\":
\"Maria\",\n" +
                                        "       \"lastName\":
\"Gonzalez\",\n" +
```

```
\"123456789\",\n" +

\"PASSPORT\",\n" +

\"USS\",\n" +

05-20\"\n" +



\"1234567890\",\n" +

gonzalez@example.com\"\n" +


                        })
        )
    ResponseEntity<ReservationDTO> save(@RequestBody @Valid
ReservationDTO reservation);
```

```
"       \"documentNumber\":

"       \"documentType\":

"       \"nationality\":

"       \"birthday\": \"1990-

"    }\n" +
"  ],\n" +
"  \"contact\": {\n" +
"    \"telephoneNumber\":

"    \"email\": \"maria.

"  }\n" +
"}")
```

**LISTING 7.10** Add examples to the request.

After making these modifications, the next time someone accesses the documentation, it will look as in Figure 7.5.

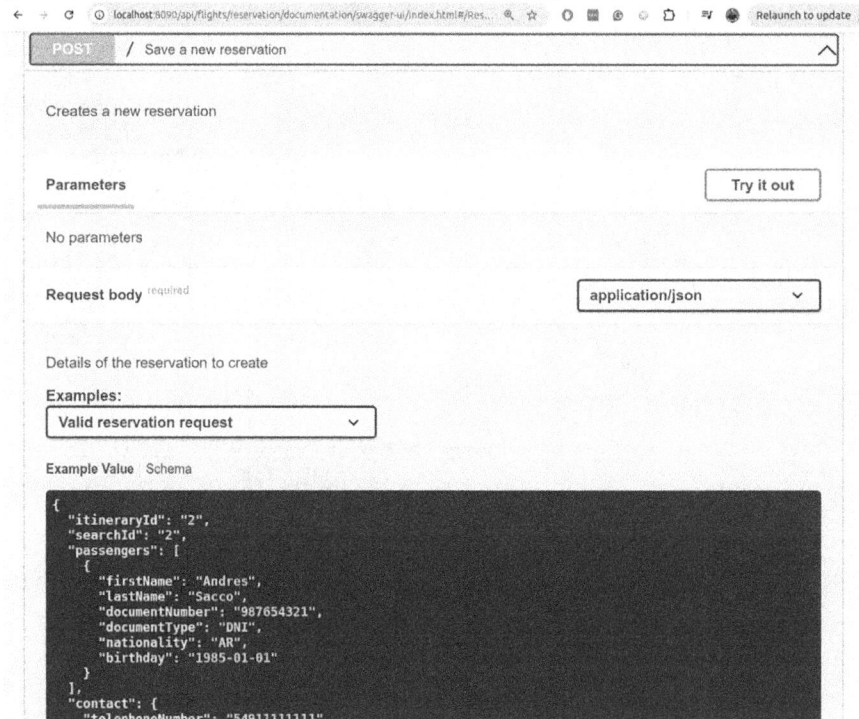

**FIGURE 7.5** Example of the save endpoint with examples.

As a suggestion, try to add examples to all the endpoints, not just the PUT/POST method, because this could help developers understand which values are valid in a GET.

## CHECKING THE DOCUMENTATION

Documenting an application is vital for minimizing communication among multiple people when gathering information, lowering the risk of numerous incorrect requests to invoke an endpoint. If no one checks that the documentation adheres to the agreed-upon standards, however, it would have the same effect as if it did not exist.

### Which Mechanism Exists to Check the Documentation?

Some tools reduce the work of manual revisions to check that everything follows the standard. Of course, it's possible to do it manually. Still, there is always the risk that someone will forget the rules or not check whether something affects other teams.

There are two tools that validate whether the documentation adheres to the OpenAPI specifications: zally[13] and Stoplight[14]. Of course, there are many other tools, but they lack the same level of maturity and user base, increasing the risk that problems may be challenging to resolve.

### zally

zally is an open-source API linting tool developed by Zalando, a company with extensive experience in creating tools and standards for common challenges many users face. It ensures that an API's documentation adheres to the specifications of OpenAPI. This tool provides a command-line interface and a REST API, allowing users to submit the API's structure and verify whether the documentation is accurate. If any issues arise, it will provide information about which part of the specification is incorrect.

This tool was designed to be self-hosted, with the idea of integrating it into a CI/CD pipeline and validating it before deploying it in production. Of course, it offers many predefined rules, which can also be disabled, or custom rules can be created.

### Stoplight

This is another option for validating an application's documentation. The focus of this tool goes beyond API linting; it serves as a governance platform that allows for defining documentation similarly to a conventional tool. This tool emphasizes team collaboration and quality assurance through an intuitive UI where everything is easy to accomplish, such as designing or modifying an API specification.

This tool also allows creating mocks for APIs during the development process or performing integration tests. Additionally, it can be integrated into the CI/CD pipeline as part of the validation process before deployment to production. It is, however, essential to note that using this tool requires a paid license.

### Which Is the Best Option?

Both options are strong candidates for validating the documentation, but let's examine their main differences, which are shown in Table 7.4.

---

[13]https://opensource.zalando.com/zally/
[14]https://stoplight.io/

*TABLE 7.4* Main things to consider when choosing an option.

| Feature | Zally | Stoplight |
|---|---|---|
| Supports OpenAPI. | ✓ | ✓ |
| It's possible to create custom rules. | ✓ | ✓ |
| Supports use in a pipeline. | ✓ | ✓ |
| Integrating the validations locally as part of a project is possible. | ✓ | ✗ |
| It's well documented. | ✓ | ✓ |
| It's simple to implement without the need to maintain external tools. | ✓ | ✗ |

There are significant differences between the options. Of course, they are all great alternatives to validating the documentation instead of doing it manually, because doing it manually carries the risk of human error. Therefore, as depicted in Figure 7.6, creating an ADR to synthesize all the arguments into one document is a good idea.

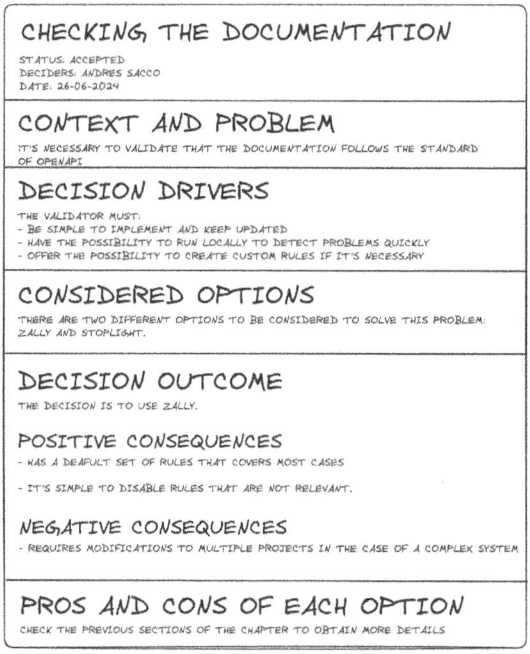

*FIGURE 7.6* ADR for the decision of which option to use.

Consequently, the ADR in the previous figure highlights the use of a library or tool that produces OpenAPI documentation while offering a visual interface for viewing and interfacing.

### How to Implement the Validations in the Application

The next step, after deciding on the best tool to validate the documentation, is implementing the solution on the application. To do that, creating a new profile that only validates the documentation is necessary, excluding all the other tests. In this example, let's use the name DT and include the SureFire plugin with the correct exclusion, as in Listing 7.11.

```
<profile>
   <id>DT</id>
   <build>
        <plugins>
             <plugin>
                   <groupId>org.apache.maven.plugins</groupId>
                   <artifactId>maven-surefire-plugin</artifactId>
                   <version>${maven.surefire.version}</version>
                   <configuration>
                        <excludes>
                              <exclude>**/unit/**Test.java</
exclude>
                              <exclude>**/performance/**Test.
java</exclude>
                              <exclude>**/integration/**Test.
java</exclude>
                              <exclude>**/architecture/**Test.
java</exclude>
                        </excludes>
                        <argLine>-Dfile.encoding=UTF-8</argLine>
                        <argLine>-XX:+EnableDynamicAgentLoading</
argLine>
                   </configuration>
             </plugin>
        </plugins>
   </build>
</profile>
```

**LISTING 7.11** Adding a new profile to execute the validations.

After that, it's necessary to include the required plugins to run and stop the application during the pre-integration test phase. If this step is not taken, the application will continue running after execution. Additionally, a plugin must be added to extract the OpenAPI definition from the application and generate a file with that information for use by the validator. Listing 7.12 contains all the configurations of both plugins.

```
<plugin>
   <groupId>org.springframework.boot</groupId>
   <artifactId>spring-boot-maven-plugin</artifactId>
   <configuration>
        <wait>10000</wait>
        <maxAttempts>180</maxAttempts>
        <jmxPort>${random.jmx.port}</jmxPort>
        <directories>
             <directory>src/conf/integration</directory>
        </directories>
   </configuration>
   <executions>
        <execution>
             <goals>
                   <goal>repackage</goal>
             </goals>
        </execution>
        <execution>
             <id>start-app</id>
```

```
            <phase>pre-integration-test</phase>
            <goals>
                    <goal>start</goal>
            </goals>
        </execution>
        <execution>
            <id>stop-app</id>
            <phase>post-integration-test</phase>
            <goals>
                    <goal>stop</goal>
            </goals>
        </execution>
    </executions>
</plugin>

<plugin>
    <groupId>org.springdoc</groupId>
    <artifactId>springdoc-openapi-maven-plugin</artifactId>
    <version>${springdoc-openapi-maven-plugin.version}</version>
    <executions>
        <execution>
            <id>integration-test</id>
            <goals>
                    <goal>generate</goal>
            </goals>
        </execution>
    </executions>
    <configuration>
        <apiDocsUrl>http://localhost:8090/api/flights/reservation/
documentation/api-docs</apiDocsUrl>
        <outputFileName>api.yaml</outputFileName>
        <outputDir>src/main/resources/openapi</outputDir>
        <skip>false</skip>
    </configuration>
</plugin>
```

**LISTING 7.12** Plugins to run and obtain the documentation.

The last step is adding zally-maven-plugin[15], which performs the validations. Instead of having zally run on a server, this plugin allows users to use the rules of the tools without requiring a tool to run on a server. Listing 7.13 has a default configuration, which indicates where the execution result will be and which rules are disabled.

```
<plugin>
    <groupId>com.ethlo.zally</groupId>
    <artifactId>zally-maven-plugin</artifactId>
    <version>${zally-maven-plugin.version}</version>
    <configuration>
        <!--Configure severities that fail the build. Default is MUST,
SHOULD -->
        <failOn>MUST</failOn>
        <!-- The input file to validate -->
        <source>src/main/resources/openapi/api.yaml</source>
```

---

[15]https://github.com/ethlo/zally-maven-plugin

```
        <!--Ignore certain rules. Default is none -->
        <skipRules>
                <skipRule>ApiAudienceRule</skipRule>
                <skipRule>ApiIdentifierRule</skipRule>
                <skipRule>CommonFieldTypesRule</skipRule>
                <skipRule>UseProblemJsonRule</skipRule>
                <skipRule>JsonProblemAsDefaultResponseRule</skipRule>
                <skipRule>SecureAllEndpointsRule</skipRule>
                <skipRule>SecureAllEndpointsWithScopesRule</skipRule>
                <skipRule>NoVersionInUriRule</skipRule>
                <skipRule>FunctionalNamingForHostnamesRule</skipRule>
                <skipRule>ExtensibleEnumRule</skipRule>
                <skipRule>SnakeCaseInPropNameRule</skipRule>
                <skipRule>ProprietaryHeadersRule</skipRule>
                <skipRule>IdentifyResourcesViaPathSegments</skipRule>
                <skipRule>VersionInInfoSectionRule</skipRule>
        </skipRules>

        <!-- The input file to validate -->
        <resultFile>target/openapi-results.json</resultFile>
</configuration>
<executions>
        <execution>
                <phase>verify</phase>
                <goals>
                        <goal>report</goal>
                        <goal>validate</goal>
                </goals>
        </execution>
</executions>
<dependencies>
        <dependency>
                <!-- The pluggable rule-set you want to run -->
                <groupId>org.zalando</groupId>
                <artifactId>zally-ruleset-zalando</artifactId>
                <version>${zally-ruleset-zalando.version}</version>
        </dependency>
        <dependency>
                <groupId>com.fasterxml.jackson.dataformat</groupId>
                <artifactId>jackson-dataformat-yaml</artifactId>
                <version>2.12.3</version>
        </dependency>
</dependencies>
</plugin>
```

**LISTING 7.13** Add a plugin to execute the validations.

With all the configurations, executing Maven to validate and check what happens with the documentation is time-consuming. The command and the result of the execution are shown in Listing 7.14.

```
$ mvn verify -P DT
..........

[INFO] API path hierarchy:
```

```
[INFO]
[INFO]         ├── {id}
[INFO]         │     ├── GET - getReservationById
[INFO]         │     ├── PUT - update
[INFO]         │     └── DELETE - delete
[INFO]         ├── GET - getReservations
[INFO]         └── POST - save


..........

[INFO] Rule violations (8)
[INFO] ------------------
[WARNING] 218 - MUST - ApiMetaInformationRule - Description has to be
provided - /info/description
[WARNING] 218 - MUST - ApiMetaInformationRule - Version has to follow
the Semver rules - /info/version
[WARNING] 218 - MUST - ApiMetaInformationRule - Contact name has to be
provided - /info/contact/name
[WARNING] 218 - MUST - ApiMetaInformationRule - Contact URL has to be
provided - /info/contact/url
[WARNING] 218 - MUST - ApiMetaInformationRule - Contact e-mail has to be
provided - /info/contact/email
[WARNING] 110 - MUST - SuccessResponseAsJsonObjectRule - Always return
JSON objects as top-level data structures to support extensibility - /
paths/~1/get/responses/200/content/application~1json/schema
[WARNING] 153 - MUST - Use429HeaderForRateLimitRule - Response has
to contain rate limit information via headers - /paths/~1{id}/get/
responses/429
[WARNING] 235 - SHOULD - DateTimePropertiesSuffixRule - Property
"birthday" of type "string" and format "date" should match one of the
patterns [.*_at]" - /components/schemas/PassengerDTO/properties/birthday
[WARNING]
[INFO]
[INFO] Writing result file to target/openapi-results.json
[INFO]
[INFO] ------------------------------------------------------------
[INFO] BUILD FAILURE
[INFO] ------------------------------------------------------------
[INFO] Total time:  24.296 s
[INFO] Finished at: 2025-03-08T11:53:51-03:00
[INFO] ------------------------------------------------------------
```

**LISTING 7.14** Result of the validations.

The validation results indicate some mistakes in the documentation. The official documentation of Zalando[16] has a detailed explanation of each rule.

To address the issues stemming from the documentation's lack of information regarding the owner and the application name, let's create a class named OpenApiConfiguration with the @ Configuration annotation and some annotations related to OpenAPI to incorporate this information, as shown in Listing 7.15.

---

[16]https://opensource.zalando.com/restful-api-guidelines/

```
package com.twa.flights.api.reservation.configuration;

import io.swagger.v3.oas.annotations.OpenAPIDefinition;
import io.swagger.v3.oas.annotations.info.Contact;
import io.swagger.v3.oas.annotations.info.Info;
import io.swagger.v3.oas.annotations.info.License;
import org.springframework.context.annotation.Configuration;

@Configuration
@OpenAPIDefinition(
        info =
                @Info(
                        title = "API Reservations",
                        version = "1.0",
                        description = "API for managing reservations",
                        contact =
                                @Contact(
                                        name = "Andres Sacco",
                                        email = "sacco.andres@gmail.com",
                                        url = "https://example.com"),
                        license =
                                @License(
                                        name = "Apache 2.0",
                                        url =
"https://www.apache.org/licenses/LICENSE-2.0")))
public class OpenApiConfiguration {}
```

**LISTING 7.15** Class with the information from the documentation.

To simplify the process, instead of solving all the problems, let's skip some rules, such as those that appear in Listing 7.16.

```
<skipRules>
                <!-- Previous skip rules →
    <skipRule>DateTimePropertiesSuffixRule</skipRule>
    <skipRule>SuccessResponseAsJsonObjectRule</skipRule>
    <skipRule>Use429HeaderForRateLimitRule</skipRule>
</skipRules>
```

**LISTING 7.16** Add exclusion of some rules.

Last but not least, execute the same command again to check whether the changes work with the validator. The result of the execution is shown in Listing 7.17.

```
$ mvn verify -P DT
……….. .

[INFO] API path hierarchy:
[INFO]
[INFO]        ├── {id}
[INFO]        │    ├── GET - getReservationById
[INFO]        │    ├── PUT - update
[INFO]        │    └── DELETE - delete
[INFO]        ├── GET - getReservations
[INFO]        └── POST - save
……….. .
```

```
[INFO] Rule violations (0)
[INFO] ------------------
[WARNING]
[INFO]
[INFO] Writing result file to target/openapi-results.json
[INFO]
[INFO] ------------------------------------------------------------
[INFO] BUILD SUCCESS
[INFO] ------------------------------------------------------------
[INFO] Total time:  25.342 s
[INFO] Finished at: 2025-03-08T15:12:01-03:00
[INFO] ------------------------------------------------------------
```

***LISTING 7.17*** Result of the execution.

Executing the validations, analyzing the results, introducing modifications, or skipping some rules could take time. Therefore, I suggest ignoring any rules where the solution is not trivial.

## SUMMARY

Documentation plays a vital role in development because the information within it reduces the possibility that a mistake will be introduced when integrating with the application, such as using a different URL or a request with the wrong format.

Another key point highlighted in this chapter was validating the documentation to check that it follows the required standard.

# CHAPTER 8

# EXTERNALIZING THE CONFIGURATION

A good practice is to avoid hardcoding values in the application's code. If changing a value is necessary, searching through multiple files to find where those values are located is essential. Additionally, many aspects depend on each environment, such as the URL of other microservices and the database information. Therefore, it makes sense to have a single file that contains all of the hardcoded values, simplifying the process of making changes. What happens, though, if changing those values with a specific frequency is required? What if changing a value for a few minutes is essential? Both of those questions, and many others, will be answered in this chapter.

## INTERNAL CONFIGURATION

One of the most significant changes to applications over the years is the ability to create one file representing each environment, reducing the number of places required to find a property to change the value. Of course, different frameworks and libraries have their standards related to the naming of files, but in the case of Spring Boot, the file's name is `application.yml` by default. This does not, however, mean that the application file will always use this naming convention because the framework allows one to create a file with any name and pass it as a parameter when the application is run. Considering this, making one file for each environment and using an environment variable to define which file is necessary is possible. Figure 8.1 shows how it's possible to have multiple configuration files for one application.

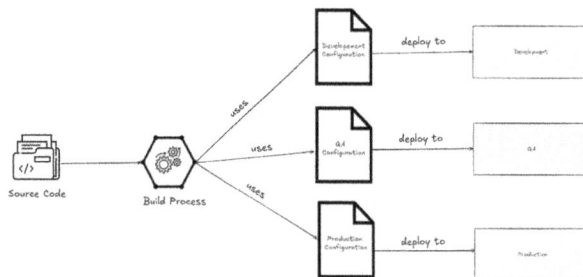

**FIGURE 8.1** Multiple configuration files inside one application.

Having one file for each environment allows tracking the history of changes to those files in case a versioning tool such as Git is being used. Therefore, it's easy to revert changes that cause problems in one environment or identify a file that someone forgot to add a configuration to. This is not a strange situation when many changes are introduced to the configuration, and the application has multiple environments.

### Problems with This Approach

This approach is a good option if it's the first time that a team is working with microservices, or the number of changes is significantly small. Still, there are some problems that should be considered, some of which are outlined in the following list:

- Configuration Duplication: Not everything in the configuration files changes across the different environments; many similar properties may be shared among all the environments. If a property changes or a new property is added, it is essential to remember to modify all the files. A potential solution for this issue is to have a base file, application.yml, and create separate files that override only the properties that change for each specific environment.
- Hard to Update Without Redeploying: If any change (e.g., URL, limit, or feature flag) is made to the application, there is no other option but to deploy the entire application, and this process takes time to complete in most situations.
- Testing Environment Conflicts: There is a high risk that someone will modify the configuration for testing proposals and push the changes into the source code.
- Security Risks: Some critical attributes, such as usernames and passwords from external services, such as databases or FTP, could be accessible to anyone.
- Lack of Validation: Given that the application's configuration could be split across multiple files, there is a risk that some properties will never be validated until the application runs, producing problems. A possible solution to this problem is to use the annotation @Configu-rationProperties to detect the problems earlier.

It's necessary to recognize that the list of problems could be more extensive depending on an organization's situation and the number of deployments or changes the application undergoes. Perhaps some companies only introduce changes to the configuration once a month. In contrast, others make changes each week, so the perception of these problems could be different, but the problems still exist.

## EXTERNAL CONFIGURATION

Externalizing the configuration provides a viable option to addressing many issues associated with consolidating all the values that determine the behavior of microservices in a single location. This approach offers the flexibility to modify the values of various attributes outside of the application without requiring a redeployment of the application, reducing the time to see the effects of the changes.

This approach requires moving part or all of the configuration that appears in `application.yml` externally, so the application is packaged. When executed, the values or the URL where the information is stored are transferred, which is a security threat because anyone could have the username/password for a database or service that contains sensitive information. On the other hand, this approach requires adopting specific standards regarding how to name the different profiles/environments (such as dev, prod, and test) because there are multiple applications, making it necessary to ensure that all the configurations from one environment are simple to identify.

### What Are the Main Benefits?

This approach became popular when microservices first appeared; many companies adopted it as a new paradigm for creating systems. It has some benefits, independent of the mechanism to externalize the configuration. Let's see some of them:

- Environment-Specific Configurations: Make it simple to switch or change the values of different settings in the environments without needing to change the code and wait for the execution of a pipeline to see the modifications. This could be a solution when something urgent needs to be changed or for A/B testing purposes.
- Centralized Configuration Management: Since one location contains all the information, the likelihood of the same value appearing multiple times is minimized. Additionally, it is easy to find and replace values, and it is simple to maintain and keep updated. Improved Security: Sensitive information such as API keys and database passwords can be managed and kept outside of the code, ensuring that not all company members have access to this information, reducing the risk of bad use.
- Better Scalability and Consistency Across Services: Depending on the tool, some common configurations, such as the log level or where the applications need to save them, could be shared.
- Simplifies CI/CD Pipelines: The configuration is injected dynamically during the deployment process in the environments, so the package maintains the same configuration in case something changes.
- Version Control for Configuration Changes: Utilize Git or another tool to version the modifications, enabling the ability to roll back or view previous values.

Note that, depending on the tool or strategy chosen, the benefits could increase, but at the same time, it's necessary to consider the downsides, such as maintainability, scalability, and availability. None of the options has 100% benefits without a risk or associated problem.

## What Ways Exist to Do It?

There are many options for externalizing the configuration, but in this book, only the three most relevant options that companies usually use, with a few minor variations, will be covered.

## Environment Variables

Using variables where the application retrieves values from the system is not a new concept; however, it requires coordination between the developers and the infrastructure team regarding naming the variables and the values based on the environment.

In the early days of Java applications, when Spring Boot did not exist, this was the default method for removing sensitive information from a configuration file. It is, however, still used when only one attribute changes frequently or has certain security restrictions.

One problem with this approach is the number of variables that must be declared in an application. Imagine that the application requires fifty variables to be declared across three different environments; extrapolating this situation to ten microservices could create a chaotic scenario for anyone.

## Command-Line Arguments

Instead of having all the variables declared in the system and loaded for the application, the alternative is to pass the values of all the attributes that support dynamic values as arguments when running the application.

This approach could be combined with the previous one to indicate the application file that needs to be used to load the configuration. In this situation, it is like a combination of external and internal configuration, which is not the best option, but it's possible.

There is no limit on the number of arguments to pass to the `run` command, but the main problem is the command's size, which affects the ability to read and detect potential issues with the values.

## Config Server

The last option requires using a service that contains and exposes all the configurations of the different applications. Thus, they all need to connect to the configuration server to obtain information about a specific environment. Multiple tools exist to solve this problem, such as Consul[1], Vault[2], and Spring Cloud Config.

Of course, this approach introduces another point of failure in the system and requires that all applications communicate with the configuration server before starting. There are, however, several mechanisms to mitigate this problem, such as adding more instances or implementing a caching mechanism in front of the configuration server.

## What Is the Best Option for Each Scenario?

The decision of the best option often hinges on factors such as the team's experience, the costs associated with infrastructure, and the support frameworks or languages offered for various approaches. In this book, these considerations are set aside and the pros and cons of each option

[1]https://developer.hashicorp.com/consul
[2]https://developer.hashicorp.com/vault

are analyzed. Table 8.1 briefly overviews the different options for externalizing the configuration and identifies which is appropriate for various situations.

**TABLE 8.1** Main things to consider when choosing an option for externalizing the configuration.

| Situation | Environment Variables | Command-Line Arguments | Spring Cloud Config Server (Git) |
|---|:---:|:---:|:---:|
| Storing sensitive data | ✓ | ✗ | ✗ |
| Quick overrides in CI/CD pipelines | ✓ | ✓ | ✗ |
| Different config per environment (prod/dev/test) | ✓ | ✓ | ✓ |
| Centralized configuration management | ✗ | ✗ | ✓ |
| Version control for configuration | ✗ | ✗ | ✓ |
| Supports dynamic updates without a restart | ✗ | ✗ | ✓ |
| Externalization from application artifacts | ✓ | ✓ | ✓ |
| Minimal setup required | ✓ | ✓ | ✗ |

Significant differences exist between the three approaches, but to synthesize all the arguments in one document, creating an ADR is a good idea, as shown in Figure 8.2.

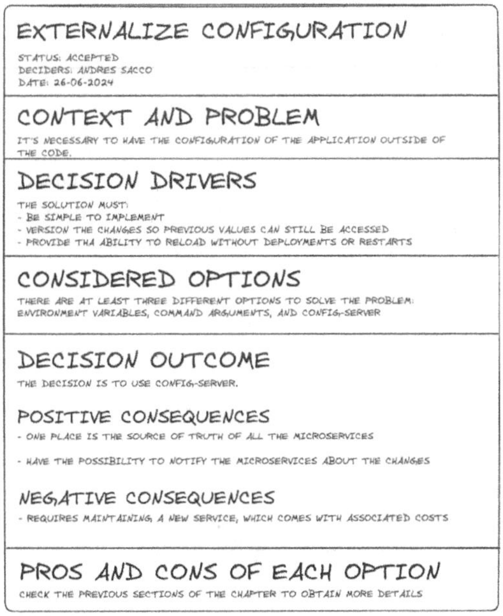

**EXTERNALIZE CONFIGURATION**

STATUS: ACCEPTED
DECIDERS: ANDRES SACCO
DATE: 26-06-2024

**CONTEXT AND PROBLEM**

IT'S NECESSARY TO HAVE THE CONFIGURATION OF THE APPLICATION OUTSIDE OF THE CODE.

**DECISION DRIVERS**

THE SOLUTION MUST:
- BE SIMPLE TO IMPLEMENT
- VERSION THE CHANGES SO PREVIOUS VALUES CAN STILL BE ACCESSED
- PROVIDE THA ABILITY TO RELOAD WITHOUT DEPLOYMENTS OR RESTARTS

**CONSIDERED OPTIONS**

THERE ARE AT LEAST THREE DIFFERENT OPTIONS TO SOLVE THE PROBLEM: ENVIRONMENT VARIABLES, COMMAND ARGUMENTS, AND CONFIG-SERVER.

**DECISION OUTCOME**

THE DECISION IS TO USE CONFIG-SERVER.

**POSITIVE CONSEQUENCES**

- ONE PLACE IS THE SOURCE OF TRUTH OF ALL THE MICROSERVICES

- HAVE THE POSSIBILITY TO NOTIFY THE MICROSERVICES ABOUT THE CHANGES

**NEGATIVE CONSEQUENCES**

- REQUIRES MAINTAINING A NEW SERVICE, WHICH COMES WITH ASSOCIATED COSTS

**PROS AND CONS OF EACH OPTION**

CHECK THE PREVIOUS SECTIONS OF THE CHAPTER TO OBTAIN MORE DETAILS

**FIGURE 8.2** ADR about the decision of which way to access the database.

This document allows anyone to understand why one approach was selected instead of another and to see which factors were considered when deciding.

## WHAT IMPLICATIONS DO THE MODIFICATIONS HAVE ON THE APPLICATION?

Modify the application, or a series of them, to externalize the configuration. This means creating a new application that represents the configuration server, which retrieves information from files or repositories such as GitHub and exposes it in one place, with the idea that all the applications connect to it. Figure 8.3 shows the interaction between the different components of this approach.

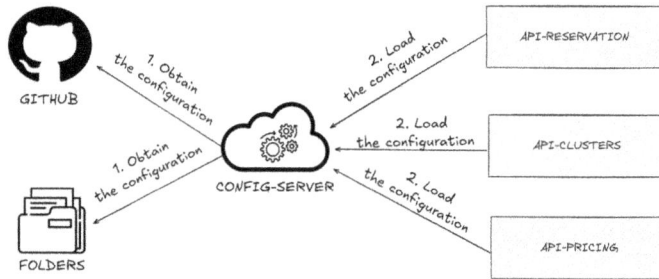

**FIGURE 8.3** The interaction between the different components.

To keep it simple, the changes are made in different sections, each showing the problems associated with a specific component, such as the configuration server or the microservices.

### Creating a New Config Server

Using a config server requires many modifications to the current `api-reservation`. Before introducing any changes to that application, however, it is necessary to create the server responsible for obtaining and returning the different configurations.

Let's create the application using the `curl` command, indicating the name of the project, the version of Spring Boot, and the necessary modules to be included in the same way as in the first chapter of this book. The command looks as in Listing 8.1.

```
→   ~ curl https://start.spring.io/starter.zip \
   -d dependencies=web,cloud-config-server \
   -d type=maven-project \
   -d language=java \
   -d bootVersion=3.4.5 \
   -d baseDir=config-server \
   -d groupId=com.twa \
   -d artifactId=config-server \
   -d name=config-server \
   -d description="Application that contains the configuration of all the
microservices." \
   -d javaVersion=21 \
   -o config-server.zip
```

**LISTING 8.1** Command to create the configuration project.

Of course, alternative methods, such as the IDE or the Spring Initializr Web site, can be used to generate the project.

*The actuator is not included from the beginning because the idea is to show a problem that could happen with the configuration modifications, and how the server reacts to those changes.*

After the generation, let's decompress the file and import it into the IDE to work on that project. The POM file containing all the application's dependencies will look similar to Listing 8.2.

```xml
<?xml version="1.0" encoding="UTF-8"?>
<project xmlns="http://maven.apache.org/POM/4.0.0" xmlns:xsi="http://
www.w3.org/2001/XMLSchema-instance"
    xsi:schemaLocation="http://maven.apache.org/POM/4.0.0 https://maven.
apache.org/xsd/maven-4.0.0.xsd">
    <modelVersion>4.0.0</modelVersion>
    <parent>
        <groupId>org.springframework.boot</groupId>
        <artifactId>spring-boot-starter-parent</artifactId>
        <version>3.4.5</version>
        <relativePath/> <!-- lookup parent from repository -->
    </parent>
    <groupId>com.twa</groupId>
    <artifactId>config-server</artifactId>
    <version>0.0.1-SNAPSHOT</version>
    <name>config-server</name>
    <description>Application that contains the configuration of all the
microservices.</description>
    <properties>
        <java.version>21</java.version>
        <spring-cloud.version>2024.0.1</spring-cloud.version>
    </properties>
    <dependencies>
        <dependency>
            <groupId>org.springframework.boot</groupId>
            <artifactId>spring-boot-starter-web</artifactId>
        </dependency>
        <dependency>
            <groupId>org.springframework.cloud</groupId>
            <artifactId>spring-cloud-config-server</artifactId>
        </dependency>

        <dependency>
            <groupId>org.springframework.boot</groupId>
            <artifactId>spring-boot-starter-test</artifactId>
            <scope>test</scope>
        </dependency>
    </dependencies>
    <dependencyManagement>
        <dependencies>
            <dependency>
                <groupId>org.springframework.cloud</groupId>
                <artifactId>spring-cloud-dependencies</artifactId>
                <version>${spring-cloud.version}</version>
                <type>pom</type>
                <scope>import</scope>
            </dependency>
```

```
        </dependencies>
    </dependencyManagement>

    <build>
        <plugins>
            <plugin>
                <groupId>org.springframework.boot</groupId>
                <artifactId>spring-boot-maven-plugin</artifactId>
            </plugin>
        </plugins>
    </build>

</project>
```

**LISTING 8.2** POM file with the different dependencies.

There is one class inside the project, which is the main class. The main class, responsible for executing the application, is simple, like any other application generated using Spring Initializr. To become a config server, however, the annotation @EnableConfigServer must be introduced, which enables the support. The modifications to the main class look as shown in Listing 8.3.

```
package com.twa.config.server;

import org.springframework.boot.SpringApplication;
import org.springframework.boot.autoconfigure.SpringBootApplication;
import org.springframework.cloud.config.server.EnableConfigServer;

@EnableConfigServer
@SpringBootApplication
public class ConfigServerApplication {

    public static void main(String[] args) {
        SpringApplication.run(ConfigServerApplication.class, args);
    }
}
```

**LISTING 8.3** Modifications on the main class to enable the support of the config server.

After modifying the application's main class, the next step is to remove the static and templates folders from the resources folder, with the idea of keeping that folder simple. Additionally, it's necessary to create a folder that contains all the configurations from the different applications across various environments. To achieve this, let's make a folder called config-data inside the resources folder, with two files that each need to refer to the reservation's API, called api-reservation-dev.yml and api-reservation-prod.yml, with the same information that exists in the files of the application. Listing 8.4 partially represents the information that both files need to contain.

```
spring:
  application:
    name: api-reservation
```

```
datasource:
  driver-class-name: com.mysql.cj.jdbc.Driver
  url: jdbc:mysql://localhost:3312/flights_reservation
  username: root
  password: muppet
jpa:
  show-sql: false
  generate-ddl: false
  hibernate:
    ddl-auto: validate
liquibase:
  change-log: classpath:db/changelog/db.changelog-root.xml
...
```

**LISTING 8.4** Content of the files with the configuration of the application.

After creating the files the server will expose, it's time to set up the configuration like any other Spring Boot application. Let's create a file called `application.yml` with the contents shown in Listing 8.5, which typically includes the application name, the port, and some configuration related to the compression of responses.

```
spring:
  application:
    name: config-server
  profiles:
    active: native

  cloud:
    config:
      server:
        native:
          search-locations: classpath:/config-data

server:
  port: 8888
  error:
    include-stacktrace: never
  servlet:
    context-path: /config-server

  compression:
    enabled: true
    min-response-size: 2048
    mime-types: application/json,application/xml,text/html,text/
xml,text/plain
```

**LISTING 8.5** Configuration of the config server.

The configuration file has an extra node with information that other applications, such as `api-reservation`, do not have. The node cloud, which refers to the location of the files in the configuration, in this case, relates to the `config-data` folder.

The last step in checking whether the server is functioning correctly and exposing information about the different applications involves running it like any other Spring Boot application and executing a request to the default endpoint, passing the application's name and environment as parameters to obtain the configuration. Listing 8.6 shows the request and response that the server will return.

```
➜  ~ curl http://localhost:8888/config-server/api-reservation/dev

{
  "name": "api-reservation",
  "profiles": [
    "dev"
  ],
  "label": null,
  "version": null,
  "state": null,
  "propertySources": [
    {
      "name": "classpath:/config-data/api-reservation-dev.yml",
      "source": {
        "spring.application.name": "api-reservation",
        "spring.datasource.driver-class-name": "com.mysql.cj.jdbc.
Driver",
        "spring.datasource.url": "jdbc:mysql://localhost:3312/flights_
reservation",
        "spring.datasource.username": "root",
        "spring.datasource.password": "muppet",
        "spring.jpa.show-sql": false,
        "spring.jpa.generate-ddl": false,
        "spring.jpa.hibernate.ddl-auto": "validate",
        "spring.liquibase.change-log": "classpath:db/changelog/
db.changelog-root.xml",
        "server.port": 8090,
        ......
        "cache.configuration.CATALOG_COUNTRY.maxSize": 180,
        "springdoc.api-docs.path": "/documentation/api-docs",
        "springdoc.swagger-ui.path": "/documentation/swagger-ui"
      }
    }
  ]
}
```

**LISTING 8.6** Result of the execution of the curl command.

Listing 8.6 has a request without any security mechanism, so anyone can access that information. It's possible to introduce a simple username and password verification. Information such as the reservation one in the preceding listing is usually considered sensitive, so access should be limited.

NOTE    *Spring Cloud Config offers different endpoints to obtain the configuration information about a particular application. The request in Listing 8.6 shows just one of the most popular ways to do it, but others like it are shown in Table 8.2.*

*TABLE 8.2* Explanation of the different ways to obtain the configuration.

| Endpoint Format | Description | Example |
|---|---|---|
| `/{application}/{profile}` | Return the information from an application and a specific profile. | `/api-reservation/prod` |
| `/{application}-{profile}.yml` | Return the information in YAML format. | `/api-reservation-prod.yml` |
| `/{label}/{application}-{profile}.yml` | The same as the previous one, but indicating which branch on Git is needed to use it. | `/main/api-reservation-prod.yml` |
| `/{application}/{profile}/{label}` | Return the configuration from a specific profile using a specific Git branch. | `/api-reservation/prod/main` |
| `/{application}-{profile}.properties` | Return the configuration in a `properties` file. | `/api-reservation-prod.properties` |
| `/{application}-{profile}.json` | Return the configuration, but in JSON format. | `/api-reservation-prod.json` |

One question that could arise after seeing the server result is, what happens if those files undergo some modifications? Well, the best way to see it is to make modifications to any of the `api-reservation-xxx.yml` files and execute the request, for example, just modify the application's name from `api-reservation` to `api-reservation-dev` as appears on Listing 8.7.

```
spring:
  application:
    name: api-reservation-dev
...
```

*LISTING 8.7* Modification on the api-reservation-prod file.

Now, if someone makes the same request that appears in Listing 8.6, the changes will not appear. This situation occurs because the server does not refresh the changes on the files after the startup process, so the only option is to stop and rerun it.

Spring Boot has an actuator containing an endpoint called `refresh`, which could be considered to solve the problem. Let's modify the actuator to check what happens with this approach and support the different endpoints, such as `health` and `info`, on the server. First, add the actuator's dependency to the POM file, as shown in Listing 8.8.

```
<dependency>
    <groupId>org.springframework.boot</groupId>
    <artifactId>spring-boot-starter-actuator</artifactId>
</dependency>
```

*LISTING 8.8* Dependency related to the actuator.

The next step involves adding all the configuration related to the actuator in the `application.yml` to expose specific endpoints, such as the `info`, `health`, and `refresh` endpoints, which could be a possible solution to detect changes. The modifications appear as in Listing 8.9.

```
management:
  endpoints:
    web:
      base-path: /management
      exposure:
        include: info,health,refresh

  info:
    java:
      enabled: false #change if you want to obtain information about
Java
    os:
      enabled: false #change if you want to obtain information about OS
    env:
      enabled: true
  endpoint:
    health:
      show-details: always
      probes:
        enabled: false
info:
  app:
    name: "@project.artifactId@"
    version: "@project.version@"
  contact:
    email: "sacco.andres@gmail.com"
    slack: "adsacco"
```

**LISTING 8.9** Configuration of the actuator.

Let's run the application and repeat the process of introducing modifications to one of the config files. After that, we will execute a request to the `refresh` endpoint, as shown in Listing 8.10.

```
→   ~ curl -X POST http://localhost:8888/config-server/management/
refresh
```

**LISTING 8.10** Invoke the refresh endpoint.

Suppose there is no exception after the modification, and the request is executed to obtain the information from `api-reservation`. In that case, the result will be the same as before refreshing the endpoint. This is because the refresh only detects changes in the configuration files, not those that the application loads from the file system. Therefore, this approach is not the best option, as it requires rerunning the application in all cases.

Considering the problems discussed in the previous paragraph, and all the configurations within a single application, exploring alternatives is pertinent. At this point, tools related to code versioning come to the rescue, notably Git, which offers the ability to have a single repository or a folder within a repository that contains the application's configurations. At the same time, the `config-server` pulls those files to expose them at an endpoint.

The modifications to support Git are pretty simple, only requiring changes to `application.yml` by removing everything related to the location of the files locally and indicating the URI, branch, and folder where the files are, as shown in Listing 8.11.

```
spring:
  application:
    name: config-server

  cloud:
    config:
      server:
        git:
          uri: https://github.com/andres-sacco/deguyer-spring-boot-
microservices.git
          default-label: main
          clone-on-start: true
          search-paths: config
          # For private repositories use this attributes
          # username: your-username
          # password: your-personal-access-token

# Previous configuration
```

**LISTING 8.11** Changes to the application.yml to support Git.

In Listing 8.11, the repository's username and password appear as a comment. This is because the repository is public, so including them is unnecessary. Including this information becomes necessary, however, if a private repository is used.

**NOTE** *In the case of this book, the repository with the configuration of the applications is the same; it contains all the source code but uses a specific folder called* config. *Try to use a dedicated repository with all the configurations of the different applications.*

The following step involves rerunning the application and requesting the endpoint that returns the configuration, as shown in Listing 8.12. Remember to remove the folder `config-data` from the server to ensure that the result is obtained from GitHub instead of locally.

```
→   ~ curl http://localhost:8888/config-server/api-reservation/dev

{
  "name": "api-reservation",
  "profiles": [
    "dev"
  ],
  "label": null,
  "version": null,
  "state": null,
  "propertySources": [
    {
```

```
    "name": "classpath:/config-data/api-reservation-dev.yml",
    "source": {
      "spring.application.name": "api-reservation",

    }
  }
 ]
}
```

**LISTING 8.12** Result of the execution of the curl command.

If the result is the same as before, make the changes related to Git's repository. The next step will be to modify any files associated with the configuration, such as api-reservation-dev.yml. After making the modifications, try executing the same command shown in Listing 8.12 and check that the result returns the latest version of the file on GitHub.

Check the console of the application; it will show a log similar to Listing 8.13, which mentions that a change was detected in the repository at approximately the same moment that the commit was made.

```
2025-05-09T15:41:04.998-03:00  INFO 446274 --- [config-server] [on(3)-
127.0.0.1] o.s.web.servlet.DispatcherServlet       : Completed
initialization in 1 ms
2025-05-09T15:41:07.148-03:00  INFO 446274 --- [config-server] [nio-
8888-exec-1] o.s.c.c.s.e.NativeEnvironmentRepository : Adding property
source: Config resource 'file [/tmp/config-repo-14073871291081126857/
config/api-reservation-dev.yml]' via location 'file:/tmp/config-
repo-14073871291081126857/config/'
2025-05-09T15:42:19.170-03:00  INFO 446274 --- [config-server] [nio-
8888-exec-2] o.s.c.c.s.e.NativeEnvironmentRepository : Adding property
source: Config resource 'file [/tmp/config-repo-14073871291081126857/
config/api-reservation-dev.yml]' via location 'file:/tmp/config-
repo-14073871291081126857/config/'
2025-05-09T15:42:34.435-03:00  INFO 446274 --- [config-server] [nio-8888-
exec-4] .c.s.e.MultipleJGitEnvironmentRepository : Fetched for remote
main and found 1 updates
2025-05-09T15:42:34.509-03:00  INFO 446274 --- [config-server] [nio-
8888-exec-4] o.s.c.c.s.e.NativeEnvironmentRepository : Adding property
source: Config resource 'file [/tmp/config-repo-14073871291081126857/
config/api-reservation-dev.yml]' via location 'file:/tmp/config-
repo-14073871291081126857/config/'
2025-05-09T15:42:45.967-03:00  INFO 446274 --- [config-server] [nio-
8888-exec-6] o.s.c.c.s.e.NativeEnvironmentRepository : Adding property
source: Config resource 'file [/tmp/config-repo-14073871291081126857/
config/api-reservation-dev.yml]' via location 'file:/tmp/config-
repo-14073871291081126857/config/'
```

**LISTING 8.13** Logs of the application.

The approach improves the benefits of having a config server because it's possible to make changes. When someone pushes the changes to the repository, the config server automatically detects them without restarting the application.

For now, let's pause the modifications on the config server and move on to another relevant component. These microservices must load the configuration from an external instance with a file inside the application.

## Modifying the Application to Use the Server

Creating the config server is just one of the components necessary to externalize the configuration. The other is modifying the microservices to replace the actual configuration, allowing them to connect and obtain values from an external service. To achieve this, some modifications must be introduced to the POM file of `api-reservation`. The first modification involves adding the dependency related to the config, as shown in Listing 8.14.

```
<dependency>
    <groupId>org.springframework.cloud</groupId>
    <artifactId>spring-cloud-starter-config</artifactId>
</dependency>
```

**LISTING 8.14** Dependency that needs to be added to the POM file.

Also, other changes to the POM file related to the version of Spring Cloud and the dependencies associated with that library are required. The modifications require adding the dependency that appears in Listing 8.15 to the `dependencyManagement` section.

```
<dependencyManagement>
    <dependencies>
        <dependency>
            <groupId>org.springframework.cloud</groupId>
            <artifactId>spring-cloud-dependencies</artifactId>
            <version>2023.0.3</version>
            <type>pom</type>
            <scope>import</scope>
        </dependency>
    </dependencies>
</dependencyManagement>
```

**LISTING 8.15** Modifications to the POM file to use all the dependencies.

The next step involves removing most of the configuration from `application.yml` and adding the attributes related to the config server, as shown in Listing 8.16. It's essential to add the path of the config server and the username/password to access and obtain the information.

```
spring:
  application:
    name: api-reservation
  profiles:
    active: dev

  config:
      import: optional:configserver:http://localhost:8888/config-server
```

**LISTING 8.16** Changes in application.yml.

The next step is to run the application and check whether everything works well, but it is necessary to run `config-server` beforehand. If everything works well, the log that could appear on the console will look like Listing 8.17, showing that the application connects to the `config-server` and obtains all the attributes.

```
  .   ____          _            __ _ _
 /\\ / ___'_ __ _ _(_)_ __  __ _ \ \ \ \
( ( )\___ | '_ | '_| | '_ \/ _` | \ \ \ \
 \\/  ___)| |_)| | | | | || (_| |  ) ) ) )
  '  |____| .__|_| |_|_| |_\__, | / / / /
 =========|_|==============|___/=/_/_/_/

 :: Spring Boot ::                (v3.3.0)

2025-05-10T12:41:02.076-03:00  INFO 542685 --- [api-reservation-dev]
[ restartedMain] c.t.f.a.r.ApiReservationApplication    : Starting
ApiReservationApplication using Java 21.0.2 with PID 542685 (/home/
asacco/Code/deguyer/deguyer-spring-boot-microservices/chapter-8/api-
reservation/target/classes started by asacco in /home/asacco/Code/
deguyer/deguyer-spring-boot-microservices/chapter-8/api-reservation)
2025-05-10T12:41:02.077-03:00  INFO 542685 --- [api-reservation-dev] [
restartedMain] c.t.f.a.r.ApiReservationApplication    : The following
1 profile is active: "dev"
2025-05-10T12:41:02.093-03:00  INFO 542685 --- [api-reservation-dev] [
restartedMain] o.s.c.c.c.ConfigServerConfigDataLoader   : Fetching config
from server at : http://localhost:8888/config-server
2025-05-10T12:41:02.093-03:00  INFO 542685 --- [api-reservation-dev]
[ restartedMain] o.s.c.c.c.ConfigServerConfigDataLoader   : Located
environment: name=api-reservation, profiles=[default], label=null, versio
n=0209f896d2384c0817f0e12922c5bf41c660c4d2, state=
2025-05-10T12:41:02.093-03:00  INFO 542685 --- [api-reservation-dev] [
restartedMain] o.s.c.c.c.ConfigServerConfigDataLoader   : Fetching config
from server at : http://localhost:8888/config-server
2025-05-10T12:41:02.093-03:00  INFO 542685 --- [api-reservation-dev]
[ restartedMain] o.s.c.c.c.ConfigServerConfigDataLoader   : Located
environment: name=api-reservation, profiles=[dev], label=null, version=02
09f896d2384c0817f0e12922c5bf41c660c4d2, state=
```

**LISTING 8.17** Result of the execution of the application.

Now, let's replicate the scenario in the previous section by introducing some modifications to one of the configuration files. Let's apply these changes to `api-reservation-dev.yml`, specifically updating the information node with the value shown in Listing 8.18.

```
info:
  app:
    name: "api-reservation-dev"
    version: "@project.version@"
  contact:
    email: "sacco.andres@gmail.com"
    slack: "adsacco"
```

**LISTING 8.18** Modifications to the configuration file.

After pushing the modification to the Git repository, the config server will have the new version of the file. Let's see what happens, though, when we execute a request to the `info` endpoint with the changes. Let's do a request like the one in Listing 8.19 and check the results.

```
→  ~ curl --location 'http://localhost:8090/api/flights/reservation/
management/info'

{
    "app": {
        "name": "@project.artifactId@",
        "version": "@project.version@"
    },
    "contact": {
        "email": "sacco.andres@gmail.com",
        "slack": "adsacco"
    },
    "reservation-stats": {
        "amount": 4
    }
}
```

**LISTING 8.19** Result of executing a curl command to the info endpoint.

The result of the request shows that the changes do not appear on the microservice, which is a problem because restarting it each time something changes is not an option. The best option is to use the `refresh` endpoint, which was mentioned in the previous section, but instead of doing it on the config server, let's do it on the application, as shown in Listing 8.20.

```
→  ~ curl --location --request POST 'http://localhost:8090/api/flights/
reservation/management/refresh'

[
    "config.client.version",
    "info.app.name"
]
```

**LISTING 8.20** Result of the execution of the refresh endpoint.

After that, let's make the same request in Listing 8.19 again to check whether the changes now appear in the application. If everything is okay, the result will look similar to Listing 8.21.

```
→  ~ curl --location 'http://localhost:8090/api/flights/reservation/
management/info'

{
    "app": {
        "name": "api-reservation-dev",
        "version": "@project.version@"
    },
    "contact": {
        "email": "sacco.andres@gmail.com",
        "slack": "adsacco"
```

```
    },
    "reservation-stats": {
        "amount": 4
    }
}
```

**LISTING 8.21** Result of executing a curl command on the info endpoint.

To clarify how the process works before starting with the modifications, see Figure 8.4.

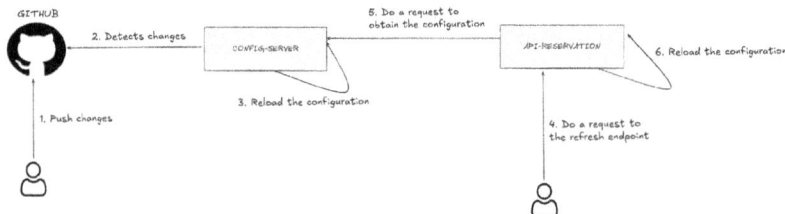

**FIGURE 8.4** Process to notify the changes to all the applications.

With these modifications in mind, it's possible to introduce many changes to the configuration files; after that, it's only necessary to invoke the `refresh` endpoint. What happens, though, in a real environment where many instances of the same microservice exist simultaneously? The only alternative is to do it on each instance with one request per instance; this is not a great solution, but at least a solution exists.

### Adding Queues to Detect the Changes

The main problem in the previous section is how to notify all instances of one microservice or different microservices about the changes without needing to request each one. Of course, the first thing that might be thought of is to create a script with all the URLs and execute it each time something changes in the configuration, but this approach could have many problems, such as knowing who is responsible for keeping the list of URLs. What happens if a microservice has more or fewer instances than appear in the script?

Spring offers a straightforward solution to this problem by sending a single request to the `config-server`, notifying all the microservices that utilize it to retrieve the latest version of the configuration. To inform all instances of the microservices that rely on something that is not new in the development of the application, messages are sent to a queue where both the microservices and the `config-server` are subscribed to send and receive messages.

To clarify how the process works before starting with the modifications, see Figure 8.5.

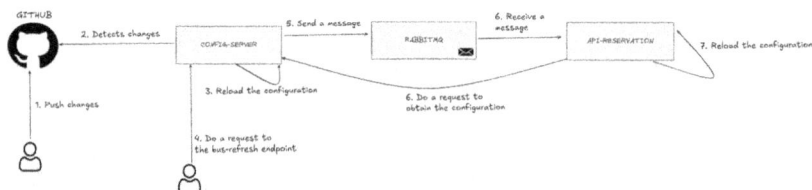

**FIGURE 8.5** Process to notify all the applications of the changes.

There are many tools for sending and receiving messages. Some, such as Kafka[3], involve creating many replicas by default, while others, such as RabbitMQ[4], are simpler. It is generally unnecessary to use multiple tools; however, the choice depends on whether the company is replacing a tool, rather than introducing a new one that needs to be maintained. In the case of this book, as the focus is on notifying the team of the modifications to the microservices, the tool that will be used is RabbitMQ.

The first thing to do is modify the Docker Compose file to include an image of RabbitMQ that exposes the necessary ports to communicate with other applications and to observe what happens inside them. The modifications to the file look as in Listing 8.22.

```
version: '3.1'
services:
 # Previous configuration
 config-server-messaging:
    image: rabbitmq:3-management
    container_name: rabbitmq
    ports:
      - "5672:5672"       # AMQP protocol (used by Spring Cloud Bus)
      - "15672:15672"     # RabbitMQ Management UI
    environment:
      RABBITMQ_DEFAULT_USER: guest
      RABBITMQ_DEFAULT_PASS: guest
```

**LISTING 8.22** Adding support to use RabbitMQ.

After making the modifications, it's time to run the Docker Compose file and check that everything functions correctly before continuing with the changes. To observe what occurs with RabbitMQ, let's open a browser at *http://localhost:15672*. This displays a page similar to Figure 8.6, where it's required to enter the username and password.

**FIGURE 8.6** RabbitMQ initial Web page.

After introducing the credentials, the tool will show an overview of the number of messages published during a specified period. This is extremely useful for knowing whether the config server notifies all the microservices about the changes to the configuration. Figure 8.7 shows what the initial Web page looks like after logging in to RabbitMQ.

---

[3]https://kafka.apache.org/
[4]https://www.rabbitmq.com/

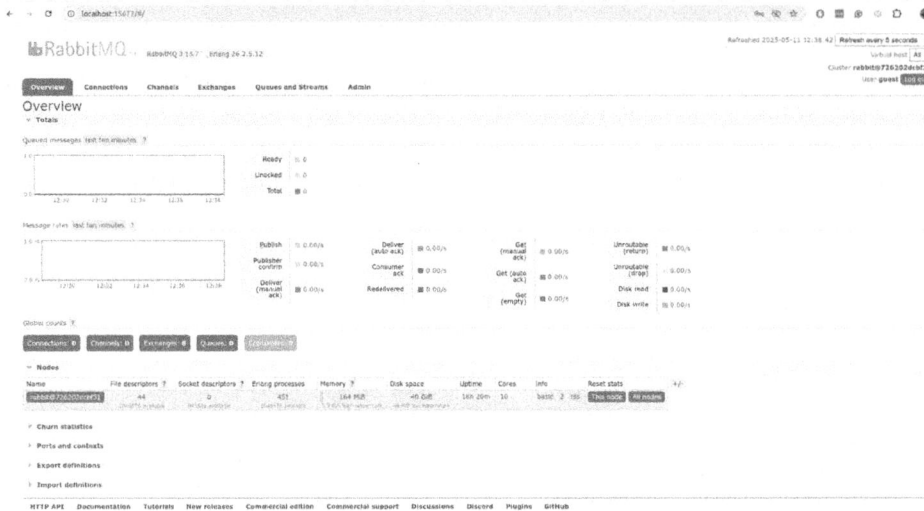

**FIGURE 8.7** RabbitMQ's initial Web page with the status.

The next step is to introduce the dependency for all the projects, `config-server` and `api-reservation`, to listen for the messages that appear on RabbitMQ. The modification necessary to introduce in the POM file is shown in Listing 8.23.

```
<dependency>
  <groupId>org.springframework.cloud</groupId>
  <artifactId>spring-cloud-starter-bus-amqp</artifactId>
</dependency>
```

**LISTING 8.23** Dependencies to support receiving events.

Now, it's time to introduce the modifications to the `application.yml` files to configure the messaging tool's location and the necessary credentials. The modifications look as in Listing 8.24.

```
spring:
  # Previous configuration
  rabbitmq:
    host: localhost
    port: 5672
    username: guest
    password: guest
```

**LISTING 8.24** Add changes to the configuration to connect with RabbitMQ.

Modifications must be made to the files in the GitHub repository in the case of `api-reservation`, instead of doing it in the file that resides inside the application.

In the case of the `config-server`, another minor modification is necessary to expose the endpoint responsible for capturing the request and sending the event. The endpoint is called `bus-refresh`, and the changes to the `application.yml` look as in Listing 8.25.

```
management:
  endpoints:
    web:
      base-path: /management
      exposure:
        include: info,health,refresh,bus-refresh
```

**LISTING 8.25** Add modifications to enable the bus-refresh endpoint.

After making the modifications, run both applications to connect to RabbitMQ. To check the tools' connections, open a browser and navigate to *http://localhost:15672*. Enter the credentials and go to the Connections section, which shows all the connected applications. If everything is correct, the page will look as in Figure 8.8.

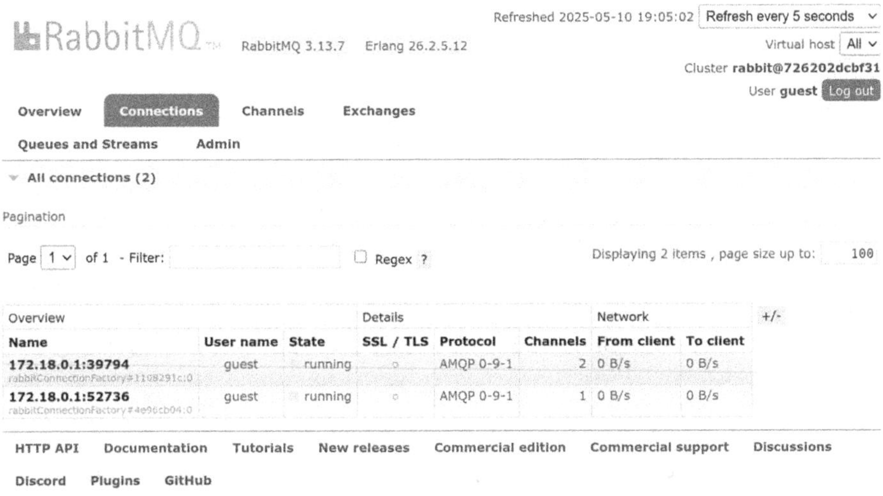

**FIGURE 8.8** RabbitMQ management with active connections.

The last step in this process involves modifying the configuration files on GitHub, such as changing the email of the `info` endpoint. After that, it's time to inform the `config-server` that something has changed and the applications need to reload the configuration. To do this, it's necessary to invoke the `bus-refresh` endpoint, as shown in Listing 8.26.

```
→   ~ curl -i --location --request POST http://localhost:8888/config-
server/management/busrefresh

HTTP/1.1 204
Date: Sun, 11 May 2025 00:11:55 GMT
```

**LISTING 8.26** Add changes to the configuration to connect with RabbitMQ.

After executing the command, the applications listed in that messaging tool will reload their configuration by calling the `config-server` again. The console of `api-reservation` will display the log outputs shown in Listing 8.27, which represent the receipt of the message and indicate that something is being done.

```
2025-05-10T21:13:02.754-03:00   INFO 583317 --- [api-reservation-dev]
[auYWJyeuJDdqA-1] o.s.cloud.bus.event.RefreshListener      : Received
remote refresh request.
2025-05-10T21:13:02.759-03:00   INFO 583317 --- [api-reservation-dev]
[auYWJyeuJDdqA-1] o.s.c.c.c.ConfigServerConfigDataLoader    : Fetching
config from server at : http://localhost:8888/config-server
2025-05-10T21:13:03.450-03:00   INFO 583317 --- [api-reservation-dev]
[auYWJyeuJDdqA-1] o.s.c.c.c.ConfigServerConfigDataLoader    : Located
environment: name=api-reservation, profiles=[default], label=null, versio
n=ffd33caf5467a034d261a283eeb1e38c5658fedc, state=
2025-05-10T21:13:03.454-03:00   INFO 583317 --- [api-reservation-dev]
[auYWJyeuJDdqA-1] o.s.c.c.c.ConfigServerConfigDataLoader    : Fetching
config from server at : http://localhost:8888/config-server
2025-05-10T21:13:04.102-03:00   INFO 583317 --- [api-reservation-dev]
[auYWJyeuJDdqA-1] o.s.c.c.c.ConfigServerConfigDataLoader    : Located
environment: name=api-reservation, profiles=[dev], label=null, version=ff
d33caf5467a034d261a283eeb1e38c5658fedc, state=
[auYWJyeuJDdqA-1] o.s.cloud.bus.event.RefreshListener      : Keys
refreshed []
```

*LISTING 8.27* Output of the console after sending the event.

This approach reduces the number of requests to notify all the microservices; however, some-one still needs to do it manually. The best solution is to add a webhook on GitHub that automati-cally requests the config-server when a modification appears in the repository. Unfortunately, this requires many changes to the code, such as publishing the applications on services with a public address and configuring the webhooks, which are not covered in this book.

## SUMMARY

When making a decision on how to declare an application's configuration, a number of aspects must be considered, such as the company's size, the number of changes those files undergo, the cost associated with having a dedicated resource, or the problems that could occur if someone introduces a bad configuration.

As mentioned in this chapter, externalizing the configuration and detecting changes is a pow-erful tool in many ways. Still, in contrast to the benefits that the company receives, it may require too much time to set up and maintain.

It's necessary to understand that there is no unique option to tackle those problems in all cases; just keep in mind that there is more than one way to solve it. Use whichever is simplest to implement for the scenario.

# CHAPTER 9

# BUILD AND PACKAGE THE APPLICATION

Creating an application could be complex because it requires many things, such as access to the database, communicating with another system, or documenting the different endpoints. An API may look great in a local environment, but at some point, it must be deployed somewhere else to check the behavior in production and, finally, deployed to production.

In this scenario, using an IDE or running Maven commands to execute the application is impossible. So, it's necessary to find a way to minimize the risk of something going wrong.

## WHAT IS THE IDEA BEHIND THE BUILD AND PACKAGE PROCESSES?

Both processes assist in many aspects of developers' daily work, minimizing issues that might arise in various environments. The building process doesn't just involve compiling the code; it aims to execute all the operations that can help standardize and reduce problems visible only when someone runs the application. For instance, if there's a conflict in the dependencies, this issue typically does not become apparent until production.

On the other hand, packaging seeks to streamline the application's distribution by minimizing the files or configurations required to transition from one location to another for a new version release. Additionally, this process aims to reduce the dependency on the specifics of how to run the application, taking into consideration the types of servers used by companies.

Let's look at each process in more detail to understand what is recommended.

## BUILD

There are several aspects to this process, such as compiling and running tests when necessary before packaging the application for distribution, that are clear. Others may not be immediately apparent but can benefit developers in various ways, such as preventing potential dependency conflicts, striving for a consistent code format to enhance readability, identifying and addressing potential quality issues, or simply updating or upgrading the application.

It's recommended that this mechanism or plugin be added to the application from its creation to detect any problem quickly and fix it as soon as possible.

## Code Format

Each language has its own standards for writing code. Sometimes, if someone does not follow that standard, the code may still work and nothing will happen to the application. If everyone writes code without following a standard, though, it can affect its readability.

There are multiple solutions to tackle this problem, such as the IDE showing the mistakes in the code in red, but at some point, someone needs to make the modifications. One possible approach is to add a plugin that will format the code following a standard on each command that anyone executes.

Since *Chapter 1*, the example application of this book has used a plugin called Spotless[1], which supports Maven and Gradle. This plugin uses `google-java-format`[2] behind the scenes, which contains the most relevant things to be formatted. It's also possible to use the Java and Kotlin formats, as well as many other languages.

## Prevent Dependency Conflicts

Adding dependencies to an application is expected in most cases, especially to avoid reinventing solutions for typical situations such as accessing a database, communicating with other applications, or performing many other tasks. In some instances, however, two different libraries may require a third library to function, and both libraries don't need to use the same version of that third library. In this scenario, dependency management tools, such as Maven, address the issue using specific criteria, ensuring no significant problems arise. Yet, there are other situations where the decisions made can affect the expected behavior of the application. Therefore, it is essential to use a tool that detects such conflicts and identifies which libraries use different versions of another library.

The application used in this book has also relied on a plugin called Enforcer[3], which detects conflicts and provides information about libraries that could cause problems. Use it to resolve any issues that arise promptly. Do not wait for something serious to occur during the packaging process or when attempting to run the application in specific environments.

## Detect Unused Dependencies

Another problem that could affect the building process and the application package size is the number of libraries. In most cases, all the libraries listed in the POM file for Maven are necessary for the application; however, if someone adds a new feature and includes multiple libraries, not all of them may be required. Additionally, if someone removes a feature such as connecting to a database, they might forget to eliminate all the dependencies related to Spring Data.

These situations will not affect the application's behavior. They will, however, impact its build and packaging time, so it could be a good idea to detect and remove all the unused libraries. This process could be cumbersome to perform manually because it involves analyzing all the code to determine which libraries are not in use. Therefore, the best approach is to use a

---

[1]https://github.com/diffplug/spotless/tree/main
[2]https://github.com/google/google-java-format
[3]https://maven.apache.org/enforcer/maven-enforcer-plugin/

plugin that provides this information, allowing someone to remove the unnecessary dependencies accordingly.

One of the most used plugins is DepClean[4], which is simple to use on applications. The first thing to do is to add the plugin with all the dependencies, as in Listing 9.1.

```
<plugin>
   <groupId>se.kth.castor</groupId>
   <artifactId>depclean-maven-plugin</artifactId>
   <version>2.0.6</version>
   <executions>
        <execution>
             <goals>
                   <goal>depclean</goal>
             </goals>
        </execution>
   </executions>

   <dependencies>
        <dependency>
             <groupId>org.ow2.asm</groupId>
             <artifactId>asm-util</artifactId>
             <version>9.7</version>
        </dependency>
        <dependency>
             <groupId>org.ow2.asm</groupId>
             <artifactId>asm-tree</artifactId>
             <version>9.7</version>
        </dependency>
        <dependency>
             <groupId>org.ow2.asm</groupId>
             <artifactId>asm-commons</artifactId>
             <version>9.7</version>
        </dependency>
        <dependency>
             <groupId>org.ow2.asm</groupId>
             <artifactId>asm</artifactId>
             <version>9.7</version>
        </dependency>
   </dependencies>
</plugin>
```

**LISTING 9.1** DepClean dependencies.

In Listing 9.1, the plugin has many dependencies; this is required because other libraries produce problems when executing the validations. As usual, check which version of each plugin is the latest because with each new version, bugs are fixed.

[4]https://github.com/ASSERT-KTH/depclean/tree/master

The next step requires executing a specific command, as shown in Listing 9.2. This command reports which dependencies the application uses directly or indirectly and which are unnecessary.

```
$ mvn se.kth.castor:depclean-maven-plugin:2.0.6:depclean
......
......
------------------------------------------------------------
[INFO] Starting DepClean dependency analysis
------------------------------------------------------------
 D E P C L E A N   A N A L Y S I S   R E S U L T S
------------------------------------------------------------
USED DIRECT DEPENDENCIES [7]:
        com.mysql:mysql-connector-j:8.3.0:compile (2 MB)
......
......
USED TRANSITIVE DEPENDENCIES [108]:
        org.graalvm.js:js:22.3.3:test (22 MB)
......
......
USED INHERITED DIRECT DEPENDENCIES [0]:
USED INHERITED TRANSITIVE DEPENDENCIES [0]:
POTENTIALLY UNUSED DIRECT DEPENDENCIES [15]:
        org.liquibase:liquibase-core:4.20.0:compile (2 MB)
......
......
POTENTIALLY UNUSED INHERITED DIRECT DEPENDENCIES [0]:
POTENTIALLY UNUSED INHERITED TRANSITIVE DEPENDENCIES [0]:
[INFO] Analysis done in 0min 20s
[INFO] ------------------------------------------------------------
[INFO] BUILD SUCCESS
[INFO] ------------------------------------------------------------
[INFO] Total time:  21.609 s
[INFO] Finished at: 2025-03-11T16:54:40-03:00
[INFO] ------------------------------------------------------------
```

**LISTING 9.2** Report on the execution of the plugin.

In this case, the analysis indicates that an unused library may exist. Remember, however, that this could result in false positives, as Liquibase is used to populate the database. Therefore, checking that everything functions correctly after removing a dependency is essential.

## Code Analysis and Auto-Fix

Developing an application involves many aspects essential for good performance, such as caching, compressing requests, and other elements. Not all developers, however, pay attention to their code, adhere to best practices, or pay attention to minor details such as variable declaration or exception handling. Several steps exist to validate these practices, including code reviews with multiple team members or the use of static code analysis tools such as SonarLint or Checkstyle.

In some cases, the main issue with static code analysis is that it only highlights problems; someone still needs to fix them, which adds time to the process. This isn't necessarily a flawed approach, but it could lead to new errors. A good strategy to detect and resolve most issues is to delegate the responsibility to a tool that handles both tasks. One example is error-prone[5] from Google, which contains a vast number of rules related to good practices and offers the possibility to add another set of regulations, such as the rules from Picnic[6], which includes validations related to Spring.

The first thing to do is add the modifications to the POM file on the plugin related to the compilation of the code that appears in Listing 9.3.

```
<plugin>
  <groupId>org.apache.maven.plugins</groupId>
  <artifactId>maven-compiler-plugin</artifactId>
  <version>${maven-compiler-plugin.version}</version>
  <configuration>
        <source>${java.version}</source>
        <target>${java.version}</target>
        <encoding>UTF-8</encoding>
        <compilerArgs>
                <arg>-XDcompilePolicy=simple</arg>
                <arg>-Xplugin:ErrorProne</arg>
        </compilerArgs>
        <annotationProcessorPaths>
                <path>
                        <groupId>org.mapstruct</groupId>
                        <artifactId>mapstruct-processor</artifactId>
                        <version>${mapstruct.version}</version>
                </path>

                <!-- Error Prone itself. -->
                <path>
                        <groupId>com.google.errorprone</groupId>
                        <artifactId>error_prone_core</artifactId>
                        <version>2.30.0</version>
                </path>
        </annotationProcessorPaths>
  </configuration>
</plugin>
```

**LISTING 9.3** Add a dependency related to error-prone.

Another change needs to be included before using error-prone. It's necessary to create a file called `jvm.config` in the `.mvn` directory with the information that appears in Listing 9.4.

```
--add-exports jdk.compiler/com.sun.tools.javac.api=ALL-UNNAMED
--add-exports jdk.compiler/com.sun.tools.javac.file=ALL-UNNAMED
--add-exports jdk.compiler/com.sun.tools.javac.main=ALL-UNNAMED
--add-exports jdk.compiler/com.sun.tools.javac.model=ALL-UNNAMED
--add-exports jdk.compiler/com.sun.tools.javac.parser=ALL-UNNAMED
--add-exports jdk.compiler/com.sun.tools.javac.processing=ALL-UNNAMED
--add-exports jdk.compiler/com.sun.tools.javac.tree=ALL-UNNAMED
```

---

[5]https://github.com/google/error-prone
[6]https://error-prone.picnic.tech/

```
--add-exports jdk.compiler/com.sun.tools.javac.util=ALL-UNNAMED
--add-opens jdk.compiler/com.sun.tools.javac.code=ALL-UNNAMED
--add-opens jdk.compiler/com.sun.tools.javac.comp=ALL-UNNAMED
```

**LISTING 9.4** Configuration to enable the error-prone plugin.

The final step is to execute a command such as `compile` on Maven, which will run the plugin behind the scenes and check all the code shown in Listing 9.5.

```
$ mvn clean compile
......
......
[INFO] ------------------------------------------------------------
[ERROR] COMPILATION ERROR :
[INFO] ------------------------------------------------------------
[ERROR] /home/asacco/deguyer-spring-boot-microservices/chapter-9/
api-reservation/src/main/java/com/twa/flights/api/reservation/service/
ReservationService.java:[53,13] [DeadException] Exception created but
not thrown
    (see https://errorprone.info/bugpattern/DeadException)
  Did you mean 'throw new TWAException(APIError.RESERVATION_WITH_SAME_
ID);'?
[INFO] 1 error
[INFO] ------------------------------------------------------------
[INFO] ------------------------------------------------------------
[INFO] BUILD FAILURE
[INFO] ------------------------------------------------------------
[INFO] Total time:  1.979 s
[INFO] Finished at: 2025-03-11T17:37:33-03:00
[INFO] ------------------------------------------------------------
```

**LISTING 9.5** Output of the execution of the compilation.

The result of the execution is a list of problems that error-prone detects, which need to be solved. In this case, however, the library offers the option for automatic fixes. To enable this feature, configuration modifications must be made to specify which problems will be addressed automatically. Listing 9.6 displays the required changes to the plugin's configuration.

```
<compilerArgs>
    <arg>-XDcompilePolicy=simple</arg>
    <arg>-Xplugin:ErrorProne -XepPatchChecks:DeadException,EmptyMethodCh
eck -XepPatchLocation:IN_PLACE</arg>
</compilerArgs>
```

**LISTING 9.6** Modifications on the plugins configuration.

After these modifications, if the same command from Listing 9.5 is executed, all detected errors will be automatically fixed without any intervention. This process reduces the time spent understanding and resolving a problem. As a suggestion, however, do not delegate all fixes to the plugin from the start. Try to analyze which issues are trivial and which need to be manually reviewed before being included in the plugin for fixing.

## Update Dependencies

Another problem that typically arises sometime after a launch is the versioning of dependencies or libraries. Initially, the application employs the latest versions of various libraries. As the application matures, however, these libraries release new versions, and eventually, the application may end up using older versions that may contain bugs or security vulnerabilities.

There are many ways to solve this problem; most require someone to analyze the dependency management files and check the repositories for new versions. This process takes significant time and must be done with a specific frequency, so it isn't the best option. Another alternative, which is not so popular, is to use a plugin called Version Maven Plugin[7], which analyzes all of the application's dependencies and provides a report about which libraries need to be updated.

To use this plugin, the first thing to do is to add a plugin like the one in Listing 9.7 to the POM file.

```
<plugin>
   <groupId>org.codehaus.mojo</groupId>
   <artifactId>versions-maven-plugin</artifactId>
   <version>2.18.0</version>
</plugin>
```

**LISTING 9.7** Modifications to the POM file to use the plugin.

After the modifications to the POM file, the next step is to execute a simple command that scans all the dependencies and checks for the latest version in the same way that is shown in Listing 9.8.

```
$ mvn versions:display-dependency-updates
......
......
[INFO] The following dependencies in Dependency Management have newer
versions:
[INFO]    biz.aQute.bnd:biz.aQute.bnd.annotation ............... 7.0.0 -> 7.1.0
[INFO]    ch.qos.logback:logback-classic ....................... 1.5.6 -> 1.5.17
......
......
[INFO] ------------------------------------------------------------------
[INFO] BUILD SUCCESS
[INFO] ------------------------------------------------------------------
[INFO] Total time:  8.618 s
[INFO] Finished at: 2025-03-11T21:22:37-03:00
[INFO] ------------------------------------------------------------------
```

**LISTING 9.8** Dependencies that need to be updated.

---

[7]https://www.mojohaus.org/versions/versions-maven-plugin/usage.html

The result of executing the command in Listing 9.8 shows all the dependencies that need to be updated, including the transitive dependencies, which, in some cases, is not a good idea because it's impossible to distinguish which of them are part of the application. Another command reads only the versions declared in the properties and suggests which must be updated, as shown in Listing 9.9.

```
$ mvn versions:display-property-updates
......

......
[INFO] The following version properties are referencing the newest
available version:
[INFO]    ${depclean-maven-plugin.version} ............................ 2.0.6
[INFO]    ${karate.version} ........................................... 1.4.1
[INFO]    ${quickperf.version} ........................................ 1.1.0
[INFO]    ${versions-maven-plugin.version} ........................... 2.18.0
[INFO] The following version property updates are available:
[INFO]    ${archunit-junit5.version} ........................... 1.2.1 -> 1.4.0
[INFO]    ${liquibase-core.version} ......................... 4.20.0 -> 4.31.1
[INFO]    ${mapstruct.version} ........................... 1.5.5.Final -> 1.6.3
[INFO]    ${maven-compiler-plugin.version} ............. 3.8.1 -> 4.0.0-beta-2
[INFO]    ${maven-enforcer-plugin.version} .................. 3.0.0-M2 -> 3.5.0
[INFO]    ${resilience4j-spring-boot3.version} .............. 2.1.0 -> 2.3.0
[INFO]    ${spotless-maven-plugin.version} .................. 2.43.0 -> 2.44.3
[INFO]    ${springdoc-openapi-starter-webmvc-ui.version} ....... 2.1.0 -> 2.8.5
[INFO]    ${testcontainers.version} ......................... 1.19.7 -> 1.20.6
[INFO]
[INFO] ------------------------------------------------------------------------
[INFO] BUILD SUCCESS
[INFO] ------------------------------------------------------------------------
[INFO] Total time:  1.056 s
[INFO] Finished at: 2025-03-11T21:23:57-03:00
[INFO] ------------------------------------------------------------------------
```

**LISTING 9.9** Execution of the plugin to check only the properties.

The execution result in Listing 9.9 is assertive, but all the versions of the dependencies need to be declared as properties.

## Upgrade Application

Updating the application's dependencies is relatively straightforward if it is done regularly, but what if it is a legacy system? How can a transition to a new version of a framework, such as Spring Boot, be managed? It often requires someone spending many hours finding out which changes require migrating to a new version of Java or Spring Boot, which comes with a high risk of introducing problems in the application.

Considering all of these problems, a solution appeared some years ago: a tool called OpenRewrite[8]. This tool has a vast catalog of recipes that outline the steps to migrate from one version to a new one, reducing the manual intervention required from developers to just including a plugin. The official Web site details the recipes.

---
[8]https://docs.openrewrite.org/

The first step is to define which application elements need to be migrated. For example, the project could greatly benefit from using a new version of Spring Boot and adopting Java 21 instead of 17. To achieve this, the plugin with the configuration shown in Listing 9.10 must be included in the POM file.

```xml
<plugin>
    <groupId>org.openrewrite.maven</groupId>
    <artifactId>rewrite-maven-plugin</artifactId>
    <version>6.3.0</version>
    <configuration>
        <activeRecipes>
            <recipe>org.openrewrite.java.OrderImports</recipe>
            <recipe>org.openrewrite.java.migrate.UpgradeToJava21</
recipe>
            <recipe>org.openrewrite.java.spring.boot3.
UpgradeSpringBoot_3_3</recipe>
        </activeRecipes>
    </configuration>
    <dependencies>
        <dependency>
            <groupId>org.openrewrite.recipe</groupId>
            <artifactId>rewrite-spring</artifactId>
            <version>6.3.0</version>
        </dependency>
        <dependency>
            <groupId>org.openrewrite.recipe</groupId>
            <artifactId>rewrite-migrate-java</artifactId>
            <version>3.3.0</version>
        </dependency>
    </dependencies>
</plugin>
```

**LISTING 9.10** Dependencies to use OpenRewrite on the application.

Each recipe has its dependencies, so the list must include more than just the active recipes. If the dependency isn't included, the migration will fail. The list of dependencies related to each recipe appears on the official Web site alongside the entire package name.

After the modifications to the POM file, the next step is to run a command that explicitly indicates the migration. The command and the result are shown in Listing 9.11.

```
$ mvn rewrite:run
......

......
[WARNING] Changes have been made to chapter-9/api-reservation/
src/test/java/com/twa/flights/api/reservation/architecture/general/
ArchitectureConstants.java by:
[WARNING]      org.openrewrite.java.migrate.UpgradeToJava21
[WARNING]          org.openrewrite.java.migrate.UpgradeToJava17
[WARNING]              org.openrewrite.java.migrate.lang.StringFormatted:
{addParentheses=false}
[WARNING]          org.openrewrite.java.migrate.UpgradeBuildToJava21
[WARNING]          org.openrewrite.java.migrate.UpgradeJavaVersion:
{version=21}
```

```
[WARNING] Changes have been made to chapter-9/api-reservation/
src/test/java/com/twa/flights/api/reservation/architecture/layer/
ControllerRulesTest.java by:
[WARNING]       org.openrewrite.java.OrderImports
[WARNING]           org.openrewrite.java.migrate.UpgradeToJava21
[WARNING]               org.openrewrite.java.migrate.UpgradeToJava17
[WARNING]                   org.openrewrite.java.migrate.lang.
StringFormatted: {addParentheses=false}
[WARNING]               org.openrewrite.java.migrate.UpgradeBuildToJava21
[WARNING]                   org.openrewrite.java.migrate.
UpgradeJavaVersion: {version=21}
[WARNING] Please review and commit the results.
[WARNING] Estimate time saved: 12m
[INFO] ------------------------------------------------------------
[INFO] BUILD SUCCESS
[INFO] ------------------------------------------------------------
[INFO] Total time:  34.302 s
[INFO] Finished at: 2025-03-12T14:47:50-03:00
[INFO] ------------------------------------------------------------
```

**LISTING 9.11** Result of the execution on the migration.

If everything is okay, the application will migrate to the new Java and Spring Boot versions without a problem. If something is wrong, however, the plugin will provide details about the situation; in that case, someone needs to make the corrections before rerunning the plugin.

The migration could take several minutes, depending on the size of the application and the number of active recipes declared on the plugin.

## PACKAGING

After building the application, the next step is to define how to distribute it across different environments. This topic is particularly relevant because, nowadays, with the appearance of microservices, deployments are frequent, perhaps more than one microservice a week, so a lousy strategy means more work for the developers or the infrastructure team.

There are numerous options for distributing the application, but this book focuses on two complementary approaches:

- JAR/WAR, which is the traditional way to package applications.
- Docker containers are a modern way to encapsulate everything related to the application's environment. In most cases, they are inside a JAR/WAR file.

### What Problems Could Appear During This Process?

Issues depend on the chosen strategy for packaging and distribution. For instance, several problems may arise when using a JAR file, such as microservices utilizing a version incompatible with specific environments. Locally, everything functions well, but when someone carries out an upload, issues might surface, which subsequently results in time spent figuring out what is happening with the application. Another problem with this approach is that it is difficult to simulate what happens in specific environments. This approach commonly appears in legacy projects or companies that do not use CI/CD, or only use it partially.

Docker minimizes most of these problems, offering the possibility to run the application locally or in another environment with the same result, thereby reducing the complexity of understanding potential issues with the application. At the same time, this approach has some extra steps, such as building and uploading the image to a repository to make it accessible in any environment. Note, however, that this approach takes more time than the previous one and has extra costs when using a Docker repository.

## How to Build an Image

Building an image involves various approaches; some are straightforward to implement but simultaneously introduce other issues, such as the duration required for building or the space each image occupies. This section demonstrates how it is possible to build an image using the most relevant methods, ranging from the simplest to the most complex. Some prioritize the application's performance, such as using GraalVM[9], while others, such as the layer strategy, aim to reduce the size of the file and the time of the operation.

Before creating a Dockerfile, it's necessary to create a file named `application-docker.yml`. This file contains the same information as `application.yml`, but with some modifications, such as replacing `localhost` with the names of Docker containers, as shown in Listing 9.12.

```
spring:
  application:
    name: api-reservation

  datasource:
    driver-class-name: com.mysql.cj.jdbc.Driver
    url: jdbc:mysql://api-reservation-db:3306/flights_reservation
    username: root
    password: muppet

  # Previous configuration

http-connector:
  defaultConfig: &commonDefaultConfig
    connectionTimeout: 5000
    readTimeout: 5000
    responseTimeout: 5000
  hosts:
    api-catalog:
      host: "api-catalog"
      port: 6070
      # Previous configuration

    api-clusters:
      host: "api-clusters"
      port: 4070
      # Previous configuration
```

**LISTING 9.12** The application file to use on the Docker image.

---

[9]https://www.graalvm.org/

The changes in bold refer to the container names in the Docker Compose file. If the application has more properties connected with other services, they must be replaced.

The next step is to create a new profile on the POM file to exclude the execution of all the tests, as shown in Listing 9.13, to reduce the packaging time. This new profile will exclude all the packages and folders associated with the tests.

```
<profile>
    <id>PA</id>
    <build>
            <plugins>
                    <plugin>
                            <groupId>org.apache.maven.plugins</groupId>
                            <artifactId>maven-surefire-plugin</artifactId>
                            <version>${maven.surefire.version}</version>
                            <configuration>
                                    <excludes>
    <exclude>**/performance/**Test.java</exclude>
                                    <exclude>**/unit/**Test.java</exclude>
                                    <exclude>**/architecture/**Test.java</exclude>
    <exclude>**/integration/**Test.java</exclude>
                                    </excludes>
                                    <argLine>-Dfile.encoding=UTF-8</argLine>
                                    <argLine>-
XX:+EnableDynamicAgentLoading</argLine>
                            </configuration>
                    </plugin>
            </plugins>
    </build>
</profile>
```

**LISTING 9.13** New profile to exclude all the tests.

The last step before creating the Docker image is to build the application to ensure everything is okay with the new profile. To do this, execute the command mvn package as it appears in Listing 9.14.

```
$ mvn package -P PA
......
......

[INFO] Analysis done in 0min 18s
[INFO] ------------------------------------------------------------
[INFO] BUILD SUCCESS
[INFO] ------------------------------------------------------------
[INFO] Total time:  21.902 s
[INFO] Finished at: 2025-04-04T12:24:45-03:00
[INFO] ------------------------------------------------------------
```

**LISTING 9.14** Result of the package command.

The result of Listing 9.14 indicates that everything works fine, but to be sure, a good idea is to check the target folder of the file api-reservation-0.0.1-SNAPSHOT.jar.

## Create a Base Image

After making the application modifications and checking that everything works fine, the next step is to create the image responsible for running the application. To do that, a Dockerfile must be created in the application's root directory. This file will use a base image from OpenJDK[10], as shown in Listing 9.15.

```
FROM openjdk:21-slim

COPY target/api-reservation-*.jar application/api-reservation.jar

CMD java -jar application/api-reservation.jar --spring.config.
location=classpath:/application-docker.yml

EXPOSE 8090
```

**LISTING 9.15** Dockerfile to run the application.

The Dockerfile will copy the JAR file from the `target` folder, remove the version from the file name, and execute the application, indicating which application file it must use.

> **NOTE**
>
> *A good practice when creating a Dockerfile is to reduce the size of the image. To do this in the case of Java, it is recommended to use the slim versions, which contain a small number of installed packages, reducing the security vulnerabilities simultaneously. Another recommendation related to security or vulnerabilities is to check frequently whether there is a new version of the image from the same JDK version but with a different minor or patch version. A common practice when a new security issue appears is to fix the JDK and create a new image.*

The next step is to build the image so that it is available at least locally. To do this, it's necessary to invoke the command `docker build`, specifying the name of the image, as shown in Listing 9.16.

```
$ docker build -t adschosen/api-reservation:1.0.0 .
[+] Building 3.9s (8/8) FINISHED
 => [internal] load build definition from Dockerfile
0.0s
 => => transferring dockerfile: 245B
0.0s
 => [internal] load .dockerignore
0.0s
 => => transferring context: 2B
0.0s
 => [internal] load metadata for docker.io/library/openjdk:21-slim
3.0s
```

---

[10]https://hub.docker.com/_/openjdk

```
 => [auth] library/openjdk:pull token for registry-1.docker.io
0.0s
 => [internal] load build context
0.6s
 => => transferring context: 70.80MB
0.6s
 => CACHED [1/2] FROM docker.io/library/openjdk:21-slim@sha256:707205384
7a8a05d7f3a14ebc778a90b38c50ce7e8f199382128a53385160688              0.0s
 => [2/2] COPY target/api-reservation-*.jar application/api-reservation.
jar                                                                   0.1s
 => exporting to image
0.2s
 => => exporting layers
0.2s
 => => writing image sha256:843d84bef0f6582543b567fba7b9356da83cc8876877
31819cfbe665ba24e0c5                                                  0.0s
 => => naming to docker.io/adschosen/api-reservation:1.0.0
0.0s
```

**LISTING 9.16** Result of the building process.

The next step is to push the image to a repository accessible to everyone, not just locally. To do this, it's necessary to use the command `docker push`, indicating which image needs to be uploaded, in the same way that appears in Listing 9.17.

```
$ docker push adschosen/api-reservation:1.0.0
The push refers to repository [docker.io/adschosen/api-reservation]
8bf27ac2cf9f: Pushed
5f70bf18a086: Pushed
992cf93d96ab: Pushed
582b2106abf5: Pushed
9bc6f96b61fb: Pushed
659a8c4ba776: Pushed
0ac7ecf8a41c: Pushed
d310e774110a: Pushed
1.0.0: digest: sha256:6624ac17003fa45f9de6469ea8c2c194b44fd5a89f0bafba4d
943b694aec5966 size: 1996
```

**LISTING 9.17** Uploading the image to the Docker repository.

The result of executing Listing 9.17 shows that the image is available for anyone accessing the repository. Note that logging in is required to upload the image to any repository.

After building the image, it's time to modify the Docker Compose file to use it. The modifications require defining a new service with a name and the ports that are exposed in the same way as shown in Listing 9.18.

```
version: '3.1'
services:

  # Previous configuration

  api-reservation:
    image: adschosen/api-reservation:1.0.0
    container_name: api-reservation
```

```
    ports:
      - 8090:8090
    restart: always

  api-reservation-db:
    container_name: api-reservation-db
    image: mysql:8.2.0
    restart: always
    environment:
      MYSQL_DATABASE: 'flights_reservation'
      MYSQL_ROOT_PASSWORD: 'muppet'
    ports:
      - 3312:3306
```

*LISTING 9.18* Adding the api-reservation image to the Docker Compose file.

The final step is to run the Docker Compose file and check that everything works correctly using any endpoint. For example, Listing 9.19 shows a `curl` command to obtain information from a specific reservation.

```
$ curl -X 'GET' \
  'http://localhost:8090/api/flights/reservation/1' \
  -H 'accept: application/json'

{"id":1,"itineraryId":"2","searchId":"2","passengers":[{"id":1,"firstName
":"Andres","lastName":"Sacco","documentNumber":"987654321","documentType
":"DNI","nationality":"ARG","birthday":"1985-01-01"}],"contact":{"id":1,
"telephoneNumber":"54911111111","email":"sacco.andres@gmail.com"}}
```

*LISTING 9.19* Result of the execution of a curl command.

As a suggestion, when building an image for the first time, if something bad happens, do not increment the version number and push to Docker's repository; instead, try to check locally before invoking the `push` command.

## Use a Layers Strategy to Reduce the Time to Build

Building an image on Docker requires time to execute all the steps of the Dockerfile and space in the Docker repository where the images are saved to be distributed across different environments or shared. These two points are relevant because images could be built once or more than once each week, so it's essential to find a way to reuse layers.

**NOTE** *If nothing changes, Docker creates a layer for each step that can be reused across different images. For example, if the first step of an image involves downloading a specific version of a tool, Docker will create a layer and push it to a repository. If someone later creates a new version of the image using the same tool version, Docker will detect and reuse the layer from the previous build.*

The applications do not change everything with each new version; they might just fix a minor bug without altering the libraries or dependencies they use to function. Therefore, splitting the application into different layers or steps might be beneficial, where one layer contains the code and another holds the dependencies. Java has tools that allow extracting the file's content to analyze or copy it into another place. Considering this advantage, let's modify the Dockerfile from Listing 9.16 to copy the JAR file and extract the content to create different layers. Listing 9.20 shows how to do it using the multi-stage feature of Docker, but only push the last layer.

```
FROM openjdk:21-slim-bookworm AS builder
WORKDIR workspace
ARG JAR_FILE=target/*.jar
COPY ${JAR_FILE} api-reservation.jar
RUN java -Djarmode=layertools -jar api-reservation.jar extract

FROM openjdk:21-slim-bookworm
WORKDIR workspace
COPY --from=builder workspace/dependencies/ ./
COPY --from=builder workspace/spring-boot-loader/ ./
COPY --from=builder workspace/snapshot-dependencies/ ./
COPY --from=builder workspace/application/ ./
ENTRYPOINT ["java", "org.springframework.boot.loader.launch.JarLauncher",
"--spring.config.location=classpath:/application-docker.yml"]
```

**LISTING 9.20** Multi-stage image to reduce the building time.

The first stage of the Dockerfile represents the JAR file copy and extracts the content. After that, copying all the folders in the same directory is necessary to run the application. The last command is used to run a Spring Boot application using Java. It's essential to write the correct package location of the launcher, which, since version 3.3.x of Spring, has changed from

`org.springframework.boot.loader.JarLauncher` to `org.springframework.boot.loader.launch.JarLauncher`.

After these modifications to the Dockerfile, the next step is to build the image to check that everything works fine, as in Listing 9.21.

```
$ docker build -t adschosen/api-reservation:1.0.0 .
[+] Building 2.8s (13/13) FINISHED
 => [internal] load .dockerignore
0.0s
 => => transferring context: 2B
0.0s
 => [internal] load build definition from Dockerfile
0.0s
 => => transferring dockerfile: 610B
0.0s
 => [internal] load metadata for docker.io/library/openjdk:21-slim-bookw
orm                                                         1.1s
 => [internal] load build context
0.6s
 => => transferring context: 70.81MB
0.6s
 => [builder 1/4] FROM docker.io/library/openjdk:21-slim-bookworm@sha256
:7072053847a8a05d7f3a14ebc778a90b38c50ce7e8f199382128a533851606  0.0s
 => CACHED [builder 2/4] WORKDIR workspace
0.0s
 => [builder 3/4] COPY target/*.jar api-reservation.jar
0.2s
```

```
 => [builder 4/4] RUN java -Djarmode=layertools -jar api-reservation.jar
extract                                                          0.6s
 => CACHED [stage-1 3/6] COPY --from=builder workspace/dependencies/ ./
0.0s
 => CACHED [stage-1 4/6] COPY --from=builder
workspace/spring-boot-loader/ ./
0.0s
 => CACHED [stage-1 5/6] COPY --from=builder
workspace/snapshot-dependencies/ ./
0.0s
 => [stage-1 6/6] COPY --from=builder workspace/application/ ./
0.0s
 => exporting to image
0.1s
 => => exporting layers
0.1s
 => => writing image sha256:2646469315588e4cb4bf8829be341d4e1a0da883b9d1
2b8c93944109f83eec42                                             0.0s
 => => naming to docker.io/adschosen/api-reservation:1.0.0
0.0s
```

*LISTING 9.21* Result of building the image using the layers strategy.

The result of Listing 9.21 mentions the word CACHED at several steps; this happens when someone tries to build an image without any modifications. If the application only suffers alterations in the code, one of the layers will be built, but the other one will be reused.

If the Docker Compose file is rerun without any modifications, Docker will use the new version, and everything will work similarly to the previous approach.

This approach will help reduce the time spent building and the space the image consumes on the Docker repository, but it will not improve the application's startup performance.

### Use GraalVM to Reduce the Startup Time

One of the challenges with the application is reducing the startup time and the size of the images with the previous approaches and modifications. It's possible, but insignificant compared to other languages, such as Go or Rust. GraalVM[11] offers the ability to compile and run applications natively, reducing the startup time compared to traditional JVM-based applications. This approach could be combined with other techniques, such as explicitly defining the heap size using -Xmx flags or enabling the lazy initialization of beans to ensure that beans are only created when necessary.

NOTE *GraalVM is a vast topic to explain in a single section; so, refer to the official documentation, which gives many details about how things work behind the scenes with this approach.*

Spring Boot introduced straightforward support for GraalVM in version 3.0.0, which is compatible with most ecosystem libraries. This feature, however, is not entirely new; Spring added support in an experimental capacity in version 2.7.0, allowing developers to use GraalVM, albeit without all its features.

---

[11]https://www.graalvm.org/

*What Are the Main Problems with Using It?*

Adopting GraalVM has many advantages but also introduces some challenges, most related to library compatibility, as not all libraries function correctly. For example, libraries such as Liquibase and Flyway lack support, so the only options are to disable them in the configuration or remove them from the POM file. Other libraries work but introduce some modifications to the application; for example, Caffeine, which uses reflection, requires dynamic proxies to be explicitly declared in a configuration file called `reflect-config.json`, indicating which classes need to do something that is not compatible by default with a native image. This process introduces more complexity to developing an application because it must wait until the native image detects this problem, so it could be necessary to build the image several times before fixing all the issues.

Additionally, the problem with dependencies is that this process increases the build time significantly compared to traditional JVM builds. It could take several minutes to finish creating a native image, which may ultimately affect the deployment time in a pipeline and the resources required by a CI/CD system to execute the entire pipeline. There are multiple solutions to this problem, such as creating a pipeline that generates the image with more resources than other pipelines.

*How to Implement It*

To use GraalVM, a supported JDK version must be installed on the machine, so check the official documentation[12] for instructions. Some alternatives, such as SDKMAN!, solve the problem of installing different versions and changing them with a simple command.

The first step requires explicitly adding some dependencies to prevent issues during the building process. Some are connected to the logging and others to the server, as shown in Listing 9.22.

```
<dependencies>

    <!-- Other dependencies -->

    <dependency>
          <groupId>org.springframework.boot</groupId>
          <artifactId>spring-boot-starter-logging</artifactId>
    </dependency>

    <dependency>
          <groupId>io.netty</groupId>
          <artifactId>netty-handler</artifactId>
    </dependency>

    <!-- Other dependencies -->
</dependencies>
```

**LISTING 9.22** Dependencies to use GraalVM.

Note that the building process slightly differs from the default method, which may cause the application to crash during or while executing.

After adding the dependencies, it's time to add a plugin responsible for part of the building process; this plugin is native-maven-plugin from GraalVM. It is recommended to add it to the

---

[12]https://www.graalvm.org/downloads/

pluginManagement section to prevent any conflict with other parts of the file. Listing 9.23 shows how to add the plugin with the correct configuration.

```
<build>

  <pluginManagement>
        <plugins>
              <plugin>
                    <groupId>org.graalvm.buildtools</groupId>
                    <artifactId>native-maven-plugin</artifactId>
                    <extensions>true</extensions>
              </plugin>
        </plugins>
  </pluginManagement>

  <!-- Other configuration -->
</build>
```

**LISTING 9.23** Add a plugin to build the application.

The next step related to the configuration of the POM file is to declare a new profile that contains all the configurations associated with GraalVM. Listing 9.24 shows the configuration to exclude all the tests during the packing process, with one plugin responsible for generating the image and another connected with Hibernate.

```
<profile>
  <id>PN</id>
  <build>
        <plugins>
              <plugin>
                    <groupId>org.hibernate.orm.tooling</groupId>
                    <artifactId>hibernate-enhance-maven-plugin</
artifactId>
                    <version>${hibernate.version}</version>
                    <executions>
                          <execution>
                                <configuration>

  <enableLazyInitialization>true</enableLazyInitialization>
  <enableDirtyTracking>false</enableDirtyTracking>
  <enableAssociationManagement>false</enableAssociationManagement>
  <enableExtendedEnhancement>false</enableExtendedEnhancement>
                                </configuration>
                                <goals>
                                      <goal>enhance</goal>
                                </goals>
                          </execution>
                    </executions>
              </plugin>

              <plugin>
                    <groupId>org.springframework.boot</groupId>
                    <artifactId>spring-boot-maven-plugin</artifactId>
                    <configuration>
                          <image>
```

```xml
                                    <buildpacks>
                                        <buildpack>gcr.io/paketo-
buildpacks/graalvm</buildpack>
                                        <buildpack>gcr.io/paketo-
buildpacks/java-native-image</buildpack>
                                    </buildpacks>
                                    <env>
    <BP_JVM_VERSION>21.*</BP_JVM_VERSION>
    <BP_NATIVE_IMAGE>true</BP_NATIVE_IMAGE>
                                    </env>
                                </image>
                        </configuration>
                        <executions>
                            <execution>
                                <id>process-aot</id>
                                <goals>
                                    <goal>process-aot</goal>
                                </goals>
                            </execution>
                        </executions>
                </plugin>

                <plugin>
                        <groupId>org.graalvm.buildtools</groupId>
                        <artifactId>native-maven-plugin</artifactId>
                        <configuration>
    <classesDirectory>${project.build.outputDirectory}</classesDirectory>
                            <metadataRepository>
                                <enabled>true</enabled>
                            </metadataRepository>
                            <requiredVersion>22.3</requiredVersion>
                        </configuration>
                        <executions>
                            <execution>
                                <id>add-reachability-metadata</id>
                                <goals>
                                    <goal>add-reachability-
metadata</goal>
                                </goals>
                            </execution>
                        </executions>
                </plugin>

                <plugin>
                        <groupId>org.apache.maven.plugins</groupId>
                        <artifactId>maven-surefire-plugin</artifactId>
                        <version>${maven.surefire.version}</version>
                        <configuration>
                            <excludes>
    <exclude>**/performance/**Test.java</exclude>
    <exclude>**/unit/**Test.java</exclude>
    <exclude>**/architecture/**Test.java</exclude>
    <exclude>**/integration/**Test.java</exclude>
                            </excludes>
                            <argLine>-Dfile.encoding=UTF-8</argLine>
```

```
                    <argLine>-XX:+EnableDynamicAgentLoading</
argLine>
                        </configuration>
                    </plugin>
                </plugins>
        </build>
</profile>
```

**LISTING 9.24** Add a new profile to build the application using GraalVM.

It's relevant to include how to build the application in the `spring-boot-maven-plugin`. There are several ways to do it, but in the case of creating a native image, it is recommended to include `graalvm` and `java-native-image` from Paketo Backpacks[13]. This buildpack offers the opportunity to build the application natively, but there are also other options, so check the official documentation to see which other ways exist.

Some dependencies or libraries have problems with this mechanism of building and packaging an application up to the version of Spring that appears in this book. One of them is Hibernate and the use of `LAZY`, so for that reason, Listing 9.24 has a plugin related to the ORM and some configurations designed to solve those problems.

Hibernate is not the only library or dependency that has problems working with a native image; Caffeine is another that faces similar issues. Fortunately, it offers a solution to this problem, allowing users to continue benefiting from this library. To solve it, it's necessary to create a file called `reflect-config.json` in `/src/main/resources/META-INF/native-image` with the same information that appears in Listing 9.25.

```
[
  {
    "name": "com.github.benmanes.caffeine.cache.PSAMS",
    "allDeclaredConstructors": true,
    "allDeclaredMethods": true
  },
  {
    "name": "com.github.benmanes.caffeine.cache.PSAW",
    "allDeclaredConstructors": true,
    "allDeclaredMethods": true
  },
  {
    "name": "com.github.benmanes.caffeine.cache.SSMSWR",
    "allDeclaredConstructors": true,
    "allDeclaredMethods": true
  },
  {
    "name": "com.github.benmanes.caffeine.cache.PSWRMS",
    "allDeclaredConstructors": true,
    "allDeclaredMethods": true
  }
]
```

**LISTING 9.25** Configuration to solve problems with Caffeine.

---

[13]https://github.com/paketo-buildpacks/spring-boot

Another change connected with the dependencies added in Listing 9.22 is configuring the logs; specifically, the format must be indicated. To do this, let's create a file called `logback-spring.xml` in `/src/main/resources` with the content that appears in Listing 9.26.

```
<configuration>
    <appender name="STDOUT" class="ch.qos.logback.core.ConsoleAppender">
        <encoder>
            <pattern>%d{HH:mm:ss.SSS} [%thread] %-5level %logger{36} -
%msg%n</pattern>
        </encoder>
    </appender>

    <root level="info">
        <appender-ref ref="STDOUT"/>
    </root>
</configuration>
```

**LISTING 9.26** Logs configuration format.

Other problems that do not have solutions, at least up to the version of Spring Boot used in this book, are the exceptions related to Circuit Breaker and the use of Liquibase. In both cases, the only way to package the application without issues is to disable Liquibase and remove the exceptions from the circuit breaker's configuration. To achieve this, the best approach is to create a new file called `application-graalvm.yml`, containing the duplicated content from `application-docker.yml`, and to make the modifications shown in Listing 9.27.

```
spring:
  application:
    name: api-reservation

  # Previous configuration

  liquibase:
    enabled: false
    change-log: classpath:db/changelog/db.changelog-root.xml

resilience4j.circuitbreaker:
  configs:
    default:
      failure-rate-threshold: 50
      sliding-window-type: count_based
      sliding-window-size: 5

      automatic-transition-from-open-to-half-open-enabled: true
      wait-duration-in-open-state: 10s
      permitted-number-of-calls-in-half-open-state: 1

      register-health-indicator: false
      # Remove exceptions
  backends:
    catalog:
```

```
        baseConfig: default
```

**# Previous configuration**

*LISTING 9.27* New application.yml to use on GraalVM.

The last step involves compiling the application and building the image simultaneously, combining different commands, as shown in Listing 9.28.

```
$ mvn clean compile spring-boot:build-image -P PN

. . . . . .
. . . . . .

[INFO]  > Executing lifecycle version v0.20.7
[INFO]  > Using build cache volume 'pack-cache-7a5150cf6cbc.build'
[INFO]
[INFO]  > Running creator
[INFO]     [creator]    ===> ANALYZING
[INFO]     [creator]    Image with name "docker.io/library/api-
reservation:0.0.1-SNAPSHOT" not found
[INFO]     [creator]    ===> DETECTING
[INFO]     [creator]    target distro name/version labels not found,
reading /etc/os-release file
[INFO]     [creator]    7 of 16 buildpacks participating
[INFO]     [creator]    paketo-buildpacks/graalvm          9.1.1
[INFO]     [creator]    paketo-buildpacks/ca-certificates  3.10.0
[INFO]     [creator]    paketo-buildpacks/bellsoft-liberica 11.2.0
[INFO]     [creator]    paketo-buildpacks/syft             2.10.0
[INFO]     [creator]    paketo-buildpacks/executable-jar   6.13.0
[INFO]     [creator]    paketo-buildpacks/spring-boot      5.33.0
[INFO]     [creator]    paketo-buildpacks/native-image     5.16.0

. . . . . .
. . . . . .

[INFO]     [creator]    [1/8] Initializing...
(4.3s @ 0.26GB)
[INFO]     [creator]    [2/8] Performing analysis...   [*****]
(58.5s @ 3.44GB)
[INFO]     [creator]    [3/8] Building universe...
(7.7s @ 4.63GB)
[INFO]     [creator]    [4/8] Parsing methods...       [**]
(4.5s @ 4.35GB)
[INFO]     [creator]    [5/8] Inlining methods...      [****]
(3.3s @ 2.78GB)
[INFO]     [creator]    [6/8] Compiling methods...     [*****]
(29.4s @ 3.25GB)
[INFO]     [creator]    [7/8] Layouting methods...     [***]
(11.5s @ 4.12GB)
[INFO]     [creator]    [8/8] Creating image...        [***]
(9.4s @ 4.94GB)
```

```
. . . . . .
. . . . . .
[INFO] Successfully built image 'docker.io/library/api-
reservation:0.0.1-SNAPSHOT'
[INFO]
[INFO] ------------------------------------------------------------
[INFO] BUILD SUCCESS
[INFO] ------------------------------------------------------------
[INFO] Total time:  05:51 min
[INFO] Finished at: 2025-04-07T13:54:45-03:00
[INFO] ------------------------------------------------------------
```

**LISTING 9.28** Result of the process of compilation.

The duration of the building process depends on various aspects, such as the available memory and the number of CPUs on the machine, which can consume a significant amount of resources. Be aware that the process may fail the first time or display a message regarding the available space needed. If this situation occurs, try modifying the Docker configuration on the machine by adding more CPU, memory, and space for its use.

The last step is to modify `docker-compose.yml` with the name of the image and the command to execute the image, and use the correct `application.yml`. Listing 9.29 shows the modifications.

```
api-reservation:

    image: api-reservation:0.0.1-SNAPSHOT
    container_name: api-reservation
    ports:
     - 8090:8090
    restart: always
    command: ["--spring.config.location=classpath:/application-graalvm.
yml"]
```

**LISTING 9.29** Modifications on the Docker Compose file.

If everything is okay, it's time to rerun the Docker Compose file and execute a request similar to the previous packaging strategies. The startup time of the microservice will be considerably lower than that of the previous versions. Listing 9.30 shows the result of executing a `curl` command on the GraalVM microservices.

```
$ curl -X 'GET' \
  'http://localhost:8090/api/flights/reservation/1' \
  -H 'accept: application/json'

{"id":1,"itineraryId":"2","searchId":"2","passengers":[{"id":1,"firstName
":"Andres","lastName":"Sacco","documentNumber":"987654321","documentType
":"DNI","nationality":"ARG","birthday":"1985-01-01"}],"contact":{"id":1,
"telephoneNumber":"54911111111","email":"sacco.andres@gmail.com"}}
```

**LISTING 9.30** Result of the execution.

When comparing the sizes of images from different strategies, the image with GraalVM is 363 MB, while the others are approximately 509 MB. Therefore, building an image natively helps reduce the size and improve the application's startup performance; however, it requires more time.

## SUMMARY

Building and packaging an application is extremely helpful for deploying it in an environment, allowing it to run locally, and detecting possible strange behavior that does not appear to conflict with incorrect dependencies or configurations in the IDE.

Defining the best way to build and reduce the package size could take some time because it involves analyzing which mechanisms exist to achieve this and the trade-offs of implementing them, such as how using GraalVM could cause some dependencies of Spring Boot to not work. Also, it's a good idea to consider other aspects, such as code formatting and dealing with transient dependencies, which could produce random errors in the applications.

It's necessary to understand that this process is iterative. The main goal is to have a working method of packaging and distribution, and then try to improve it with minor changes.

# CHAPTER 10

# OBSERVABILITY AND MONITORING

Creating an application involves considering several key aspects, such as how to persist information, prevent unauthorized access to data, and distribute the application across various environments in a straightforward manner. Problems, however, often emerge only after the application is in use in a specific environment. Observability and monitoring are two key aspects that help developers understand what is happening within the system and identify where errors are occurring.

## WHAT IS OBSERVABILITY AND MONITORING?

These two concepts, in general, can cause confusion among developers, as it can be unclear whether they refer to the same or different things and what their scope is. Let's clarify this with a simple definition:

- *Monitoring* involves the systematic collection, visualization, and analysis of predefined metrics, logs, and health indicators to assess the current condition of a system. It aims to address questions such as: Is the system operational? Are the response times within acceptable limits? Are there any faults or failures?
- *Observability*, on the other hand, represents a more comprehensive concept. It pertains to the system's capacity to expose sufficient internal data—through logs, metrics, and traces—to enable operators and developers to comprehend not only that an issue has occurred but also its underlying causes. While monitoring involves observing symptoms, observability is concerned with diagnosing root causes.

In a monolithic architecture, logs are relevant, but a message indicating which part produced an error is enough. With the emergence of microservices architecture, where each service operates independently and communicates over the network, many problems can arise, such as increased complexity in debugging.

Possessing information regarding the internal behavior of a microservice is crucial, as it facilitates the identification of errors, bottlenecks, and performance degradation; assists in the monitoring of request flow across services amid distributed failures; supports incident response and root cause analysis to minimize downtime; offers historical data concerning changes, deployments, and regressions; and enables informed decision-making related to scaling, refactoring, and performance optimization.

To implement observability and monitoring in microservices, it's necessary to follow some practices and tools:

- Structured Logging: Write logs in a structured format (e.g., JSON) to enable querying, filtering, and correlation.
- Distributed Tracing: Use tools to trace requests across services and understand latency and failure points.
- Metrics Collection: Export service metrics (e.g., response time, error rate, and resource usage) using tools.
- Dashboards and Alerts: Visualize system behavior using tools, and configure alerts to notify teams about abnormal behavior or failures.

Note that each of these features includes other features, such as the correlation of IDs involved in tracing and logging.

## LOGGING

This practice involves recording information during the application's execution in a location such as the console, a file, or another tool that collects all this data. The information, commonly referred to as logs, typically includes a timestamp, details about the part of the application involved, the type of information (INFO, DEBUG, WARN, or ERROR), and a message describing the action.

This information is crucial in some production environments, but it's also relevant locally to understand what happens when an error or bug occurs. Let's see some of the most pertinent benefits of this practice:

- Visibility: It's possible to see what happens inside the application and understand the health of the application in the case that some component, internal or external, fails. Different Levels: There are multiple levels of logs, each of which could provide more information about a specific error or failure.
- Alerting: The logs could be used as a mechanism to detect bad behavior, trigger an alert, or just collect metrics.
- Concatenate: It's possible to create a request ID that can be used to connect requests that travel across multiple microservices or applications.

Without gathering accurate information about the various applications of a system, understanding what occurs in a production environment can be too much effort. To effectively use the logs, there are some aspects to consider:

- Structure: The logs should have a format that makes it easy to parse and query the information, usually JSON.
- Log Aggregation Tool: A tool that is responsible for collecting all logs and providing features to query and retrieve information.

- Log Agent: A tool that is responsible for collecting information from the application and sending it to the log aggregation tool.
- Correlation IDs: The logs should include some form of correlation to facilitate understanding of how information is transmitted across multiple applications. This concept is generally associated with tracing.
- Log Level: Logs should have different levels to identify the importance of the information easily.

Of course, other aspects could be considered in the logging process, but this list only represents the most relevant ones.

## What Ways Exist to Expose Logs?

Collecting logs of different applications and putting them in one central place requires the use of some tool, the most relevant of which are:

- Loki[1]: This tool was developed by Grafana and can be used as a data source and to simply show logs, with the chance to create dashboards.
- Logstash[2]: This tool, developed by Elastic, offers a robust data processing pipeline that ingests, enriches, and transforms logs before forwarding them to storage systems, such as Elasticsearch. Filebeat[3]: This tool was created by Elastic and acts as a lightweight log shipper that monitors log files and transmits them directly to Logstash or Elasticsearch with minimal system impact.
- Fluentd[4]: This tool was developed by Treasure Data and functions as a versatile data collector that enables routing, buffering, filtering, and transforming logs before sending them to various destinations, such as Elasticsearch, Kafka, or cloud services. OpenTelemetry Collector[5]: This tool is an integral component of the OpenTelemetry project, facilitating the collection of logs, metrics, and traces within a unified pipeline. These can be processed and exported to a wide range of back ends, including Jaeger, Prometheus, and Elasticsearch.
- Vector.dev[6]: This tool was developed by Datadog and provides a high-performance observability pipeline, meticulously crafted in Rust, which efficiently gathers, transforms, and routes logs and metrics to various destinations with minimal latency and exemplary reliability.

Each tool has its pros and cons that must be considered before choosing one. In the case of this book, the following section explains the most relevant differences between some tools for collecting logs, some of which do not require a paid license to use.

**NOTE** *Other tools not mentioned in this section are Logagent, Promtail, Datadog Log Management, Splunk, Graylog, and AWS CloudWatch Logs.*

---

[1]https://grafana.com/oss/loki/
[2]https://www.elastic.co/logstash
[3]https://www.elastic.co/beats/filebeat
[4]https://www.fluentd.org/
[5]https://opentelemetry.io/docs/collector/
[6]https://vector.dev/

## What Is the Best Option for Each Scenario?

Choosing the best option generally relies on factors such as the team's expertise, the intricacy of tool setups, the changes required for applications, and the level of support provided for different languages or frameworks through various methods. In this book, we will temporarily put this consideration aside and examine the advantages and disadvantages of each option to help with deciding on the best option. Table 10.1 provides a concise overview of the various options for collecting logs from the applications.

**TABLE 10.1** Main things to consider when choosing an option.

| Features | ELK | Loki | Fluentd |
|---|---|---|---|
| Log Collection Agent | ✓ | ✗ | ✓ |
| Centralized Log Aggregation | ✓ | ✓ | ✓ |
| Log Parsing/Transformation | ✓ | ✓ | ✓ |
| Log Storage Engine | ✓ | ✓ | ✗ |
| Query Language | ✓ | ✓ | ✗ |
| Log Volume Efficiency | ✗ | ✓ | ✓ |
| Structured Logs Support (JSON, etc.) | ✓ | ✓ | ✓ |
| Maintenance Complexity | ✗ | ✓ | ✓ |

There are significant differences between the three approaches; synthesizing all the arguments into one document by creating an ADR is a good idea, as shown in Figure 10.1.

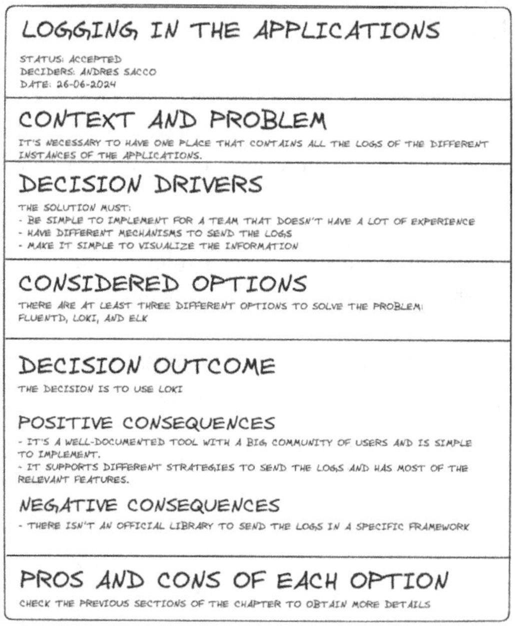

**FIGURE 10.1** ADR about the decision of how to collect the logs.

This document helps anyone grasp the reasons for choosing one approach over another and confirms the factors evaluated during the decision-making process.

## What Implications Do the Modifications Have on the Application?

After choosing an option, the next step is to start making modifications to use it. In the case of Loki, the first step involves creating a Docker Compose file that will contain the tool. Listing 10.1 shows the basic configuration of the Docker Compose file.

```
version: '3.1'
services:
  loki:
    image: grafana/loki:2.9.2
    container_name: loki
    ports:
      - "3100:3100"
    command: -config.file=/etc/loki/local-config.yaml

  grafana:
    image: grafana/grafana:10.3.1
    container_name: grafana
    ports:
      - "3000:3000"
    environment:
      - GF_SECURITY_ADMIN_USER=admin
      - GF_SECURITY_ADMIN_PASSWORD=admin
    volumes:
      - grafana-storage:/var/lib/grafana

volumes:
  grafana-storage:
```

**LISTING 10.1** Docker Compose configuration.

Before starting the modifications on the application, start Loki and Grafana. Grafana is responsible for displaying the logs in an accessible format, offering the possibility to perform advanced queries.

In the application, it is necessary to create a file named `logback-spring.xml` that contains various appenders to expose the logs and send them to Loki. Listing 10.2 displays the content of the file.

```
<?xml version="1.0" encoding="UTF-8"?>
<configuration scan="true">

    <!-- LOG LEVEL -->
    <property name="LOG_LEVEL" value="INFO" />

    <!-- Console Appender -->
    <appender name="CONSOLE" class="ch.qos.logback.core.ConsoleAppender">
        <encoder>
            <pattern>%d{yyyy-MM-dd HH:mm:ss} [%thread] %-5level
%logger{36} - %msg%n</pattern>
        </encoder>
    </appender>
```

```
    <!-- Loki Appender -->
    <appender name="LOKI" class="com.github.loki4j.logback.
Loki4jAppender">
        <http>
            <url>http://localhost:3100/loki/api/v1/push</url>
        </http>
        <format>
            <label>
                <pattern>app=api-reservation,host=localhost,level=%lev
el</pattern>
                <readMarkers>true</readMarkers>
            </label>
            <message>
                <pattern>
                    {
                    "level":"%level",
                    "class":"%logger{36}",
                    "thread":"%thread",
                    "message": "%message"
                    }
                </pattern>
            </message>
        </format>
    </appender>

    <!-- Root Logger -->
    <root level="${LOG_LEVEL}">
        <appender-ref ref="CONSOLE" />
        <appender-ref ref="LOKI" />
    </root>

</configuration>
```

**LISTING 10.2** logback-spring.xml definition.

In the previous listing, there are two different appenders: One is responsible for sending the logs to Loki, while the other displays the logs on the console. This allows the user to retain the ability to run the application locally and observe the results.

The next step involves adding dependencies to the POM file, which enables the capability to generate logs in a standard format and send them to Loki. Listing 10.3 shows the minimum dependencies that are required.

```
<dependency>
    <groupId>org.springframework.boot</groupId>
    <artifactId>spring-boot-starter-logging</artifactId>
</dependency>

<dependency>
    <groupId>com.github.loki4j</groupId>
    <artifactId>loki-logback-appender</artifactId>
    <version>1.4.1</version>
</dependency>
```

**LISTING 10.3** Add dependencies to the POM file.

Consider checking which is the latest version of the dependency related to Loki, as new versions are periodically released that address some performance issues.

NOTE *There are other options for collecting the logs instead of using HTTP; it's possible to use Promtail, which involves saving the logs to a file. The tool reads that file and sends the information to Loki.*

With all these changes made, run the application and send multiple requests to any of the endpoints that provide information about the reservations, and send some logs to the tool before ingress.

After completing all the requests, open a browser and go to *http://localhost:3000*, which displays a Web page similar to that shown in Figure 10.2.

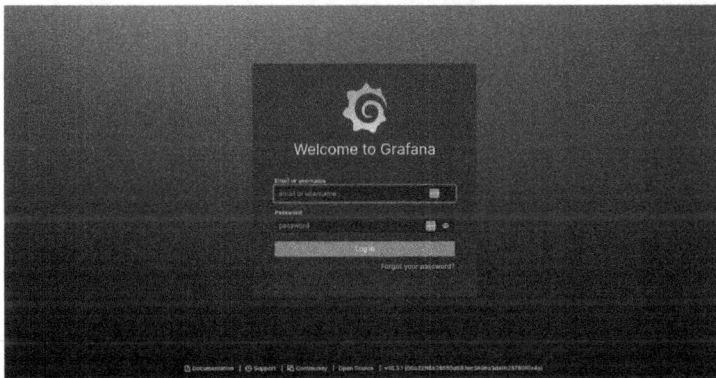

**FIGURE 10.2** Default Web page of Grafana.

Log in to the application by using `admin` as the username and password and then clicking Log in. If everything is okay, the next Web page that appears will be the initial page, suggesting actions such as creating a dashboard or adding a new data source. In this case, adding a new data source is necessary to obtain information from Loki. So, click on Add your first data source and find Loki, as shown in Figure 10.3.

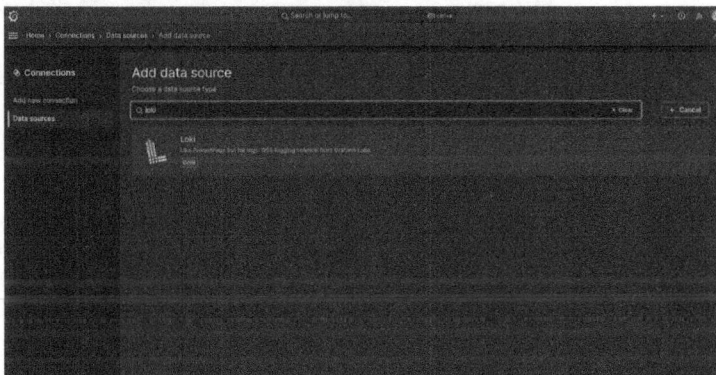

**FIGURE 10.3** Configuring a new data source.

On the following Web page, it's necessary to configure all the details about the data source. In this case, just fill the URL field in the Connection section with *http://loki:3100*, as shown in Figure 10.4.

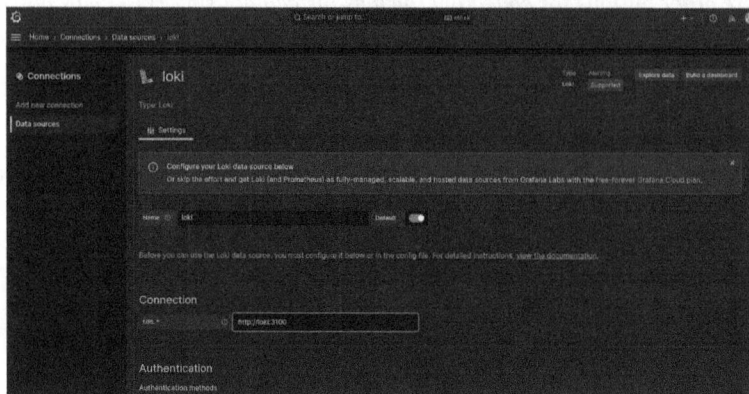

**FIGURE 10.4** Configuring Loki.

The final step in the configuration is to click Save & Test, which will indicate whether the connection is successful or not. If everything is okay, click on the link Explore view and modify the label filter with the value app and the name of the application, as shown in Figure 10.5.

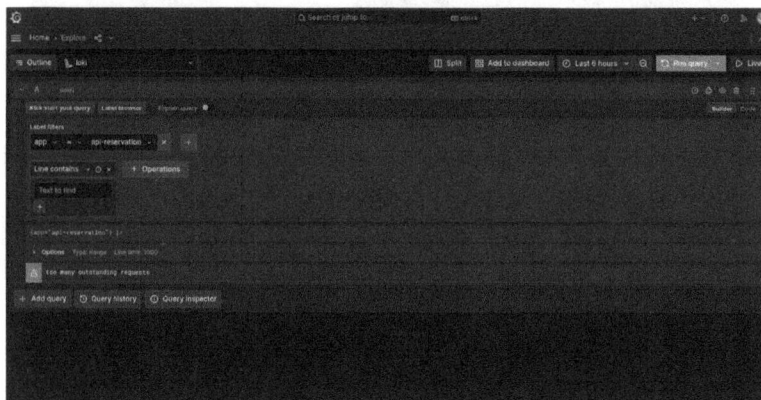

**FIGURE 10.5** Check whether the logging process is working.

If everything is okay and the application logs appear, it is recommended to create a new dashboard to display the logs with some level of detail. To do this, go to the Dashboard option, click on Create dashboard, and then click on the section Import to use a predefined dashboard instead of creating one from scratch. Figure 10.6 shows what the Web page looks like to import the dashboard.

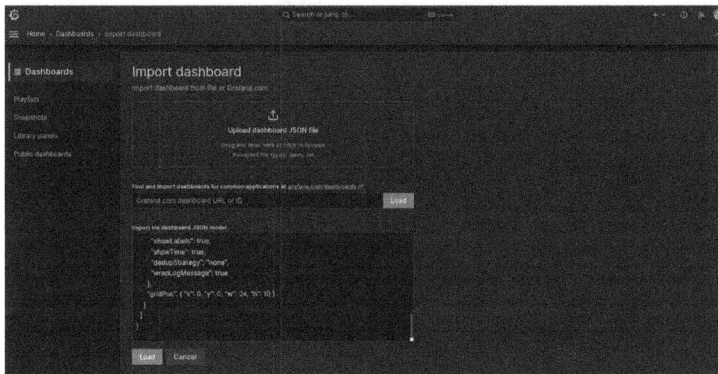

***FIGURE 10.6*** Importing a new dashboard.

To import dashboards, there are two options: One is to access the dashboard directly on the Grafana Web page, and the other is to create it in JSON format for import. Listing 10.4 displays the content of the dashboard to be copied and pasted onto the Web page shown in Figure 10.6. Change the UID of the data source, which is associated with the ID of the recently created data source.

```
{
  "id": null,
  "title": "Loki Logs Overview",
  "timezone": "browser",
  "schemaVersion": 36,
  "version": 1,
  "refresh": "10s",
  "panels": [
      {
      "title": "Logs by Level (Graph)",
      "type": "timeseries",
      "id": 5,
      "datasource": { "type": "loki", "uid": "d76c287e-4900-4798-9753-
efba546a69b7" },
      "targets": [
        {
          "expr": "count_over_time({app=\"api-reservation\"} |=
\"ERROR\" [5m])",
          "refId": "A",
          "legendFormat": "ERROR"
        },
        {
          "expr": "count_over_time({app=\"api-reservation\"} |= \"WARN\"
[5m])",
          "refId": "B",
          "legendFormat": "WARN"
        },
        {
```

```
              "expr": "count_over_time({app=\"api-reservation\"} |= \"INFO\"
      [5m])",
              "refId": "C",
              "legendFormat": "INFO"
            }
          ],
          "gridPos": { "x": 0, "y": 16, "w": 24, "h": 8 }
        },
        {
          "title": "Error Log Count (Last 1h)",
          "type": "stat",
          "id": 2,
          "datasource": { "type": "loki", "uid": "d76c287e-4900-4798-9753-
      efba546a69b7" },
          "targets": [
            {
              "expr": "count_over_time({app=\"spring-boot-app\"} |=
      \"ERROR\" [1h])",
              "refId": "A"
            }
          ],
          "gridPos": { "x": 0, "y": 10, "w": 6, "h": 6 }
        },
        {
          "title": "Warning Log Count (Last 1h)",
          "type": "stat",
          "id": 3,
          "datasource": { "type": "loki", "uid": "d76c287e-4900-4798-9753-
      efba546a69b7" },
          "targets": [
            {
              "expr": "count_over_time({app=\"api-reservation\"} |= \"WARN\"
      [1h])",
              "refId": "A"
            }
          ],
          "gridPos": { "x": 6, "y": 10, "w": 6, "h": 6 }
        },
        {
          "title": "Debug Log Count (Last 1h)",
          "type": "stat",
          "id": 3,
          "datasource": { "type": "loki", "uid": "d76c287e-4900-4798-9753-
      efba546a69b7" },
          "targets": [
            {
              "expr": "count_over_time({app=\"api-reservation\"} |=
      \"DEBUG\" [1h])",
              "refId": "A"
            }
          ],
          "gridPos": { "x": 12, "y": 10, "w": 6, "h": 6 }
        },
        {
          "title": "Info Log Count (Last 1h)",
          "type": "stat",
```

```
      "id": 4,
      "datasource": { "type": "loki", "uid": "d76c287e-4900-4798-9753-
efba546a69b7" },
      "targets": [
        {
          "expr": "count_over_time({app=\"api-reservation\"} |= \"INFO\"
[1h])",
          "refId": "A"
        }
      ],
      "gridPos": { "x": 18, "y": 10, "w": 6, "h": 6 }
    },
        {
      "title": "Logs per Level",
      "type": "logs",
      "id": 1,
      "datasource": { "type": "loki", "uid": "d76c287e-4900-4798-9753-
efba546a69b7" },
      "targets": [
        {
          "expr": "{app=\"api-reservation\"}",
          "refId": "A"
        }
      ],
      "options": {
        "showLabels": true,
        "showTime": true,
        "dedupStrategy": "none",
        "wrapLogMessage": true
      },
      "gridPos": { "x": 0, "y": 0, "w": 24, "h": 10 }
    }
  ]
}
```

**LISTING 10.4** Dashboard to see the logs of the application.

If the import is correct, the next Web page that appears will resemble Figure 10.7, which displays the details of the logs once Loki is working.

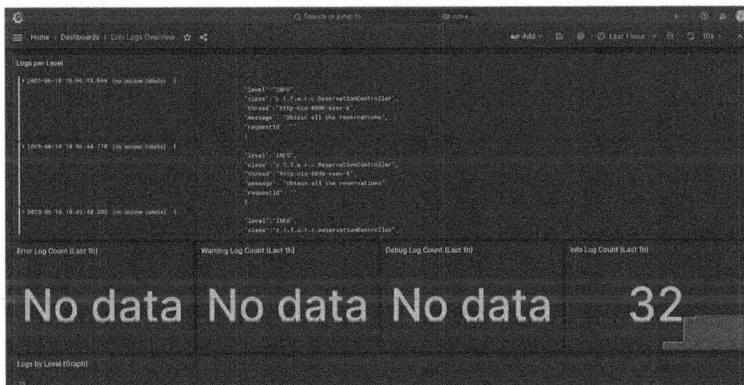

**FIGURE 10.7** Loki dashboard.

It's important to know that it's possible to create multiple dashboards with different formats and different levels of information. The dashboard that appears in this chapter is just one of the most basic ones that can be built.

## TRACES

This practice involves tracking the flow of a request as it passes through various components, which may include other applications, databases, or external systems. In a microservices architecture, it is common for a request to travel across many components before returning a result, so it's important to understand which components are involved in a flow to detect bottlenecks or strange behavior in part of the flow.

Traces record detailed information about each step of the flow, such as which services were called, how long each took, and where any errors or bottlenecks occurred. Each piece of information is captured as spans, and all the spans together form a trace.

The flexibility and benefits that microservices introduce are great, but they also bring a lot of challenges in detecting issues and diagnosing performance problems. Tracing helps in many areas, such as:

- Visibility: Tracing offers a clear view of how a request moves through various services, making it easier to identify slowdowns, failures, or unexpected issues across the system.
- Bottlenecks: By measuring the duration of each service call, tracing helps identify which parts of the architecture are causing latency or performance degradation.
- Correlation: Tracing allows for the correlation of distributed events using trace IDs or span IDs, helping to connect all parts of a single request even when it crosses multiple services.
- Root Cause Analysis: When failures happen, tracing shows exactly where the problem occurred in the request chain, reducing the time needed to diagnose and fix issues.
- Context: Traces carry contextual metadata (e.g., user ID, request type, and transaction ID) that provides valuable information for understanding not only what failed but also why.

To maximize the benefits of this practice, it's necessary to use a tool that considers all relevant aspects, such as correlation and context, because if any aspect is not covered, the information will not be helpful for solving a problem.

### What Ways Exist to Collect Traces?

Collecting and visualizing traces from different applications and consolidating them in one central place involves the use of specialized tools, the most relevant of which are:

- New Relic[7]: This platform is a commercial observability tool offering comprehensive full-stack monitoring and robust distributed tracing features. It enables users to track requests across microservices, visualize dependencies, and pinpoint performance bottlenecks.
- Elastic APM[8]: This Elastic-developed tool is a component of the Elastic Stack, providing distributed tracing, metrics, and performance monitoring that are seamlessly integrated with Elasticsearch and Kibana, simplifying the correlation of logs, traces, and metrics.

---

[7]https://newrelic.com
[8]https://www.elastic.co/apm

- Tempo[9]: This tool, created by Grafana Labs, is an open-source back end for distributed tracing that efficiently stores trace data by indexing only trace IDs and integrates smoothly with Grafana for visualization.
- AWS X-Ray[10], Google Cloud Trace[11], and Azure Monitor[12]: These tools are cloud-native tracing solutions provided by AWS, Google Cloud, and Azure. They offer integrated support for distributed tracing and performance analysis of applications operating within their specific cloud environments.
- Zipkin[13]: This open-source distributed tracing system collects timing data for requests passing through microservices and features a Web interface for visualizing trace data and diagnosing latency problems.
- Jaeger[14]: This tool, originally created by Uber and now maintained by the CNCF, is an open-source platform for distributed tracing. It helps monitor and troubleshoot microservices-based systems by collecting, storing, and visualizing trace data.

Each tool has its advantages and disadvantages that must be carefully evaluated before selection. The next section outlines the key distinctions between various tools for log collection, some of which do not require a paid license.

**NOTE** *Other tools not mentioned in this section are Honeycomb, AppDynamics, Dynatrace, Lightstep, Instana, and SigNoz.*

## What Is the Best Option for Each Scenario?

The decision on which option to use often depends on factors such as team experience, infrastructure costs, and the available support frameworks or programming languages for different methodologies. In this book, this consideration will be set aside; instead, the advantages and disadvantages of each option will be analyzed to make the most informed decision. Table 10.2 provides a concise overview of the various options for consolidating the traces of different applications in one location.

**TABLE 10.2** Main things to consider when choosing an option.

| Feature | New Relic | Elastic APM | Tempo |
|---|---|---|---|
| Distributed Tracing | ✔ | ✔ | ✔ |
| UI to View Traces | ✔ | ✔ | ✘ |
| Back-End Storage for Traces | ✔ | ✔ | ✔ |
| Logs-Traces Correlation | ✔ | ✔ | ✔ |
| Trace Sampling | ✔ | ✔ | ✔ |

*(Continued)*

[9]https://grafana.com
[10]https://docs.aws.amazon.com/xray/latest/devguide/aws-xray.html
[11]https://cloud.google.com/trace/docs
[12]https://learn.microsoft.com/azure/azure-monitor/app/distributed-tracing-overview
[13]https://zipkin.io
[14]https://www.jaegertracing.io

**TABLE 10.2** Continued

| Feature | New Relic | Elastic APM | Tempo |
|---|:---:|:---:|:---:|
| OTLP Support | ✔ | ✔ | ✔ |
| Back-End Storage for Traces | ✔ | ✔ | ✔ |
| Works with Loki | ✘ | ✘ | ✔ |
| Free License | ✘ | ✔ | ✔ |

There are notable differences between the three approaches. Consolidating all the arguments into a single document is beneficial, as illustrated in Figure 10.8.

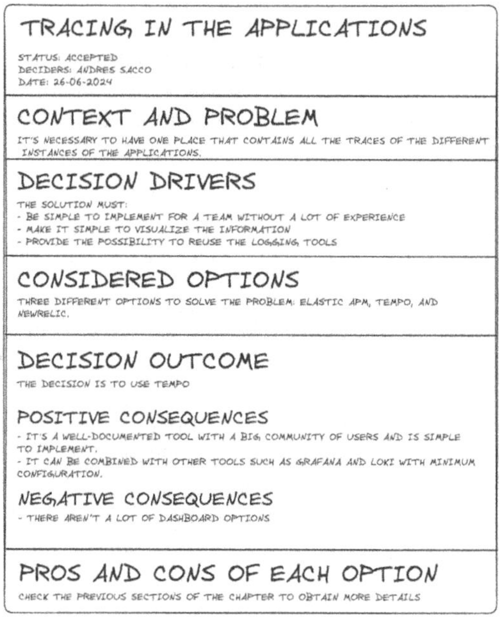

**TRACING IN THE APPLICATIONS**

STATUS: ACCEPTED
DECIDERS: ANDRES SACCO
DATE: 26-06-2024

**CONTEXT AND PROBLEM**

IT'S NECESSARY TO HAVE ONE PLACE THAT CONTAINS ALL THE TRACES OF THE DIFFERENT INSTANCES OF THE APPLICATIONS.

**DECISION DRIVERS**

THE SOLUTION MUST:
- BE SIMPLE TO IMPLEMENT FOR A TEAM WITHOUT A LOT OF EXPERIENCE
- MAKE IT SIMPLE TO VISUALIZE THE INFORMATION
- PROVIDE THE POSSIBILITY TO REUSE THE LOGGING TOOLS

**CONSIDERED OPTIONS**

THREE DIFFERENT OPTIONS TO SOLVE THE PROBLEM: ELASTIC APM, TEMPO, AND NEWRELIC.

**DECISION OUTCOME**

THE DECISION IS TO USE TEMPO

**POSITIVE CONSEQUENCES**

- IT'S A WELL-DOCUMENTED TOOL WITH A BIG COMMUNITY OF USERS AND IS SIMPLE TO IMPLEMENT.
- IT CAN BE COMBINED WITH OTHER TOOLS SUCH AS GRAFANA AND LOKI WITH MINIMUM CONFIGURATION.

**NEGATIVE CONSEQUENCES**

- THERE AREN'T A LOT OF DASHBOARD OPTIONS

**PROS AND CONS OF EACH OPTION**

CHECK THE PREVIOUS SECTIONS OF THE CHAPTER TO OBTAIN MORE DETAILS

**FIGURE 10.8** ADR about the decision of how to collect the traces.

This document helps users understand the reasons for choosing one approach over another, as well as the factors considered during the decision-making process.

### What Implications Do the Modifications Have on the Application?

After selecting Tempo to send traces, the next step is to start making modifications to the application. To do this, begin by adding the dependencies needed to collect the information. One possible way to achieve this is to delegate the responsibility to OpenTelemetry for collecting and sending the information to Tempo. A similar approach could be applied to Loki if the same method were considered for everything. Listing 10.5 shows the necessary dependencies for collecting the information; however, keep in mind that newer versions may be available, so be sure to check the Maven Repository[15].

---

[15] https://mvnrepository.com/

```
<!-- OpenTelemetry -->
<dependency>
   <groupId>io.opentelemetry</groupId>
   <artifactId>opentelemetry-exporter-otlp</artifactId>
   <version>1.33.0</version>
</dependency>

<dependency>
   <groupId>io.opentelemetry</groupId>
   <artifactId>opentelemetry-sdk-extension-autoconfigure</artifactId>
   <version>1.33.0</version>
</dependency>

<dependency>
   <groupId>io.opentelemetry.instrumentation</groupId>
   <artifactId>opentelemetry-spring-boot-starter</artifactId>
   <version>1.33.0-alpha</version>
</dependency>
```

**LISTING 10.5** Dependencies to send logs to Tempo.

The next step involves modifying the `application.yml` file to configure the location of Tempo and the protocol used to send traces. The modifications appear similar to those in Listing 10.6.

```
#Previous configuration

otel:
  sdk:
    disabled: false
  exporter:
   otlp:
      endpoint: http://localhost:4317  # Replace with Tempo URL
      protocol: grpc
      metrics:
        enabled: false
  resource:
    attributes:
      service.name: api-reservation
```

**LISTING 10.6** Modifications to application.yml.

Tempo requires some basic configuration to function properly, such as security mechanisms, the ports it uses, and where it stores information. In most cases, these are a set of default values, as shown in Listing 10.7, which represent the `tempo.yaml` file.

```
auth_enabled: false

server:
  http_listen_port: 3100

ingester:
  lifecycler:
    ring:
      kvstore:
        store: inmemory
```

```
      replication_factor: 1
  chunk_idle_period: 5m
  max_chunk_age: 1h

schema_config:
  configs:
    - from: 2022-01-01
      store: boltdb-shipper
      object_store: filesystem
      schema: v11
      index:
        prefix: index_
        period: 24h

storage_config:
  boltdb_shipper:
    active_index_directory: /tmp/loki/index
    cache_location: /tmp/loki/boltdb-cache
    shared_store: filesystem
  filesystem:
    directory: /tmp/loki/chunks

limits_config:
  enforce_metric_name: false
  reject_old_samples: true
  reject_old_samples_max_age: 168h

chunk_store_config:
  max_look_back_period: 0s

table_manager:
  retention_deletes_enabled: false
  retention_period: 0s
```

**LISTING 10.7** Default Tempo configuration.

The final step in this process of modifications is to add the Tempo image to the Docker Compose file, along with the corresponding ports to expose, as shown in Listing 10.8.

```
version: '3.1'
services:

 tempo:
    image: grafana/tempo:2.4.1
    container_name: tempo
    ports:
      - "4317:4317"  # OTLP gRPC
      - "4318:4318"  # OTLP HTTP
      - "3200:3200"  # Tempo HTTP API
    command: ["-config.file=/etc/tempo.yaml"]
    volumes:
      - ./tempo.yaml:/etc/tempo.yaml

  #Previous configuration
```

**LISTING 10.8** Add Tempo to the Docker Compose file.

After making all the modifications, it's time to run the application and the Docker Compose file, executing multiple requests to any of the available endpoints to populate Tempo before going to Grafana to configure the tool.

The configuration of the data source in Grafana resembles what was shown in the *Logging* section of this chapter. If all of the settings are correct, on navigating to the Explorer view, the Web page that appears will be similar to Figure 10.9.

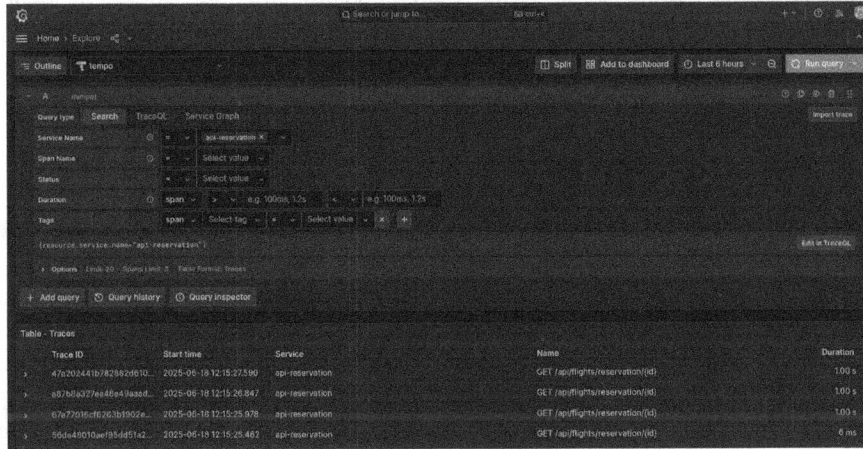

**FIGURE 10.9** Tempo traces.

Similarly, it's possible to create a dashboard with this information using the logs, but the complexity of these types of dashboards lies in determining what information is necessary to show.

## METRICS AND ALERTS

This practice involves gathering numerical indicators that show the status and performance of an application or infrastructure over time. In a microservices architecture, where numerous services operate independently and communicate continuously, having measurable data such as response times, error rates, memory consumption, or request throughput is essential for understanding system behavior in real-world conditions.

Metrics are collected regularly and reflect specific aspects of system activity, aiding teams in spotting patterns, anomalies, or deterioration over time. When a particular condition is met—for example, when a metric exceeds a set threshold—an alert is triggered to notify operators that there may be an issue. These alerts act as early warnings, allowing teams to investigate and address problems before they escalate.

Microservices introduce another significant challenge that encompasses multiple aspects to consider. Metrics and alerts help to reduce the risk of missing something because they provide:

- Visibility: Monitoring provides real-time insights into the availability, performance, and resource utilization of each microservice, enabling issues to be detected before they impact users.

- Metric Levels: Different types of metrics—such as CPU usage, memory consumption, response times, and error rates—help teams assess how services behave under different conditions.
- Alerting: Alerts can be set up based on specific thresholds or unusual metric patterns, allowing teams to respond swiftly to service issues or failures and reduce downtime.
- Correlation: Monitoring data can be linked with traces and logs to develop a complete understanding of an issue, especially when pinpointing the root cause of incidents.
- Capacity Planning: Historical metrics help forecast trends and guide decisions on scaling services or adjusting infrastructure to meet demand.

To implement effective collection metrics and create alerts to detect problems on the microservices, it is necessary to follow most of these practices:

- Monitoring Tools: Use platforms to gather metrics from services and infrastructure at regular intervals.
- Instrumentation Libraries: Integrate a library that exposes the application's information, which can be used as the monitoring tool.
- Dashboards: Create or reuse a dashboard to visualize metrics and monitor application performance.
- Alerts: Configure alerts to detect problems or anomalies using existing metrics and send a notification via a channel such as Slack, email, or PagerDuty.

Certainly, additional aspects could be included in the metrics collection process, but this list focuses on just the most important ones.

## What Ways Exist to Collect Metrics and Create Alerts?

Collecting metrics from different applications and centralizing them for analysis and alerting requires the use of specialized tools, the most relevant of which are:

- New Relic[16]: This tool provides a comprehensive observability platform that gathers metrics, traces, and logs. It offers robust alerting features via an intuitive UI, simplifying real-time monitoring and response to application and infrastructure issues.
- Elastic APM[17]: This tool, developed by Elastic, is part of the Elastic Stack and enables the collection of metrics, traces, and logs from applications, with alerting and visualization capabilities integrated directly into Kibana.
- Datadog[18]: This tool offers a cloud-native observability platform that combines metrics, logs, traces, and alerts, featuring integrated dashboards, AI-powered anomaly detection, and seamless compatibility with modern infrastructure.

---

[16]https://newrelic.com
[17]https://www.elastic.co/apm
[18]https://www.datadoghq.com

- Grafana Cloud/Grafana OSS[19]: This tool, created by Grafana Labs, allows users to collect and visualize metrics from sources such as Prometheus and Graphite. It offers robust dashboarding and flexible alerting features, available in both its open-source and cloud versions.
- Dynatrace[20]: This enterprise-level tool offers automatic instrumentation and real-time monitoring of applications, infrastructure, and user experience. It includes intelligent alerting powered by its AI engine to assist teams in quickly identifying and solving performance problems.

Each tool has its pros and cons that must be considered before making a decision on which one to use. The following section explains the most relevant differences between some tools for collecting logs, some of which do not require a paid license.

**NOTE**    *Other tools not mentioned in this section are Zabbix, Nagios, InfluxDB, AppDynamics, and Sensu.*

## What Is the Best Option for Each Scenario?

Making a decision on which tool to use typically depends on factors such as the team's expertise, the ability to integrate tools with the current stack, the available support frameworks, and the cost implications of using paid versus free licenses for different methods. Table 10.3 provides a concise overview of the various options for externalizing configuration, highlighting their suitability for different scenarios.

**TABLE 10.3** Main things to consider when choosing an option.

| Feature | New Relic | Elastic APM | Prometheus |
|---|:---:|:---:|:---:|
| Collects Metrics | ✔ | ✔ | ✔ |
| Integration with OpenTelemetry | ✔ | ✔ | ✔ |
| Custom Metrics | ✔ | ✔ | ✔ |
| Scraping Model | ✘ | ✘ | ✔ |
| Spring Boot Micrometer Support | ✘ | ✘ | ✔ |
| Correlation with Logs (Loki) | ✘ | ✘ | ✔ |
| Correlation with Traces (Tempo) | ✘ | ✘ | ✔ |
| Free License | ✘ | ✔ | ✔ |

There are significant differences between the three approaches. Synthesizing all the arguments into one document is a good idea, as shown in Figure 10.10.

---

[19]https://grafana.com
[20]https://www.dynatrace.com

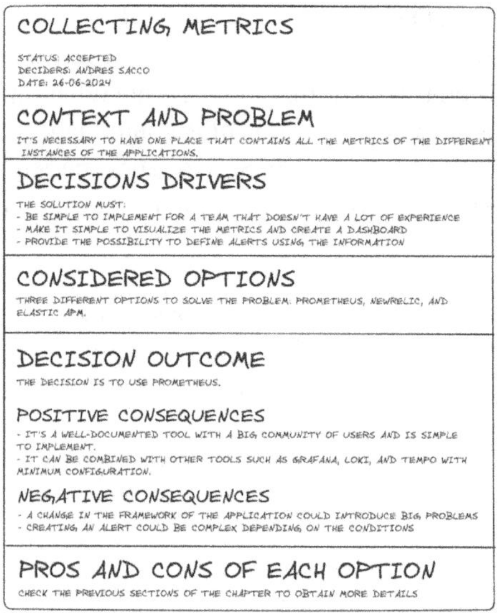

**FIGURE 10.10** ADR about the decision of how to collect the metrics.

This document provides an understanding of the rationale behind the selection of one approach over another, while also providing insight into the factors considered during the decision-making process.

## What Implications Do the Modifications Have on the Application?

Using Prometheus is straightforward if the application utilizes other tools that integrate with Grafana, such as Loki or Tempo. The first step is to introduce a new dependency in the application, as shown in Listing 10.9, to expose the metrics in a format that Prometheus can use.

```
<dependency>
    <groupId>io.micrometer</groupId>
    <artifactId>micrometer-registry-prometheus</artifactId>
</dependency>
```

**LISTING 10.9** Dependencies to send collected metrics to Prometheus.

After adding the dependency, it's time to modify the configuration to enable the Prometheus endpoint in the `management` section, as shown in Listing 10.10.

```
management:
  #Previous configuration
  endpoint:
    health:
      show-details: always
      probes:
        enabled: false
    prometheus:
      enabled: true
```

**LISTING 10.10** Modifications to application.yml.

To check whether the modifications to the application are working, simply run the application and make a request to the Prometheus endpoint, as shown in Listing 10.11.

```
$ curl http://localhost:8090/api/flights/reservation/management/
prometheus

# HELP application_ready_time_seconds Time taken for the application to
be ready to service requests
# TYPE application_ready_time_seconds gauge
application_ready_time_seconds{main_application_class="com.twa.flights.
api.reservation.ApiReservationApplication"} 13.708
# HELP application_started_time_seconds Time taken to start the
application
# TYPE application_started_time_seconds gauge
application_started_time_seconds{main_application_class="com.twa.flights.
api.reservation.ApiReservationApplication"} 13.706
# HELP cache_eviction_weight_total The sum of weights of evicted
entries. This total does not include manual invalidations.
# TYPE cache_eviction_weight_total counter
cache_eviction_weight_total{cache="CATALOG_COUNTRY",cache_manager="cache
Manager",name="CATALOG_COUNTRY"} 0.0
# HELP cache_evictions_total The number of times the cache was evicted.
..............
```

**LISTING 10.11** Command to check whether the endpoint is working.

The next step involves configuring Prometheus to make frequent requests to the endpoint shown in Listing 10.11 to obtain the information. To accomplish this, it is essential to create a file named `prometheus.yaml` that includes the details specified in Listing 10.12, wherein the application name, port, and metrics URL are to be provided.

```
global:
  scrape_interval: 15s

scrape_configs:
  - job_name: 'spring-boot-app'
    metrics_path: '/api/flights/reservation/management/prometheus'
    static_configs:
      - targets: ['api-reservation:8090'] # Or 'springboot:8080' if
containerized
```

**LISTING 10.12** Prometheus configuration file.

One more modification is necessary to do this; it requires adding the Prometheus image to the Docker Compose file, indicating the port to expose and which file contains the configuration, as shown in Listing 10.13.

```
version: '3.1'
services:
```

```
prometheus:
  image: prom/prometheus:v2.51.2
  ports:
    - "9090:9090"
  volumes:
    - ./prometheus.yaml:/etc/prometheus/prometheus.yml

#Previous configuration
```

**LISTING 10.13** Modifications to the Docker Compose file.

With these changes, Prometheus will not work because it is running inside a container and does not have access to the microservice. Therefore, the only option to collect the metrics is to build a Docker image of the application, as described in *Chapter 9*, making modifications to the application.yml connected to Docker.

Remember to change all the URLs, including logback-spring.xml, to match the name of the service in the Docker Compose file to prevent any problems.

After making the modifications and running the Docker Compose file, go to Grafana and add a new data source by finding Prometheus and entering the URL *http://prometheus:9090*. Then, click on Save and Test, and afterward on the link Explorer view, which will show something similar to Figure 10.11.

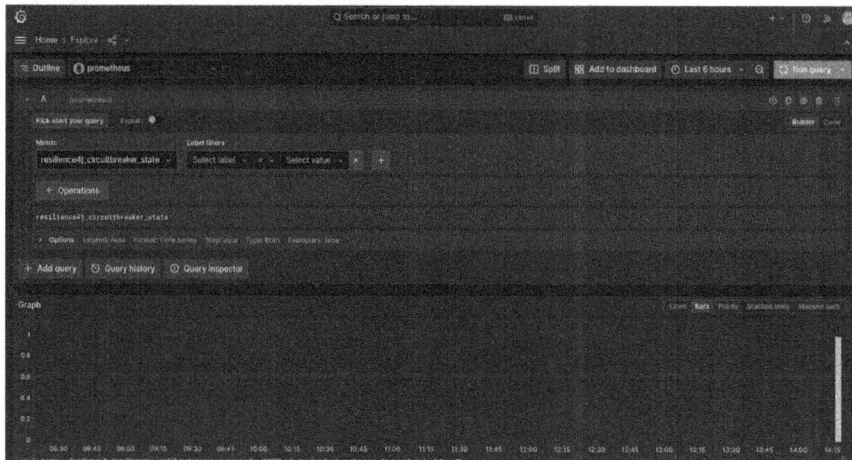

**FIGURE 10.11** Prometheus metrics.

There are some predefined dashboards on the official Grafana Web page; one of the most popular is JVM (Micrometer)[21], which provides a lot of details about the application's status. To use it, simply click on the option to create a new dashboard, then go to the Import section and enter the ID of the template that appears on the Grafana Web page. If everything is okay, a dashboard similar to Figure 10.12 will appear.

---

[21]https://grafana.com/grafana/dashboards/4701-jvm-micrometer/

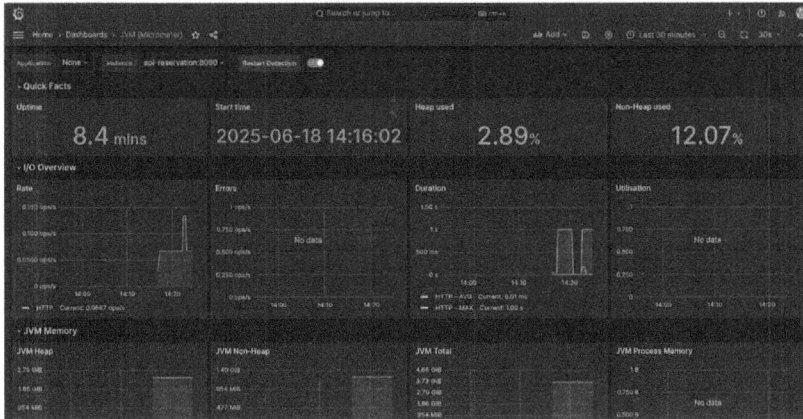

*FIGURE 10.12* JVMmetrics.

An alternative approach is to push all data to an OTEL connector, which is responsible for collecting all information and forwarding it to the corresponding tools. This approach reduces the number of different URLs to configure because all tools only know the connector, and the connector knows the URLs of the various tools.

Last but not least, with the metrics on Grafana, it's possible to create alerts using information from various tools. The creation process is simple: go to the Alerting option on the sidebar menu and click on Alert rules. On that Web page, click on New alert rule, which displays something similar to Figure 10.13.

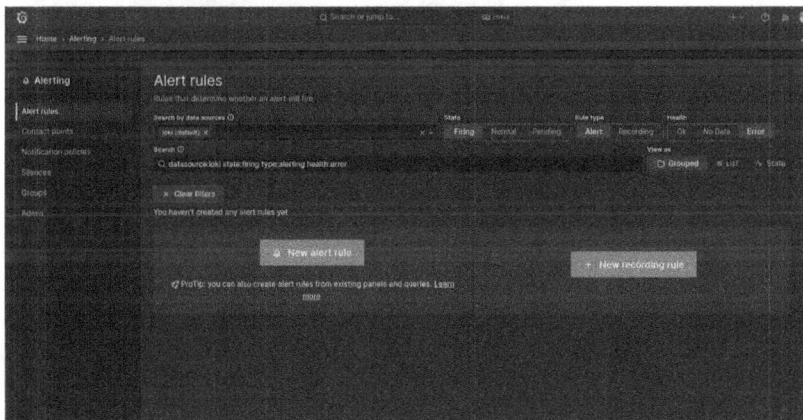

*FIGURE 10.13* Existing alerts.

After that, it's required define all the information related with the alert rule like appears on Figure 10.14 , where it's necessary to indicate the name of the rule and what data source is used, in this case, Prometheus, and select a metric, such as `resillence4j_circuitbreaker_ failure_rate`. You should also set a name for the circuit breaker.

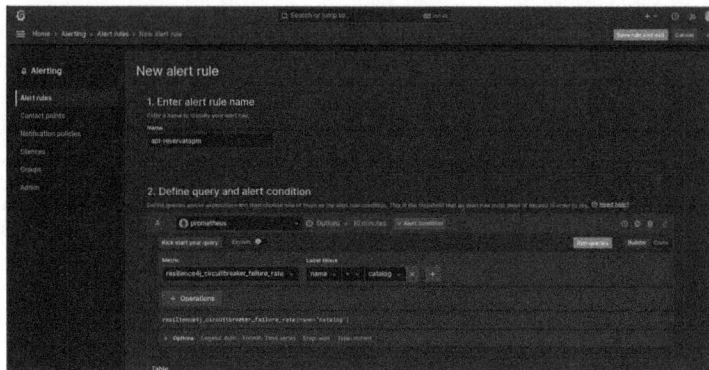

**FIGURE 10.14** Creating a new alert.

After creating the alerts, the best way to check them is to make multiple requests to the microservice to simulate how the circuit breaker behaves. If everything is okay, a Web page like in Figure 10.15 will appear, indicating that an alert was activated.

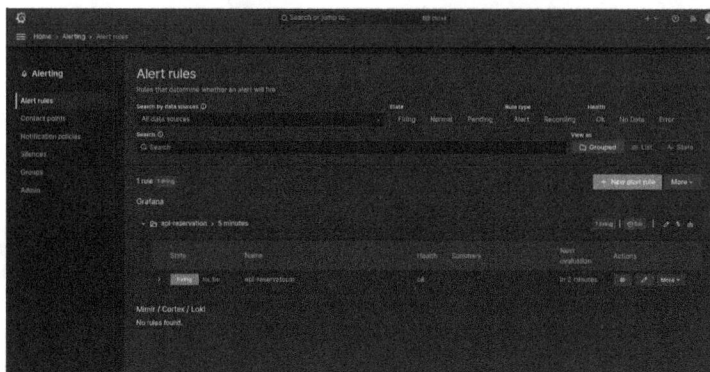

**FIGURE 10.15** Alert status.

This stack of technologies simplifies the process of creating alerts using the available information. Of course, the alert creation is simple, but it's possible to combine multiple fields to create something more robust.

## SUMMARY

This chapter presents various mechanisms for collecting information about the application, designed to enhance capabilities for determining whether everything is functioning correctly. If an issue arises, it should provide the means to identify where the problem might exist.

Initially, when creating a platform, not all features presented in this chapter may be necessary; however, they may become essential as the applications receive organic requests in production.

Consider using a stack of tools that address all problems, as this simplifies the creation of dashboards that incorporate various data sources and makes maintenance easier for the infrastructure team.

# CHAPTER 11

# SECURING THE INFORMATION

S ecurity is a critical aspect of any system because no one wants to be the victim of an attack that steals information or affects part of the system, creating a bad experience for users. Companies sometimes have an entire team dedicated to checking everything, while in others, there is just one person. Regardless of the scenario, the first ones who need to consider security are the development team. For this reason, this chapter presents various options for enhancing the security of an application.

Note that this chapter cannot cover all existing security mechanisms; however, the most well-known ones are presented.

## WHAT DOES SECURING THE INFORMATION MEAN?

An application, in some cases, manages sensitive information about clients, users, and invoices that is critical to the company's operations and to the individuals who rely on the application to share certain information. Therefore, it is essential to reduce the possibility of unauthorized access to that information.

Indeed, there are some security issues related to the libraries or frameworks that the application uses. The approach to address this is straightforward, however: Simply use one of the tools, such as Synk[1], Dependency Check[2], or Dependency Track[3], that analyze dependencies and provide information about whether any of them are vulnerable.

Another problem related to security is the Docker base image that is used to build and distribute the application. In many cases, base images expose some vulnerabilities that someone could exploit. So, some of the previously mentioned tools can be used, which offer plugins to analyze Dockerfiles, or others, such as Trivy[4], Grype[5], Docker Scout[6], or Anchore Engine[7].

---

[1]https://snyk.io/
[2]https://owasp.org/www-project-dependency-check/
[3]https://dependencytrack.org/
[4]https://trivy.dev/latest/
[5]https://github.com/anchore/grype
[6]https://docs.docker.com/scout/
[7]https://anchore.com/blog/anchore-engine/

In both cases, the tools tackle vulnerabilities in the external components of the code, such as the dependencies or the Docker image. What happens, though, with the code of the application? How is the information secured? How are actions restricted to specific endpoints?

## Which Mechanism Is Used to Secure the Information?

There are various mechanisms to secure the information; some of them require changes to the application, while the infrastructure team can implement others. Let's see a list of the most relevant approaches:

- Transport Layer Security (TLS): This requires encrypting information during transit between clients and services, using HTTPS for all communications, including those among different microservices. This approach may suggest some modifications to the host definition in `application.yml`, but the more complex aspects are delegated to the infrastructure team. Authentication and Authorization: This means having a mechanism to validate users or clients who request any application. There are several different ways to accomplish this, such as using a username and password to log in and pass a session ID, or utilizing OAuth 2 to generate a token.
- API Gateway: Utilize a layer or part of the system that restricts access to any endpoint, requiring all requests to pass through the API gateway. This layer is responsible for implementing the necessary security mechanisms.
- Other Mechanisms: Utilizing mechanisms such as CORS, CSRF, session state management, and input validation are other possible methods to reduce the risk of unauthorized access to information.

Some companies will implement one of them to reduce the risk, but often, that's not enough. In terms of security, it's required to implement most of them, considering what each one does. It is recommended not to implement all of them at once, however. Try to implement one, validate that it is working correctly, and then move on to the next one.

## What Things Are Possible to Restrict?

Restricting access or adding security is not the same for all possible components or parts of a system; some parts require an extra level of security, while others don't. Let's look at examples of different things that can be restricted. Table 11.1 provides a short overview of all the possibilities.

**TABLE 11.1** Restrictions that are possible to apply.

| Type | Example |
|------|---------|
| Endpoints | `/reservation/**`, `/management/**` |
| HTTP methods | Only allow access to the GET method on the application. |
| Roles/scopes | Add roles to execute specific operations, such as USER to create reservations, but ADMIN to update. |
| Services | It's possible to execute a request to `api-reservation` but not to `api-catalog` or another one. |
| Resources | It's possible to access only the reservations created for the same user. |

The things that can be validated need to be analyzed with the different mechanisms that exist, because not all of them allow for granular application.

## SECURING THE APPLICATIONS

After understanding the different reasons to secure the information of one endpoint of the entire microservice, it is necessary to ensure absolute security. In the case of the microservices that use Spring Boot as a framework, there are two different options:

- Create from Scratch: This approach involves using the filters that Spring Boot offers to capture requests and validate the credentials of the access control mechanism that the company decides to use. The primary issue with this approach is that it requires considerable effort, not only in coding and implementing the mechanism but also in testing to ensure everything functions correctly.
- Use a Library: To reduce the complexity of creating everything from scratch, some libraries address most security-related problems by offering the possibility to configure which aspects the application will check simply. Some libraries are popular for use in microservices, such as Spring Security[8], Apache Shiro[9], and pac4j[10].

Each approach has its pros and cons that must be considered before selecting one. The following section explains the most relevant differences between the options that involve using a library, as it does not require extensive knowledge about security or how to implement various security mechanisms.

---

**NOTE** *Other tools that can be used that are not mentioned in this section are JEE Security, Auth0 Java SDK, and Vert.x Auth.*

---

### What Is the Best Option for Each Scenario?

Implementing security across the entire platform involves considering several aspects, such as supporting multiple methods to verify that the user or application making a request does not have malicious intentions. Another essential aspect to consider is the level of documentation and the quality of the developer community. Table 11.2 provides a brief overview of the various aspects of the most relevant tools related to application security.

*TABLE 11.2* Key factors to consider when choosing an option to explore the applications.

| Feature | Spring Security | Apache Shiro | pac4j |
|---|---|---|---|
| Active maintenance and community | ✔ | ⚠ | ✔ |
| Built-in support for OAuth 2/OIDC/JWT | ✔ | ✘ | ✔ |
| Built-in support for SAML/CAS | ✘ | ✔ | ✔ |

*(Continued)*

---

[8]https://spring.io/projects/spring-security
[9]https://shiro.apache.org/
[10]https://www.pac4j.org/

*TABLE 11.2* Continued

| Feature | Spring Security | Apache Shiro | pac4j |
|---|:---:|:---:|:---:|
| Password-based auth (form, HTTP Basic) | ✔ | ✔ | ✔ |
| Role-based authorization | ✔ | ✔ | ✔ |
| Supports reactive apps | ✔ | ✘ | ✘ |
| Supports annotation-based security | ✔ | ✔ | ✔ |
| Stateless (token-based) support | ✔ | ✔ | ✔ |
| Extensible/custom filters | ✔ | ✔ | ✔ |
| Good documentation and examples | ✘ | ✔ | ✘ |

There are notable differences between the approaches; so, consolidating all the arguments into a single document is beneficial, as illustrated in Figure 11.1.

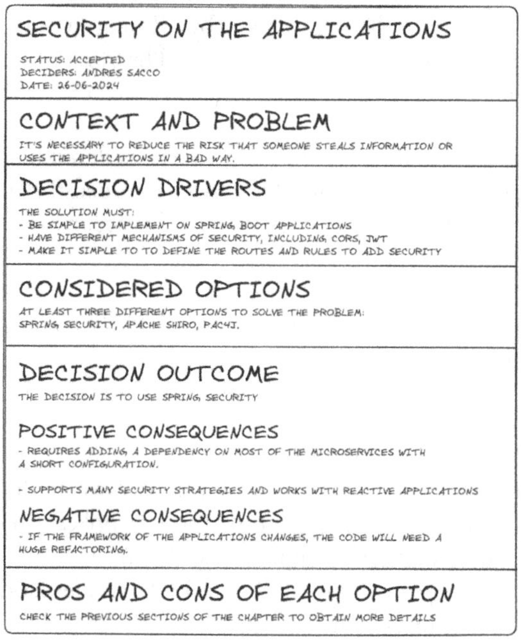

SECURITY ON THE APPLICATIONS

STATUS: ACCEPTED
DECIDERS: ANDRES SACCO
DATE: 26-06-2024

CONTEXT AND PROBLEM

IT'S NECESSARY TO REDUCE THE RISK THAT SOMEONE STEALS INFORMATION OR USES THE APPLICATIONS IN A BAD WAY.

DECISION DRIVERS

THE SOLUTION MUST:
- BE SIMPLE TO IMPLEMENT ON SPRING BOOT APPLICATIONS
- HAVE DIFFERENT MECHANISMS OF SECURITY, INCLUDING CORS, JWT
- MAKE IT SIMPLE TO TO DEFINE THE ROUTES AND RULES TO ADD SECURITY

CONSIDERED OPTIONS

AT LEAST THREE DIFFERENT OPTIONS TO SOLVE THE PROBLEM: SPRING SECURITY, APACHE SHIRO, PAC4J.

DECISION OUTCOME

THE DECISION IS TO USE SPRING SECURITY

POSITIVE CONSEQUENCES

- REQUIRES ADDING A DEPENDENCY ON MOST OF THE MICROSERVICES WITH A SHORT CONFIGURATION.
- SUPPORTS MANY SECURITY STRATEGIES AND WORKS WITH REACTIVE APPLICATIONS

NEGATIVE CONSEQUENCES

- IF THE FRAMEWORK OF THE APPLICATIONS CHANGES, THE CODE WILL NEED A HUGE REFACTORING.

PROS AND CONS OF EACH OPTION

CHECK THE PREVIOUS SECTIONS OF THE CHAPTER TO OBTAIN MORE DETAILS

*FIGURE 11.1* ADR about the decision of how to include security in the microservices.

The purpose of the document and the table is to provide reasons for why one approach was selected over another and which factors were considered in deciding on which tool to use to reduce the security risk in a system. Companies must create this type of documentation when such decisions are made that affect many teams or parts of the company.

## How Can This Library Be Integrated into the System?

The integration of Spring Security into an application that uses Spring Boot is relatively simple, requiring only a single dependency. Still, before starting with the code, it's necessary to understand how this library works behind the scenes.

When someone executes a request to any endpoint of the application, some filters are applied; most of them are not related to security and perform different functions. The idea behind these filters is to create a chain where one filter performs an action and passes control to the next one. Each filter can either continue the execution flow or produce an error and halt the execution. Figure 11.2 shows a representation of the filter execution process on a request.

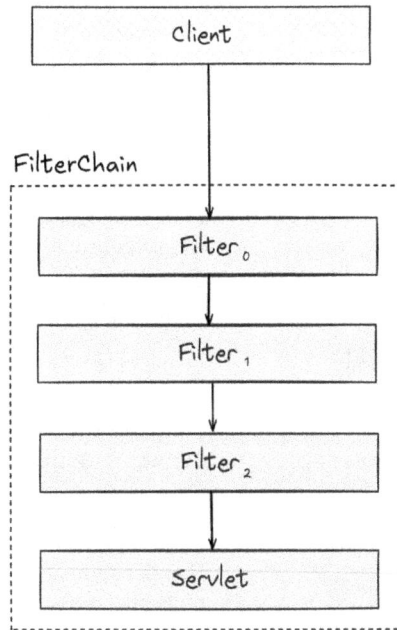

**FIGURE 11.2** The filters that are applied when the application receives a request.

In the case of Spring, one of these filters is called `DelegatingProxyFilter`, which permits interaction with the `ApplicationContext`. With this, it's possible to create a series of filters that work with the `DelegatingProxyFilter` related to security, as shown in Figure 11.3.

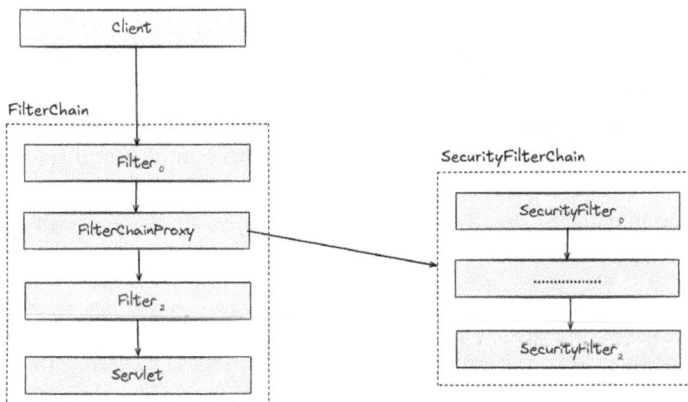

**FIGURE 11.3** The security filters that are executed during a request.

The security filters have various proposals, including authentication and authorization, and exploit vulnerabilities such as CORS and CSRF. Additionally, it's possible to create custom filters to validate specific elements and target the manager of the security filters. Some of the most relevant filters are shown in Table 11.3.

**TABLE 11.3** Security filters that can be used.

| Filter | Description |
| --- | --- |
| `CsrfFilter` | Handles CSRF token generation and validation for state-changing HTTP requests |
| `BasicAuthenticationFilter` | Intercepts HTTP to obtain the authentication information from the headers |
| `UsernamePasswordAuthenticationFilter` | Processes login form submissions for the username and password |
| `BearerTokenAuthenticationFilter` | Extracts and verifies JWT bearer tokens from the Authorization header |
| `OAuth2LoginAuthenticationFilter` | Manages OAuth 2 login via external providers (e.g., Google or GitHub) |
| `SecurityContextHolderFilter` | Loads and stores `SecurityContext` in the `SecurityContextHolder` |
| `LogoutFilter` | Manages logout requests, including session invalidation and redirect |
| `ExceptionTranslationFilter` | Handles authentication/authorization exceptions and redirects/errors |
| `AnonymousAuthenticationFilter` | Provides an anonymous Authentication object for unauthenticated users |
| `SessionManagementFilter` | Manages session creation policies, concurrency control, and session strategies |

In the following sections, most of these filters are used in examples as security mechanisms.

## Basic Security

The most basic mechanism of security involves the use of a username and password, which are stored in a database or another secure location. This mechanism introduces several challenges, such as determining where to store the information and whether all microservices need to perform the validations. For now, let's just implement it and see what other options exist.

The first step in using Spring Security involves adding a library that works with Spring Boot, as shown in Listing 11.1.

```
<dependency>
    <groupId>org.springframework.boot</groupId>
    <artifactId>spring-boot-starter-security</artifactId>
</dependency>
```

**LISTING 11.1** Dependencies that need to be added to use Spring Security.

After adding the dependency, it's time to implement the behavior for cases where an unauthorized person attempts to access the application or an endpoint. To do this, Spring Security introduces several changes that involve creating a custom class extending `BasicAuthenticationEntryPoint`, within which it's necessary to define the status and message the application will return, as shown in Listing 12.2.

```
package com.twa.flights.api.reservation.security;

import jakarta.servlet.ServletException;
import jakarta.servlet.http.HttpServletRequest;
import jakarta.servlet.http.HttpServletResponse;
import org.springframework.security.core.AuthenticationException;
import org.springframework.security.web.authentication.www.
BasicAuthenticationEntryPoint;

import java.io.IOException;
import java.io.PrintWriter;

public class CustomAuthenticationEntryPoint extends
BasicAuthenticationEntryPoint {

    @Override
    public void commence(
            HttpServletRequest request, HttpServletResponse response,
AuthenticationException authEx)
            throws IOException {
        response.addHeader("WWW-Authenticate", "Basic realm=" +
getRealmName());
        response.setStatus(HttpServletResponse.SC_UNAUTHORIZED);
        PrintWriter writer = response.getWriter();
        writer.println("HTTP Status 401 - " + authEx.getMessage());
    }

    @Override
    public void afterPropertiesSet() {
        setRealmName("twa");
        super.afterPropertiesSet();
    }
}
```

*LISTING 11.2* Custom authentication to provide behavior to unauthorized users.

The code in Listing 11.2 suggests adding a header to request the credentials and include the status, but it's possible to simply send the HTTP status as part of the response without any extra information. It's essential to consider creating this class due to the security configuration, as version 6.1 of Spring Security is required to avoid using some deprecated methods.

The next step is to create a class that represents the entire logic of security, including where users are located, the mechanism for encoding passwords to prevent them from being saved as plain text, and the security filters that must be applied. In this book, users will be defined in memory without requiring extensive modifications to the database.

Listing 11.3 shows the basic configuration of valid users and the class responsible for encoding the passwords.

```
package com.twa.flights.api.reservation.configuration;

import org.springframework.context.annotation.Bean;
import org.springframework.security.config.annotation.web.builders.
HttpSecurity;
import org.springframework.security.core.userdetails.User;
import org.springframework.security.core.userdetails.UserDetailsService;
import org.springframework.security.crypto.bcrypt.BCryptPasswordEncoder;
import org.springframework.security.crypto.password.PasswordEncoder;
import org.springframework.security.provisioning.
InMemoryUserDetailsManager;
import org.springframework.security.web.SecurityFilterChain;
import org.springframework.stereotype.Component;

@Component
public class SecurityConfiguration {

    // Defining users in memory, and the password encoder
    @Bean
    public UserDetailsService userDetailsService() {
        return new InMemoryUserDetailsManager(
                User.withUsername("admin")
                        .password(passwordEncoder().encode("admin123"))
                        .roles("USER")
                        .build()
        );
    }

    // The password encoder, used to encrypt the passwords in the
database
    @Bean
    public PasswordEncoder passwordEncoder() {
        return new BCryptPasswordEncoder();
    }

}
```

*LISTING 11.3* Basic configuration of the security mechanism.

The previous block of code includes `BCryptPasswordEncoder`, one of the possible encoders to use. Other options include `Pbkdf2PasswordEncoder`, `Argon2PasswordEncoder`, and `SCryptPasswordEncoder`; however, it is beyond the scope of this book to explain how each of them works and their respective pros and cons.

In the same class, it's necessary to add a method responsible for filtering requests and performing security validations. This method will validate that all requests require a username and password, as well as what occurs if the credentials are incorrect. Listing 11.4 shows the method with the validations.

```
    // Basic security configuration, to allow only authenticated users to
access the endpoints
    @Bean
    public SecurityFilterChain filterChain(HttpSecurity http) throws
Exception {
        http.authorizeHttpRequests(auth -> auth
                        .anyRequest().authenticated()
```

```
                ).httpBasic(httpSecurityHttpBasicConfigurer ->
httpSecurityHttpBasicConfigurer.authenticationEntryPoint(new
CustomAuthenticationEntryPoint()));


        return http.build();
    }
```

**LISTING 11.4** Basic security validations.

With all the changes in place, the next step is to run the application and check whether the endpoints are secure. To do this, let's request the `info` endpoint without any credentials, as shown in Listing 11.5.

```
→  ~ curl -i http://localhost:8090/api/flights/reservation/management/info

HTTP/1.1 401
Set-Cookie:  JSESSIONID=BAAD4729468B8B8814EDDF9C8545DC6E;  Path=/api/
flights/reservation; HttpOnly
WWW-Authenticate: Basic realm="Realm"
X-Content-Type-Options: nosniff
X-XSS-Protection: 0
Cache-Control: no-cache, no-store, max-age=0, must-revalidate
Pragma: no-cache
Expires: 0
X-Frame-Options: DENY
Content-Length: 0
Date: Fri, 30 May 2025 18:40:08 GMT


HTTP Status 401 - Full authentication is required to access this resource
```

**LISTING 11.5** Command to check whether the security mechanism is working.

Now the microservice is secure, and it's impossible to access any endpoint without the credentials. Just to be sure, however, let's request the same endpoint by providing the credentials, as shown in Listing 11.6.

```
→  ~ curl -i --user admin:admin123
http://localhost:8090/api/flights/reservation/management/info

HTTP/1.1 200
X-Content-Type-Options: nosniff
X-XSS-Protection: 0
Cache-Control: no-cache, no-store, max-age=0, must-revalidate
Pragma: no-cache
Expires: 0
X-Frame-Options: DENY
Content-Type: application/vnd.spring-boot.actuator.v3+json
```

```
Transfer-Encoding: chunked
Date: Fri, 30 May 2025 18:41:29 GMT
...
```

**LISTING 11.6** Command to access the info endpoint, passing the username/password.

This approach is one of the most basic, but it's possible to add additional mechanisms, such as CORS and CSRF. These additional filters are likely to use not just the basic username/password mechanism but also other cross-security mechanisms, so let's see each of them before looking into more complex mechanisms.

### Restricting Access from Some Origins (CORS)

Cross-origin resource sharing (CORS) is a security feature that ensures Web browsers control requests made by Web applications and other applications to a specific origin. This origin may or may not be the same, but all parties agree on which origins are considered secure and which are not. By default, the browser blocks cross-origin HTTP requests unless the application explicitly allows them.

There is a series of headers associated with this security feature that are necessary to consider; some of them appear in Table 11.4.

**TABLE 11.4** Common headers associated with CORS.

| Header | Description |
|---|---|
| Access-Control-Allow-Origin | Indicates which locations or URLs are allowed to send requests |
| Access-Control-Allow-Methods | Indicates which methods connected with the locations are allowed, such as GET, POST, or PUT |
| Access-Control-Allow-Headers | Indicates which headers are possible to send in a request |
| Access-Control-Allow-Credentials | Indicates whether some credentials need to be sent to it |
| Access-Control-Max-Age | Indicates the duration of the CORS on the cache |

Let's start with the modifications to the applications to enable this feature and allow access from an alternative location. To make this configurable for the environment and allow for quick changes, let's create the configuration in the `application.yml` as shown in Listing 11.7.

```
cors:
  allowed-origins:
    - http://localhost:3000
  allowed-methods:
    - GET
    - POST
    - PUT
    - DELETE
    - OPTIONS
  allowed-headers:
    - Authorization
    - Cache-Control
    - Content-Type
  allow-credentials: true
```

**LISTING 11.7** Configuration properties to define which things are allowed.

In the previous configuration, it's possible to define a list of origins rather than just one, or to reduce the number of supported HTTP methods.

The next step involves creating a class responsible for loading the configuration from the `application.yml` and exposing the information to be used in the Spring Boot context. Listing 11.8 represents a possible implementation of that class.

```
package com.twa.flights.api.reservation.configuration.settings;

import org.springframework.boot.context.properties.
ConfigurationProperties;
import org.springframework.stereotype.Component;

import java.util.List;

@Component
@ConfigurationProperties(prefix = "cors")
public class CorsSettings {

    private List<String> allowedOrigins;
    private List<String> allowedMethods;
    private List<String> allowedHeaders;
    private boolean allowCredentials;

   // Getters and setters

}
```

**LISTING 11.8** Definition of the class that represents the properties.

With the configuration loaded in one class, the next step is to define a `CorsConfigurationSource` using the information outlined in the previous steps. This class is the way to set the CORS configuration that is necessary to attach to the security configuration mechanism in Spring Security. Listing 11.9 shows a basic configuration of that class exposed as a bean.

```
package com.twa.flights.api.reservation.configuration;

import com.twa.flights.api.reservation.configuration.settings.CorsSettings;
import org.springframework.context.annotation.Bean;
import org.springframework.context.annotation.Configuration;
import org.springframework.web.cors.CorsConfiguration;
import org.springframework.web.cors.CorsConfigurationSource;
import org.springframework.web.cors.UrlBasedCorsConfigurationSource;

@Configuration
public class CORSConfiguration{

    private final CorsSettings settings;

    public CORSConfiguration(CorsSettings settings) {
        this.settings = settings;
    }

    @Bean
    public CorsConfigurationSource corsConfigurationSource() {
        CorsConfiguration config = new CorsConfiguration();
```

```
        config.setAllowedOrigins(settings.getAllowedOrigins());
        config.setAllowedMethods(settings.getAllowedMethods());
        config.setAllowedHeaders(settings.getAllowedHeaders());
        config.setAllowCredentials(settings.isAllowCredentials());

        UrlBasedCorsConfigurationSource source = new
UrlBasedCorsConfigurationSource();
        source.registerCorsConfiguration("/**", config);
        return source;
    }
}
```

LISTING 11.9 Configuration of the CORS.

The approach from the previous steps is just one option to consider, but it's possible to define everything in one class with hardcoded values. Although not recommended, it remains a viable option.

The final step is to attach the CORS configuration to the `SecurityFilterChain`. To do this, it is necessary to make modifications to inject it as a bean in the class and add the CORS configuration in the `filterChain` method, as shown in Listing 11.10.

```
package com.twa.flights.api.reservation.configuration;

// Imports

@Component
public class SecurityConfiguration {

    CorsConfigurationSource corsConfigurationSource;

    public SecurityConfiguration(CorsConfigurationSource
corsConfigurationSource) {
        this.corsConfigurationSource = corsConfigurationSource;
    }

    // Previous code

    @Bean
    public SecurityFilterChain filterChain(HttpSecurity http) throws
Exception {
        http.cors(httpSecurityCorsConfigurer ->
httpSecurityCorsConfigurer.configurationSource(corsConfigurationSource))
                .authorizeHttpRequests(auth -> auth
                    .anyRequest().authenticated()
                ).httpBasic(httpSecurityHttpBasicConfigurer ->
httpSecurityHttpBasicConfigurer.authenticationEntryPoint(new
CustomAuthenticationEntryPoint()));

        return http.build();
    }

    // Previous code
}
```

LISTING 11.10 Modifications to the security mechanism.

With the latest modifications, if run, some front-end applications that try to access *http://localhost:3000* will be accepted by Spring Security. An alternative approach is to use the annotation `@CrossOrigin(origins = "http://localhost:3000")` on each controller or method, but it's not recommended if the application has multiple controllers and each of them needs CORS enabled.

### Restricting Unwanted Requests (CSRF)

Cross-site request forgery (CSRF) is a type of vulnerability where the attacker uses the victim's browser to send unwanted requests to different Web sites where the user is authenticated. In most cases, this type of problem could not appear where the application receives the credentials in the header or uses a bearer token or an API key. Table 11.5 shows a brief overview of the situations where CSRF does not affect an API.

**TABLE 11.5** Risk associated with different methods.

| Method | Auth Method | CSRF Risk |
|---|---|---|
| JWT | Manually set in the header | ✗ |
| HTTP basic auth | Manually set in the header | ✗ |
| OAuth 2 access token | Bearer token in the header | ✗ |
| API keys in the header | Header or query param | ✗ |
| User logs in to an app with cookies | Cookie-based session | ✓ |

In the case of the microservices in this book, the credentials are currently sent as part of the header and do not return any session-related attributes, so CSRF can be disabled. To do this, modify the `filterChain` method, as shown in Listing 11.11.

```
@Bean
public SecurityFilterChain filterChain(HttpSecurity http) throws
Exception {
    http.cors(httpSecurityCorsConfigurer -> httpSecurityCorsConfigurer.conf
igurationSource(corsConfigurationSource))
        .csrf(AbstractHttpConfigurer::disable)
        .authorizeHttpRequests(auth -> auth
            .anyRequest().authenticated()
        ).httpBasic(httpSecurityHttpBasicConfigurer ->
httpSecurityHttpBasicConfigurer.authenticationEntryPoint(new
CustomAuthenticationEntryPoint())));

    return http.build();

}
```

**LISTING 11.11** Modifications to disable CSRF.

Disabling this mechanism introduces some risk; check first to ensure the situation is similar to the state of the microservices shown in the preceding listing.

### Stateless Session Management

A common situation that arises in other types of applications involves sending a cookie or other information to recognize that the user is logged in, with the understanding that the application utilizes that information to check a database or another mechanism where the session information is stored. In the case of the API, this mechanism is not helpful because each request must send all the information as if it were the first time someone is doing it.

Since the session is not significant in an API, it may be a good idea to disable it explicitly in Spring Security. To do this, as usual, it is necessary to modify the `filterChain` by adding the configuration to indicate that the application's session is stateless, which means that there is no `sessionID` to be stored.

```
@Bean
public SecurityFilterChain filterChain(HttpSecurity http) throws Exception {
    http.cors(httpSecurityCorsConfigurer -> httpSecurityCorsConfigurer.configur
ationSource(corsConfigurationSource))
            .csrf(AbstractHttpConfigurer::disable)
            .sessionManagement(session -> session
                    .sessionCreationPolicy(SessionCreationPolicy.STATELESS)
            )
            .authorizeHttpRequests(auth -> auth
                    .anyRequest().authenticated()
            ).httpBasic(httpSecurityHttpBasicConfigurer ->
httpSecurityHttpBasicConfigurer.authenticationEntryPoint(new
CustomAuthenticationEntryPoint()));

    return http.build();
}
```

**LISTING 11.12** Defining the session creation policy.

Disabling this mechanism is not crucial because, by default, most features in Spring Security are disabled. As a recommendation, however, always try to disable it explicitly, just in case a future version changes the default behavior.

## Validating with JWT

The next mechanism for validating security is to use a JWT token. Rather than employing an authentication server to validate the JWT token, however, let's adopt the most insecure approach, where the application only checks for the existence of a token that adheres to a specific format without knowing who the creator is, but at least with some kind of private key to generate the token. It's possible to use a similar method, but instead of a token, an API key is sent.

NOTE    *Consider using this approach to remove most of the previous logic related to the secure aspect, except for the CORS configuration, which will be used across all approaches.*

Let's start adding some dependencies to the POM file to manipulate a JWT token, as shown in Listing 11.13.

```
<dependency>
   <groupId>io.jsonwebtoken</groupId>
   <artifactId>jjwt-api</artifactId>
   <version>0.11.5</version>
</dependency>

<dependency>
   <groupId>io.jsonwebtoken</groupId>
   <artifactId>jjwt-impl</artifactId>
   <version>0.11.5</version>
   <scope>runtime</scope>
</dependency>

<dependency>
   <groupId>io.jsonwebtoken</groupId>
   <artifactId>jjwt-jackson</artifactId>
   <version>0.11.5</version>
   <scope>runtime</scope>
</dependency>
```

*LISTING 11.13* Dependencies to support JWT.

The next step is to define a class that extends `UserDetails` to represent the logged-in user and their associated credentials. Note that this information will be populated with each request because using JWT does not require having a session ID or anything similar to reduce the number of validations. Listing 11.14 shows a possible implementation of the class that represents a user.

```
package com.twa.flights.api.reservation.configuration.security;

import java.util.Collection;
import java.util.List;
import org.springframework.security.core.GrantedAuthority;
import org.springframework.security.core.authority.SimpleGrantedAuthority;
import org.springframework.security.core.userdetails.UserDetails;

public class CustomUserDetailsDTO implements UserDetails {

    private String username;
    private String password; // Typically, it wouldn't need the password if
JWT is used for authentication
    private List<SimpleGrantedAuthority> authorities;

    public CustomUserDetailsDTO(String username, String password,
List<SimpleGrantedAuthority> authorities) {
        this.username = username;
        this.authorities = authorities;
        this.password = password;
    }
    //Setters and getters
}
```

*LISTING 11.14* Class that represents the details about the user.

The next step involves creating a custom filter that is responsible for parsing the JWT token and validating whether all attributes are correct. Additionally, using the token information, populate the object defined in Listing 11.14.

```
package com.twa.flights.api.reservation.configuration.security;

//Imports

@Component
public class JwtRequestFilter extends OncePerRequestFilter {

    // The secret key shared by the generating application.
    private String secret =

"qwertyuiopasdfghjklzxcvbnm123456891012132twaprobandogeneraciondecontrase";

    @Override
    protected void doFilterInternal(
            HttpServletRequest request, HttpServletResponse response,
FilterChain filterChain)
            throws ServletException, IOException {
        final String authorizationHeader = request.getHeader("Authorization");

        String jwt = null;
        if (authorizationHeader != null && authorizationHeader.
startsWith("Bearer ")) {
            jwt = authorizationHeader.substring(7);
        }

        if (jwt != null && SecurityContextHolder.getContext().
getAuthentication() == null) {
            // Logic to parse JWT
        }

        filterChain.doFilter(request, response);
    }

}
```

**LISTING 11.14** Part of the custom filter to parse the JWT token.

In the previous listing, the filter defines a secret that acts as a private key with a long value. This requirement stems from the JWT library's minimum length specification for the secret for security reasons, though there is no restriction on the content of that secret. The filter must always call the next filter to continue the chain, passing the request to a controller in the application until it is fulfilled.

The modifications in Listing 11.14 don't serve any specific purpose; they merely capture the request and check whether a header exists. Let's make some changes to the method to parse the JWT token and obtain the information as it appears in Listing 11.15.

```
    @Override
    protected void doFilterInternal(
            HttpServletRequest request, HttpServletResponse response, FilterChain
filterChain)
            throws ServletException, IOException {
        final String authorizationHeader = request.getHeader("Authorization");

        String jwt = null;
        if (authorizationHeader != null && authorizationHeader.startsWith("Bearer "))
{
            jwt = authorizationHeader.substring(7);
        }

        if (jwt != null && SecurityContextHolder.getContext().getAuthentication()
== null) {
            try {
                // Parse and validate the token
                Claims claims =
                        Jwts.parser()
                                .setSigningKey(
                                        Base64.getEncoder().
encodeToString(secret.getBytes()))
                                .parseClaimsJws(jwt)
                                .getBody();

                // If valid, continue processing
                // Extract username and roles from the token
                String username = claims.getSubject(); // Typically, the subject
is the username

                // Convert roles to GrantedAuthority
                SimpleGrantedAuthority authority =
                        new SimpleGrantedAuthority((String) claims.get("email"));
                List<SimpleGrantedAuthority> authorities = List.of(authority);

                // Create UserDetails
                UserDetails userDetails = new CustomUserDetailsDTO(username,
null, authorities);

                // Create AuthenticationToken
                UsernamePasswordAuthenticationToken authentication =
                        new UsernamePasswordAuthenticationToken(
                                userDetails, jwt, userDetails.getAuthorities());

                authentication.setDetails(
                        new WebAuthenticationDetailsSource().
buildDetails(request));

                // Set the authentication in the SecurityContext
                SecurityContextHolder.getContext().setAuthentication(authenticati
on);
            } catch (JwtException e) {
```

```
                    // Handle invalid JWT token
                    response.sendError(HttpServletResponse.SC_UNAUTHORIZED, "Invalid
JWT token");
                    return;
            }
        }

    filterChain.doFilter(request, response);
    }
```

**LISTING 11.15** Modifications on the custom filter to parse the JWT.

After creating the custom filter, it's time to make the necessary modifications to the security configuration to use it. The changes involve adding the injection of the filter in the constructor and modifying the securityFilterChain to add the filter using the method addFilterBe-fore, as shown in Listing 11.16.

```
package com.twa.flights.api.reservation.configuration;

//Imports


@Component
@EnableWebSecurity
public class SecurityConfiguration {

    private final JwtRequestFilter jwtRequestFilter;
    private final CorsConfigurationSource corsConfigurationSource;

    public SecurityConfiguration(JwtRequestFilter jwtRequestFilter,
CorsConfigurationSource corsConfigurationSource) {
        this.jwtRequestFilter = jwtRequestFilter;
        this.corsConfigurationSource = corsConfigurationSource;
    }

    @Bean
    public SecurityFilterChain securityFilterChain(HttpSecurity http) throws
Exception {
        return http
                .cors(cors -> cors.configurationSource(corsConfigurationSource))
                .csrf(AbstractHttpConfigurer::disable)
                .sessionManagement(session -> session
                        .sessionCreationPolicy(SessionCreationPolicy.STATELESS)
                )
                .authorizeHttpRequests(
                        auth ->
                                auth.requestMatchers("/documentation/**")
                                        .permitAll() // Public endpoints
                                        .requestMatchers("/swagger-ui.html")
                                        .permitAll() // Public endpoints
                                        .requestMatchers("/swagger-ui/**")
                                        .permitAll() // Public endpoints
```

```
                                    .requestMatchers("/v3/api-docs/**")
                                    .permitAll() // Public endpoints
                                    .anyRequest()
                                    .authenticated() // Protected endpoints
                    )
                    .addFilterBefore(jwtRequestFilter,
UsernamePasswordAuthenticationFilter.class)
                    .build();
    }

    @Bean
    public AuthenticationManager authenticationManager(
            AuthenticationConfiguration authenticationConfiguration) throws
Exception {
        return authenticationConfiguration.getAuthenticationManager();
    }
}
```

**LISTING 11.16** Modifications to use the custom filter.

The previous block of code includes some additional modifications, such as the `authorize-HttpRequestFilter` now excluding specific URLs, such as the documentation for the microservice. The remaining requests, however, need to be validated for the security mechanism to be effective. These changes demonstrate that it is possible to combine different strategies based on specific rules, depending on the endpoints. Another potential set of endpoints that could be valuable yet lack security are those related to the application's health or context refresh.

After all the modifications, let's start the application and execute a `curl` command on the `info` endpoint. Listing 11.17 displays the command and its execution result.

```
→  ~ curl -s -w "\nStatus: %{http_code}\n" http://localhost:8090/api/
flights/reservation/management/info

Status: 403
```

**LISTING 11.17** Command to validate that the JWT security works.

The execution response returns a 403 error, indicating a security issue. This is a positive sign, as it suggests that the mechanism is functioning properly. The `curl` command varies slightly from what is presented in this chapter, aiming to keep it simple and highlighting the relevant parts rather than the entire response.

After that, it's time to create a JWT token to check whether the logic is working correctly or continues to return an error. There are several tools that can be used to generate a Web page, such as jwtbuilder[11], so just remember to copy the secret that is defined in the filter to create the token. Listing 11.18 provides an example of what happens when the same command from Listing 11.17 is executed, but with the JWT token included.

---

[11]http://jwtbuilder.jamiekurtz.com/

```
➜   ~ curl -s -w "\nStatus: %{http_code}\n"  --location http://
localhost:8090/api/flights/reservation/management/info --header
'Authorization: Bearer eyJ0eXAiOiJKV1QiLCJhbGciOiJIUzI1NiJ9.
eyJpc3MiOiJUV0EiLCJpYXQiOjE3NDg1NDDkwNTksImV4cCI6MTgxMTYyMTA1OSwiYXVkIjo
id3d3LmV4YW1wbGUuY29tIiwic3ViIjoic2FjY28uYW5kcmVzQGdtYWlsLmNvbSIsIkdpdmV
uTmFtZSI6IkFuZHJlcyIsIlN1cm5hbWUiOiJTQUNDTyIsImVtYWlsIjoic2FjY28uYW5kcmVz
VzQGdtYWlsLmNvbSIsInJvbGUiOlsiQURNSU4iLCJVU0VSIl19.qzgCoDWrVbbRowIyGzOT
O-OM1ayKuZXlrhlLrIVdbZE'

    Status: 200

{
    "app": {
      "name": "api-reservation",
      "version": "0.0.1-SNAPSHOT"
    },
    "contact": {
      "email": "sacco.andres@gmail.com",
      "slack": "adsacco"
    },
    "reservation-stats": {
      "amount": 9
    }
}
```

**LISTING 11.18** Result of the execution of a command with a JWT token.

This mechanism is more secure than the previous one because it requires the token to adhere to specific standards and utilize a secret value for generation. There is, however, no server present to create and verify the validity of a token. Naturally, this approach could be modified to check whether a valid API key appears in the header instead of a JWT token.

### Using a Secure Server

One of the main problems introduced by the previous approach is the risk that someone could discover the secret to generating the JWT token and use it to harm the system. Therefore, it's necessary to have a mechanism that generates and validates the token at the same time. This type of approach requires the use of a secure server that has these responsibilities and many others related to security.

There are multiple options for a secure server or an authentication server; some of the most relevant are Keycloak[12], Zitadel[13], Okta[14], AWS Cognito[15], Microsoft Entra ID[16],

---

[12]https://www.keycloak.org/
[13]https://zitadel.com/
[14]https://www.okta.com/
[15]https://aws.amazon.com/cognito/
[16]https://www.microsoft.com/en-us/security/business/identity-access/microsoft-entra-id

and Google Identity Platform[17]. Keep in mind that some options require a license fee, whereas others, such as Keycloak, are open source and backed by a robust user community. For this reason, this section will focus on Keycloak, although many options function similarly.

### Configuring the Server

The first step in using this tool involves stopping the execution of the Docker Compose file and making some modifications to run Keycloak and the database as containers. The changes will be similar to Listing 11.19, but it's not necessary to use the same username and password that appear in this block of code.

```
version: '3.1'
services:

  # Previous configuration
  keycloak-db:
    container_name: keycloak-db
    image: mysql:8.0
    environment:
      MYSQL_ROOT_PASSWORD: root
      MYSQL_DATABASE: keycloak
      MYSQL_USER: keycloak
      MYSQL_PASSWORD: password

  keycloak:
    container_name: keycloak
    image: quay.io/keycloak/keycloak:21.1.1
    environment:
      KC_DB: mysql
      KC_DB_URL_HOST: keycloak-db
      KC_DB_URL_DATABASE: keycloak
      KC_DB_USERNAME: keycloak
      KC_DB_PASSWORD: password
      KEYCLOAK_ADMIN: admin
      KEYCLOAK_ADMIN_PASSWORD: Pa55w0rd
    ports:
      - 8030:8080
    depends_on:
      - keycloak-db

    command: start-dev
```

**LISTING 11.19** Add changes to the configuration to connect to Keycloak.

The next step involves rerunning the Docker Compose file and starting with the tool's configuration before making modifications to the application. If everything is okay, open a browser to *http://localhost:8030/*, and the page shown in Figure 11.4 will appear, linking to basic information about Keycloak.

---

[17]https://cloud.google.com/security/products/identity-platform

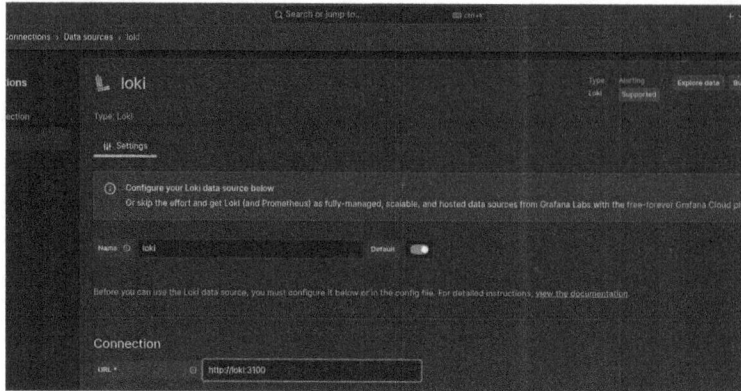

**FIGURE 11.4** Initial Web page of Keycloak.

Click on the Administration Console option and enter the username and password, as shown in Listing 11.19. If everything is okay, a Web page like the one shown in Figure 11.5 will appear, showing all features that are enabled and disabled by default.

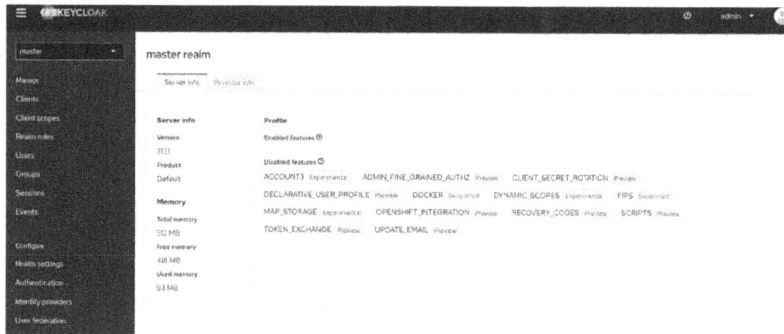

**FIGURE 11.5** Default configuration of Keycloak.

The step involves creating a new configuration that represents the system. To do this, click on the combo box in the top-left corner that contains the value master, and then click on the button Create Realm, as shown in Figure 11.6.

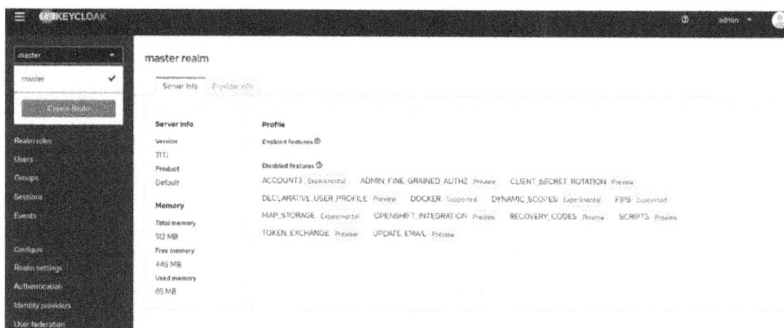

**FIGURE 11.6** New realm to manage the users, credentials, and roles.

On the following Web page, it's necessary to define a realm to manage the username, password, and many other details. While it's optional for testing, it's recommended to implement this if the tool will be used in either a production or other non-production environment. Figure 11.7 shows what the Web page for creating a new realm looks like; consider adding a descriptive name such as `twa-realm`, and ensure the toggle button is set to Enabled.

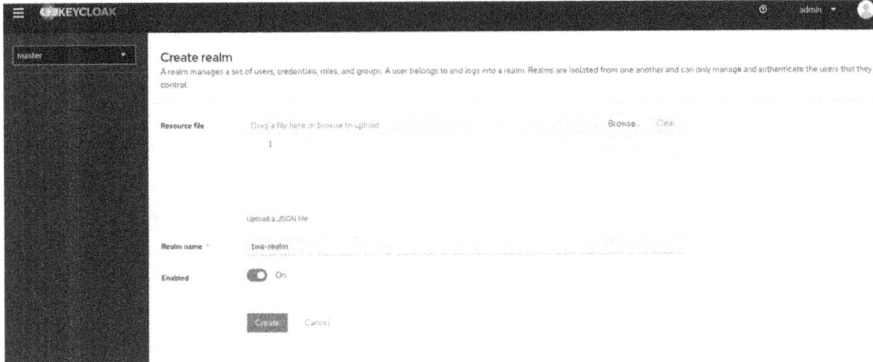

**FIGURE 11.7** Definition of a new realm.

After completing everything on the Web page, click to create the new realm. Avoid using strange characters in the name or the same name as an existing realm, as this will cause the creation to fail. If everything looks good, go to the option Realm settings that appears in the top-right corner and check whether the realm is enabled. Change the display name to something more meaningful. Figure 11.8 shows the Realm Settings Web page.

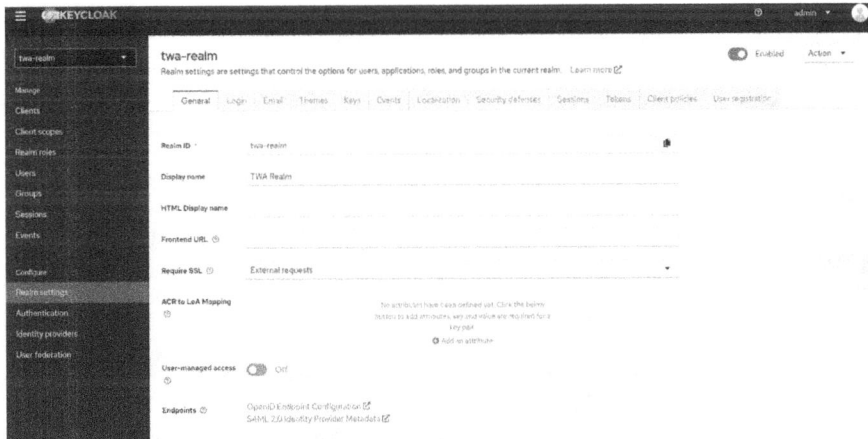

**FIGURE 11.8** Realm configuration.

The next step is to define a client that interacts with Keycloak. This client represents a service or an application that communicates with the tool to authenticate users or access protected resources. Therefore, it's essential not to use the default values and to create at least one client to represent the interaction between the application and the tool.

The option to do this appears on the left menu with the name Clients, and Figure 11.9 shows the content that will appear by default.

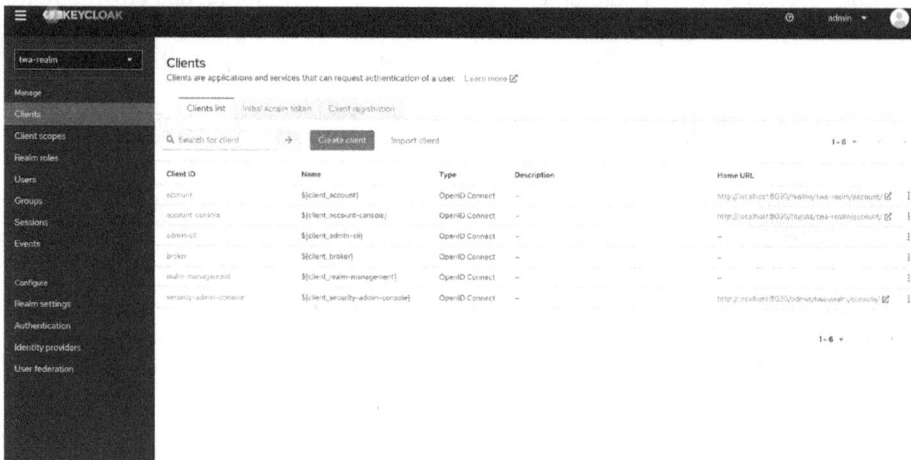

**FIGURE 11.9** List of the existing clients on the realm.

Let's create a new client with the name `twa`, which represents the communication of the `api-reservation` with Keycloak. Figure 11.10 shows the first page of the wizard to create a client.

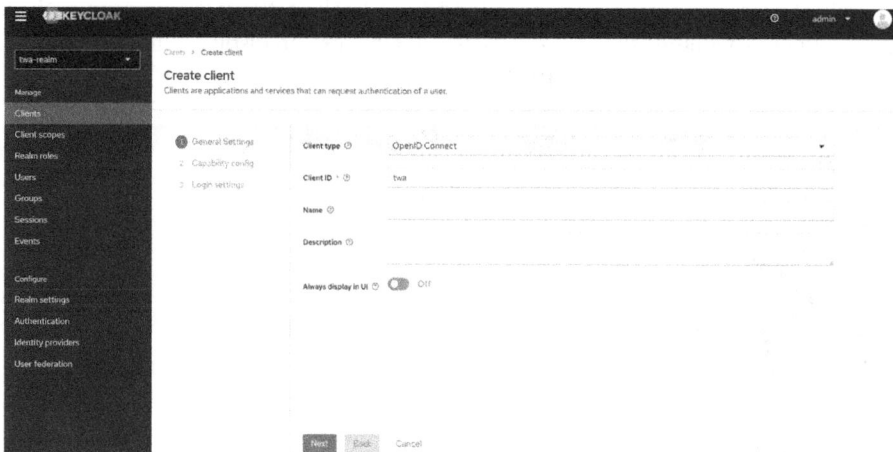

**FIGURE 11.10** First step on the wizard to create a client.

It's not necessary to complete the description and the name, but it would be great to do so. Also, disable the toggle Always display in UI because the client in this case is a microservice, so there is nothing to show.

On the next step of the wizard, disable Client Authentication and check Standard flow, as shown in Figure 11.11.

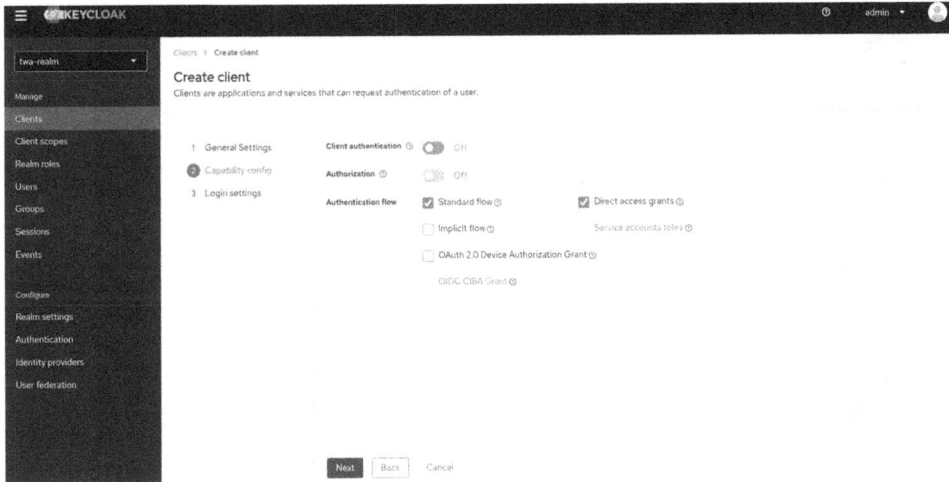

**FIGURE 11.11** Second step in the wizard to create a client.

The purpose of the second step is to implement a more secure and widely used flow in Web applications. Although the system referenced in this book does not have a Web application, there will come a time when the login process needs to be established and share information with Keycloak to generate a token that can be used across all applications.

In the last step, it is not necessary to make any modifications to the default options, as shown in Figure 11.12.

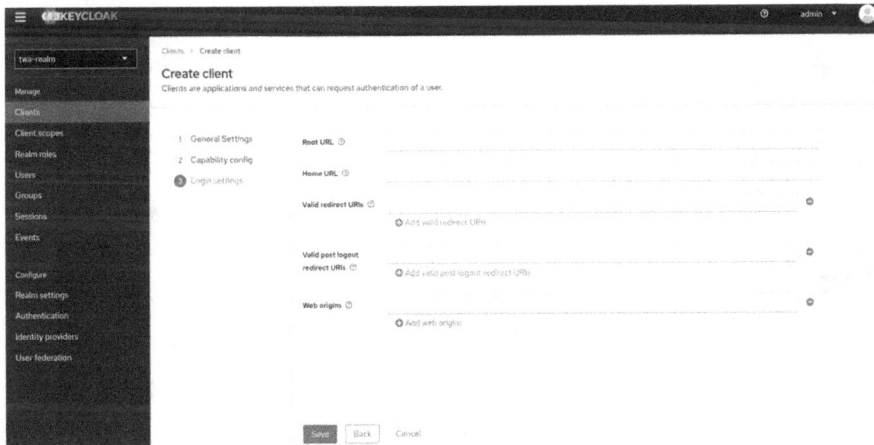

**FIGURE 11.12** Last step in the wizard to create a client.

After creating the clients to access Keycloak, it's time to define the roles related to security. To do this, click on Realm roles in the left bar, which will show a list of the default roles that exist, as shown in Figure 11.13.

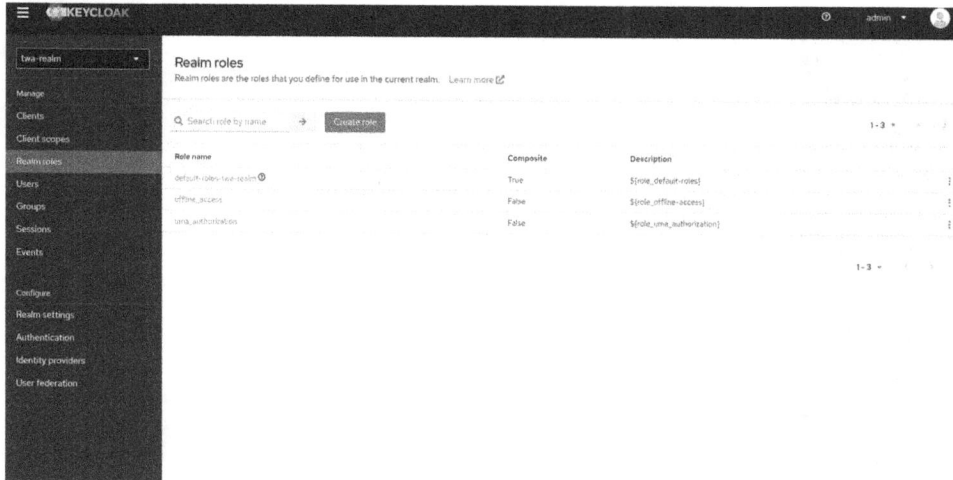

*FIGURE 11.13* Existing roles.

Click the button Create role and define at least two different roles (USER and ADMIN). Figure 11.14 illustrates the basic form for creating a new role.

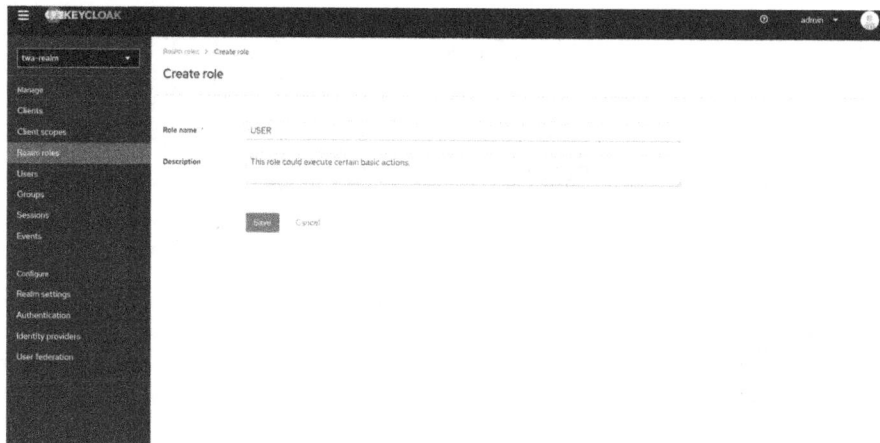

*FIGURE 11.14* Form to create new roles.

The final part of this configuration involves creating users who interact with the system. In this book, the goal is to keep the process simple, so let's manually add users in Keycloak. To do this, we'll go to the menu on the left side and click on Users. By default, a page like in Figure 11.15 will be displayed without any user content.

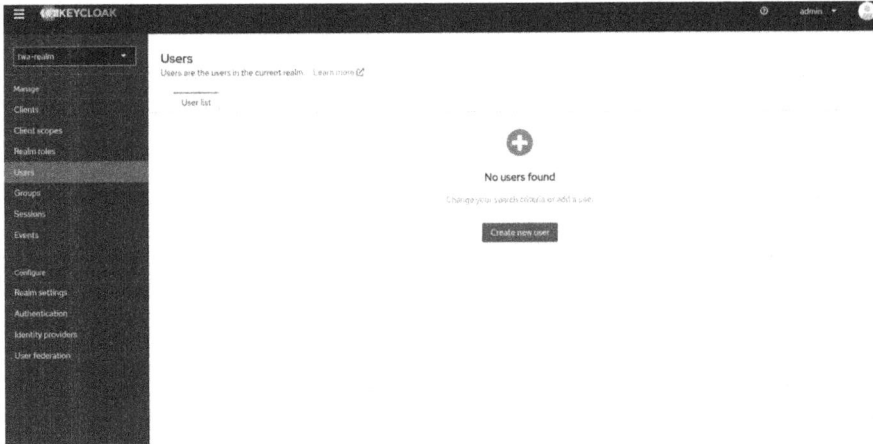

**FIGURE 11.15** List of existing users.

Click on the button Create new user and complete the form that appears in Figure 11.16 with information such as email, username, first name, and last name. It is recommended not to add any required actions because, in that case, the action implies do some additional steps before to use the new user.

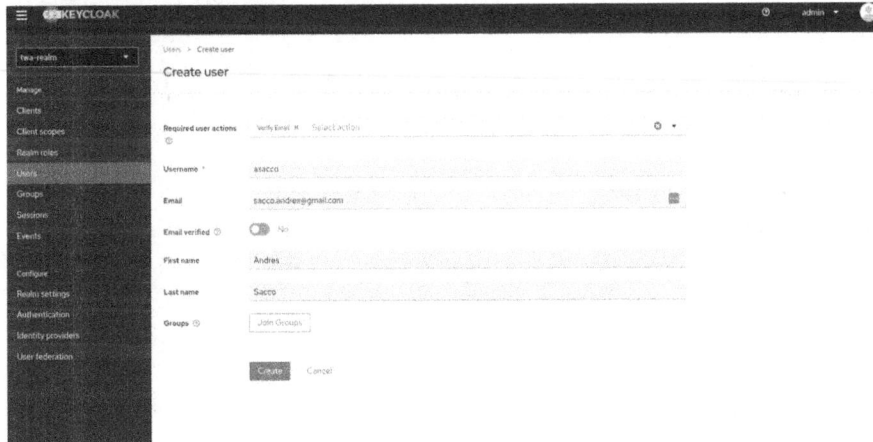

**FIGURE 11.16** Creating a new user.

After creating a user, the tool will display the details of the new user. Click on the tab Role mapping, and then select the roles previously defined in this section, as shown in Figure 11.17.

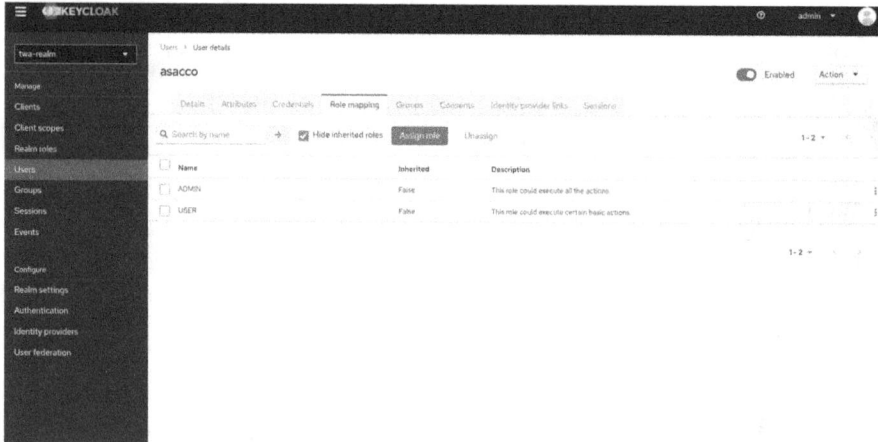

***FIGURE 11.17*** Assigning roles to the user.

The last step involves assigning a password to the user for the login process. To do this, click on the Credentials tab and create a new password, as seen in Figure 11.18.

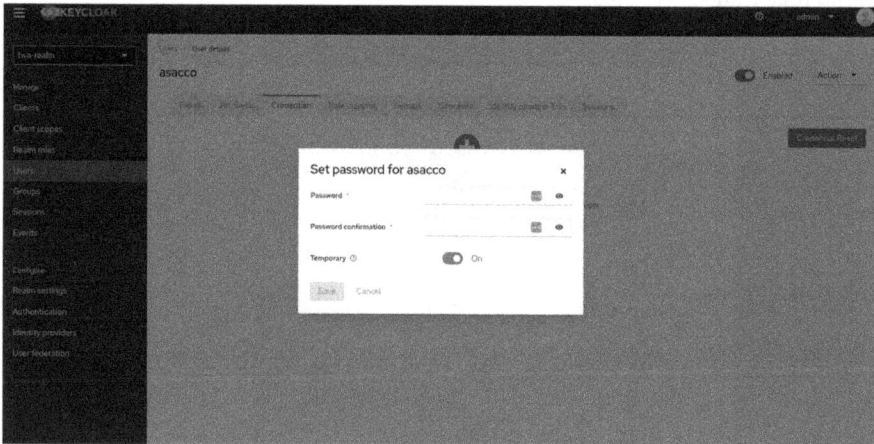

***FIGURE 11.18*** Assigning a password to the user.

Note that this only needs to be done once because after that, everything is reused, at least within the realm defined in this section.

### Configuring the Application

After configuring everything on the server, the next step involves making modifications to the application so that it can be used. The first modification consists of removing the dependencies introduced in the previous configuration mechanism and instead adding the dependencies listed in Listing 11.20.

```
<dependency>
   <groupId>org.springframework.boot</groupId>
   <artifactId>spring-boot-starter-oauth2-resource-server</artifactId>
</dependency>

<dependency>
   <groupId>org.springframework.security</groupId>
   <artifactId>spring-security-oauth2-jose</artifactId>
</dependency>
```

*LISTING 11.20* Add dependencies to use Keycloak on the application.

From the `SecurityConfiguration` class, remove the definition of the `AuthenticationManager` that was added in the previous security mechanism. After that, in the same class, add the definition of the OAuth server, as shown in Listing 11.21.

```
@Bean
   public SecurityFilterChain securityFilterChain(HttpSecurity http) throws
Exception {
        return http
                .cors(cors -> cors.configurationSource(corsConfigurationSource))
                .csrf(AbstractHttpConfigurer::disable)
                .sessionManagement(session -> session
                        .sessionCreationPolicy(SessionCreationPolicy.STATELESS)
                )
                .authorizeHttpRequests(
                        auth ->
                                auth.requestMatchers("/documentation/**")
                                        .permitAll() // Public endpoints
                                        .requestMatchers("/swagger-ui.html")
                                        .permitAll() // Public endpoints
                                        .requestMatchers("/swagger-ui/**")
                                        .permitAll() // Public endpoints
                                        .requestMatchers("/v3/api-docs/**")
                                        .permitAll() // Public endpoints
                                        .anyRequest()
                                        .authenticated() // Protected endpoints
                )
                .oauth2ResourceServer(oauth2 -> oauth2
                        .jwt(Customizer.withDefaults())
                )
                .build();
    }
```

*LISTING 11.21* Modifications on the securityFilterChain method.

The final step involves adding the server's location to the configuration to validate the tokens generated after the user logs in to the system. The changes are similar to those shown in Listing 11.22, where it is necessary to specify two different URLs: one for validating the JWT and another for identifying the issuer.

```
spring:
  application:
    name: api-reservation

  # Previous configuration

  security:
    oauth2:
      resource-server:
        jwt:
          jwk-set-uri: http://localhost:8030/auth/realms/twa-realm/
protocol/openid-connect/certs
          issuer-uri: http://localhost:8030/auth/realms/twa-realm
```

***LISTING 11.22*** Modifications to the application.yml.

After introducing the changes, it's time to run the application and begin testing to check whether everything is okay. The first step before making any requests to the application is to log in to Keycloak and obtain a token. To do this, it's possible to use the `curl` command that appears in Listing 11.23; however, in a real situation, the request will be made for a Web page.

```
→   ~ curl -X POST 'http://localhost:8030/realms/twa-realm/protocol/
openid-connect/token'  --header 'Content-Type: application/x-www-form-
urlencoded'  --data-urlencode 'grant_type=password'  --data-urlencode
'client_id=twa'  --data-urlencode 'username=asacco'  --data-urlencode
'password=78UJCbU*ansR'
```

{"access_token":"eyJhbGciOiJSUzI1NiIsInR5cCIgOiAiSldUIiwia2lkIiA6ICJUUW
90RDRGOE1kMmJWLVV0czdlZkNVaXZCWHJDZXpaQVM5cXJ2MmNOWTUwIn0.
eyJleHAiOjE3NDkxNTM4NTIsImlhdCI6MTc0OTE1MzU1MiwianRpIjoiYjc4NjAzOWUtOWVj
ZC00Y2ViLWFjOTAtZDM0M2Y2YjkwY2E4IiwiaXNzIjoiaHR0cDovL2xvY2FsaG9zdDo4MDMw
L3JlYWxtcy90d2EtcmVhbG0iLCJzdWIiOiJkZDY5ZDFjYy02OTNmLTQ5Y2EtYWNkNi0yYTg3
MGM4M2QyNTkiLCJ0eXAiOiJCZWFyZXIiLCJhenAiOiJ0d2EiLCJzZXNzaW9uX3N0YXRlIjoi
ZWMyMDkyNDgtNDczOC00OYjQ4LWI5NzktMDc3NTEwMzYzYjViIiwiYWNyIjoiMSIsImFsbG9
3ZWQtb3JpZ2lucyI6WyIvKiJdLCJyZWFsbV9hY2Nlc3MiOnsicm9sZXMiOlsiQURNSU4iLC
JVU0VSIl19LCJzY29wZSI6ImVtYWlsIHByb2ZpbGUiLCJzaWQiOiJlYzIwOTI0OC00NzM4LT
RiNDgtYjk3OS0wNzc1MTAzNjNiNWIiLCJlbWFpbF92ZXJpZmllZCI6dHJ1ZSwibmFtZSI6Ik
FuZHJlcyBTYWNjbyIsInByZWZlcnJlZF91c2VybmFtZSI6ImFzYWNjbyIsImdpdmVuX25hbW
UiOiJBbmRyZXMiLCJmYW1pbHlfbmFtZSI6IlNhY2NvIiwiZW1haWwiOiJzYWNjby5hbmRyZX
NAZ21haWwuY29tIn0.
JDvc2YSpmsGndMItQNJEMXAGRksSqxW8FILGwOhzRJR1QXr1nRawkkb0j6W13w7iByZs_
fbub95W1wPaJkygqnd05HJUISITthzRfUEl_
kMFPbZ4T5pgMd3RT6JIvyu4bl_1XGB_V8EVjen3yuV570ktzUGpbFKAK0y_
HoT-cGIkEBw33-7Ls0Ecrlr9mRcQHWatPHV322sVEbZ66H-SaptwmwEX3_0S
8n1uIN02PSCZ32wzHkuGvsF5ZZYU91wuB7ENkshlNJGtvDlog9YV5w7j8Yl
ImjlqhXxWy-3MxgNbCIdPv2XVjNQZzGVkj1RENHu3jXxA6boXC3czWhVq7-
w","expires_in":300,"refresh_expires_in":1800,"refresh_
token":"eyJhbGciOiJIUzI1NiIsInR5cCIgOiAiSldUIiwia2lkIiA6ICI1YzNmN2RlZC03
NjU5LTQwMWItOTE4OC1mMjJhN2UxMmE3YzgifQ.eyJleHAiOjE3NDkxNTUzNTIsImlhdCI6
MTc0OTE1MzU1MiwianRpIjoiNDE5NTk0MjctZTJi
Ny00YmMyLTliODEtMzA5YWU1MjcxMTIwIiwiaXNzIjoiaHR0cDovL2xvY2FsaG9zdDo4MDM
wL3JlYWxtcy90d2EtcmVhbG0iLCJhdWQiOiJodHRwOi8vbG9jYWxob3N0OjgwMzAvcmVhbG1
zL3R3YS1yZWFsbSIsInN1YiI6ImRkNjlkMWNjLTY5M2YtNDljYS1hY2Q2LTJhODcwYzgzZDI

10SISInR5cCI6IlJlZnJlc2giLCJhenAiOiJ0d2EiLCJzZXNzaW9uX3N0YXRlIjoiZWMyMDk
yNDgtNDczOC00YjQ4LWI5NzktMDc3NTEwMzYzYjViIiwic2NvcGUiOiJlbWFpbCBwcm9maWx
lIiwic2lkIjoiZWMyMDkyNDgtNDczOC00YjQ4LWI5NzktMDc3NTEwMzYzYjViIn0.mLpbeNK
ZoFiRal-gF6WetK73opWpLl1Ym2mAYcmvn3c","token_type":"Bearer","not-before-
policy":0,"session_state":"ec209248-4738-4b48-b979-077510363b5b","scope"
:"email profile"}

*LISTING 11.23* Command to simulate the login of the user and obtain the token.

The response from the `curl` command returns a JSON object containing several attributes, the most relevant of which is `access_token`, which is necessary for sending information to any application. Another attribute is `expires_in`, which provides information about the lifespan of the token before it becomes invalid.

Instead of copying and pasting the token into another `curl` command to invoke the application, let's define a variable with the result of Keycloak's execution and pass that information in the request to the application, as shown in Listing 11.24.

```
→  ~ TOKEN=$(curl -X POST 'http://localhost:8030/realms/twa-realm/
protocol/openid-connect/token' \
 --header 'Content-Type: application/x-www-form-urlencoded' \
 --data-urlencode 'grant_type=password' \
 --data-urlencode 'client_id=twa' \
 --data-urlencode 'username=asacco' \
 --data-urlencode 'password=78UJCbU*ansR' | jq -r .access_token)

curl -i -H "Authorization: Bearer $TOKEN" http://localhost:8095/api/
flights/reservation/management/info

HTTP/1.1 200
Vary: Origin
Vary: Access-Control-Request-Method
Vary: Access-Control-Request-Headers
X-Content-Type-Options: nosniff
X-XSS-Protection: 0
Cache-Control: no-cache, no-store, max-age=0, must-revalidate
Pragma: no-cache
Expires: 0
X-Frame-Options: DENY
Content-Type: application/vnd.spring-boot.actuator.v3+json
Transfer-Encoding: chunked
Date: Fri, 06 Jun 2025 11:23:27 GMT

{"app":{"name":"api-reservation","version":"0.0.1-SNAPSHOT"},"contact
":{"email":"sacco.andres@gmail.com","slack":"adsacco"},"reservation-
stats":{"amount":9}}
```

*LISTING 11.24* Command to access the info endpoint passing the token.

This approach is an evolution of the previous one, where no one validates the token. It, however, also introduces the need for many applications to understand Keycloak, and each application must validate it. It is necessary to consider whether this approach is suitable for an extensive system of microservices, or whether a combination of this approach and the previous one would be better, where the microservices that expose information for the Web page are validated with the secure server, while the others, which are deeply embedded in the system without any direct access, only validate whether the JWT token is valid or not.

## SUMMARY

In this chapter, different mechanisms were shown, each with its pros and cons. Some carry more weight in decision-making depending on the information that the system saves. There is no silver bullet that solves all possible problems, but it is at least possible to mitigate or restrict access using some of these mechanisms.

Some concepts introduced in this chapter are recommended for use, such as CORS, CSRF, and stateless sessions, as they help reduce the risk of exploitation of these vulnerabilities and can be used with any approach.

# 12

# Discovering, Exposing, and Balancing

Creating different applications on a system presents a series of problems or challenges that need to be addressed at some point. One of the most critical aspects of security is identifying which endpoints are exposed to the outside world. This consideration is crucial, as someone with bad intentions could steal sensitive information or attempt to populate the databases with incorrect data. Therefore, it's essential to take action to minimize the risks associated with this situation. For this reason, this chapter will introduce the use of the API Gateway pattern, as well as other related patterns, such as Service Discovery and Load Balancing.

## EXPOSING

An architecture based on microservices offers many benefits, some of which are detailed throughout this book; however, it also introduces some minor problems. One of these issues is the existence of too many endpoints, which may or may not belong to the same application. As a result, clients utilizing these endpoints need to memorize numerous different URLs, simultaneously exposing part of the internal organization of the platform. Figure 12.1 presents an overview of the current situation in which anyone could access any application in our example scenario.

It is necessary to reduce the complexity of having multiple endpoints while also increasing security for specific endpoints that most clients should not be aware of.

### What Does Exposing All the Endpoints Mean?

- Exposing all the endpoints means that anyone can see and access all endpoints in the applications. There are, however, some risks associated with this approach:
- Security: Everyone has access to all endpoints and so could obtain sensitive information, such as credit card numbers, client addresses, and phone numbers. It's possible to restrict access through some security mechanism, such as an API key or username/password, but at some point, the endpoint will be exposed. Once someone discovers that a particular endpoint is exposed, they may try to access it.
- Resilience: The microservices could fail at some point during the life cycle of an application, but if everyone can make requests to all the endpoints, the risk of this occurring

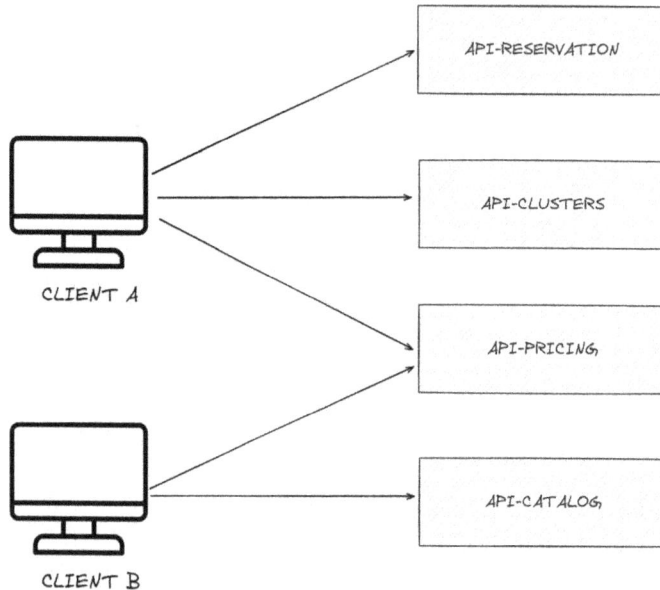

**FIGURE 12.1** Situation where anyone can see all the hosts of the applications.

increases because it's possible for too many requests to be made in a short period, which would affect those microservices. At the same time, if something goes wrong, there is no mechanism to retry or define a fallback method, as the system delegates responsibility to each consumer to handle it.

- Routing: Another issue is that the routes of the different endpoints may change if a new microservice is introduced or another functionality is migrated, creating new routes necessary for communication with all consumers. These consumers must wait until the changes are made.
- Caching: Using a caching mechanism provides the unique opportunity to reduce the number of requests that most microservices receive. The main problem with this, however, is that the majority of these mechanisms delegate responsibility to the consumer, which means the system could receive a large number of requests to obtain the same information, whether it is static or changes daily.

More situations could occur when the system is open. What has been mentioned previously is just a small sample of problems. For all these reasons, it's necessary to create a barrier between the application and the external world, which could be anyone on the Internet or just another part of the company, and to mitigate these problems and hide the internal structure of the system.

## What Ways Exist to Do This?

There are two main options to solve the problem, each with its own set of tools and approaches, along with their respective pros and cons. Both aim to establish the possibility of creating a proxy from the clients and the applications.

## Manually

The first impulse when problems arise is to try to create something manually that solves all the issues by analyzing the tools the company uses and repurposing some of them. This approach has several disadvantages, such as:

- Effort: Creating something from scratch requires significant effort for many people. Not only does it involve creating and maintaining a custom tool, but the possibility of bugs presents the biggest challenge.
- Scalability: The likelihood of misusing resources and creating something from scratch increases the risk of developing a negative experience for clients or consumers, particularly in applications. Some common problems include blocking requests and inefficient methods for capturing and transforming the information.
- Security: Declaring the different endpoints with their respective roles and permissions could create inconsistencies in the solution regarding the definition of security across the various applications. Additionally, manually managing JWT, OAuth 2, or API keys is prone to errors and can be insecure without established libraries.
- Routing and Balancing: Defining the endpoints manually limits the dynamic discovery when new endpoints appear, affecting scalability and maintainability.

This list of disadvantages is just an example of why it is not a good idea to create something from scratch, at least in this type of problem, where numerous solutions utilize the API Gateway pattern.

## API Gateway

API Gateway emerges as a solution to create an application that serves as a proxy between clients or consumers and the entire system, concealing all details about the number of microservices or endpoints that exist. Figure 12.2 shows what an architecture implementing this pattern looks like.

The primary distinction between this API and any other that may exist on the platform is that it can incorporate numerous additional features related to security, resilience, caching, and

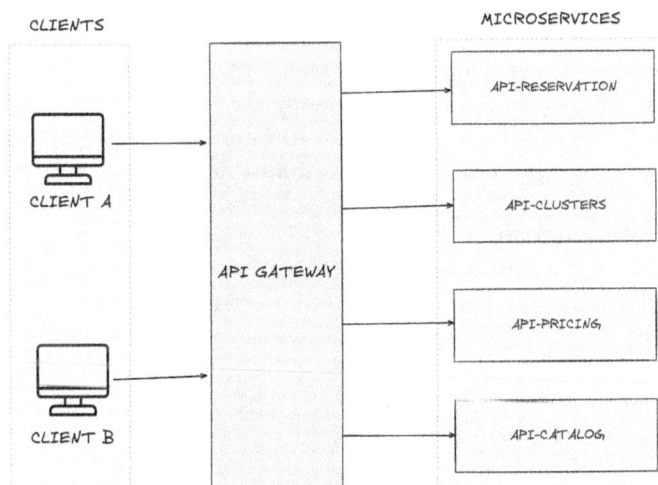

**FIGURE 12.2** A system using API Gateway.

load balancing, which can, in some cases, mitigate the number of issues that applications may encounter or need to process. At the same time, it offers a set of features to all the endpoints. For example, it's possible to include Circuit Breaker for each specific microservice with a Fallback method; however, the microservices may not contain any resilience mechanisms for communication with other applications. Figure 12.3 illustrates several key features that can be included in an implementation of API Gateway.

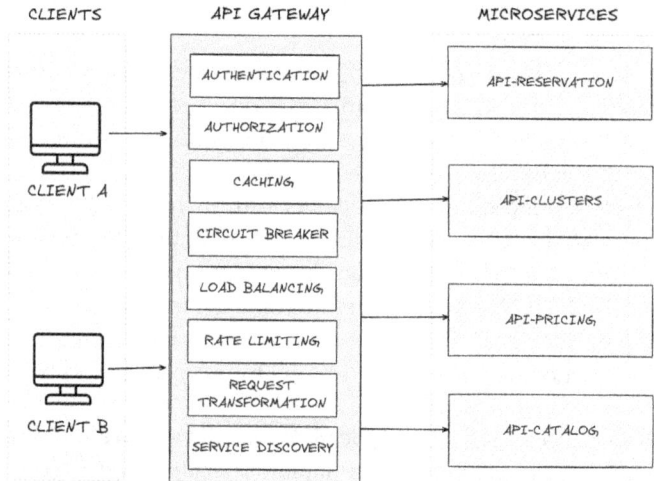

**FIGURE 12.3** Details of features that could be featured in API Gateway.

The core of this API is the definition of all the supported routes or endpoints. After this, it's necessary to include the behavior according to which features will be enabled, for example, the rate limit on specific endpoints.

Many tools implement this pattern, some of which incur costs associated with managing resources or require a paid license for use. On the other hand, there is a long list of free options available; some of the most relevant are:

- Spring Cloud Gateway[1]: A Java-based API gateway built on Spring WebFlux, providing routing, filters, load balancing, and integration with Spring Cloud features such as service discovery and Resilience4j. This is ideal for Spring Boot microservices.
- Kong[2]: An open-source, high-performance API gateway built on Nginx and Lua that offers authentication, rate limiting, logging, transformations, and plugins. It is available in both OSS and enterprise versions, making it popular in cloud-native environments.
- NGINX[3]: A general-purpose Web server and reverse proxy that serves as a lightweight API gateway. It supports load balancing, caching, SSL termination, and routing, but it lacks built-in service discovery and dynamic API management features.
- Netflix Zuul[4]:

---

[1]https://spring.io/projects/spring-cloud-gateway
[2]https://konghq.com/
[3]https://nginx.org/
[4]https://github.com/Netflix/zuul

NOTE *Other tools that could be used that are not mentioned in this section are AWS API Gateway, Azure API Management, Google Cloud API Gateway, Gravitee.io, and KrakenD.*

Each of the tools in the list has a series of pros and cons that need to be considered before using them. The following section explains the significant differences between them and which is the best option for the scenario presented in this book.

## What Is the Best Option for a Scenario?

Analyzing which is the best option often involves considering several aspects, such as the cost associated with a dedicated resource, the team's experience with a particular technology, and the modifications required to the source code. This section will analyze the pros and cons of the different options to make the best decision. Table 12.1 provides a brief overview of the tools available for protecting the exposure of endpoints, indicating support for various features with a cross, a tick, or a warning if a feature is supported but requires an external plugin.

**TABLE 12.1** Main things to consider when choosing an option to expose endpoints.

| Feature | Spring Cloud Gateway | Kong | NGINX | Netflix Zuul |
|---|---|---|---|---|
| Cloud-native support | ✔ | ✔ | ⚠ | ✘ |
| Service discovery | ✔ | ✔ | ✘ | ⚠ |
| Load balancing | ✔ | ✔ | ⚠ | ⚠ |
| Circuit breaker | ✔ | ✔ | ✘ | ⚠ |
| Rate limiting | ✔ | ✔ | ⚠ | ⚠ |
| Authentication/authorization | ✔ | ⚠ | ⚠ | ⚠ |
| Dynamic route config | ✔ | ✔ | ⚠ | ⚠ |
| Hot reload/live config | ✔ | ✔ | ✘ | ⚠ |
| OpenAPI/Swagger support | ✔ | ⚠ | ✘ | ⚠ |

The difference between the options is evident in the previous table; however, synthesizing all the arguments in one document is a good idea, as shown in Figure 12.4.

This document enables anyone to understand why one approach was chosen over another and to verify the factors considered when making the decision.

## How Can This Pattern Be Integrated into the System?

Creating an API gateway involves creating a new project that acts as a layer hiding all the actual endpoints of the various APIs in the system. To do this, let's make a project using the same `curl` command that was used in previous chapters but with minor modifications, such as the dependencies that need to be introduced and the name, as seen in Listing 12.1.

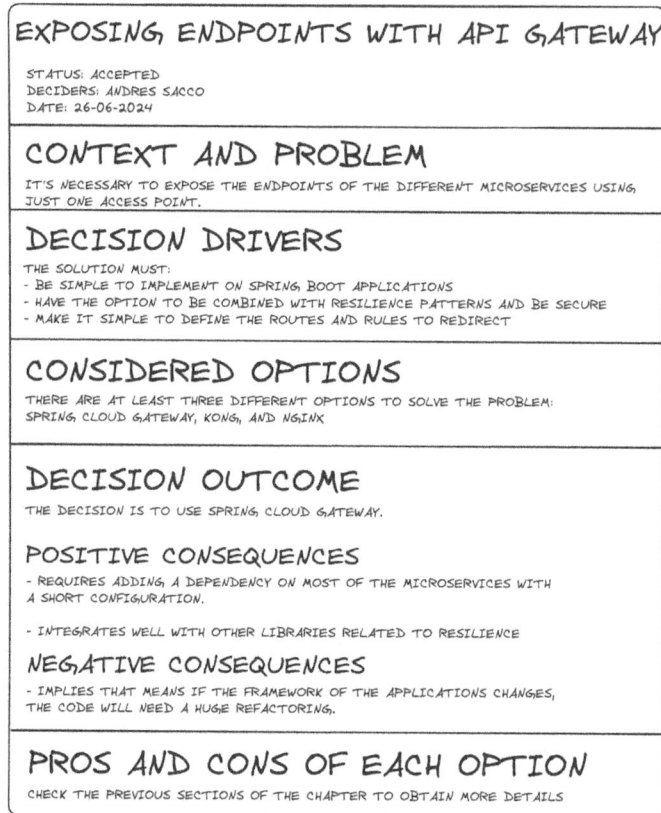

**FIGURE 12.4** ADR about the decision of how to protect the endpoints.

```
→    ~ curl https://start.spring.io/starter.zip \
    -d dependencies=actuator,cloud-gateway,webflux \
    -d type=maven-project \
    -d language=java \
    -d bootVersion=3.4.5 \
    -d baseDir=api-gateway \
    -d groupId=com.twa \
    -d artifactId=api-gateway \
    -d name=api-gateway \
    -d description="Application that represents the gateway." \
    -d javaVersion=21 \
    -d packaging=jar \
    -o api-gateway.zip
```

**LISTING 12.1** Command to create the API Gateway project.

**NOTE**

*Note that this project does not include a security mechanism, so keep it simple and focus on the most relevant aspects, such as API Gateway, Service Discovery, and load balancing. Combining Spring Security to incorporate the various elements introduced in previous chapters is also possible.*

After creating the project, decompress the file as usual and import it into the IDE. The project's POM file will look as in Listing 12.2 if everything is correct.

```xml
<?xml version="1.0" encoding="UTF-8"?>
<project xmlns="http://maven.apache.org/POM/4.0.0" xmlns:xsi="http://
www.w3.org/2001/XMLSchema-instance"
   xsi:schemaLocation="http://maven.apache.org/POM/4.0.0 https://maven.
apache.org/xsd/maven-4.0.0.xsd">
    <modelVersion>4.0.0</modelVersion>
    <parent>
        <groupId>org.springframework.boot</groupId>
        <artifactId>spring-boot-starter-parent</artifactId>
        <version>3.4.5</version>
        <relativePath/> <!-- lookup parent from repository -->
    </parent>
    <groupId>com.twa</groupId>
    <artifactId>api-gateway</artifactId>
    <version>0.0.1-SNAPSHOT</version>
    <name>api-gateway</name>
    <description>Application that represents the gateway.</description>
    <properties>
        <java.version>21</java.version>
        <spring-cloud.version>2024.0.1</spring-cloud.version>
    </properties>
    <dependencies>
        <dependency>
            <groupId>org.springframework.boot</groupId>
            <artifactId>spring-boot-starter-actuator</artifactId>
        </dependency>

        <dependency>
            <groupId>org.springframework.boot</groupId>
            <artifactId>spring-boot-starter-webflux</artifactId>
        </dependency>

        <dependency>
            <groupId>org.springframework.cloud</groupId>
            <artifactId>spring-cloud-starter-gateway</artifactId>
        </dependency>

        <dependency>
            <groupId>org.springframework.boot</groupId>
            <artifactId>spring-boot-starter-test</artifactId>
            <scope>test</scope>
        </dependency>
    </dependencies>
    <dependencyManagement>
        <dependencies>
            <dependency>
                <groupId>org.springframework.cloud</groupId>
                <artifactId>spring-cloud-dependencies</artifactId>
                <version>${spring-cloud.version}</version>
                <type>pom</type>
                <scope>import</scope>
            </dependency>
```

```
                </dependencies>
        </dependencyManagement>

        <build>
                <plugins>
                        <plugin>
                                <groupId>org.springframework.boot</groupId>
                                <artifactId>spring-boot-maven-plugin</artifactId>
                        </plugin>
                </plugins>
        </build>

</project>
```

**LISTING 12.2** POM file with the different dependencies.

The structure of the POM file is concise because it requires only a few dependencies to function correctly. The actuator and Web dependencies are included to provide the same basic functionality as the other applications on the platform, but are not strictly necessary for inclusion.

**NOTE** *The POM file in Listing 12.2 has the dependency* `spring-cloud-starter-gateway-mvc` *instead of the correct one,* `spring-cloud-starter-gateway`*. Hence, it's necessary to make the corrections before continuing.*

The next step is to create the base `application.yml` file, which most applications have on the system, providing information related to the application's health, name, and exposed port, as shown in Listing 12.3.

```
spring:
  application:
    name: api-gateway

server:
  port: 8020
  error:
    include-stacktrace: never

  compression:
    enabled: true
    min-response-size: 2048
    mime-types: application/json,application/xml,text/html,text/
xml,text/plain
management:
  endpoints:
    web:
      base-path: /management
      exposure:
        include: info,health

  info:
    java:
      enabled: false #change if you want to obtain information about Java
```

```
      os:
        enabled: false #change if you want to obtain information about OS
      env:
        enabled: true
    endpoint:
      health:
        show-details: always
        probes:
          enabled: false
info:
  app:
    name: "@project.artifactId@"
    version: "@project.version@"
  contact:
    email: "sacco.andres@gmail.com"
    slack: "adsacco"
```

**LISTING 12.3** Configuration of the API gateway.

Let's run the application and check whether everything is okay. To do this, simply execute a `curl` command with a request to the `info` endpoint, as shown in Listing 12.4.

```
➜   ~ curl http://localhost:8020/management/info

{
  "app": {
    "name": "api-gateway",
    "version": "0.0.1-SNAPSHOT"
  },
  "contact": {
    "email": "sacco.andres@gmail.com",
    "slack": "adsacco"
  }
}
```

**LISTING 12.4** Command to check whether the actuator is working.

After creating the project's base, it's time to define the redirections according to the different paths.

## Adding Redirections

When using Spring Cloud Gateway, there are three different components related to redirections:

- Route: Refer to a unique ID, which contains a list of predicates, each connected with a URL or path. For example, in the case of this book, it could be a good idea to use the name of each microservice as a unique ID.
- Predicates: This section contains the rules that need to match to redirect the request, including the path, host, and parameters. It's not necessary to define a route for the entire microservice or system; if it's required, it's possible to specify one for specific endpoints.
- Filter: This section captures and modifies the request to restrict access or employ a resilience pattern during a specific service's downtime.

Now, after briefly introducing the different components, it's time to modify the system to automatically redirect requests to various microservices when the API gateway receives a request for a specific path. To achieve this, Spring Cloud Gateway provides a straightforward method, where it's essential to identify the path and the host associated with that path. Listing 12.5 illustrates an example of the structure of a simple route's definition.

```
- id: clusters # Identification of the routing
  uri: http://localhost:4070 # Host of the microservice
  predicates:
    - Path=/api/flights/clusters/** # Path to capture and redirect
```

**LISTING 12.5** Section that represents one redirect.

This straightforward approach introduces the possibility of having multiple configurations depending on the environment, all in one place. Another option, however, allows this without modifying the configuration file: Simply create a configuration class that declares the route using `RouteLocatorBuilder` to generate a `RouteLocator` with the same parameters appearing in any of the previous routes in Listing 12.5. The equivalent for the cluster routes is shown in Listing 12.6.

```
@Configuration
public class GatewayRoutesConfig {

    @Bean
    public RouteLocator customRouteLocator(RouteLocatorBuilder builder)
{
        return builder.routes()
            .route("clusters", r -> r
                .path("/api/flights/clusters/**")
                .uri("http://localhost:4070"))
            .build();
    }
}
```

**LISTING 12.6** Section that represents one redirect but defining on the code

With the previous explanation in mind, it's time to modify the configuration file to include all the redirections and, in some cases, restrict access to specific paths, as seen in Listing 12.7.

```
spring:
  application:
    name: api-gateway
  profiles:
    active: native

  cloud:
    gateway:
      routes:
        # ☑ Clusters with Circuit Breaker
        - id: clusters
```

```
      uri: http://localhost:4070
      predicates:
        - Path=/api/flights/clusters/**

  # ☑ Reservation with Circuit Breaker
  - id: reservation
    uri: http://localhost:3070
    predicates:
      - Path=/api/flights/reservation/**

  # ☑ Catalog with Circuit Breaker
  - id: catalog
    uri: http://localhost:6070
    predicates:
      - Path=/api/flights/catalog/**

  # 🔒 Explicit Blocked (return 403)
  - id: block-pricing
    uri: no://op
    predicates:
      - Path=/api/flights/pricing/**
    filters:
      - name: SetStatus
        args:
          status: 403

  - id: block-itineraries-search
    uri: no://op
    predicates:
      - Path=/api/flights/itineraries-search/**
    filters:
      - name: SetStatus
        args:
          status: 403

  - id: block-provider-alpha
    uri: no://op
    predicates:
      - Path=/api/flights/provider/alpha/**
    filters:
      - name: SetStatus
        args:
          status: 403

  - id: block-provider-beta
    uri: no://op
    predicates:
      - Path=/api/flights/provider/beta/**
    filters:
      - name: SetStatus
        args:
          status: 403

# Previous configuration
```

**LISTING 12.7** Command to check whether the actuator is working.

The final step involves running all the microservices and the API gateway, and then attempting to access the exposed endpoints. For example, let's access the information of a city that resides on the `api-catalog` through the gateway using the `curl` command, as shown in Listing 12.8.

```
→   ~ curl http://localhost:6070/api/flights/catalog/city/BUE

{
  "name": "Buenos Aires",
  "code": "BUE",
  "timeZone": "America/Argentina/Buenos_Aires",
  "country": {
    "name": "Argentina",
    "code": "AR",
    "continent": {
      "name": "South America",
      "code": "SA"
    }
  }
}
```

**LISTING 12.8** Command to check whether the redirection is working.

A good way to check whether the gateway is working and register the route is to check the logs on the console. The following code block shows the output of the `api-gateway` if everything is working.

```
2025-05-26T18:03:52.859-03:00  INFO 1076691 --- [api-gateway]
[          main] o.s.c.g.r.RouteDefinitionRouteLocator    : Loaded
RoutePredicateFactory [Header]
2025-05-26T18:03:52.859-03:00  INFO 1076691 --- [api-gateway]
[          main] o.s.c.g.r.RouteDefinitionRouteLocator    : Loaded
RoutePredicateFactory [Host]
2025-05-26T18:03:52.859-03:00  INFO 1076691 --- [api-gateway]
[          main] o.s.c.g.r.RouteDefinitionRouteLocator    : Loaded
RoutePredicateFactory [Method]
2025-05-26T18:03:52.859-03:00  INFO 1076691 --- [api-gateway]
[          main] o.s.c.g.r.RouteDefinitionRouteLocator    : Loaded
RoutePredicateFactory [Path]
2025-05-26T18:03:52.859-03:00  INFO 1076691 --- [api-gateway]
[          main] o.s.c.g.r.RouteDefinitionRouteLocator    : Loaded
RoutePredicateFactory [Query]
2025-05-26T18:03:52.859-03:00  INFO 1076691 --- [api-gateway]
[          main] o.s.c.g.r.RouteDefinitionRouteLocator    : Loaded
RoutePredicateFactory [ReadBody]
2025-05-26T18:03:52.859-03:00  INFO 1076691 --- [api-gateway]
[          main] o.s.c.g.r.RouteDefinitionRouteLocator    : Loaded
RoutePredicateFactory [RemoteAddr]
2025-05-26T18:03:52.859-03:00  INFO 1076691 --- [api-gateway]
[          main] o.s.c.g.r.RouteDefinitionRouteLocator    : Loaded
RoutePredicateFactory [XForwardedRemoteAddr]
2025-05-26T18:03:52.859-03:00  INFO 1076691 --- [api-gateway]
[          main] o.s.c.g.r.RouteDefinitionRouteLocator    : Loaded
RoutePredicateFactory [Weight]
```

```
2025-05-26T18:03:52.859-03:00  INFO 1076691 --- [api-gateway]
[          main] o.s.c.g.r.RouteDefinitionRouteLocator    : Loaded
RoutePredicateFactory [CloudFoundryRouteService]
```

**LISTING 12.9** Output of the execution of the application with the routes.

The previous code block only shows a few lines of all the logs that appear on the console, but they are the most relevant for this section.

### Adding Resilience Patterns to the Communication

After verifying that everything works as expected, other aspects must also be addressed, specifically issues related to errors in various applications and the application of resilience patterns.

In the case of Spring Cloud Gateway, a specific dependency is used for Resilience4j instead of the default library, with the notion that there should not be too much code defining the use of different patterns, such as Circuit Breaker. It is, however, possible to determine all the configurations for the various statuses in the `application.yml`. Listing 12.10 shows the dependency that needs to be included in the POM file.

```
<dependency>
    <groupId>org.springframework.cloud</groupId>
    <artifactId>spring-cloud-starter-circuitbreaker-reactor-resilience4j</artifactId>
</dependency>
```

**LISTING 12.10** Add a dependency to support resilience patterns.

Before continuing with the modifications, let's create a class that represents the potential problems that could arise during communication between the API gateway and other microservices, to hide all possible information. Listing 12.11 shows the same class that exists in the `api-reservation`.

```
package com.twa.api.gateway.dto;

import java.util.List;

public class ErrorDTO {
    private String description;
    private List<String> reasons;

    public ErrorDTO(String description, List<String> reasons) {
        this.description = description;
        this.reasons = reasons;
    }

    public String getDescription() {
        return description;
    }

    public List<String> getReasons() {
        return reasons;
    }
}
```

**LISTING 12.11** Class showing the errors.

After defining the DTO showing the errors on the API gateway, the next step is to create a series of endpoints that will be used for the circuit breaker when a problem arises. In the case of Listing 12.12, the approach is to return additional information about the issue at a single endpoint.

```
package com.twa.api.gateway.controller;

import com.twa.api.gateway.dto.ErrorDTO;
import org.springframework.http.HttpStatus;
import org.springframework.http.ResponseEntity;
import org.springframework.web.bind.annotation.GetMapping;
import org.springframework.web.bind.annotation.RequestMapping;
import org.springframework.web.bind.annotation.RestController;

import java.util.List;

@RestController
@RequestMapping("/fallback")
public class FallbackController {

    private static final String ERROR_MESSAGE = " service is currently
unavailable";
    private static final List<String> errors = List.of("It could suffer a high
load", "It could be a temporary problem");

    @GetMapping("/clusters")
    public ResponseEntity<ErrorDTO> fallbackClusters() {
        ErrorDTO error = new ErrorDTO("Clusters".concat(ERROR_MESSAGE), errors);
        return new ResponseEntity<>(error, HttpStatus.BAD_GATEWAY);
    }

    @GetMapping("/reservation")
    public ResponseEntity<ErrorDTO> fallbackReservation() {
        ErrorDTO error = new ErrorDTO("Reservation".concat(ERROR_MESSAGE),
errors);
        return new ResponseEntity<>(error, HttpStatus.BAD_GATEWAY);
    }

    @GetMapping("/catalog")
    public ResponseEntity<ErrorDTO> fallbackCatalog() {
        ErrorDTO error = new ErrorDTO("Catalog".concat(ERROR_MESSAGE), errors);
        return new ResponseEntity<>(error, HttpStatus.BAD_GATEWAY);
    }
}
```

**LISTING 12.12** Controller that represents the fallback methods.

The final step in modifying the system to address various communication issues is to declare a circuit breaker for each host, which serves as the fallback method. Listing 12.13 shows the filters responsible for intercepting problems and delegating necessary actions to a circuit breaker.

```
# Previous configuration

 cloud:
    gateway:
      routes:
        # ☑ Clusters with Circuit Breaker
        - id: clusters
          uri: http://localhost:4070
          predicates:
            - Path=/api/flights/clusters/**
          filters:
            - name: CircuitBreaker
              args:
                name: clustersCB
                fallbackUri: forward:/fallback/clusters

        # The same approach on all the APIs

# Previous configuration
```

**LISTING 12.13** Add the configuration to support Circuit Breaker and Fallback.

It's recommended to define at least one circuit breaker for each host, ideally one for each critical endpoint. This is because it is possible that only one or two endpoints of the other micros-ervice are not functioning correctly, while the rest are working properly.

After the modifications related to the routes, it's necessary to declare the circuit breaker's configuration as with any other application that uses Resilience4j. Let's introduce a simple configuration in the `application.yml`, as shown in Listing 12.14.

```
# Previous configuration

resilience4j.circuitbreaker:
  configs:
    default:
      failure-rate-threshold: 50
      sliding-window-type: count_based
      sliding-window-size: 5
      automatic-transition-from-open-to-half-open-enabled: true
      wait-duration-in-open-state: 10s
      permitted-number-of-calls-in-half-open-state: 1
      register-health-indicator: false

  backends:
    catalogCB:
      baseConfig: default
    clustersCB:
      baseConfig: default
    reservationCB:
      baseConfig: default

# Previous configuration
```

**LISTING 12.14** Add the configuration to support Circuit Breaker on different applications or backend.

After all the modifications, it's time to check whether everything is working. To do that, let's run the API gateway and send a request to one of the fallback endpoints, as shown in Listing 12.15.

```
→   ~ http://localhost:8020/fallback/catalog

{
    "description": "Catalog service is currently unavailable",
    "reasons": [
        "It could suffer a high load",
        "It could be a temporary problem"
    ]
}
```

**LISTING 12.15** Command to check whether the fallback endpoints are working.

After checking that the fallback endpoints are working, the next step is to stop a microservice with an associated circuit breaker, such as `api-catalog`, and execute a request as shown in Listing 12.16.

```
→   ~ http://localhost:8020/api/flights/catalog/city/BUE

{
    "description": "Catalog service is currently unavailable",
    "reasons": [
        "It could suffer a high load",
        "It could be a temporary problem"
    ]
}
```

**LISTING 12.16** Command to check whether the fallback of the catalog is working.

The message shown in Listing 12.16 could be customized to provide additional information for the endpoint consumer. Additionally, it's possible to omit Fallback and use only Circuit Breaker in the configuration or to apply a rate limit to a specific endpoint.

## DISCOVERING

In a distributed environment with multiple applications, each capable of having more than one instance, a new problem arises: How do the different microservices know the URLs and ports of the various instances? What happens if new cases appear, or if some of them are stopped?

The range of problems associated with this situation is extensive, encompassing various instances in each environment, a large number of microservices on a platform, and numerous other issues. It is necessary to find a mechanism or methodology to address this issue.

### What Does Discovering the Different Instances Involve?

The process of discovering applications to create a list or table of all existing instances has several architectural considerations. The following are requirements or implications of this approach:

• Service Registration: Each application must notify the system in some way that a new instance of the application is available, including specific information such as the host, port, health status, and version. All of this metadata is necessary to distinguish between different instances of the same or other applications.

- Dynamic Lookup: The consumers/clients of the different applications need to know, in some way, the list of available instances that exist instead of relying on static configurations. This is one of the key points of a discovery service because it reduces the number of times that it's necessary to deploy all the applications.
- Health Monitoring: Part of the discovery process involves checking the health status of all instances to remove them from the registry (table or list) of available instances, ensuring that unhealthy instances are not sending data.
- Load Balancing Support: The ability to maintain a list of all instances offers additional features, including client-side or server-side load balancing, which helps distribute traffic across healthy instances.
- Security Considerations: The system for registering new applications must be secure during registration and lookup to prevent fake services from being misused.

There are other aspects to consider in the discovery process, but these are the most relevant that apply to any approach or tool.

### What Ways Exist to Do This?

There are two main options for discovering the different instances of each application. One involves more manual work and some coordination with clients or consumers, and the other reduces manual work by delegating the discovery process to a tool.

### Manually

There are many aspects to consider when manually carrying out this process, such as the need for someone to share a list of all instances available in a document and to notify everyone in the company about the changes. Additionally, different clients/consumers need to specify in their respective `application.yml` files the list of instances that exist for each microservice and utilize some mechanism for load balancing, all while facing the risk that this approach could fail. Figure 12.5 illustrates how the different clients communicate with the microservices using this specific approach.

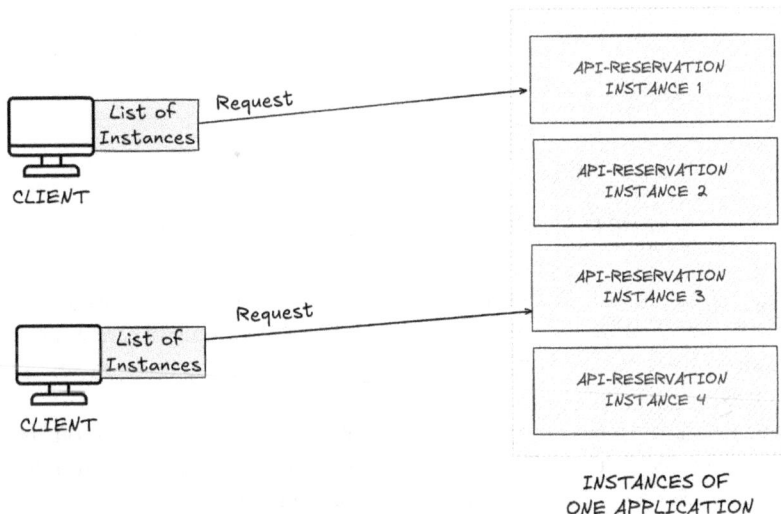

**FIGURE 12.5** Each client has a list of instances.

Of course, there are some alternatives to this approach, such as defining a DNS that groups all the instances of the same application. Some tool is required, however, to determine which instance receives each particular request. For all these reasons, it's not a good idea to use this approach unless each microservice has one instance each.

## Service Discovery

This pattern, or method for solving the problem, involves having an additional component in the infrastructure that contains all instances of the various applications. Each application, during the startup process, registers itself with the discovery server, providing all the necessary information to recognize its specifics, including the host, port, health status, and application name.

On the other hand, clients and consumers connect to the discovery server to obtain information about the available applications and use that information to communicate with them using a name that acts as a DNS, thereby avoiding the use of the real host and port. Figure 12.6 shows how the interaction between the components works.

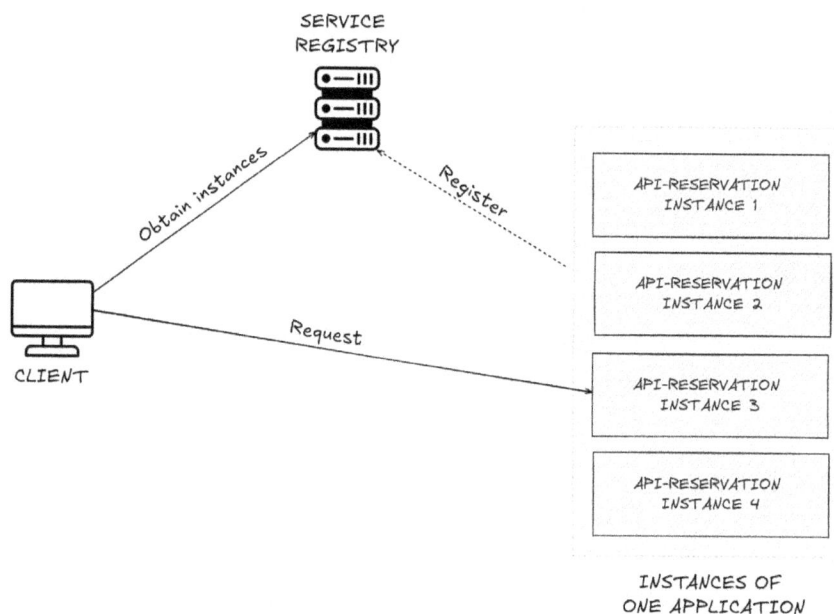

**FIGURE 12.6** Representation of using a service discovery server.

The registration process involves periodically checking the Service Discovery component to determine whether the different instances remain available. If any of them are unhealthy, they will be removed from the registry, preventing consumers or clients from sending requests to those instances.

Another key aspect of this approach is security, as most tools available on the market offer different mechanisms to ensure that only clients using a specific format can register and obtain the registry of available instances. It's also possible to combine this with some advanced security mechanisms, such as using an API key.

The following options are some of the most popular to use this pattern:

- Eureka[5]: A service registry developed by Netflix that is part of the Spring Cloud ecosystem. It supports service registration and discovery, primarily for Java-based microservices, and is simple and easy to integrate with Spring Boot applications.
- Consul[6]: A distributed service mesh and service discovery platform by HashiCorp. It provides service registration, health checks, key-value storage, and multi-datacenter support. It is language agnostic and integrates with Spring Boot via Spring Cloud Consul.
- ZooKeeper[7]: A centralized coordination service designed for distributed systems, often used in conjunction with Apache Kafka or Hadoop. It supports Service Discovery, leader election, and configuration management; however, it is more complex and not solely specialized for service discovery.
- Kubernetes: A container orchestration platform that features built-in service discovery through DNS, load balancing, and health checks. When a service is created, Kubernetes automatically assigns it a stable DNS name (e.g., `service-name.namespace.svc.cluster.local`) and load balances requests across healthy Pods. This dynamic discovery mechanism enables seamless communication between microservices without manual configuration. Kubernetes is widely adopted for cloud-native and scalable deployments.

---

**NOTE** *Other tools that can be used that are not mentioned in this section are etcd, AWS Cloud Map, CoreDNS, and SmartStack.*

Not all of these tools are suitable for every possible scenario; each has a series of pros and cons that it's necessary to consider. The following section provides a brief overview of the most relevant aspects of all of them, as well as the best option for the scenario presented in this book.

## What Is the Best Option for a Scenario?

When discussing the various options available for discovery tools, most share standard features, suggesting some type of modifications to the source code or infrastructure. It's also necessary to consider that choosing a specific tool isn't required, as the tool connects with Spring Cloud, as mentioned in the section regarding endpoint exposure. Table 12.2 provides a brief overview of the various aspects of the most relevant tools related to the discovery process.

*TABLE 12.2* Key factors to consider when choosing an option.

| Feature | Eureka | Consul | ZooKeeper | Kubernetes |
|---|---|---|---|---|
| Register | ✓ | ✓ | ✓ | ✗ |
| Discover | ✓ | ✓ | ✓ | ✗ |
| Health checks | ✓ | ✓ | ✗ | ✓ |
| Spring Cloud support | ✓ | ✓ | ✗ | ✓ |

*(Continued)*

---

[5]https://github.com/spring-cloud/spring-cloud-netflix
[6]https://developer.hashicorp.com/consul
[7]https://zookeeper.apache.org/

**TABLE 12.2** Continued

| Feature | Eureka | Consul | ZooKeeper | Kubernetes |
|---|:---:|:---:|:---:|:---:|
| DNS | ✔ | ✔ | ✘ | ✔ |
| UI | ✔ | ✔ | ✘ | ✔ |
| Metadata support | ✔ | ✔ | ✘ | ✔ |
| Security | ✔ | ✔ | ✘ | ✔ |
| Dynamic scaling | ✔ | ✔ | ✘ | ✔ |
| Cloud-native | ✘ | ✔ | ✘ | ✔ |

There are notable differences between the approaches; so, consolidating all the arguments into a single document is beneficial, as illustrated in Figure 12.7.

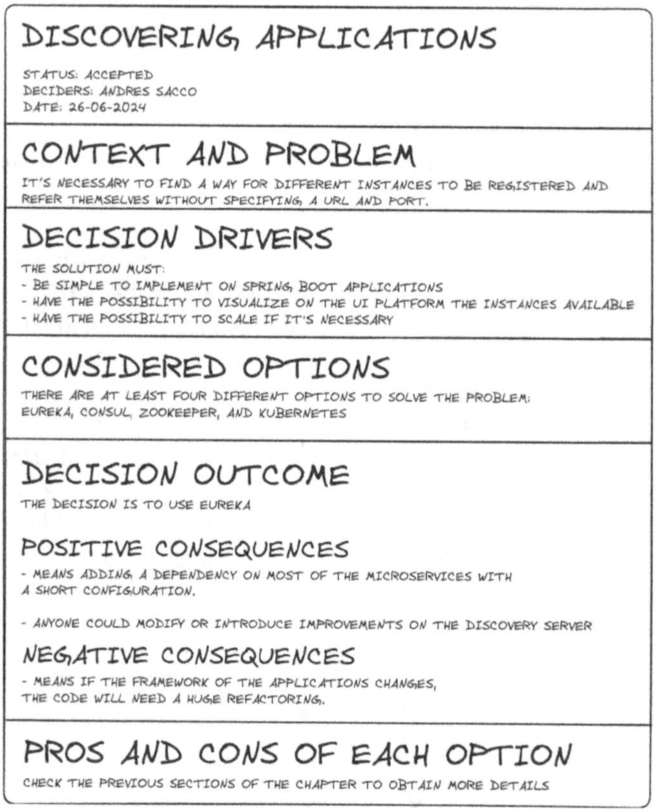

**DISCOVERING APPLICATIONS**

STATUS: ACCEPTED
DECIDERS: ANDRES SACCO
DATE: 26-06-2024

**CONTEXT AND PROBLEM**

IT'S NECESSARY TO FIND A WAY FOR DIFFERENT INSTANCES TO BE REGISTERED AND REFER THEMSELVES WITHOUT SPECIFYING A URL AND PORT.

**DECISION DRIVERS**

THE SOLUTION MUST:
- BE SIMPLE TO IMPLEMENT ON SPRING BOOT APPLICATIONS
- HAVE THE POSSIBILITY TO VISUALIZE ON THE UI PLATFORM THE INSTANCES AVAILABLE
- HAVE THE POSSIBILITY TO SCALE IF IT'S NECESSARY

**CONSIDERED OPTIONS**

THERE ARE AT LEAST FOUR DIFFERENT OPTIONS TO SOLVE THE PROBLEM: EUREKA, CONSUL, ZOOKEEPER, AND KUBERNETES

**DECISION OUTCOME**

THE DECISION IS TO USE EUREKA

**POSITIVE CONSEQUENCES**

- MEANS ADDING A DEPENDENCY ON MOST OF THE MICROSERVICES WITH A SHORT CONFIGURATION.

- ANYONE COULD MODIFY OR INTRODUCE IMPROVEMENTS ON THE DISCOVERY SERVER

**NEGATIVE CONSEQUENCES**

- MEANS IF THE FRAMEWORK OF THE APPLICATIONS CHANGES, THE CODE WILL NEED A HUGE REFACTORING.

**PROS AND CONS OF EACH OPTION**

CHECK THE PREVIOUS SECTIONS OF THE CHAPTER TO OBTAIN MORE DETAILS

**FIGURE 12.7** ADR about the decision of how to discover the microservices.

The purpose of this document is to enable anyone to understand why one approach was selected over another and which factors were considered during the decision-making process. All companies must create this documentation when such decisions are made that affect many teams or parts of the company.

## How Can This Pattern Be Integrated into the System?

To integrate Service Discovery into this platform's ecosystem, a new project must be created that contains the names and IP addresses of all application instances. All applications don't have to be registered on the Service Discovery component, as it's possible to utilize the current approach, where each microservice includes the host and port of others for communication. This is, however, the only way to leverage all the benefits fully.

The first step involves using the `curl` command with all the dependencies, the version of Java, and the application's name in the same manner shown in Listing 12.17.

```
→  ~ curl https://start.spring.io/starter.zip \
  -d dependencies=actuator,cloud-eureka-server \
  -d type=maven-project \
  -d language=java \
  -d bootVersion=3.4.5 \
  -d baseDir=discovery-server \
  -d groupId=com.twa \
  -d artifactId=discovery-server \
  -d name=discovery-server \
  -d description="Application that contains the service discovery." \
  -d javaVersion=21 \
  -d packaging=jar \
  -o discovery-server.zip
```

**LISTING 12.17** Command to create the discovery server project.

After the previous command is executed, it's necessary to decompress and import the project into an IDE and verify that the POM file looks as in Listing 12.18, where the most relevant dependencies are connected with the Eureka server and the actuator.

```xml
<?xml version="1.0" encoding="UTF-8"?>
<project xmlns="http://maven.apache.org/POM/4.0.0" xmlns:xsi="http://
www.w3.org/2001/XMLSchema-instance"
   xsi:schemaLocation="http://maven.apache.org/POM/4.0.0 https://maven.
apache.org/xsd/maven-4.0.0.xsd">
   <modelVersion>4.0.0</modelVersion>
   <parent>
        <groupId>org.springframework.boot</groupId>
        <artifactId>spring-boot-starter-parent</artifactId>
        <version>3.4.5</version>
        <relativePath/> <!-- lookup parent from repository -->
   </parent>
   <groupId>com.twa</groupId>
   <artifactId>discovery-server</artifactId>
   <version>0.0.1-SNAPSHOT</version>
   <name>discovery-server</name>
   <description>Application that contains the service discovery.</
description>
   <properties>
        <java.version>21</java.version>
        <spring-cloud.version>2024.0.1</spring-cloud.version>
   </properties>
   <dependencies>
        <dependency>
```

```
                        <groupId>org.springframework.boot</groupId>
                        <artifactId>spring-boot-starter-actuator</artifactId>
            </dependency>
            <dependency>
                        <groupId>org.springframework.cloud</groupId>
                        <artifactId>spring-cloud-starter-netflix-eureka-server</
artifactId>
            </dependency>

            <dependency>
                        <groupId>org.springframework.boot</groupId>
                        <artifactId>spring-boot-starter-test</artifactId>
                        <scope>test</scope>
            </dependency>
    </dependencies>
    <dependencyManagement>
            <dependencies>
                        <dependency>
                                    <groupId>org.springframework.cloud</groupId>
                                    <artifactId>spring-cloud-dependencies</artifactId>
                                    <version>${spring-cloud.version}</version>
                                    <type>pom</type>
                                    <scope>import</scope>
                        </dependency>
            </dependencies>
    </dependencyManagement>

    <build>
            <plugins>
                        <plugin>
                                    <groupId>org.springframework.boot</groupId>
                                    <artifactId>spring-boot-maven-plugin</artifactId>
                        </plugin>
            </plugins>
    </build>

</project>
```

**LISTING 12.18** POM file with the different dependencies.

The dependency related to the actuator doesn't require using Service Discovery, but it's good practice to know whether the application is functioning correctly and which version is running.

After importing the problems, some modifications are required to activate the Service Discovery pattern. The first modification involves opening the application's main class and adding the annotation @EnableEurekaServer, as shown in Listing 12.19.

```
package com.twa.discovery.server;

import org.springframework.boot.SpringApplication;
import org.springframework.boot.autoconfigure.SpringBootApplication;
import org.springframework.cloud.netflix.eureka.server.
EnableEurekaServer;

@EnableEurekaServer
@SpringBootApplication
public class DiscoveryServerApplication {
```

```
    public static void main(String[] args) {
        SpringApplication.run(DiscoveryServerApplication.class, args);
    }
}
```

**LISTING 12.19** Modifications on the main class to enable the support of the discovery server.

Creating an `application.yml` file with the configuration outlined in Listing 12.20 is necessary to configure the application, closely resembling the existing configuration.

```
spring:
  application:
    name: discovery-server
  profiles:
    active: native

server:
  port: 8761
  error:
    include-stacktrace: never
  servlet:
    context-path: /discovery-server

  compression:
    enabled: true
    min-response-size: 2048
    mime-types: application/json,application/xml,text/html,text/
xml,text/plain
management:
  endpoints:
    web:
      base-path: /management
      exposure:
        include: info,health

  info:
    java:
      enabled: false #change if you want to obtain information about Java
    os:
      enabled: false #change if you want to obtain information about OS
    env:
      enabled: true
  endpoint:
    health:
      show-details: always
      probes:
        enabled: false
info:
  app:
    name: "@project.artifactId@"
    version: "@project.version@"
  contact:
    email: "sacco.andres@gmail.com"
    slack: "adsacco"
```

**LISTING 12.20** Default configuration of the discovery server.

The next step is to introduce the modifications related to the Eureka configuration in the `application.yml` file, as shown in Listing 12.21.

```
# Previous configuration
eureka:
  client:
    register-with-eureka: false
    fetch-registry: false
```

**LISTING 12.21**  Configuration of the discovery server.

The configuration is short, but it may not be simple to understand the meaning of each attribute, so let's explain them:

- `register-with-eureka`: Indicates whether the application will register itself as a service on the Eureka server. In the case of Service Discovery, it is `false` because the application is the server itself.
- `fetch-registry`: Indicates whether it's necessary to download the list of registry services to use them. In the case of Service Discovery, it's not required.

To clarify any doubt about when each value must be set to `true` or `false`, Table 12.3 shows the typical combinations of these attributes in different scenarios.

**TABLE 12.3**  Explanation of the values of Service Discovery in different scenarios.

| Scenario | register-with-eureka | fetch-registry |
|---|---|---|
| Normal client | true | true |
| A gateway that only routes | false | true |
| Eureka server | false | false |
| Standalone app | false | false |

The next step is to run the application and check whether everything works correctly. Let's perform a simple `curl` request to the `info` endpoint, as shown in Listing 12.22.

```
➜  ~ curl http://localhost:8761/discovery-server/management/info

{
  "app": {
    "name": "discovery-server",
    "version": "0.0.1-SNAPSHOT"
  },
  "contact": {
    "email": "sacco.andres@gmail.com",
    "slack": "adsacco"
  }
}
```

**LISTING 12.22**  Command to check whether the actuator is working.

If everything functions correctly, the next step is to open a browser using the default Service Discovery URL, *http://localhost:8761/discovery-server/*. Figure 12.8 shows information about the uptime, resources available on the application, and registered applications.

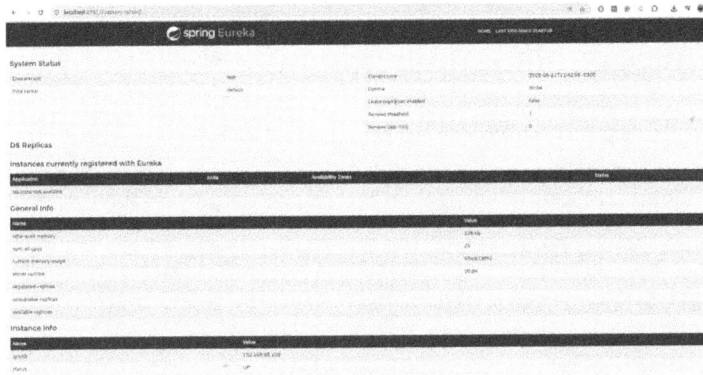

**FIGURE 12.8** Default Web page with information about the discovery server.

After modifying the server, it's time to change the different applications and register them. One comment: The modifications to `api-reservation` and `api-gateway` are similar. To avoid displaying code blocks in this chapter with duplicate code, the changes will only be shown once.

The modifications start with introducing the dependencies related to the Eureka client, as shown in Listing 12.23. As, in the case of `api-gateway`, the dependency management that appears in the listing is part of the base POM, it's not necessary to include it.

```
<project>
   <!-- Previous changes -->
   <dependencyManagement>
         <dependencies>
               <dependency>
                     <groupId>org.springframework.cloud</groupId>
                     <artifactId>spring-cloud-dependencies</artifactId>
                     <version>2024.0.1</version>
                     <type>pom</type>
                     <scope>import</scope>
               </dependency>
         </dependencies>
   </dependencyManagement>

   <dependencies>
         <!-- Other dependencies -->
         <dependency>
               <groupId>org.springframework.cloud</groupId>
               <artifactId>spring-cloud-starter-netflix-eureka-client</
artifactId>
         </dependency>
   </dependencies>

   <!-- Previous changes -->
</project>
```

**LISTING 12.23** Modifications to the application to use the discovery server.

The last modification involves making changes to the `application.yml` file, defining the server's base URL, and enabling the registration mechanism on Service Discovery, as shown in Listing 12.24.

```
spring:
  #Previous Configuration

  cloud:
    discovery:
      enabled: true

#Previous Configuration

eureka:
  client:
    register-with-eureka: true
    fetch-registry: true
    service-url:
      defaultZone: http://localhost:8761/discovery-server/eureka
```

**LISTING 12.24** Modifications to the configuration to register.

It's time to run the applications to see what the discovery server's Web page looks like. To do this, start running the server first and then the other applications. Remember that each application must register upon starting, so the server must be available.

**NOTE** *A good idea could be to create a Docker image to build the service discovery and the* `api-gateway` *to reduce the complexity of running multiple applications from the command line.*

If everything is running in the correct order, a page like in Figure 12.9 will appear on the server, listing the registered applications.

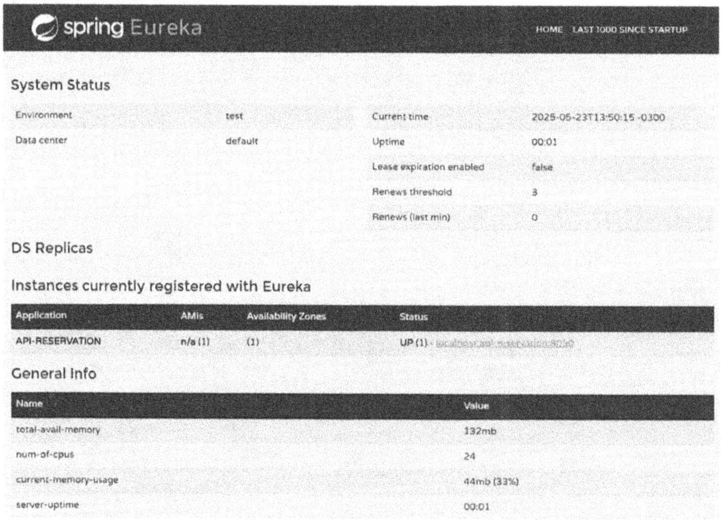

**FIGURE 12.9** Default Web page about the discovery server with applications registered.

With these changes working, it's possible to refer to any application with the name that appears on the Service Discovery component instead of the full URL. The name necessary to introduce the modifications is shown in Figure 12.25 With this in mind, let's make the changes to the `api-gateway` to use `api-reservation` instead of `localhost`. Listing 12.25 displays the changes to the `application.yml` file.

```
#Previous Configuration

#  ☑  Reservation with Circuit Breaker
- id: reservation
  uri: lb://API-RESERVATION
  predicates:
    - Path=/api/flights/reservation/**

#Previous Configuration
```

**LISTING 12.25** Modifications to use the name of the application.

The characters `lb` in the URI refer to *load balancing*; Service Discovery provides this feature by default. The next section will discuss load balancing in more depth.

The final step is to run all the applications and verify that everything continues to function as before the changes. Of course, the ideal scenario is to replicate this change across all the microservices of the system; however, for simplicity, this book only executes the changes on one microservice.

## LOAD BALANCING

Having multiple instances of the same microservices does not solve the problem of processing too many requests simultaneously if the system lacks a mechanism to distribute them equitably, thereby preventing some instances from receiving a high volume of requests while others remain idle.

The balancing or distribution of requests helps keep the system available during extreme events or when an application has only a few instances, all of which have a stable but considerable workload.

### What Does Balancing Requests Mean?

Balancing requests refers to the process of distributing incoming requests across multiple instances of the same service to ensure efficient resource utilization and maintain system responsiveness. Load balancers employ a range of strategies or algorithms to distribute requests, including round-robin, least connections, and health-based routing.

This process is beneficial when the system needs to stay available and flexible. If one part of the system stops working, the load balancer sends the requests to the parts that are still working, so users don't notice any problems. Additionally, when new parts are added to handle more users, the load balancer automatically starts using them without requiring any manual changes.

### What Ways Exist to Do This?

The two possible options to solve this specific problem are, firstly, using an external tool that gathers all requests and distributes them among the various instances of the same microservices, thereby preventing a large number of requests from being directed to the same cases. The other approach assigns the responsibility of selecting one of the instances to the different consumers, assuming they receive the list from the service discovery tool.

## External Tool

In this approach, the tool acts as a proxy, receiving all the requests and distributing them according to the number of instances that are registered and the number of requests that each particular instance processes in a short period. Figure 12.10 shows the interaction between the different components of the communication process.

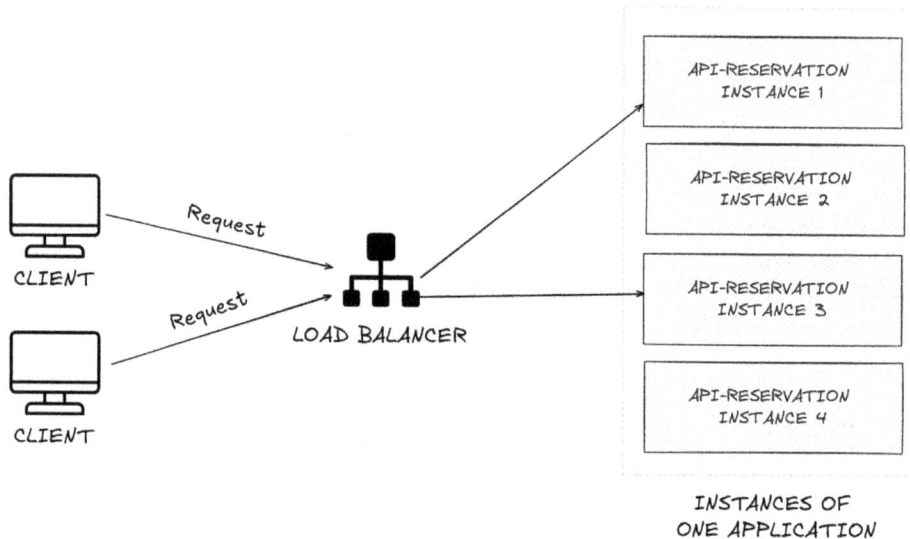

**FIGURE 12.10** Representation of using a load balancer like an external tool.

Using this type of tool offers several benefits, such as the ability to change the load-balancing algorithm without notifying all consumers; it is agnostic to the technology used by various microservices in some cases, and it's simple to implement since it's not necessary to make changes to the microservices. Someone does, however, need to ensure that it is kept up to date and operational.

Some of the most relevant tools that work with this approach are:

- NGNIX: A high-performance reverse proxy and Web server that excels at load balancing HTTP, TCP, and UDP traffic. NGINX distributes incoming requests across multiple backend servers using various algorithms such as round-robin, least connections, or IP hash.
- Kubernetes: This automatically distributes network traffic across multiple healthy Pod replicas using ClusterIP, NodePort, or LoadBalancer service types. Kubernetes also supports Ingress controllers for HTTP/HTTPS routing and external load balancers for high availability. This ensures reliable and scalable access to services in dynamic environments, making Kubernetes ideal for cloud-native architectures.

NOTE *Other tools that can be used that are not mentioned in this section are HAProxy, Envoy, AWS Elastic Load Balancing (ELB), Google Cloud Load Balancing, and Azure Load Balancer.*

To select any of these tools, it's necessary to analyze whether they align with the Service Discovery approach, as these two topics work in tandem. Therefore, it's not a good idea to choose Spring Cloud Eureka for Service Discovery and then NGINX for load balancing.

## Consumer

On the opposite side, there is a tool that intercepts all requests: the load balancer on the consumer side, which delegates the responsibility of obtaining the list of instances and balancing the number of requests that a particular client sends to a set of instances of a microservice. Figure 12.11 shows the interaction between all the components that interact in the communication.

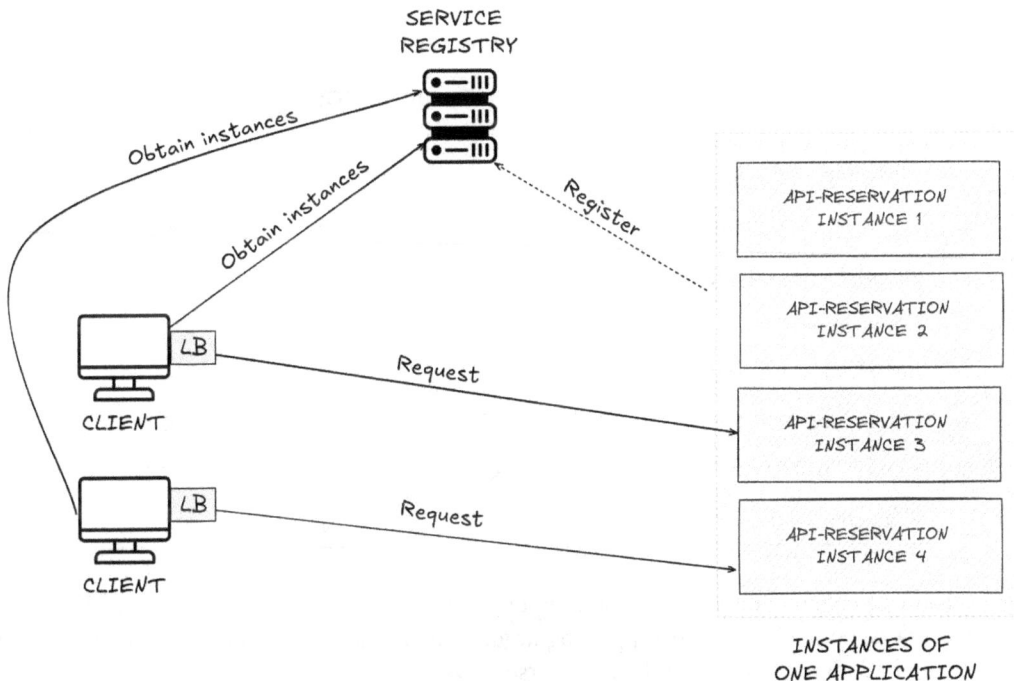

**FIGURE 12.11** Representation of using a load balancer on the client/consumer.

The tools employed in this approach are especially effective when integrated with a Service Discovery mechanism that can dynamically provide an up-to-date list of available service instances. In the context of this book, such a mechanism is already in place, ensuring that external tools such as API gateways or load balancers can route traffic intelligently, balance the load efficiently, and respond to failures gracefully. This dynamic discovery enables the infrastructure to adapt automatically to changes in the system, such as service scaling or instance failures, without requiring manual configuration or redeployment.

Some of the tools that work with this approach and Spring Boot are:

• Spring Cloud LoadBalancer[8]: A modern client-side load-balancing library created by the Spring team to replace Ribbon. It integrates seamlessly with Spring Boot and Spring Cloud, supports Service Discovery, and works with `RestTemplate`, `WebClient`, and reactive applications.

## What Is the Best Option for a Scenario?

Load balancing is a crucial aspect to consider when multiple instances of the same application are involved, particularly in the event of significant events that could impact the entire system if a single instance receives all the requests. When choosing among the different options, various factors need to be considered, including modifications to the source code, potential issues introduced when testing other features, and the level of community support in case problems are discovered. The following table summarizes the main pros and cons of the different options.

**TABLE 12.4** Main things to consider when choosing a load-balancing option.

| Feature | Spring Cloud Load Balancer | NGINX | Kubernetes |
|---|---|---|---|
| Client-side load balancing | ✓ | ✗ | ✗ |
| Server-side load balancing | ✗ | ✓ | ✓ |
| Spring Boot integration | ✓ | ✗ | ✗ |
| Discovery aware | ✓ | ✗ | ✓ |
| Retry logic | ✓ | ✗ | ✗ |
| Circuit breaker | ✗ | ✗ | ✗ |
| Supports WebClient | ✓ | ✓ | ✓ |
| Production ready | ✓ | ✓ | ✓ |

The distinctions among the various options are clearly outlined in the preceding table; nonetheless, compiling all the supporting arguments into a single document, as illustrated in Figure 12.12, provides a comprehensive perspective.

This document allows readers to understand the rationale behind the selected approach and review the key factors that influenced the decision-making process.

## How Can This Pattern Be Integrated into the System?

The changes necessary to introduce are relatively minor, considering that most of the effort relies on having a discovery server in place. To activate the load balancer on any project, it is necessary to add a dependency to the POM file, as shown in Listing 12.26.

---

[8]https://docs.spring.io/spring-cloud-commons/reference/spring-cloud-commons/loadbalancer.html

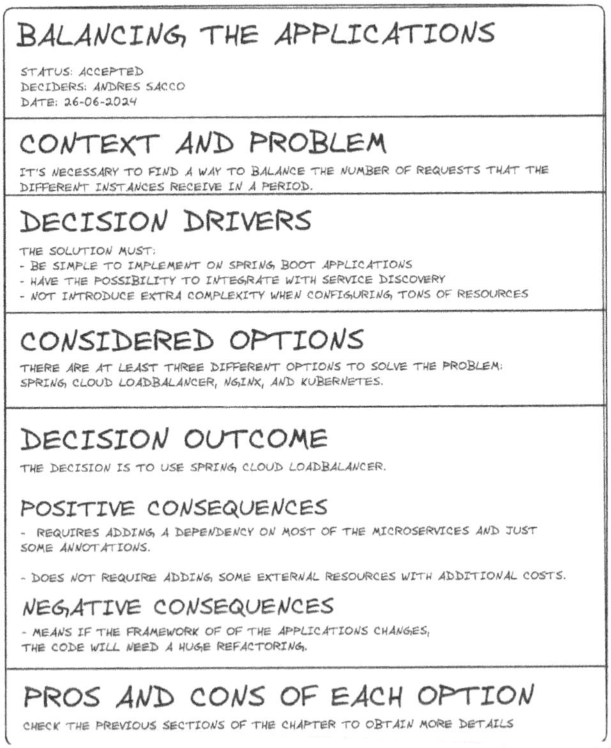

*FIGURE 12.12* ADR about the decision of which load-balancing option to use.

```
#Previous Configuration

<dependency>
    <groupId>org.springframework.cloud</groupId>
    <artifactId>spring-cloud-starter-loadbalancer</artifactId>
</dependency>

#Previous Configuration
```

*LISTING 12.26* Add dependencies related to the load balancer.

The previous dependency is not necessary to include in the API gateway because `spring-cloud-starter-gateway` has a transitive dependency on the load balancer.

The change necessary to introduce is to activate the load balancer on the client responsible for communicating with other applications. In this book, it is the class that generates the `WebClient`. Listing 12.27 shows that it is necessary to include the annotation `@LoadBalanced` to indicate that communication will be balanced considering the elements present in the Service Discovery component.

```
#Previous imports

import org.springframework.cloud.client.loadbalancer.LoadBalanced;

public abstract class TWAConnector {
```

```
    @LoadBalanced
    protected WebClient getConnector(
            HostConfiguration hostConfiguration, EndpointConfiguration
endpointConfiguration) {
        #Previous code
    }
}
```

**LISTING 12.27** Enable the load balancer on the creation of the client.

The next step is to introduce the modifications to the different connectors to indicate the name of the service registered on the Eureka server using the annotation `@LoadBalancerClient`. Listing 12.28 shows the modification on one of the connectors, but the changes are similar across all of them.

```
#Previous imports

import org.springframework.cloud.loadbalancer.annotation.
LoadBalancerClient;

@Component
@LoadBalancerClient(name = "api-clusters")
public class ClusterConnector extends TWAConnector {
    #Previous code
}
```

**LISTING 12.28** Activate the load balancer on the connector.

The value of the attribute name of the annotation must match precisely with the value on the service discovery; otherwise, the load balancer will not function properly, but the platform will not experience communication issues between the microservices.

In cases where the method of communicating with other applications changes from `WebClient` or `RestTemplate` to `FeignClient`, it will be necessary to update the dependency and most annotations; however, the changes are straightforward to implement.

## SUMMARY

In this chapter, all the modifications necessary to support different patterns, such as Service Discovery, were shown. The idea is to eliminate the need to remember a specific URL and instead use something such as DNS, which refers to all the instances of the same microservice. This is extremely useful considering that most applications have more than one instance in production environments.

Related to the previous pattern is the new, popular approach of load balancing on the client side, which delegates the responsibility to a component within the infrastructure to determine which instance needs to redirect the request. Of course, it's possible to combine the classic approach with this new one, as not all microservices will adopt or migrate to this method.

Last but not least, the API Gateway shows how it's possible to hide all the URLs and paths behind a straightforward application that is responsible for receiving all the requests and acting according to the rules defined in the configuration.

To conclude this book, it's essential to know that it's not necessary to implement everything from the beginning, because in some cases, the time to investigate one aspect or the costs associated with having a service to externalize the configuration could affect the cost. Try to integrate everything that can be easily implemented without relying on an external service. If a possible problem is detected, implement the solution that addresses this issue only at that point.

APPENDIX A

# Setup Enviroment Tools

This book utilizes several tools to run the examples. This appendix guides the reader on the installation of essential tools, excluding those that have been covered within the individual chapters.

## INSTALL JAVA

Before starting development, and following the instructions in this book, it is necessary to install the Java Development Kit (JDK). Keep in mind that there are various options available for the JDK:

- *OracleJDK*[1]: This version was free until Java 11. In later versions, it can be used for development and testing, but a license is required for production use. Since Oracle owns Sun Microsystems, this version of the JDK provides the latest bug fixes and new features.
- *OpenJDK*[2]: When Oracle acquired Sun Microsystems, it introduced this open-source alternative, which is accessible to all developers and can be used in any environment without restrictions. The primary issue with this version is the delay in releasing bug patches for non-critical cases.
- *Others*: There are many other vendors of the JDK. For instance, Amazon Web Services (AWS) offers *Amazon Corretto*[3], which is based on OpenJDK and enhances the performance of applications within AWS environments.

Throughout all the chapters of this book, OpenJDK is used. Any preferred alternative may be chosen, however. The installation methods for the JDK vary depending on the operating system:

- For macOS and Linux, *brew*[4] can be used—a tool for installing and updating various software packages.

[1]https://www.oracle.com/java/technologies/
[2]https://openjdk.java.net/
[3]https://aws.amazon.com/es/corretto/
[4]https://brew.sh/

➜   ~ brew install openjdk

Another option is to utilize SDKMAN!, which is similar to brew and offers multiple versions and implementations of the JDK.

➜   ~ sdk install java 21-open

- For Windows platforms, two options are available:
  - Install brew and run the same command as on macOS/Linux.
  - Install *AdoptOpenJDK*[5], which provides OpenJDK for various platforms. An MSI file is available for Windows, which simplifies the installation process.

Once the JDK is installed, verify the availability of the Java version on the system by typing the following:

➜   ~ java -version
openjdk 21 2023-09-19
OpenJDK Runtime Environment (build 21+35-2513)
OpenJDK 64-Bit Server VM (build 21+35-2513, mixed mode, sharing)

No specific version of Java is required to run these examples. All examples are, however, written using JDK 21. JDK 17 or higher can be used, which meets the requirements for Spring Boot 3.0. Despite this, many developers continue to use version 11 in production, with approximately 61% following this trend, according to Snyk[6].

## INSTALL MAVEN

Maven must be installed on the machine to run or follow the examples effectively. It is a valuable tool for efficiently managing and resolving dependency conflicts across various versions of a project.

Various methods exist for installing Maven, depending on the operating system. Some may require manual steps, such as downloading it from the official Web site[7] and configuring environment variables to recognize the mvn command. For the sake of simplicity, however, in this book, how to install it using package manager tools is demonstrated:

- On macOS/Linux, Homebrew[8] can be used—a tool designed for installing and updating various packages.

  ➜   ~ brew install maven

Additionally, installation can be done via SDKMAN![9], which operates similarly to Homebrew and offers a straightforward method for installing various libraries or tools.

  ➜   ~ sdk install maven

---

[5]https://adoptopenjdk.net/releases.html
[6]https://snyk.io/jvm-ecosystem-report-2021/
[7]https://maven.apache.org/download.cgi
[8]https://brew.sh/
[9]https://sdkman.io/

Finally, there's another method exclusive to Ubuntu distributions.

➜   ~ sudo apt-get install maven

- For Windows platforms, two installation options are available:
  - The first option is to install Homebrew and run the same command as on macOS/Linux.
  - The second option involves manually downloading Maven, unzipping its contents into a directory, and creating an environment variable named MAVEN_HOME that points to the bin directory inside the created Maven folder.

Once the Maven installation is complete, verify the version on the system by typing the following:

```
➜ ~ mvn --version
Apache Maven 3.9.1
Maven home: /usr/share/maven
```

## INSTALL GIT

This tool serves as a version control system, monitoring changes introduced by various individuals. While not essential for accessing the book's source code, since GitHub provides a download button for all repositories, Git is included as an option for those who wish to fork the repository and make modifications.

In the preceding section, it was noted that various package manager tools can be employed to install this tool:

- brew:

  ➜   ~ brew install git

- SDKMAN!:

  ➜   ~ sdk install git

For those who prefer an alternative, Git's[10] official Web site offers an executable download for Windows that installs all necessary components.

Once the tool is installed, the version can be verified on the system by typing the following command:

```
➜ ~ git --version
git version 2.34.1
```

To streamline commits and avoid the need to input a username and email address each time, these settings can be configured globally using the following commands:

```
➜ ~ git config --global user.name "John Doe"
➜ ~ git config --global user.email "johndoe@example.com"
```

---

[10]https://git-scm.com/downloads

## INSTALL INTELLIJ

Installation instructions for this IDE can be found on the official Web page[11], which lists the minimum system requirements and compatible operating systems. There are two versions of the IDE to consider: Community Edition, which is entirely free and supports various plugins, and Ultimate, which is paid and offers additional features not relevant to this book. Figure A.1 shows the official Web site to download the IDE.

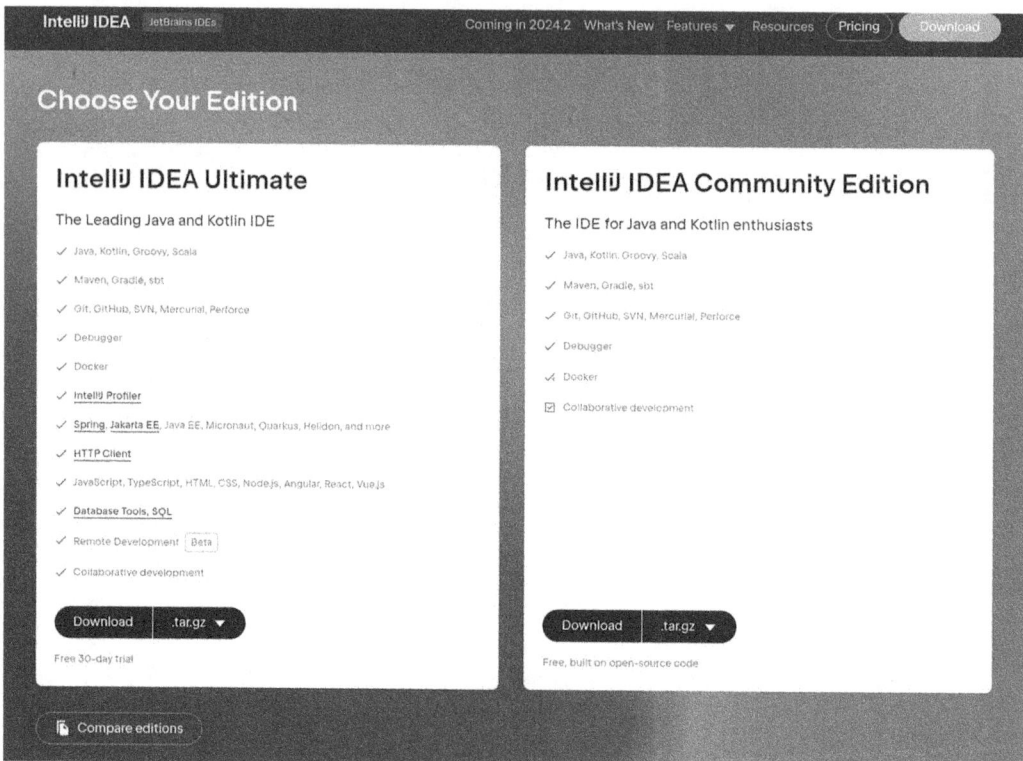

*FIGURE A.1* Official site to download the IDE.

Some plugins that may be helpful to install on this IDE include:

• Maven Helper[12]
• GitToolBox[13]
• Docker[14]

To install one of these plugins, navigate to Preferences -> Plugins, locate the desired plugin by its name, and proceed with the installation. Figure A.2 shows the section to install the plugins.

---

[11]https://www.jetbrains.com/idea/download/#section=linux
[12]https://plugins.jetbrains.com/plugin/7179-maven-helper
[13]https://plugins.jetbrains.com/plugin/7499-gittoolbox
[14]https://plugins.jetbrains.com/plugin/7724-docker

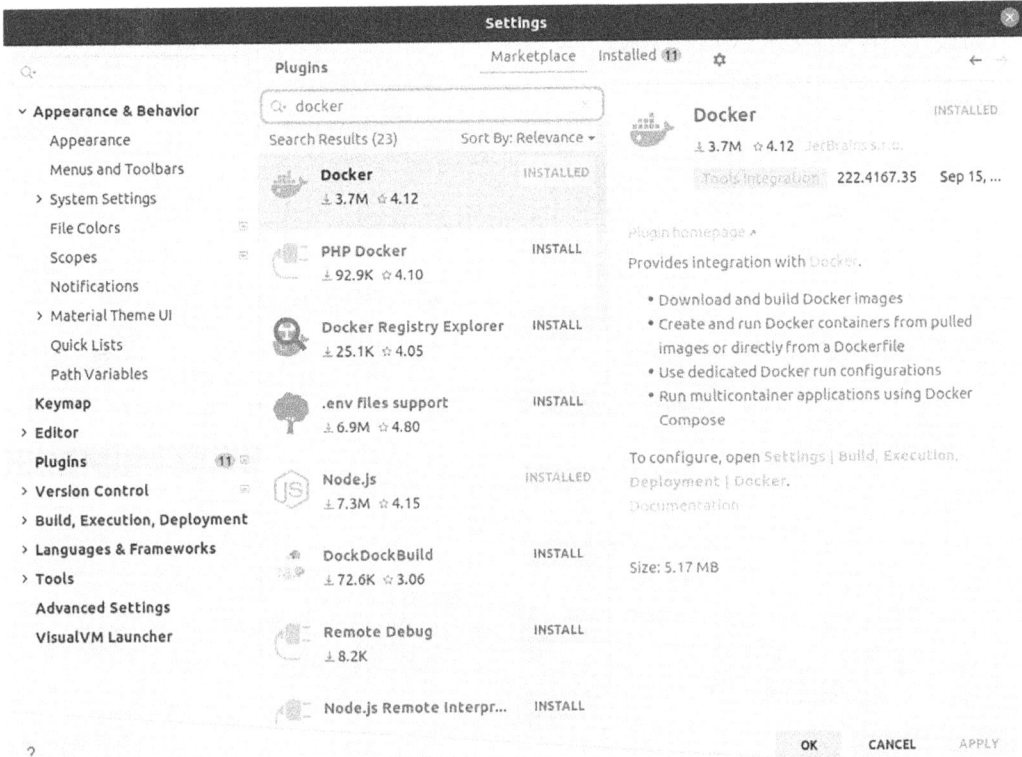

**FIGURE A.2** IntelliJ plugin installation.

## INSTALL DOCKER

Docker is a leading choice for running container engines on Linux. In this book, leveraging Docker simplifies the installation process for various databases and microservices, enabling effortless deployment and removal by simply stopping the container.

**NOTE** *The purpose of this book isn't to delve into every advantage and drawback of Docker, as numerous existing resources, including books, articles, and videos, thoroughly cover the technology's intricacies.*

To install Docker, the process varies depending on the operating system. For Linux distributions, there are various native installation methods. For Windows and macOS, Docker Desktop is utilized, adding a layer between the operating system and Docker to enable container execution. Refer to the official Web site[15] for detailed instructions.

Once this tool is installed, verify the version on the system by typing the following:

```
→ ~ docker --version
Docker version 26.1.2, build 211e74b
```

---

[15]http://docs.docker.com/install

All available container images can be found on Docker Hub's official Web page[16]. For testing purposes, it is recommended to start with commonly used images, such as `hello-world`, to ensure smooth operation.

```
➜   ~ docker pull hello-world:latest
➜   ~ docker run hello-world:latest
Hello from Docker!
This message shows that your installation appears to be working
correctly.

To generate this message, Docker took the following steps:
1. The Docker client contacted the Docker daemon.
2. The Docker daemon pulled the "hello-world" image from the Docker Hub.
   (amd64)
3. The Docker daemon created a new container from that image which runs
   the executable that produces the output you are currently reading.
4. The Docker daemon streamed that output to the Docker client, which
   sent it to your terminal.

To try something more ambitious, you can run an Ubuntu container with:
$ docker run -it ubuntu bash

Share images, automate workflows, and more with a free Docker ID:
https://hub.docker.com/

For more examples and ideas, visit:
https://docs.docker.com/get-started/
```

To delve deeper into various commands, explore the official Web site, which provides a cheat sheet[17]. It elucidates vital commands and their distinct components.

---

[16]https://hub.docker.com/
[17]https://docs.docker.com/get-started/docker_cheatsheet.pdf

# RECOMMENDED AND ALTERNATIVES TOOLS

This appendix will discuss the primary tools and alternative options presented throughout the various chapters.

## DEVELOPMENT

- IntelliJ[1]: IntelliJ is the most widely used IDE for Java. IntelliJ IDEA Community Edition provides all the essential features needed to begin working with Java and Spring. Additionally, there is the Ultimate version, which includes extra features and additional plugins.
- Eclipse[2]: Eclipse is another popular IDE for Java development and is well known among veteran developers. Most of its plugins are free and maintained by a vast community of developers who frequently update them. Additionally, there are numerous plugins available for Spring development.
- NetBeans[3]: This is another option for developing applications using various programming languages. Currently, it lacks a large community of users, as other options offer better user interfaces and plugins that cater to the needs of most developers. Some developers, however, use it when learning their first programming language.

## DATABASES

No particular option is highly recommended to administer the database, but the most relevant, depending on the type of database, are the following:

### Relational Database

- MySQL Workbench[4]: This is one of the most commonly used interfaces for executing queries and performing administrative tasks on various MySQL databases. This tool allows

---

[1]https://www.jetbrains.com/idea/
[2]https://www.eclipse.org/downloads/
[3]https://netbeans.apache.org/
[4]https://www.mysql.com/products/workbench/

monitoring resource usage for each database, modeling different tables and their relationships, and explaining each query.

- SQLyog[5]: This is a powerful alternative to MySQL Workbench, offering additional features such as comparing data between different databases or tables, synchronizing the schema from an SQL file or another database, and scheduling daily backups.

## Non-Relational Database

## MongoDB

- Compass[6]: This tool is the official solution for connecting to, querying, optimizing, and analyzing MongoDB's performance. It can be installed on multiple operating systems and features an easy-to-use user interface. Additionally, it provides a straightforward interface to visualize the impact of executing each query.
- Studio 3T[7]: This is an alternative to Compass, which many developers used initially when other tools didn't offer an exemplary user interface. Its interface is similar to tools such as MySQL Workbench and pgAdmin III. Queries can be run without blocking the user interface.

## Redis

- Redis Insight[8]: This is a free official tool for connecting to and interacting with the Redis database. It offers features such as viewing the size of stored data, checking data usage with graphs, and analyzing resource usage, such as CPU and memory. This tool provides all the elements needed to administer a Redis database locally or remotely. An exciting feature is the ability to configure an existing database or download and create one using the tool.

## REQUEST API

- Postman[9]: This is an easy-to-use tool for testing REST endpoints. It allows defining variables that represent environments or other parameters, such as the current date. Tests can also be scheduled to run at specific times.
- Insomnia[10]: This is another alternative tool for requesting REST endpoints. One of the main differences from Postman is that this tool supports multiple protocols, including REST, gRPC, SOAP, and GraphQL. It offers features and a user interface similar to Postman but can switch between at least two themes.
- curl[11]: This is a simple command-line tool for calling REST endpoints. This tool is compatible with most common operating systems and serves as an alternative to other tools.

---

[5]https://webyog.com/product/sqlyog/
[6]https://www.mongodb.com/products/compass
[7]https://studio3t.com/
[8]https://redis.com/es/redis-enterprise/redisinsight
[9]https://www.postman.com/
[10]https://insomnia.rest/
[11]https://curl.se/download.html

# OPENING A PROJECT

This book presents examples illustrating various concepts. These projects can be developed by following the guidelines outlined in the chapters or obtained from the official source code repository. To import them into an integrated development environment (IDE), refer to the instructions provided in this appendix.

**NOTE** *IntelliJ is the recommended IDE for this book; therefore, all instructions are tailored to it.*

To execute all the projects in this book, they must be installed on a local machine, preferably with JDK 17 or a later version. There are no specific requirements regarding the distribution. Detailed guidance on the necessary installation tools can be found in *Appendix A*.

Figure C.1 illustrates how to open a file or an existing project in IntelliJ IDEA. To select a specific project, navigate to File > Open....

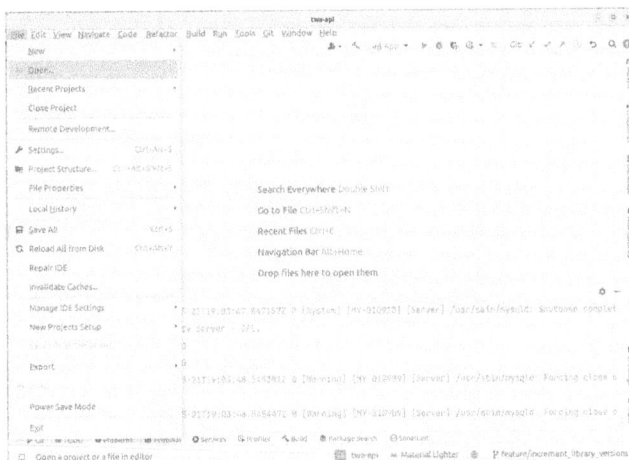

**FIGURE C.1** Menu option to open a project.

Upon clicking Open…, a popup like that shown in Figure C.2 will appear, allowing the selection of the project's location for import into the IDE.

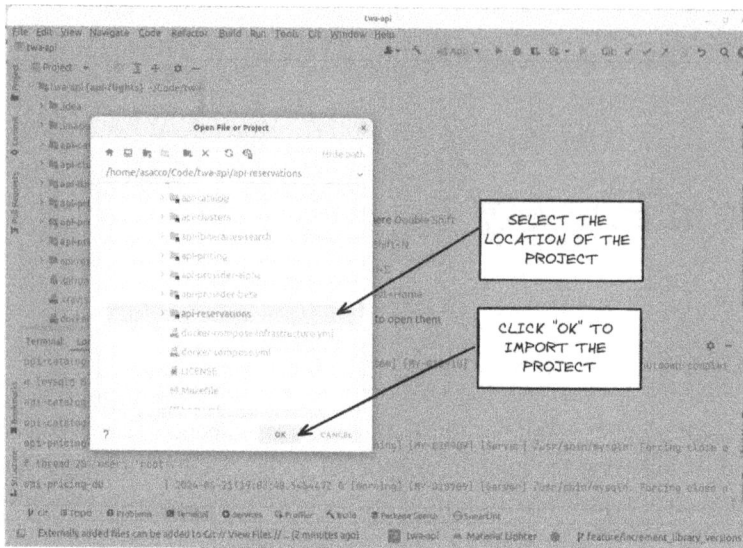

**FIGURE C.2** Pop-up window to select the project to import.

After importing the project into the IDE, it is possible to browse the various packages to locate the main class, which is typically found in the root package. Figure C.3 displays the complete project structure of the application discussed in this book.

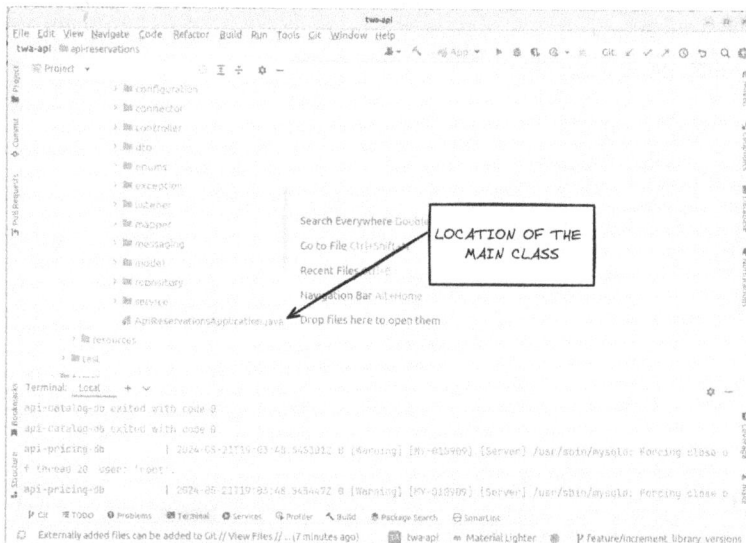

**FIGURE C.3** Location of the main class to execute the application.

To run the application, click on the main class and select the option Run Application, or run it using the terminal with the command mvn spring-boot:run.

# INSTALL AND CONFIGURE RELATIONAL DATABASE

This appendix explains how to install the MySQL database, which is used to persist information throughout various chapters of the book. It outlines two approaches for setting up and loading data into the database: installing MySQL locally or using Docker. While the examples focus on MySQL, other relational databases, such as PostgreSQL or SQL Server, can also be used without restriction.

**NOTE**

*MySQL is a relational database management system (RDBMS) that was released in 1994 by MySQL AB, now owned by Oracle. Several features make it a popular choice among developers:*
- *It's free to use.*
- *It offers excellent performance, handling a significant number of operations efficiently.*
- *According to Stack Overflow's 2021[1] survey, approximately 50% of developers use this database in some applications. This widespread usage means that many people can detect and report any issues.*

To use the database in the application, follow these steps.

## STEP 1: INSTALL THE DATABASE

The first step is to download and run the MySQL database installer. MySQL supports multiple operating systems, including Windows, macOS, and various Linux distributions. The installer can be downloaded from the official MySQL Web site, following the installation instructions[2] specific to the operating system. It is essential to set up a username and password for the administrator account, which will be used later to connect to the database in step 3.

---

[1]https://insights.stackoverflow.com/survey/2021#technology
[2]https://dev.mysql.com/doc/refman/8.0/en/installing.html

Many developers are reluctant to install databases because they consume system resources and may be used infrequently. For instance, having a local database is required to complete the exercises in this book; however, MySQL might not be used again after finishing the book. To simplify database management without a permanent installation, Docker offers a practical solution.

First, visit the Docker Hub Web site to locate a specific version of MySQL[3]. It's recommended not to use the "latest" tag, as the most recent version might have issues and may not run correctly. Instead, specify a particular version to ensure stability.

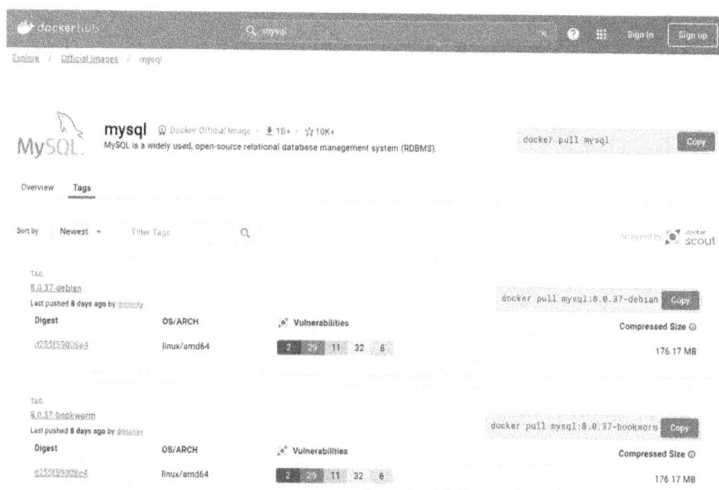

**FIGURE D.1** Docker Hub's Web page.

After selecting the database version, the next step involves downloading the image locally using the `docker pull` command. Listing D-1 show the result of the execute the command to pull the image.

```
→  ~ docker pull mysql/mysql-server:8.0.28
8.0.28: Pulling from mysql/mysql-server
221c7ea50c9e: Pull complete
d32a20f3a6af: Pull complete
28749a63c815: Pull complete
3cdab959ca41: Pull complete
30ceffa70af4: Pull complete
e4b028b699c1: Pull complete
3abed4e8adad: Pull complete
Digest: sha256:6fca505a0d41c7198b577628584e01d3841707c3292499baae87037f886c9fa2
Status: Downloaded newer image for mysql/mysql-server:8.0.28
docker.io/mysql/mysql-server:8.0.28
```

**LISTING D-1** Result of pulling the image from the Docker Hub

The final step is to run the image of the downloaded database. Listing D-2 shows the execution of the database with all the parameters.

---

[3]https://hub.docker.com/_/mysql?tab=tags

```
→  ~ docker run mysql/mysql-server:8.0.28  -e MYSQL_ROOT_
PASSWORD=password
[Entrypoint] MySQL Docker Image 8.0.28-1.2.7-server
[Entrypoint] No password option specified for new database.
[Entrypoint]  A random onetime password will be generated.
[Entrypoint] Initializing database
........
[Entrypoint] MySQL init process done. Ready for start up.

[Entrypoint] Starting MySQL 8.0.28-1.2.7-server
2022-04-08T03:01:52.053869Z 0 [System] [MY-010116] [Server] /usr/sbin/
mysqld (mysqld 8.0.28) starting as process 1
2022-04-08T03:01:52.061845Z 1 [System] [MY-013576] [InnoDB] InnoDB
initialization has started.
2022-04-08T03:01:52.208388Z 1 [System] [MY-013577] [InnoDB] InnoDB
initialization has ended.
2022-04-08T03:01:52.411922Z 0 [Warning] [MY-010068] [Server] CA
certificate ca.pem is self signed.
2022-04-08T03:01:52.411987Z 0 [System] [MY-013602] [Server] Channel
mysql_main configured to support TLS. Encrypted connections are now
supported for this channel.
2022-04-08T03:01:52.433058Z 0 [System] [MY-010931] [Server] /usr/sbin/
mysqld: ready for connections. Version: '8.0.28'  socket: '/var/lib/
mysql/mysql.sock'  port: 3306  MySQL Community Server - GPL.
2022-04-08T03:01:52.433067Z 0 [System] [MY-011323] [Server] X Plugin
ready for connections. Bind-address: '::' port: 33060, socket: /var/run/
mysqld/mysqlx.sock
```

*LISTING D-2* – Run a MySQL container with all the configuration

Rest assured, once the database is running, it becomes accessible through the same port as a locally installed instance.

## STEP 2: INSTALL THE CLIENT TO ACCESS THE DATABASE

To work with MySQL, a client is required to facilitate the creation of schemas, insertion of data, and verification of functionality. There are many client options available—some free and others offering short trial periods. In this book, MySQL Workbench is recommended, as it is the official and most popular tool for managing MySQL databases.

Refer to the official MySQL Workbench documentation to download the installer. For system requirements and installation instructions, visit the MySQL Workbench installation Web page on the MySQL site[4].

## STEP 3: CONFIGURE THE CONNECTION

After installing the database and the client, open MySQL Workbench and create a new connection using the credentials set up in step 1. If the installer did not prompt to set up a username and password, the default credentials might be root for the username and an empty password.

---

[4]https://www.mysql.com/

As shown in Figure D.2, MySQL Workbench has a button with a plus icon. Click this button to create a new connection.

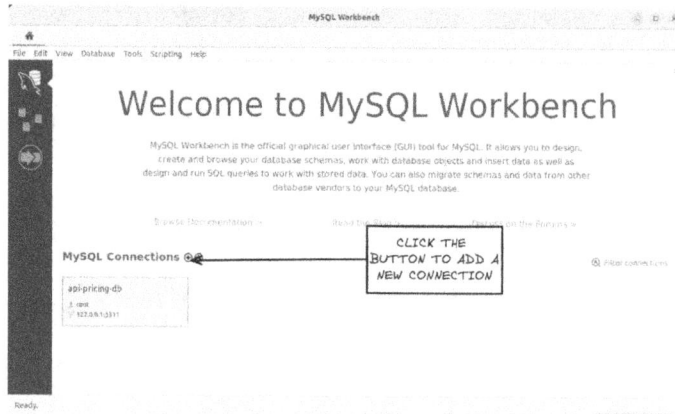

**FIGURE D.2** Client to access the database.

After clicking the button, a new window will appear, similar to Figure D.3, where the details for the new connection can be entered. In this window, the following information must be provided:

- Connection Name: Any name for the connection, as there are no restrictions on the name.
- Hostname: This is typically `localhost` or `127.0.0.1`.
- Port: The default MySQL port, which is `3306`.
- Username: A MySQL username (e.g., `root`).

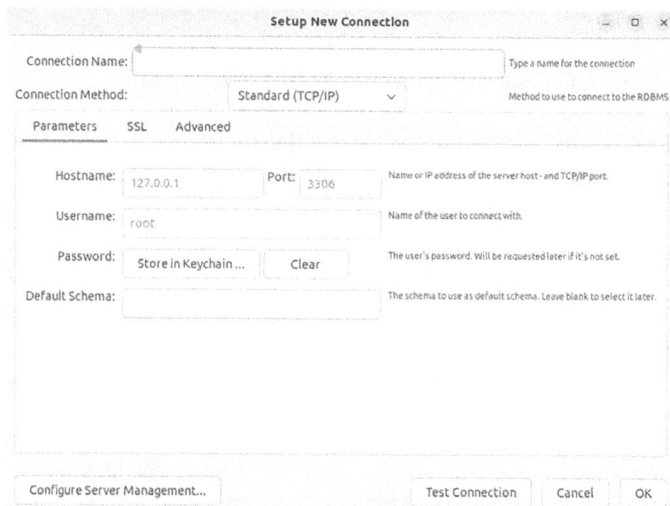

**FIGURE D.3** Create a new connection.

Click the Test Connection button to verify that everything is working correctly. A popup will appear prompting for the connection password. To set the password and avoid entering it again in the future, click the Store in Keychain… button. This will prompt for the password, which will then be saved securely on the machine.

After testing the connection, click OK to save all the connection information.

## STEP 4: CREATE THE SCHEMA

Once a connection is created in MySQL Workbench, as shown in Figure D.4, it can be double-clicked to access the database and perform the desired operations.

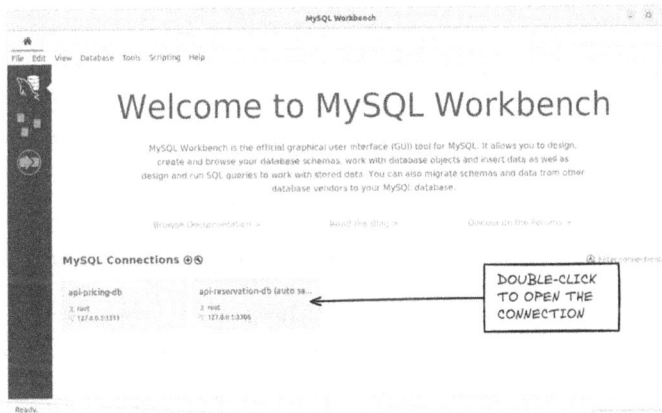

**FIGURE D.4** Active connections on MySQL Workbench.

The first task to perform in the database is to create a new schema that will contain all the tables. This is done by clicking the button with a plus icon and a database symbol. When the form appears, enter the name of the new database. Finally, clicking Apply creates an empty schema, which will be populated with different tables in the next step.

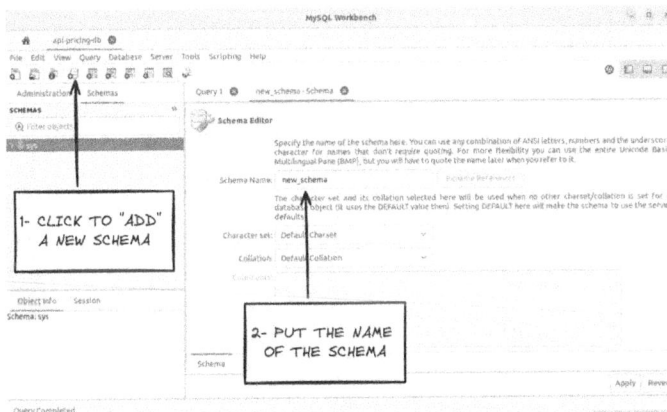

**FIGURE D.5** Create a new schema.

## STEP 5: LOAD THE DATA

The final step in this process is to create and populate the schema structure with the information used in the various chapters. This can be done by navigating to the code repository, where different folders are organized by chapter. There is also a folder named `database` that contains all the scripts. Execute these scripts on the database to set up the necessary schema and data.

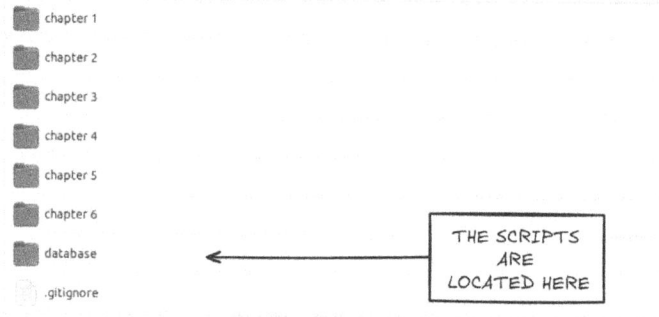

**FIGURE D.6** Source repository with the scripts of the database.

Inside this folder, various files with specific names are available. Each file is intended to be executed in numerical order. The first script to execute is `V1.0_init_database.sql`.

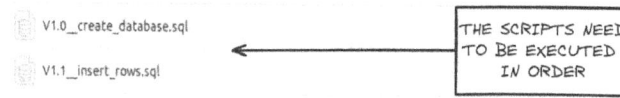

**FIGURE D.7** Different scripts that need to be executed on the database.

The final step in setting up the database with all the information needed for the book is to open and execute each script. To do this, drag and drop the files into MySQL Workbench, and the application will open them, displaying their contents. After that, simply press the button to run the scripts in the database. Repeat this process for each script to complete the setup.

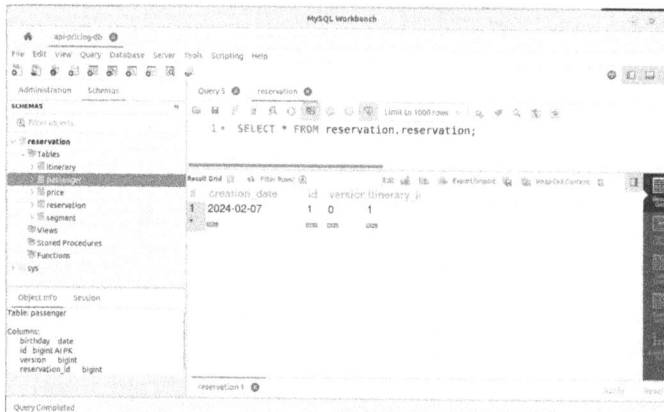

**FIGURE D.8** Loading the script on MySQL Workbench.

# INSTALL AND CONFIGURE NON-RELATIONAL DATABASE

The main issue with this type of database is that the installation process can be time-consuming and involves executing various instructions, depending on the specific database. It is recommended that Docker be used to run different images, and the UI console, which, in some cases, such as Redis Insight, does not need to be installed on the machine.

## REDIS

This is a non-relational database designed for high performance, offering various installation options.

One installation method involves using the popular tool brew, which installs and runs the database locally. If the database is no longer needed after completing this book, however, it should be removed. Listing E.1 displays the command used and the resulting output.

```
→  ~  brew install redis
==> Installing redis
==> Pouring redis--7.0.4.x86_64_linux.bottle.tar.gz
==> Caveats

To restart redis after an upgrade:
  brew services restart redis
Or, if you don't want/need a background service you can just run:
  /home/linuxbrew/.linuxbrew/opt/redis/bin/redis-server /home/
linuxbrew/.linuxbrew/etc/redis.conf
==> node
Bash completion has been installed to:
  /home/linuxbrew/.linuxbrew/etc/bash_completion.d
```

**LISTING E.1** Installation using brew.

Once the installation process is complete, the database will run on port 5432. To stop or remove it, use brew's remove or stop command.

The second option is to create a Docker Compose file, as shown in Listing E.2, that runs both the database and Redis Insight, a tool for accessing and interacting with Redis.

```
version: '3.1'

services:
 api-reservation-db:
    container_name: api-reservation-db
    image: redis:6.2
    restart: always
    ports:
      - 6379:6379

 redisinsight:
    image: redislabs/redisinsight:1.12.1
    ports:
      - '8001:8001'
```

*LISTING E.2* – Docker Compose file to run Redis.

After creating a file, just run it using the command `docker-compose up`. Then, go to the browser and enter `localhost:8001`, the port that Redis Insight uses.

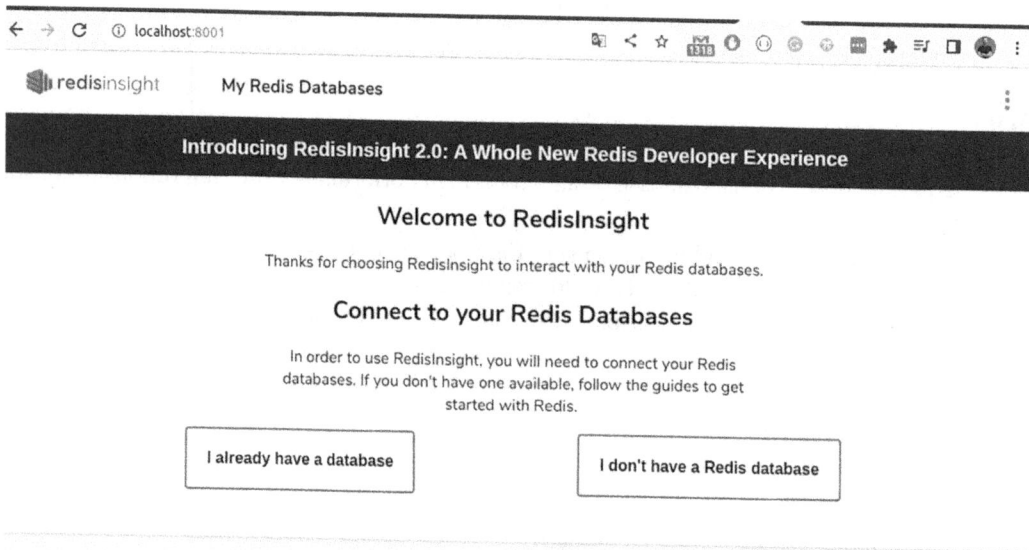

*FIGURE E.1* Redis Insight home page.

The next step is establishing a connection between the tool and the running database instance. Press the I already have a database button to see a Web page with multiple connection options. These options range from connecting to a database hosted locally to specific services on various cloud providers, such as Amazon Web Services (AWS).

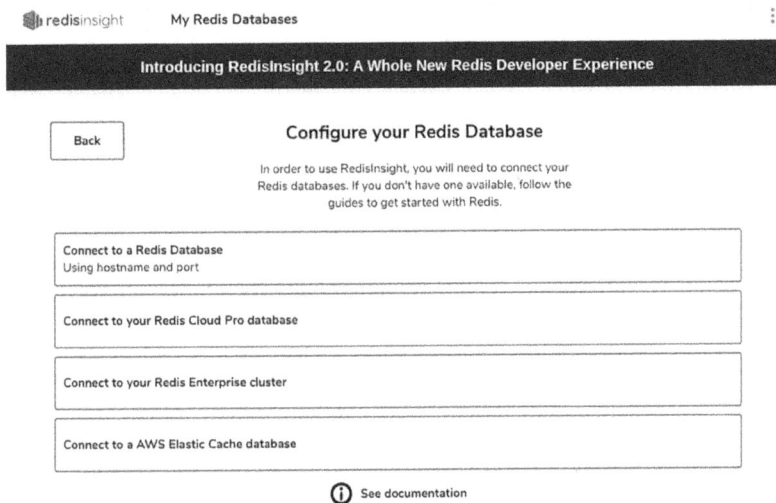

**FIGURE E.2** Configuration of the database.

The next step is to click on the button Connect to a Redis Database and complete the modal with the information of the connection:

- host: `api-reservation-db`
- port: `6379`
- name: `reservation (or any other value)`

Once all the required information is confirmed, Redis Insight will validate the provided details to ensure they are correct before proceeding to add the database.

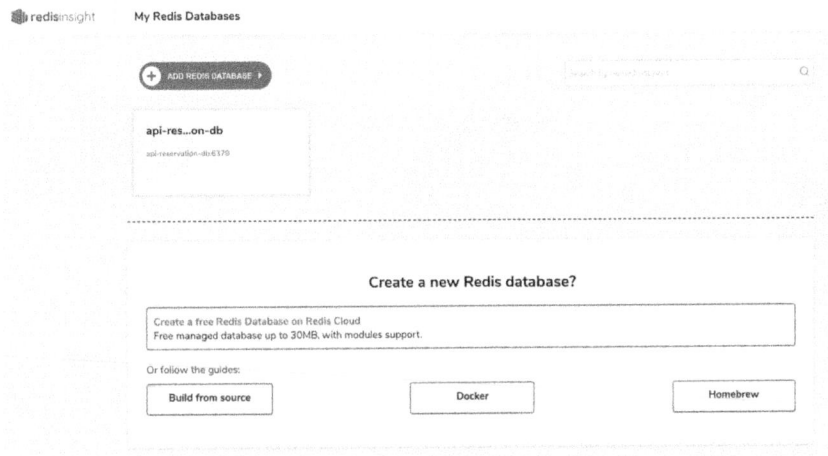

**FIGURE E.3** The connection with the database.

Double-clicking on the database opens a new page that displays all available operations and provides status information for that database.

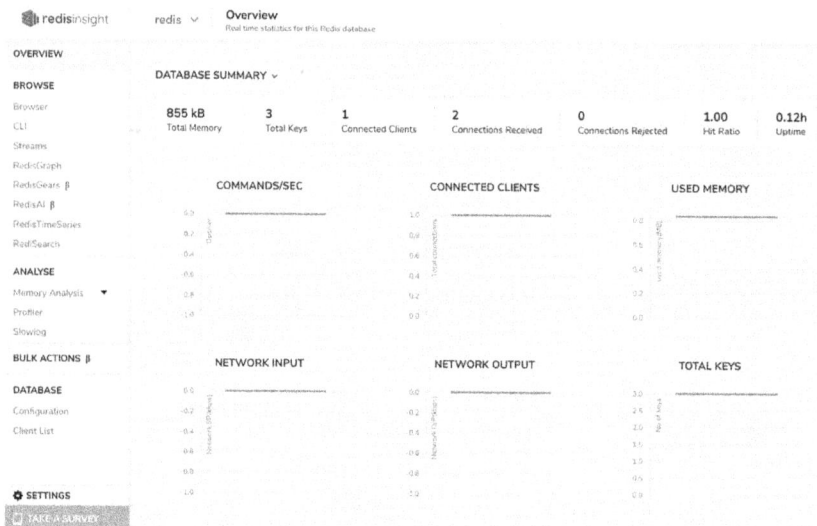

**FIGURE E.4** Active database.

The final step involves selecting the Browser option, which allows adding new elements to the database or inspecting existing ones. This feature helps verify aspects such as the key's time to live (TTL).

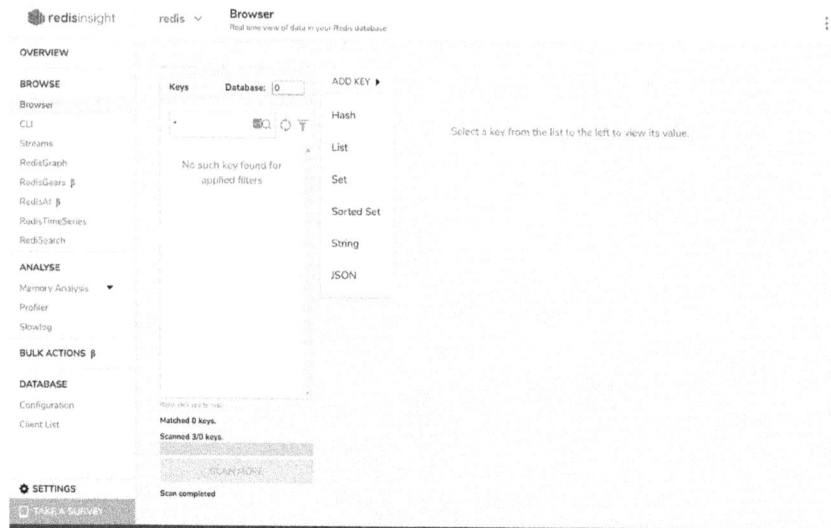

**FIGURE E.5** Browser tab, which permits adding new keys.

## MongoDB

This is a non-relational database designed to persist information as documents while offering some features of relational databases. This database provides various installation options.

Documentation is available for installing this database using various types of packages, each tailored to the specific operating system in use. Depending on the operating system version, the installation process might involve additional steps.

Another option mentioned in the official documentation, and previously covered, involves using brew for the installation. This method simplifies the installation process. The first step is to add the MongoDB repositories to brew, as they are omitted by default.

```
➜  ~ brew tap mongodb/brew

Cloning into '/home/linuxbrew/.linuxbrew/Homebrew/Library/Taps/mongodb/
homebrew-brew'...
remote: Enumerating objects: 1017, done.
remote: Counting objects: 100% (302/302), done.
remote: Compressing objects: 100% (105/105), done.
remote: Total 1017 (delta 245), reused 208 (delta 196), pack-reused 715
Receiving objects: 100% (1017/1017), 218.01 KiB | 1.79 MiB/s, done.
Resolving deltas: 100% (540/540), done.
Tapped 18 formulae (36 files, 363.6KB).
```

*LISTING E.3* Include the repositories of MongoDB for brew.

Afterward, update the repositories in brew and execute the command to install MongoDB on the machine.

```
➜  ~ brew update
Already up-to-date.

➜  ~ brew install mongodb-community@6.0
Warning: mongodb-community provides a launchd plist which can only be
used on macOS!
You can manually execute the service instead with:
  mongod --config /home/linuxbrew/.linuxbrew/etc/mongod.conf
```

*LISTING E.4* Update and install MongoDB using brew.

The last option is to use Docker commands to run the database or a Docker Compose file.

```
version: '3.1'

services:
 api-reservation-db:
    container_name: api-reservation-db
    image: mongo:5
    restart: always
    environment:
      MONGO_INITDB_ROOT_USERNAME: root
      MONGO_INITDB_ROOT_PASSWORD: rootpassword
    ports:
      - 27017:27017
```

*LISTING E.5* Docker Compose file to run MongoDB.

Once MongoDB is running locally, the next step involves using a graphical database access tool. MongoDB Compass, the official tool provided by MongoDB, serves this purpose. Installation requires following the steps outlined in the official documentation, which differ depending on the operating system.

Upon first opening MongoDB Compass, a screen similar to Figure E.6 appears, enabling configuration of the initial connection.

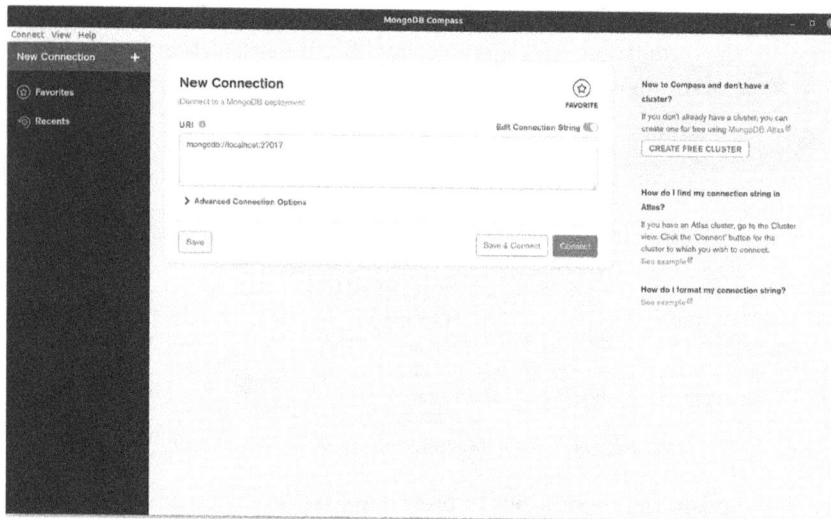

**FIGURE E.6** Mongo Compass first page.

The next step is to click Advanced Connection Options to enter the username and password for the MongoDB server running on the machine. When using the Docker Compose setup, the username is `root` and the password is `rootpassword`.

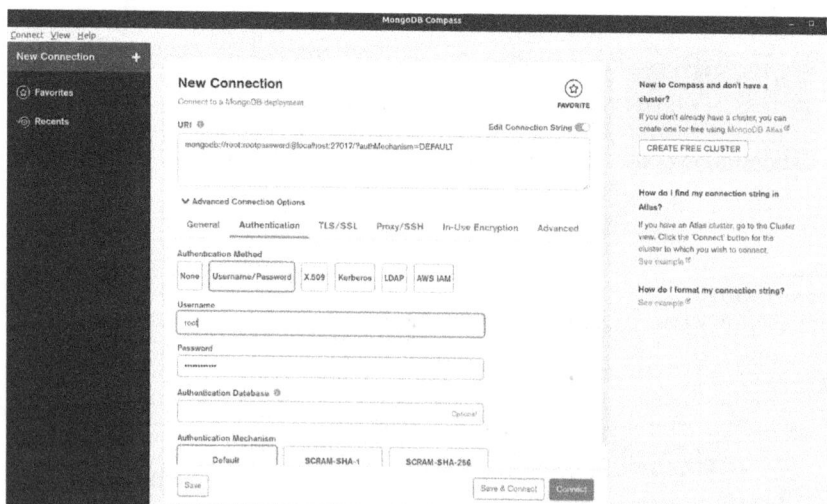

**FIGURE E.7** Configure the connection with the Mongo server.

Entering all the information correctly leads to a screen displaying all databases on the MongoDB server. By default, three databases are protected from deletion.

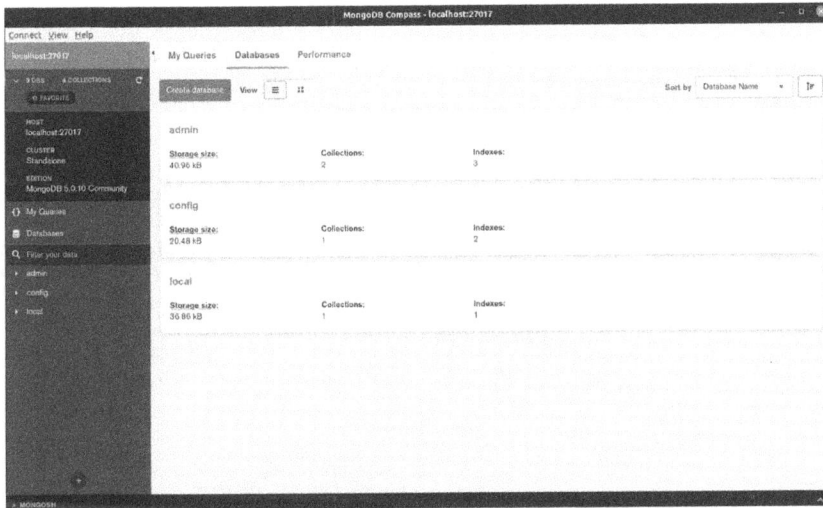

**FIGURE E.8** Databases available on the machine.

The final step involves creating a new database to store the application-related information, including catalog data. This is done by clicking the Create database button and completing the required fields.

# *Further Readings*

This book provides a comprehensive overview of various libraries, technologies, and databases essential for Spring Boot application development. The coverage of these resources, however, is limited. While it serves as a valuable starting point, this appendix outlines a curated list of books and resources for further exploration.

The resources are organized into distinct sections to facilitate easy access to information.

## ARCHITECTURE

This section includes resources designed to support learning about techniques for improving various aspects of an application, such as availability, maintainability, scalability, and performance:

- *Fundamentals of Software Architecture: An Engineering Approach* by Mark Richards and Neal Ford (O'Reilly, 2020)[1]: This book contains extensive information on various concepts related to the definition of architecture, offering valuable insights into key considerations when creating an application. Additionally, there is a specific chapter that explains how to document the various architectural decisions.
- *Software Architecture: The Hard Parts: Modern Trade-Off Analyses for Distributed Architectures* by Mark Richards and Neal Ford (O'Reilly, 2021)[2]: This book covers some advanced topics related to application creation and shows the trade-offs of using different distributed architecture options, such as communication between different applications. *Hands-On Software Architecture with Java* by Giuseppe Bonocore (Packt Publishing, 2022)[3]: This book shows different aspects of creating an application's Java architecture. Some relevant topics covered in this book are cross-cutting concerns and architectural patterns.

---

[1]https://learning.oreilly.com/videos/fundamentals-of-software/9781663728357/
[2]https://learning.oreilly.com/library/view/software-architecture-the/9781492086888/
[3]https://www.packtpub.com/product/hands-on-software-architecture-with-java/9781800207301

- *Microservices Patterns* by Chris Richardson (Manning, 2018)[4]: This book covers different patterns connected directly with microservices that help improve aspects such as resilience, availability, performance, and how to split a monolith into microservices.

## OBSERVABILITY AND MONITORING

This section includes resources covering various aspects of observability. Some delve into the theoretical details of what aspects are relevant to different monitoring applications, while others focus on the tools used for implementation:

- *Software Telemetry* by Jamie Riedesel (Manning, 2021)[5]: This book provides an overview of the different concepts connected to application observability, such as how to send metrics about the use of an application, how to create distinct dashboards, and which aspects are vital to check in a platform.
- *Observability Engineering* by Charity Majors, Liz Fong-Jones, and George Miranda (O'Reilly, 2022)[6]: This book provides information about the different metrics to consider on a platform, along with guidance on how these metrics can be calculated.
- *Cloud-Native Observability with OpenTelemetry* by Alex Boten (Packt Publishing, 2022)[7]: This resource provides information on how to implement OpenTelemetry and outlines the key aspects that should be monitored.

## PERSISTENCE

This section provides a range of resources on various aspects of data persistence, spanning both relational and non-relational databases. Some books also offer insights into the performance of the most prominent data persistence options:

- *Java Persistence with Spring Data and Hibernate* by Catalin Tudose (Manning, 2023)[8]: This book provides information about persistence performance and some techniques to improve its quality.
- *Beginning Spring Data* by Andres Sacco (Apress, 2022)[9]: This book offers the possibility to learn in detail about different databases for persisting information, and which are the most convenient for each situation.
- *Spring Boot Persistence Best Practices* by Anghel Leonard (Apress, 2020)[10]: This book addresses key topics to enhance the quality and performance of relational database persistence. While some aspects can be applied to non-relational databases, most concepts are specific to relational databases and do not have direct equivalents in non-relational systems.

---

[4]https://www.manning.com/books/microservices-patterns
[5]https://www.manning.com/books/software-telemetry
[6]https://learning.oreilly.com/library/view/observability-engineering/9781492076438/
[7]https://www.packtpub.com/product/cloud-native-observability-with-opentelemetry/9781801077705
[8]https://www.manning.com/books/java-persistence-with-spring-data-and-hibernate
[9]https://link.springer.com/book/10.1007/978-1-4842-8764-4
[10]https://link.springer.com/book/10.1007/978-1-4842-5626-8

- *Redis in Action* by Josiah Carlson (Manning, 2013)[11]: This book teaches the fundamentals of using Redis, including examples of data that can be stored in the database. It also addresses aspects related to performance and scalability.
- *MongoDB Performance Tuning* by Guy Harrison and Michael Harrison (Apress, 2021)[12]: This book covers fundamental aspects of queries and performance improvement, as well as additional topics such as creating a cluster with multiple instances and monitoring database resource usage.

## SECURITY

This section provides resources on various aspects of enhancing application security:

- *Spring Security in Action, Second Edition*, by Laurentiu Spilca (Manning, 2024)[13]: This book covers the basic concepts for increasing the security of a Spring Boot application and solving the most common problems.
- *API Security in Action* by Neil Madden (Manning, 2020)[14]: This book offers the possibility of understanding most of the relevant problems connected with application security in a way that focuses on the issue, not on one particular framework or technology.
- Laurentiu Spilca's channel on YouTube[15]: Videos on key Spring topics—such as security, performance, and basic tutorials—are available. Laurentiu, a highly recognized speaker on numerous Spring-related subjects, has also published multiple books, some focusing on specific topics, such as Spring Security, and others covering more general areas.

## TESTING

This section explores resources on various testing methods and how AI can enhance test quality:

- *Unit Testing Principles, Practices, and Patterns* By Vladimir Khorikov (Manning, 2020)[16]: This book offers an overview of different aspects of testing, such as the creation of mocks, the scope of the various types of testing, and some best practices.
- *Testing Web APIs* by Mark Winteringham (Manning, 2022)[17]: This book focuses on different testing methodologies, tools, and best practices for ensuring the quality and security of Web APIs.
- *AI-Assisted Testing* by Mark Winteringham (Manning, 2024)[18]: The use of AI increases each year; this book explains different techniques for using assertive prompts to reduce the time it takes to produce tests.

---

[11]https://www.manning.com/books/redis-in-action?query=Redis
[12]https://link.springer.com/book/10.1007/978-1-4842-6879-7
[13]https://www.manning.com/books/spring-security-in-action-second-edition
[14]https://www.manning.com/books/api-security-in-action
[15]https://www.youtube.com/c/laurentiuspilca
[16]https://www.manning.com/books/unit-testing
[17]https://www.manning.com/books/testing-web-apis
[18]https://www.manning.com/books/ai-assisted-testing

## TOOLS

This section includes resources related to tools for specific tasks, such as the IDE for developing the application and Docker for running a database or the application's build:

- *Beginning IntelliJ IDEA* by Ted Hagos (Apress, 2021)[19]: This book covers all aspects of using IntelliJ, including the installation process, debugging applications, and the essential elements needed to acquire basic skills in the IDE.
- *Docker in Action* by Jeff Nickoloff and Stephen Kuenzli (Manning, 2019)[20]: This book comprehensively explains Docker's features and interactions with various operating system layers. Additionally, it covers how to create a Docker image or run an existing one.

---

[19]https://link.springer.com/book/10.1007/978-1-4842-7446-0
[20]https://www.manning.com/books/docker-in-action-second-edition?query=Docker%20in%20Action

**A**

Actuator, 74, 78, 82, 88, 93

Amazon Web Services (AWS), 126, 132, 145, 198, 202, 226, 297, 307, 338–339, 355, 369, 379, 385, 402

Application Programming Interface (API), 32, 54, 97, 163, 165, 178, 179, 202, 212, 225, 226, 233, 235, 239, 320, 331, 332, 338, 354, 355, 368, 379, 381

API gateway, 320, 351, 353–360, 362, 364, 366, 375, 376, 381, 383

AsyncAPI, 226

**C**

Communication, 139–182
   applications, 139–147
   errors, impact of, 159–168
   request, impact of, 168–182
   Spring Boot, implementation in, 147–159

Conventional tools, 226

Custom Endpoint, 93

**D**

Docker, 132, 148, 173, 196, 198, 199, 202, 203, 265, 278–285, 292, 339, 389–390

**E**

Enterprise Java Beans (EJB), 97, 99

**G**

Git, 387

Google Identity Platform, 338–339

**H**

Health Endpoint, 81, 90

**I**

Ibatis, 99–100

Info Endpoint, 78, 89

Integrated development environment (IDE), 4, 8, 9, 11, 19, 21, 25, 32, 252, 253, 269, 270, 293, 357, 371, 388, 391, 393, 394, 412

IntelliJ, 7–9, 19, 388–389, 391, 393, 412

Inversion of control (IoC), 2

**J**

Java, 1, 385
   databases
      non-relational, 392
      relational, 391–392
   development, 391
   requestAPI, 392

Java Database Connectivity (JDBC), 97–99, 101, 103

Java Development Kit (JDK), 9, 24, 97, 281, 286, 385, 386, 393

Java Persistence API (JPA), 97, 99–101, 103, 105, 110–112, 114–117, 121, 122, 126–129

Java Virtual Machine (JVM), 79, 89, 207, 211, 285, 286, 316

**K**

Keycloak, 338–344, 347–349

**L**

Loggers Endpoint, 86

**M**

Mapping Endpoint, 87
Maven, 386
Metrics Endpoint, 83, 92
Microservices, 27–66. *see also* Spring; Spring Boot
  architecture, 34–66
    alternative, 38–39
    application logic, 41–53
    exception handling, 53–59
    hexagonal, 36–38
    implementation, 41
    layers, 34–36
    Spring Boot application, 39–41
    validation, 59–66
  developer's impact, 32–34
  discovering, 366–377
    best option, 369–370
    implications, 366–367
    manual, 367–368
    pattern integration, 371–377
    process, 367
    service, 368–369
  documentation, 225–246
    AsyncAPI, 226
    checks, 239–246
    conventional tools, 226
    endpoints, 228–239
    examples, 236–239
    OpenAPI, 225–226
  exposing, 351–366
    adding redirections, 359–363
    adding resilience, 363–366
    API gateway, 353–355
    best option, 355
    endpoints, 351–352
    pattern integration, 355–359
    problem solving, 352
  load balancing, 377–382
    balancing requests, 377
    best option, 380
    consumer, 379–380
    pattern integration, 380–382
    possible options, 377–378
    tool, 378–379
  logging, 296–306
  metrics and alerts, 311–317
    application modification and implications, 314–318
    best option, 313–314
    collecting metrics, 312–313

monoliths, 28–30
  observability and monitoring, 295–318
    application modification and implications, 299–306
    best option, 298–299
    collecting logs, 297
    problems and solutions, 30–32
    traces, 306–318
      application modification and implications, 308–311
      best option, 307–308
      collecting and visualizing traces, 306–307
Microsoft Entra ID, 338–339
MongoDB, 121–125, 392, 405–407
Monoliths, 28–30
  architecture, 295–296

**N**

Non-relational databases
  installation
    MongoDB, 405–407
    Redis, 401–404
  MongoDB, 392
  Redis, 392

**O**

Object-relational mapping (ORM), 97, 105–106
Okta, 338–339
OpenAPI, 225–230, 233, 239–244, 355

**P**

Pit test coverage report, 220

**R**

Realm Settings Web page, 341
Redis, 401–404
Relational databases, 391–392
  configuration, 397–399
  installation, 395–397
    client access, 397
  load the data, 400
  schema creation, 399
RequestAPI, 392
Role mapping, 345

**S**

Service Discovery, 368–369
Spring, 1–3. *see also* Microservices
  inversion of control (IoC), 2
  modules

container, 2, 3
data Access, 2, 3
test, 2, 3
web, 2, 3
Spring Boot, 3–4, 8. see also Microservices
application configuration, 67–95
actuator, 73–95
aspects, 67–70
context-path, 70–71
endpoints, 77–95
error pages, 71–72
implementation, 74–77
multiple configurations, 72–73
purpose, 77
application creation, 7–23
alternatives, 8
challenges, 23
code run, IDE, 19–21
command line, 10–11, 21–23
configuration, 67–96
domain creation, 14–16
endpoints creation, 16–19
logic addition, 13–14
plugin, 9–10
Spring Initializr, 8–9
structure, 11–13
application modification, 252–268
change detection, adding queues, 264–268
config server creation, 252–261
application security, 321–350
implementation, 321–322
application testing, 183–223
architecture test, 212–217
integration test, 190–206
mutation test, 217–223
performance test, 206–211
unit test, 184–190
architecture, 409–410
build, 270–278
code analysis and auto-fix, 272–275
code format, 270
dependency conflicts prevention, 270
unused dependency detection, 270–272
update application, 276–278
update dependencies, 275–276
databases, 97–138
alternative, 104–105
custom libraries, 101
EJB, 99
Ibatis, 99–100

JDBC, 98–99
JPA, 100–101
native, 101
non-relational, 101
persisting information, 105–130
relational, 98
types, 101–103
version update, 130–137
external configuration, 249–251
benefits, 249
command-line arguments, 250
config server, 250
environment variables, 250
options, 250–251
information security, 319–350
basic security, 325–332
JWT token, 332–338
libraries or frameworks, 319–320, 322–324
mechanism, 320
restricting access, 320–321
secure server, 338–350
internal configuration, 247–248
challenges, 248
methodology, 4–7
decision making approach, 6–7
definition, 4–6
observability and monitoring, 410
packaging, 278–293
base image creation, 281–283
building an image, 279–280
challenges, 278–279
GraalVM, 285–293
layers strategy, 283–285
persistence, 410–411
practices, 23–26
code formatting, 25–26
conflicts, 23–25
security, 411
testing, 411
tools, 412
validation, 59
Spring Boot Microservices, 354. see also Spring;
Spring Boot; Microservices
Spring Cloud Gateway, 359, 360, 363
Spring Data, 97, 101–108, 110, 111, 114, 115, 117,
121, 122, 124, 126–128
non-relational database, 120–130
MongoDB, 121–125
Redis, 126–130
persisting information, 105–137

automatic queries, 107–109
  manual queries, 109–110
  object mapping, 105–106
  repositories, 106–107
relational database, 110–120
  annotations, 111–117
  configuration, 110–111
  repositories, 117–120
version update, 130–137
  alternate, 133–135
  Flyway, 132–133
  Liquibase, 133
  tool, 132
Springfox, 228
Spring Initializr, 8–9
Stoplight, 239

**T**
Travel World Agency (TWA), 4

**X**
XML, 1, 140, 219

**Y**
YAML file, 9, 12, 68

**Z**
zally, 239
Zitadel, 338–339

www.ingramcontent.com/pod-product-compliance
Lightning Source LLC
Chambersburg PA
CBHW080138220326
41598CB00032B/5102